The Political Economy of Emerging Markets

The CERI Series in International Relations and Political Economy

Series Editors, Christophe Jaffrelot and Christian Lequesne

This series consists of works emanating from the foremost French research center in international studies, the Paris-based Centre d'Etudes et de Recherches Internationales (CERI), part of Sciences Po and associated with the CNRS (Centre National de la Recherche Scientifique).

Founded in 1952, CERI has about sixty fellows drawn from different disciplines who conduct research on comparative political analysis, international relations, regionalism, transnational flows, political sociology, political economy, and on individual states.

This series focuses on the transformations of the international arena, in a world where the state, though its sovereignty is questioned, reinvents itself. The series explores the effects on international relations and the world economy of regionalization, globalization (not only of trade and finance), and transnational flows at large. This evolution in world affairs sustains a variety of networks from the ideological to the criminal or terrorist. Besides the geopolitical transformations of the globalized planet, the new political economy of the world has a decided impact on its destiny as well, and this series hopes to uncover what that is.

Published by Palgrave Macmillan:

Politics in China: Moving Frontiers
edited by Françoise Mengin and Jean-Louis Rocca
Tropical Forests, International Jungle: The Underside of Global Ecopolitics
by Marie-Claude Smouts, translated by Cynthia Schoch
The Political Economy of Emerging Markets: Actors, Institutions and Financial Crises in Latin America
by Javier Santiso

The Political Economy of Emerging Markets

Actors, Institutions and Financial Crises in Latin America

Javier Santiso

THE POLITICAL ECONOMY OF EMERGING MARKETS
© Javier Santiso, 2003

First published 2003 by
PALGRAVE MACMILLAN™
175 Fifth Avenue, New York, N.Y. 10010 and
Houndmills, Basingstoke, Hampshire, England RG21 6XS.
Companies and representatives throughout the world

PALGRAVE MACMILLAN is the global academic imprint of the
Palgrave Macmillan division of St. Martin's Press, LLC and of
Palgrave Macmillan Ltd. Macmillan® is a registered trademark in the
United States, United Kingdom and other countries. Palgrave
is a registered trademark in the European Union and other countries.

ISBN 1–4039–6232–4 hardback

Library of Congress Cataloging-in-Publication Data
Santiso, Javier.
    The political economy of emerging markets: actors, institutions and
    financial crises in Latin America/by Javier Santiso.
        p. cm.
    Includes bibliographical references.
    ISBN 1–4039–6232–4
        1. Capital market—Latin America. 2. Stock exchanges—Latin America.
3. Financial crises—Latin America. I. Title.

HG5160.5.A3S26 2003
332'.098—dc21   2002044716

A catalogue record for this book is available from the British Library.

Design by Newgen Imaging Systems (P) Ltd., Chennai, India.

First edition: August, 2003
10 9 8 7 6 5 4 3 2 1

Printed in the United States of America.

. . . y el director del banco observaba el manómetro
que mide el cruel silencio de la moneda . . .

Federico Garcia Lorca
Poeta en Nueva York

Pour Suzanne

CONTENTS

LIST OF TABLES, CHARTS AND GRAPHS

Tables

Charts

Graphs

THE AUTHOR

Javier Santiso holds B.A., M.A. and Ph.D. degrees from Sciences Po Paris (Institut d'Etudes Politiques de Paris) and an M.B.A. degree from HEC School of Management. From 1995 to 1997 he completed his doctoral studies at Oxford University as a Senior Associate Member of the St. Antony's College Latin American Center (University of Oxford). From 1997 to 2002 he was tenure-track Research Fellow (now on leave) at the Paris-based think-tank Centre d'Etudes et de Recherches Internationales (CERI-Sciences Po Paris) and as a Senior Expert Associate on Latin American Emerging Markets for Crédit Agricole Indosuez investment bank. He also served as a consultant for leading private institutions (Société Générale, Dexia, Générale des Eaux, Total Fina Elf, Renault), international organizations (Inter-American Development Bank, OECD) and nongovernmental organizations (International Federation of Human Rights). Since 2002, he is the Madrid-based Chief Economist for Latin America of Banco Bilbao Vizcaya Argentaria (BBVA). This book is based on an academic research conducted before 2002 and does not engage the responsibility of any of the mentioned institutions.

He has been Visiting Professor in Latin American Political Economy at The Paul Nitze School of Advanced Studies, SAIS Johns Hopkins University. He also lectured on international political economy at Sciences Po Paris and on European corporate strategies in Latin America at HEC School of Management. He has published several articles (more than 30) in leading academic journals in France, United States, United Kingdom, Chile, Spain and Mexico.

CHAPTER ONE

Introduction: Inside the Black Box
A Journey Toward Emerging Markets

It may be that genus (of financial crises) is like a pretty woman (in
our culture): hard to define but recognizable when encountered.

Charles Kindleberger[1]

By the end of the twentieth century, emerging markets had become the
new El Dorado of international finance. Their emergence was certainly
not new. In fact, most Latin American stocks exchanges for example date
from the end of the previous century and as stressed by many economists
and historians, the integration of world finance was already very large
and deep by the very end of the nineteenth century.[2] Wall Street and
London's (re)discovery of emerging market gold mines have provided
the impetus for one of the most incredible gold rushes of the late twentieth century. At the beginning of the 1980s, the so-called emerging
markets (i.e. developing country stock markets surveyed by the World
Bank's International Finance Corporation (IFC)[3]) were only 32 and had
a market capitalization of less than US$70 bn (around a mere 2.5 per-
cent of world market capitalization). By the end of the twentieth century,
the IFC identified 81 emerging stock markets with a total market
capitalization of more than US$1.4 tn. (4.7 percent of the global bond
market). The aggregate size of emerging debt markets has jumped from
about US$450 bn. in 1989 to over US$1.4 tn. in 1999 representing
nearly 5 percent of the world market, while emerging equity markets
have experienced over the same decade an impressive growth reaching
an aggregate size of about 8.5 percent of global market capitalization.

While this story is clearly about numbers, abstract amounts of money flows, it also concerns actors and institutions: a myriad analysts, strategists and fund managers involved, during the last decade, in a series of financial booms and crises, from Latin America to Asia and Russia. Although markets consist of daily transactions and huge volumes, they remain social constructs. A proper analysis of financial dynamics requires a departure from the tenacious idea that financial emerging markets, whether efficient or deficient, are not neutral and abstract homogenous entities that adjust themselves automatically to financial information and economic variations. Their temporalities are in the form of sudden accelerations and ephemeral torpors. Some actors have short-term trading horizons; others take into account more long-term perspectives. Those markets make noise and, because of relevant statistical information, are less transparent and reliable. Emerging markets are more sensitive to this chatter than any other financial market. Fears, manias and panics are then major drivers of booms and slumps.[4]

The political economy of financial crises is thus tinged with economic sociology and financial behavior. It follows a necessary deviation that could also be considered a return, or a "journey," as Hirschman would say. So the far-off origins of a science whose founding fathers, like Adam Smith, were fascinated with theorizing about not only the wealth of nations but also with the moral sentiments of economic actors; in the present case, it means to deal with market sentiments, anticipations and perceptions. Even though an analysis of interests has since made strides over an analysis of passions, certain tenacious economists continue to occupy themselves with actors that they refuse to reduce to "rational fools" as inferred by Amartya Sen, the Nobel Prize winner of the discipline.[5]

Financial markets are neither the tyrants nor the magicians or even the omnipotent short-termists that critics frequently depict. Their temporal horizons vary according to profession, products and the constraints and resources that restrain or enlarge the horizons of very different actors. Recent financial crises have shown the necessity for a study of the socioeconomic aspects of markets that goes beyond their demonization in the person of Georges Soros. Behind the power of the market hide a myriad actors, analysts, strategists, economists, traders and fund managers whose asset-management styles and temporal horizons vary from one institution to another and even within the same investment bank or the same pension fund. In short, they constitute a veritable epistemic community that share a set of cognitive maps and also differ in many ways, involved in a world of high-speed temporal bubbles, with its own dynamics and rhythms, windows of opportunities and walls of constraints.

In order to understand financial crisis in emerging markets, it is necessary to know how financial markets think, to analyze their cognitive regimes and temporal horizons. That requires analyzing information games and the resulting web of anticipations, which link operators as well as questioning the cognitive regimes and temporal frameworks shared by traders, investors and other analysts whose anticipations make or break market prices. To proceed into the black box, or to *analyze the analysts*, also means, to learn more about the way the market itself is organized, with their market markers, five all-star analysts and institutions, hierarchies and connections. This deconstructive exercise is also an attempt to cross disciplinary boundaries, an invitation to trespass from economics to politics and vice-versa, from international political economy to economic history and economic sociology, and beyond.

1.1   The Visible Hands: Implicit Handshakes and Explicit Strangulations. A Socioeconomic Approach to Emerging Markets

Financial markets do not establish the reign of the invisible hand, but rather the reign of implicit handshakes and, from time to time, explicit strangulations, as with the corrections made to the detriment of Mexico, Korea, Russia, Brazil and many other developing countries during the past decade. The aim of this book is precisely to unravel some of the various strands in the tapestry woven of the interactions of those who make the market. It is not embroidered by the invisible hand of God, or the devil, but more simply by the unceasing expectations and interactions of a myriad analysts and investors who draw their breath from Wall Street.[6]

To understand international financial (dis)orders means to take into account what is going on inside the black box, analyze actors and institutions, their investment behaviors and cognitive regimes. However, until recently, neither sociologists, nor economists entered the black box. The former because of some ideological aversions regarding markets (and financial markets are in a way the ultimate devil). The latter because it is impossible to formalize socio-economic games. Yet, increasingly, scholars are paying more attention to the behavior of actors and market sentiments. Recent works in economic sociology, cultural anthropology and international political economy have contributed to new understandings of finance. Economists too have changed their way of looking at financial crisis. One of the most remarkable trends of the literature on financial crises has been the gradual displacement of its center of gravity.[7] Works centered on the economic fundamentals of the crises evolved to a second generation of models that insisted on the sensitivity of economic fundamentals to changes in the anticipatory behavior of financial actors.[8]

In other words, the literature has become increasingly interested in the "sentiments of the market," in the mimetic rationality of actors, in asymmetries and cascades of information, in the influence of self-fulfilling prophecies, self-realizing prophetic mechanisms and the diffusion of the "noise" and "herding behaviour" that affect financial markets. In short the literature is focusing more and more on the behavior of financial actors, their anticipations and reactions to economic fundamentals but also to the signals emitted by the actors involved in the game. The importance ascribed to financial institutions in recent research further points to what some have already labelled a "third generation model of crises" that "should assign a key role to financial structure and financial systems."[9]

One of the most stimulating developments in the literature is on behavioral finances and prospect theory. Developed by psychologists and economists such as Kahneman, Tversky and Thaler, this theory tries to explain anomalies focusing on human behavior toward risk.[10] Other developments will try to test the existence of anomalies through experimental economic tests.[11] Financial markets are no longer abstract numbers but are also concrete actors, with their bounded rationalities, irrational exuberance or rational herding behaviors. They live in a world of forecasts and are forward looking, trying to anticipate booms and slumps, and to manage risks and returns.[12] Some players are more risk averse or risk seeking than others. Risk aversion or risk taking behavior of the same actors can also change with contexts and settings. The prospect theory points out, for example, that when choice involves losses, investors are risk seekers not risk averse.[13] They can be "overconfident" about their abilities and have a propensity for taking risks and making investing mistakes such as focusing on stocks they believe will do well at the expense of those stocks in their portfolio that risk doing badly. But their investment process can also be a learning process, with trials and errors (if they have enough time to keep their job). They can have a "fear of regret" causing them to hold bad stocks for too long, postponing a revision of their views. They can be subject to conflicts, "cognitive dissonance," when they are faced with evidence that one of their core beliefs might be wrong.

Emerging markets are also worlds with their own rituals, beliefs and symbols, worlds that are mainly dynamic, actors' cognitive maps changing with environments, agendas and career perspectives. Encounters between anthropology and economy can lead to stimulating understandings in order to underline the diversity of actors as we are not talking of a homogeneous world. This is true even if we take a professional category such as pension-fund managers. Each one has his own colorful story, cultural trajectory, written rules and hidden ones that can be regarded as a belief and tribal system, with sophisticated myths, cultural codes and tribal hierarchies.[14] Other interesting works focus on institutions and conflicts of interests. Another line of research focuses on the reactions of financial operators to risk analyses diffused by rating agencies and brokerage firms. These works have proven the existence of market failures and institutional biases such as the rating agency's rigidity in downgrading a country (that happens also to be a client). Others underline the extent to which brokerage firms can be torn by conflicts of interest, subjugated to a double obligation to offer the best services to their clients as well as to sell the stocks these firms underwrite.[15]

In the same way, rating agencies can be seen as actors of the confidence game. The rating game of agencies is closely watched and frequently criticized. Sovereign credit-rating changes systematically fail to anticipate currency crises—but do better in predicting defaults. The downgrades appear to materialize not before but during or after the crises in Asia for example.[16] For emerging markets, during the period 1979–1999, the probability of a Moody's downgrade in the six months following a currency crisis was less than 20 percent while a downgrade in the twelve months following the crisis was of nearly 27 percent.[17] For the Institutional Investor, the numbers are much more striking: during the same period, the probability of a downgrade in the six months following a currency crisis has been less than 39 percent, while a downgrade in the twelve months following the crisis was of nearly 80 percent.

The intensity of critics gives an idea of the key players that these operators became during the past decades. In fact, as underlined by the survey we conducted and according to 145 answers given, the evaluations of the rating agencies are considered by emerging market analysts and fund managers as "important" or "very important" for nearly 75 percent of the people who answered the question (compared to only 5 percent considering evaluations of rating agencies as irrelevant and 20 percent as not important). But when considered as important or very important, in fact, this is explained not for the accuracy of rating agencies evaluations (very much criticized) but because the markets react to their moves.[18]

The investment grade change of a country or a downgrading of another will be closely watched by market participants. When Mexico, for example, was awarded by Moody's with an investment grade status in 2000 it became a major event. The move coincided with the departure of the S&P analyst Lacey Gallagher, very respected and well connected in Mexico, who joined CSFB. Probably this also generated a market opportunity for Moody's,[19] mainly driven by an improved economic situation. More than a year later, in January 2002, another rating agency, Fitch, upgraded Mexico's sovereign credit to investment grade, prompting leading operators to anticipate action from the last big rating agency, namely S&P and market impacts.[20] More generally the empirical research done on rating agencies changes and their impact on financial markets confirms anecdotical evidence, suggesting that rating moves have significant short-term impacts on financial markets.[21]

Rating agencies are obviously not the only actor involved in the confidence game. Financial markets can in fact be understood more as a place of belief than of memory, where games of affluence and influence are played out by myriad actors. In the midst of an unceasing bombardment of information, traders, investors and analysts must react in real time. In addition to rating agencies (Moody's, Standard & Poor's, Fitch Ibca), large international organizations (IMF, World Bank, IADB), international newspapers (*Financial Times, Wall Street Journal, The Economist*), central banks, finance ministers and country risks firms (Institute of International Finance, Economist Intelligence Unit, Business Monitor) and index providers are among the actors that accumulate and diffuse information and contribute to form the configuration of the main points of reference of traders, analysts, money managers.

In this avalanche of news produced in the world each year, one that increases at approximately two *exabytes* (estimated in 2000), the equivalent of around 40 bn. copies of *The Economist*,[22] financial operators have powerful filters. In the world of finance, agencies of financial information such as Bloomberg (created in 1984 by Michael Bloomberg a former Salomon Brothers trader and the current mayor of New York City) and Reuters (founded in 1851 by Paul Julius Reuter) are major actors, veritable market makers, that configure the reference points for thousands of operators. Bloomberg, for example, delivers business information in 100 countries through more than 150,000 terminals. For US$1,285 a month per terminal, the company provides what is regarded by financial operators as the most comprehensive financial data available. It has captured 36 percent of the US$7 bn. global market for real-time data, his main competitors being London-based Reuters and Bridge Information

Systems. With Thomson Financial, another leading integrated financial news provider,[23] these companies dominate the financial information industry.[24] Their nonstop and real time information flows literally establishes the rhythm for the lives of brokers, traders and investors who calculate their anticipations and reactions partly on results posted by promoters of these agencies that channelled the information.

Whether quarterly reports of companies or public accounts of governments, each piece of information must be treated as quickly as possible, and, occasionally, in a matter of seconds when panic movements begin to set in. The central desk of the Reuters agency alone furnishes as many as 25 dispatches per minute. In less than half an hour, the equivalent of a daily newspaper is dispatched to more than 362,000 computer terminals located across the globe.[25] In the field of emerging markets, and the Latin American market in particular, each operator follows the macroeconomic indicators of each country, awaiting the arrival of statistics at regular intervals. Thus, every bank has a daily calendar of events at its disposal. In the case of Goldman Sachs, for example, for the first 15 days of February 1997, no less than 30 economic and political events concerning the emerging markets of Latin America were recorded.[26] The dissemination and availability of economic information increased dramatically with the development of digital technologies and the improvements made by emerging market governments to supply timely information to markets.

Information and rumors, interconnected in continuous flows, are diffused at high speeds, where imitating "the other" becomes imperative to staying in the game. This imitation becomes a self-validating virus often disconnected from the facts. They make the collective opinion of participants as a determinant of the anticipation of future revenues in charting the course of stocks. For André Orléan, one of the economists to have pushed this type of analysis the farthest, understanding these movements requires an analysis of the strategic interactions between actors operating on financial markets. He aims to uncover the sociological dynamics of financial markets by integrating interpersonal influences into his analysis, by understanding the game of cross-anticipation between different actors at time "t" and also their future beliefs about the market at time "t + 1." Financial bubbles are not simply mathematical artifacts but are also rational mimetic bubbles. In order to make them intelligible it is equally important to understand the impact of market interactions. In such a way, a fall in prices during a financial crisis, such as that of October 1987, is self-reinforcing, containing an endogenous dynamic founded on the interaction between participants.[27] Furthermore, actors develop mimetic strategies because there is a certain risk in distancing oneself from average opinion. Actors give in to conjecture on the behavior of other operators, integrating not only new information into their anticipations, but also beliefs about the reactions that such anticipations will arouse in the behavior of other agents.[28] Financial markets constitute an open world in which speed is primary. One must know how to profit from windows of opportunity, which open and close at high speeds, more rapidly and durably than competitors, especially when one is faced with the instability of emerging markets.

1.2   States Versus Markets: Temporal Cognitive Regimes

Thanks to the rise of new information technologies, speed has become even more pronounced in the last decades. International finance has experienced a series of major changes: new actors appeared, innovations multiplied, markets emerged. The liberalization and the deregulation of bond markets in 1979, and, with a time lag, the stock market in 1986, accompanied the rapid acceleration of the financial sphere.[29] Thus, between 1980 and 1992, the annual growth rate of the volume of financial stocks in OECD countries attained a yearly average of 6 percent, which is 2.5 times higher than the growth rate of fixed-capital formation. One particular piece of data demonstrates the extent of the game: every day 40 times more financial than trade transactions take place. Resulting profits are made in extremely short periods. It is estimated that more than half of the total return on U.S. equities during the 1980s was made in just 20 days.

One indicator that the pulse of the world economy is accelerating under the pressure of finance is the increasing rapidity of the reconfiguration of financial stocks driven by the strict performance obligations that are imposed on companies by institutional investors. This quest leads to the ever-increasing instability of capital, which flies from investment to investment in increasingly brief lapses of time. Between 1980 and 1987 the yearly rate of abandoned stocks (obtained through fusion and acquisitions) passed from 20 to 75 percent. The turnover rate of stocks on the New York Stock Exchange moved from 30 to 70 percent between 1979 and 1989.[30]

Thanks to the rise in new information technologies, the interconnection of different stock markets has been made at a rhythm that is too rapid and constraining for states. States are faced with an incredible acceleration in capital movements. New computer technology allows for arbitrage and corrections to be made in a matter of seconds. A new development imposed by the increasing use of telecommunications technology is the disappearance of reaction times and the shortening of temporal horizons.[31] Access to telecommunications technology not only abolishes both space and scope but also duration by shortening delays and diminishing financial costs. Thus the cost, for example, of a three-minute telephone call from London to New York has been drastically reduced from US$245 in 1930 to US$3.30 in 1990. An increase in real-interest rates has also contributed to a shortening of the temporal horizon of financial operators. Interest rates, veritable barometers of the future, are authentic measures of future prices. Their increase has been translated, over the course of the last few decades, into a quest for short-term profitability to the detriment of long-term investment. The future has thus depreciated, being surpassed by an unending race for profits, which translates, in economic terms, into the fall in the value of the present experienced during the twentieth century.[32]

Globalization of finance has been accompanied by the preeminence of the time factor over the space factor.[33] Space, as a major strategic dimension within a closed world, has lost its preeminence at the end of this century, bypassed by acceleration, urgency and speed. One of the explicit objectives of deregulation was precisely to shorten transaction times by reducing to a minimum the administrative formalities that inhibited market access. For many companies, losing days, weeks or months before penetrating a market can translate into considerable losses on the balance sheet, especially because the life cycle of products is also shortening. In the computer industry, for example, losing six months on a product with a life cycle of approximately 18 months is a luxury that no company can afford. The acceleration of the economy can therefore be measured by taking into account the shortening of waiting periods imposed by deregulation. In the case of Mexico, administrative formalities concerning trade have been considerably reduced and precise waiting periods have been fixed in order to avoid the interference of unnecessary measures. Thus, commercial formalities limited by response dates have gone from 13 percent of all transactions to 91 percent after deregulation. Moreover, the percentages concerning trade have grown from 38 to 68 percent.[34]

The financial crises of the last few years have highlighted the vital importance of the temporal adjustments that face states. These crises have led to a questioning of the temporality of financial markets and, in particular, of the cognitive maps of financial operators, major actors at the origin of the temporal adjustments imposed on states. Following the Latin American and Asian crises of the past decade, the international community has once again learned that these financial paradises can rapidly transform into durable nightmares as once prosperous gold mines turn into money pits. But above all, such episodes, that join the long series of somersaults, panics and bubbles that mark the history of finance, also illustrate one of the most marked traits of the end of this century: the constant tug of war between states and financial markets. On the one hand, States are faced with the ever-increasing inflows and outflows of capital that set the pace for economic growth. Financial markets, on the other hand, unceasingly undertake multiple choices, 24 hours a day, moving from one country to another in the search for margins and profits. At the height of the Asian crisis, the diatribes from the Malaysian leader Mahathir Mohamed against financial wizard Georges Soros in 1997 crystallize this conflict. Soros has become one of the symbols of "market tyranny" over the last few years after having launched several violent attacks on national economies, which then proceeded to fall like dominoes.

However this apparent opposition between States and financial markets is only relative. It is important to remember that governments have historically been behind the creation of financial markets. The first one was created by the British Crown in an effort to raise funds to finance the military exploits of the King.[35] In addition, financial crises are not solely the consequence of short-term financial markets. As we will see the devaluation of the Mexican peso in December of 1994, for example, was mainly the result of a complex game of interactions between financial markets and government. This particular example demonstrates, in its sequence and timing, the extent to which economic and political temporalities interact, how much states are obliged to react quickly to financial markets and how much they seek to gain time and to build long-term credibility. The Mexican crisis, and the financial crises of the past decade, can also help to support the hypothesis that markets are essentially short term in focus while states are more long term in focus. This question deserves to be explored as the Mexican example demonstrates that a short-term approach is not only the prerogative of the market. The Mexican state, in emitting the famous *tesobonos*, or the "malditos bonos" as baptized by Arturo Porzecanski, not only sought to gain time, but also employed a prolonged short-term strategy in order to elude a devaluation and a correction of the economic trajectory before the deadline of 1994 presidential elections. The immediate and brutal market correction, in fact, contained a blessing in disguise. According to an operator of a NewYork bank, it stopped the government in mid-stride, forcing it to face the situation there and then. They could no longer push their problems off into some vague and temporally undefined future. States are traditionally defined by territorial sovereignty. It is, however, in challenging the monopoly of the Church over time, that the state consolidated itself.[36] Although markets have certainly not become the clock-masters, they have considerably broken the state's sovereignty over time. During the nineteenth century, the imperatives of industrialization—including the coordination of the transportation of merchandise by rail and the organization of important public works projects to be carried out by masses of workers—imposed a standardization of temporal norms. While it is true that markets have appropriated the temporal norms forged by the state, they have recently imposed their own temporalities—composed of accelerations, speed and crises—through the financial sphere. Each financial crisis launches a race between the international financial system—called in urgency to address deep disequilibriums in order to rapidly stop market reactions—and the interstate system. Large sums, mobilized with increasing rapidity, set the rhythm of this race: more than US$50 bn. came to the aid of Mexico, 17 bn. for Thailand, 58 bn. for South Korea, 43 bn. for Indonesia, more than 22 bn. for Russia and nearly 40 bn. for Argentina.

To understand and to discuss the short-term approach of financial markets and to test its acuity is to question the very socioeconomic dynamic of international finance, or, in other words, to enter into the black box by analyzing the analysts.

Here we present a journey into emerging markets based on an empirical investigation. We conducted nearly 250 interviews and analyzed brokers on emerging markets. The interviews started in 1996 and 1997 and focused mainly on the Mexican crisis. This material offered the background for the chapter on the Mexican crisis. This first investigation was carried out after the crisis and not captured "live." In many respects, change is not a parade that we can watch pass, as underlined by anthropologist Clifford Geertz in his Memoirs.[37] We always arrive too late. To determine the sequence of a financial crisis and the anticipations of operators, analysts and traders before, during and after it, however, is not out of reach.

The life of financial markets can only be understood by focusing on the game of actors. Financial markets are neither the Far West of the Golden Boys devoid of faith and law, nor a place where a perfect autoregulating invisible hand reigns. Implicit and explicit norms regulate markets where games of reputation and trust are as influential as turnover. Behind the supposed tutelary power of markets hide a myriad actors—fund managers, economists, strategists and analysts—who constitute a veritable epistemic community with its own codes, rules, prohibitions and dynamics of opportunity and constraint. Following the example of Geertz looking into the myths and rites of communities in Morocco or Indonesia, we conducted an in-depth study of the life of financial markets integrating a little anthropology and sociology, trespassing through the frontiers of economics and international relations.

1.3   An Empirical Analysis Based on a Global Survey and Direct Interviews

Following the first field research we conducted a more systematic survey of global emerging markets. Based on a questionnaire, we conducted a new round of interviews in order to track market sentiment and analyzed the cognitive regimes prevailing in global and Latin American emerging markets. We constructed a database of nearly 1,500 names of asset managers, economists, strategists and analysts working on global and Latin American emerging markets. Of those nearly 49 percent are based in the United States (mainly New York and Boston), 27 percent in the United Kingdom (London and Edinburgh), 12 percent in Paris, 9 percent in Latin American countries and the remaining in Spain and Switzerland.

We sent a first wave of questionnaires and started conducting direct interviews in Paris, London, Edinburgh, Madrid, New York and Boston. A total of 187 interviews have been conducted during 2000–2001: 145 questionnaires have been coded (see appendix 1.1 for a complete listing), the remaining 42 interviews being more informal and complementary cross-data interviews. The distribution of the interviews is as follows: 45 percent were conducted in the United Kingdom, 17 percent in continental Europe and 38 percent in the United States. Nearly 60 percent of all the people interviewed were asset managers (the "buy side" industry), 37 percent were economists, strategists and analysts from brokers and securities houses (the "sell-side" industry) and the remaining from rating agencies, country risks consulting companies and international newspapers.

In addition to interviews we also used quantitative fund flows data and several other polls on institutional investors conducted during 2000. We also worked on the production of asset managers and brokers, the reports published during the years 2000 and 2001 on emerging market issues and Latin American ones in particular. We decided to restrict the analysis to global and Latin American emerging markets mainly because of the size of the samples and productions, dailies, weeklies, monthlies and special issues publications or presentations provided directly by firms or through Multex database or web site and Internet research.

The quantitative data was used primarily for the second chapter where we focus on financial dynamics using macro and micro data fund flows. The interviews conducted in 2000 and 2001 were used primarily for chapters 3 and 4, which are centered in the analysis of the sell-side and buy-side industry, the heart of the players within the confidence game, asset managers and brokers. The following chapters intend to underline the dynamics of the game focusing first on the global confidence arenas (international newspapers and world meetings) and a range of other players such as academics or rating agencies. Finally we underline the interactions between states and markets within the context of the critical juncture of the Mexican and Argentinean financial crisis. The study ends then with the market participants and intergovernmental interacting game. It points out the need for another research program, this time focused on state players.

This journey toward emerging markets has been a three-year trek. During these years we interacted with authors and actors, scholars and operators. It would be impossible to thank everybody here. First, we are extremely grateful to the participants who agreed to interviews. We also would like to thank the following persons for their helpful comments, the data and the support provided, and above all for their always friendly encouragement and stimulating feedback, comments, papers and documents given during this research (in alphabetical order):

Marc Agazzotti, Ramón Aracena, Sarah Babb, Eric Barthalon, Damien Buchet, Jorge Blázquez, Steven Block, Domingo Cavallo, Jacques Cailloux, Ariel Colonomos, Starla Cohen, Rodrigo da Fonseca, François Denis, Alberto Diaz-Cayeros, Gerardo della Paolera, Ricardo della Santina Torres, Claire Dissaux, Philippe Dupuy, Marie-Hélène Duprat, Barry Eichengreen, Hubert Escaith, Amalia Estenssoro, Marc Flandreau, Marion Fourcade-Gourinchas, Denise Foreman, Jeffry Frieden, Joel Gross, Martin Grandes, Andy Haldane, David Hale, Stephan Haggard, Leo Harari, Kent Hargis, Witold Jerzy Henisz, Tarek Issaoui, Lawrence Krohn, Denis Lacorne, Bruno Landrieu, Guillermo Larrain, Pierre Laurent, Olivier Lemaigre, Jean-Charles Lemardeley, Patrice Lemonnier, Adam Lerrick, Koceila Maames, Beatriz Magaloni, Juan Martínez, Luis Miotti, Graciela Moguillansky, Caspar Melville Murphy, Jonathan Murno, Walter Molano, Sergio Orce, Charles Oman, André Orléan,

Avinash Persaud, Louis Pauly, Arturo Porzecanski, Carlos Quenan, Ricardo Raphael, Marc Russell-Jones, Carlos Santiso, Susan Strange, Sergio Schmukler, Alex Schwartsman, Jérôme Sgard, Marcelo Soto, Richard Sylla, Leonardo Torres Barsanti, Juan Yermo, Ziga Vodusek, James Vreeland, Peter West and Yves Zlotowski.

The empirical work wouldn't have been possible without the admirable support of research assistants Stewart Amer, Daniel Charron and Sebastian Nieto Parra. The marvelous visits to New York wouldn't have been what they were—unforgettable—without Jenny and Joseph Oughourlian, Mehdi Dazi and Riordan Roett. We benefit also from useful comments and ideas during our presentations of partial results at Central Bank of Spain, in Madrid, May 2001 and would like to thank Alicia Garcia Herrera for the invitation, Miguel Sebastián, Adolfo Albo, Enrique Alberola, Jorge Blázquez, Antonio Cortina and José Ramón Diez for their comments and meetings in Madrid.

A very special thanks to Olivier de Boysson, Christophe Cordonnier, Joseph Oughourlian and Luisa Palacios. Since the beginning they encouraged me to take this journey. Without them this research simply wouldn't have been possible. I would like to thank also Albert Hirschman for his inspiring bias for hope, his writings and all the meetings we had during the past years in Princeton, Paris, Madrid and Berlin.

And last but not least, I would like also to thank the institution that helped me as a research fellow to develop this essay, during all my years spent at the Centre d'Etudes et de Recherches Internationales (CERI-Sciences Po Paris), where I grew up intellectually speaking, immensely free thanks to Guy Hermet, my mentor and a former director of the center. Thanks are also due to Christophe Jaffrelot and Christian Lequesne, the current directors. Without them this research wouldn't have advanced.

Appendix 1.1: Total Interviews Completed in 2000 and 2001

Total interviews coded were 145 (out of 187 conducted from 97 different institutions). The number of persons interviewed from each institution is given in brackets.

Interviews in London and Edinbourgh: 65 (from 44 institutions)

AIB Govett (3); American Express Asset Management (1); Barclays Global Investors (1); BBVA (2); Baring Asset Management (1); Cazenove (1); City of London Investment Management (1); Delaware International Advisors (2); Deutsche Bank (1); Deutsche Asset Management (1); Dresdner Kleinwort Benson (1); Dresdner RCM Global Investors (1); Edinburgh Fund Managers (2); Colonial First State/Stewart Ivory (1); Fitch Ibca (1); Fleming Asset Management (2); Foreign &

Colonial Emerging Markets (1); Gartmore (1); Framlington Investment Management (1); Global Fund Analysis (1); Henderson Investors (1); Indocam Asset Management (2); Invesco (3); Martin Currie Investment Management (1); Investec Asset Management (1); Jupiter Asset Management (1); Martin Currie (2); Mercury Merrill Lynch Asset Management (1); Morgan Stanley Dean Witter (1); Old Mutual Asset Management (2); Pictet Asset Management (2); Rexiter Asset Management (1); Rothschild Asset Management (2); Salomon Smith Barney Citibank Asset Management (1); Schroders (1); Scottish Life (2); Scottish Widows Investment Partnership (2); Scudder Threadneedle Investments (1); Standard Life Investments (2); Tempest Consultants (2); The Economist Intelligence Unit (1); UBS Warburg Dillon Read (2); Walter Scott and Partners (1); WestLB Asset Management (1).

Interviews in Paris and Madrid: 25 (from 19 institutions)

Ahorro Corporación (1); Axa Investment Managers (3); Barep Asset Management (1); BBL Asset Management (1); Banque BNP Paribas (1); Carmignac Gestion (1); CDC (1); CDC Asset Management (2); Comgest (1); Crédit Agricole Indosuez (2); Crédit Lyonnais Asset Management (3); Fortis Investment Management (1); Indocam Asset Management (2); BNP Paribas Asset Management (1); Santander Central Hispano Gestión de Activos (2); Sinopia Asset Management (1); Société Générale (2); SG Asset Management (1); State Street Bank (1).

Interviews in New York and Boston: 55 (from 35 institutions)

ABN Amro (1); Alliance Capital Management (1); Barclays Securities (1); BBV Securities (1); Batterymarch (1); BCP Securities (1); Crédit Lyonnais Securities (2); Crédit Suisse Asset Management (2); Crédit Lyonnais Securities Americas (2); Chase (3); Deutsche Bank Securities (2); Dresdner Kleinwort Benson (1); Donaldson Lufkin & Jenrette (1); Evergreen Investment Management Company (1); Goldman Sachs (4); HSBC Securities (1); International Finance Coporation/The World Bank (2); JP Morgan (4); JP Morgan Investment (3); Keystone (1); Lehman Brothers (1); Merrill Lynch (2); MFS Investment Management (1); Moody's Investors Services (2); Morgan Stanley and Morgan Stanley Asset Management (3); Pioneer Investment Management (1); Salomon Smith Barney (2); Santander Central Hispano Investment (1); Schroders (1); Scudder Kemper Investments (1); State Street Global Advisors (1); Standard & Poor's (1); US Trust (1); Violy, Byorum & Partners (1); Wellington Management (1).

Appendix 1.2: Total Interviews Completed in 1996–1997 from (33) institutions

Ricardo Almada (Secretaria de Hacienda y Crédito Publico de México, Mexico); Juan Amieva (Director General de Asuntos Hacendarios Internacionales, Secretaria de Hacienda y Crédito Publico de México, Mexico); Carlos Asilis (Chief Economist Latin American Emerging Markets, Oppenheimer & Co, New York); Philippe Boin (Deputy Head of the Latin American Division, French Treasury Department, Paris); Omar Borla (Senior Vice President of the Latin American Economist, Flemings, New York); Olivier de Boysson (Emerging Markets Chief Economist, Economic Research Department, Banque Paribas, Paris); Christian Brachet (Manager of IMF Paris Office, Paris); Seno Bril (Business Development, Banque Paribas, Paris).

Christophe Cordonnier (Emerging Markets Chief Economist, Country Risk Credit Department, Banque Crédit Agricole Indosuez, Paris); Mehdi Dazi (Assistant Vice President, Scudder, Stevens & Clark, New York); Jean-Louis Daudier (Latin America Country Risk Analyst, COFACE, Paris); Geoffrey Dennis (Managing Director, Global Emerging Markets Strategist, HSBC James Capel, New York); Bernard Dufresne (Country Ris Specialist, Financial Division, COFACE, Paris); Richard Flax (Latin America Research Economist, Morgan Stanley, New York); Lacey Gallagher (Director Latin America Sovereign Ratings, Standard & Poor's, New York); Juan Carlos Garcia (Research Director, Santander Investment, New York); Larry Goodman (Head of Latin American Economic Research, Salomon Brothers, New York); Cynthia Harlow (Director, Latin America Equity Research, Credit Suisse First Boston, New York); Carlos Hurtado (Mexican OECD Ambassador, Permanent Representative, OECD, Paris).

Bénédicte Larre (Head of Mexico Desk, Economics Department, OECD); Guy Longueville Emerging Markets Chief Economist, Economic Research Department, Banque Nationale de Paris, Paris); Claudio Loser (Director Western Hemisphere, International Monetary Fund, Washington); Jorge Mariscal (Vice President and Manager of the Latin America Equity Group, Investment Research Department, Goldman Sachs, New York); Stefano Natella (Research Director, Credit Suisse First Boston, New York); Jim Nash (Latin American Chief Economist, Nomura Securities, New York); Francis Nicollas (Senior Economist, Economic and Financial Research Division, Crédit Lyonnais, Paris); Patrick Paradiso (Director of Economic Research, Deutsche Morgan Grenfell, New York); Denis Parisien (Vice President, Bankers Trust Securities Corporation, New York); Robert Pelosky (Research Director and Strategist, Morgan Stanley, New York); Jesus Perez Trejo (Secretaria de Hacienda y Crédito Publico de México, México); Arturo Porzecanski (Managing Director and Chief Economist, Head of Fixed Income Research, ING Barings, New York); Florent Prats (Head of Local Markets-Trading and Research Emerging Markets, Capital Markets Division, Société Générale, Paris); John Purcell (Research Director, Salomon Brothers, New York).

CHAPTER TWO

The Confidence Game: Exit, Voice and Loyalty in Financial Markets

> People believe certain stories because everyone important tells them, and people tell those stories because everyone important believes them.
>
> Paul Krugman[1]

At the very heart of financial transactions lies the question of confidence. Economists, from Smith to Coase, have underlined the importance of confidence, whether it be to explain the wealth of nations or the birth and death of firms. More recently, Paul Krugman highlighted how contemporary games of confidence and trust are at the center of financial turbulences. Given their financial needs and lack of savings, emerging markets are highly dependent on international capital flows. The game for policy-makers is thus to keep premiums low by maintaining investors' confidence in their countries' economy. It has been argued that in order to regain confidence some emerging countries should simply give up their political and monetary economy, abandoning the national currency. "The credibility of their financial policies, as argued, would be greatly enhanced by the implicit subordination to the policy-making institutions of the hard currency issues."[2] The central idea is that countries, like Argentina, could gain more confidence abroad by abandoning their national currencies as a vehicle for "institutions substitution," paraphrasing the label of the "imports substitution" approach once dominant in Latin America and developing countries during the 1960s. Two leading economists from the MIT went further in this "substitution institution" strategy in order to boost confidence suggesting that Argentina should simply give up its monetary, fiscal, regulatory and management sovereignty for an extended period of at least five years.[3]

To ensure this confidence, to maintain investors' *loyalty*, avoid their *voice* or their *exit*, it is not enough to adopt or adapt economic policies that make sense in terms of fundamentals.[4] They must fit with the fast changing *air du temps* of international financial markets. In other words they have to deal with the unstable and fast changing conventions that govern emerging markets. The unstable conventions derive from *cognitive regimes*, strategic forward looking analysis and timing considerations. They are cognitive frameworks with their own rules, constraints and taboos: conventions that change according to the macroeconomic, financial, social and political perceptions of emerging market analysts.

2.1   Exit, Voice and Loyalty in Emerging Markets

Rating agencies, government officials, international organizations and newspapers or information agencies, are all actors in this confidence game. Among these actors, financial analysts, economists, strategists, industry equity or bond analysts and fund managers are the key players. In the arenas of the international confidence game, investors, strategists and analysts have plenty of opportunities to buy or sell stocks, bonds and in the end entire countries—the so-called emerging markets. Some, scared off by rising risks or because of more attractive opportunities elsewhere, can simply exit the country. Others, unhappy with the policies implemented, can stop buying specific emerging market products, stocks or bonds, using what Hirschman labelled the *exit option*. The expression of their dissatisfaction can be direct or indirect as markets have a large range of tools and channels to protest and address their dissatisfaction. This *voice option* is less straightforward and more costly, from a temporal point of view, than exit. It implies involvement and, in the end, as stressed by Hirschman, a political dimension, the articulation of interests. In the case of financial markets, a direct measure of voice is the evolution of risk premiums, narrowing or increasing spreads of emerging market bonds over U.S. Treasury bills. Not only do they signal investors' appetite for risk, or conversely their risk aversion, but also their level of confidence, satisfaction or dissatisfaction.

For governments, in both cases, the task will be to restore confidence. Policy-makers will try to regain or maintain loyalty through sound policies, accurate data, road shows or one to one meetings. As stressed by fund managers, the improvement of investor relations and the more timely release of information is one of the most impressive trends within the confidence game.[5] It can also be seen as an indicator of the fierce competition among governments to attract investors, and to regain or maintain their loyalty.[6] The *voice* interactions between states and market operators can be direct or indirect; media distributions (international newspapers or specialized agencies such as Reuters or Bloomberg), world meetings or more selective meetings being arenas of information exchange. Financial and debt games are above all informational games, where it can be rational to imitate, voice or exit at the same time as other investors, and where asymmetries and inefficiencies of information play a large role.[7]

Informational games are therefore made up of mimetic behavior, phases of illusion and disillusion, informational mimeticism and normative mimeticism, where it is rational to imitate the dominant conventions.[8] The herding behavior is even more intensive when, unlike the globalization of the latter part of the twentieth century, in the late twentieth century investors have diversified portfolios. As indicated by Guillermo Calvo and Enrique Mendoza, with such diversified portfolios there is less incentive for investors to engage in the costly acquisition and processing of information about each market, stock or bond in which they invest, and hence the propensity toward rational herding increases.[9]

In some cases, *voice* from market participants can be organized through private associations. As during the early age of financial globalization, which saw the creation of the "Corporation of Foreign Bondholders" in 1868, by the end of twentieth century,[10] bondholders and market participants create associations in order to achieve greater voice. Some of the leading *voice* channels of emerging market operators are, for example, the *Emerging Markets Traders Association* (EMTA), the *Institute of International Finance* (IIF) or more recently the *Emerging Markets Creditors Association* (EMCA). In April 2001, these three market "voicers" participated for the first time in one of the meetings amongst the private sector as a result of their displeasure with the Argentina debt treatment. In response to private sector voice, Club de Paris created in 2001, for the first time, a website, taking into account criticisms by market participants regarding the lack of transparency and the lack of comparability of treatment.[11] Among the private sector firms brought together by the private sector associations were leading emerging operators, securities firms and fund managers like ABN Amro, Société Générale, UBS Warburg, Invesco, Ashmore Investment Management or PIMCO (the latter being amongst one of the most active).

IIF was created in 1983 by the world's largest commercial and investment banks. During the 1990s a growing number of insurance companies and investment management firms joined the association as well as multinational corporations, trading companies, export credit agencies and multilateral agencies. In 2000, IIF was one of the largest associations representing and voicing financial institutions interests in the international arenas from its Washington base (near the IMF and U.S. Treasury). In 2000, the institute represented the voices of more than 320 members headquartered in 60 countries, half of them in Europe. The institute has also established a worldwide reputation for the quality of its extensive macroeconomic and financial analysis of emerging market risk, acting not only as a forum but also as a provider of economic and financial information on emerging economies (the famous and much used IIF country risk reports).[12]

EMTA, with offices in New York, is the principal group for the emerging market trading and investment community. Formed in 1990, in response to the new opportunities created by the Brady Plan and the development of emerging bond markets, by the end of the 1990s EMTA became a leading voice trying to promote investors' rights. In 2000, in order to boost market voices, EMTA helped create EMCA, a group of bondholders, formed by private actors who assumed an increasing and critical role in emerging markets in the 1990s. Created in 2000 by a group of eight large buy side firms, EMCA's aim was to represent and directly present the interests (i.e. to voice them) of bondholders to the official sector and to sovereign issuers.[13]

As underlined by PIMCO's fund manager, "on their side, bondholders have recognized that they have been too much of a silent partner and for too long. The resulting vacuum has been filled by misperceptions that undermine the long-term health of the asset class. This situation is slowly being addressed through various initiatives, including better buy–side representation on EMTA (Emerging Markets Traders Association) and the formation of EMCA (Emerging Markets Creditors Association)."[14] The major goal of EMCA is to ensure that sovereign creditors, for example the Paris Club, adhere to the principles of equal treatment of debtors and agree to write off that portion of the debt that private creditors had written off. In practice, as underlined by one EMCA's leading members, the limited purpose of bondholders participation with officials is simply to share information: "The market is too diverse, and much of it totally uninterested in any discussion, let alone negotiation. Bondholders simply want to know what are the rules of the game are and get on with their money. The use of bondholders participating in such meetings is thus to educate the official sector how bond markets work, to give information and not to acquire it."[15]

When the Argentina default was expected to take place, in the first days of November 2001, EMCA organized a meeting with some of Argentina's international bondholders. By mid-November, a group of bondholders, among them Morgan Stanley Asset Management and Massachusetts Mutual Life Insurance, considered hiring legal and financial advisers with the purpose of participating in Argentina debt restructuring process. The government, which had by that time a public debt of US$ 132 bn., said it couldn't keep paying its obligations and asked for an "orderly" and "voluntary" debt rescheduling. It announced the terms of an initial exchange aimed, first, at domestic bondholders to swap as much as US$ 60 bn. of bonds for new loans with lower interest rates and longer maturities. In a second phase, the Argentinian government planned to follow similar plans with international bondholders. This action from international bondholders is a clear example of an attempt to organize voice; international bondholders feared that Argentina was favoring domestic banks and pension funds in the first round of restructuring as a prelude to more coercive tactics with foreign bondholders. BBVA Banco Francés, an Argentina bank owned by Spain's BBVA, was among the first "local" actors who agreed to the exchange of its US$3.5 bn. of government debt, by November 9, 2001, just a few days before the start of the debt exchange with domestic bondholders scheduled for November 16, 2001.

The week before the exchange, more than 200 bondholders gathered in an auditorium on Bear Stearns New York office for a conference on creditors rights. Many of the investors attending had held bonds sold by Ecuador when the country restructured its debt in 1999 and were in fact hoping to avoid problems they had encountered before by organizing their voice earlier. As quoted by one of the most respected Wall Street analysts, commenting on the event, "to make matters worse, investors were treated to a virtual house of horrors at the EMCA meeting in Manhattan. Don't get me wrong, the conference was fabulous. In contrast to sell-side conferences, the creditors ran this one. Therefore, the content was useful, not self-serving advertisement. Nevertheless, the information was outright scary because it revealed the legal morass that will follow the Argentina restructuring."[16]

During the first weeks of November, Allan Meltzer and Adam Lerrick, chairman and director respectively of the Center for Public Policy at Carnegie Mellon University, completed a study based on a simulation exercise involving investors and policy-makers. The results of the case study based on the "Republic of Mañana" (in fact Argentina) suggested that only the intervention of a multilateral (the IMF) could stimulate a liquid and efficient solution to a debt restructuring by guaranteeing a minimum price to investors seeking to sell their paper. Among the participants in the simulation exercise were a former finance minister of Mexico, senior officials from the IMF, from the White House, from Moody's Investors Service (the rating agency sent one of its senior analysts on Argentina) and also high-level representatives from French and German Treasuries. Interestingly, private investors also participated, including Mohamed El-Erian of PIMCO (a founding member of EMCA), Peter Geraghty of Darby International Finance and Jay Newman of Elliott Associates (a fund very much involved in the Ecuador debt rescheduling).[17] A few weeks after this theoretical exercise, Anne Krueger, IMF's First Deputy Managing Director, announced in a critical speech the need for a formal framework and mechanism for sovereign debt restructuring....[18]

During Argentina's debt default by the end of 2001, another attempt to organize "voice" from within the market and by market participants came in the form of the Argentine Bondholders Committee (ABC), a group formed in November with the help of the lawyer's office Mayer Brown & Platt. The explicit purpose of this attempt was to convey some big investor's views to the Argentine government, to obtain and exchange views in order to implement debt negotiations strategies. Mainly composed of European (and Italian) retail investors, the ABC group represents interests different from the EMCA. One of the major fears of the ABC group was the threat of different treatment for domestic and international creditors during the restructuring debt negotiation process that started in November (and ended with the Argentina official default by the end of 2001). This view was shared by prominent economists such as, for example, Nouriel Roubini from NYU, who published several important papers, one of them on December 21, 2001,[19] arguing that foreign rather than domestic bondholders should accept more pain in sovereign debt-restructuring.

Other leading arenas of interaction are the highly selective meetings organized between officials and market participants. As they are exclusive and selective, these one to one meetings are praised not only by investments banks (because they indicate their ability to access information and reach high-level contacts) or asset managers (because they strengthen their monitoring capacities and their investment efficiency) but also by officials who can try to curb perceptions, interact with leading market markers and, in sensitive situations, try to transmit views.

Thus, when Argentina was facing its huge swap operation in June 2001 and later when it was negotiating another rescue package with the

IMF, which became effective in September 2001, several leading market makers organized selective meetings with Argentinian and international officials. For example, on July 26, Merrill Lynch's emerging market fixed-income research team hosted a series of investor meetings in Washington D.C. with high-level officials at the IMF, IADB, U.S. Treasury, U.S. State Department and the World Bank in order to assess the attitude of Bush's administration and the international community regarding crisis-ridden emerging economies and rescue packages.[20]

Another way of gathering information and interacting directly with officials of emerging countries is by making field trips and missions. Here also, at crucial or critical junctures, it gives the opportunity for analysts and economists to hold meetings with top officials, collect data and information and develop a more qualitative perception of the situation. For leading investment banks it is essential to building their competency to develop more timely and precise views and analysis on the country and maintain high-level contacts.[21]

Governments in emerging countries can also take into account the voice of dissatisfied investors and improve the quality of their policy making. It might be that "discontented customers or members could become so harassing that their protests would at some point hinder rather than help whatever efforts at recovery are taken."[22] One can then distinguish between *negative* and *positive* voice effects, voice options leading to self-fulfilling crises and voice options leading to policy adjustments if protesters' voice are taken into account on time. From this perspective it can be argued that in order to manage financial risk and prevent crises in international financial markets, one of the most relevant options is monitoring voice as it involves many "blessings in disguise." Perceiving and answering market voices is therefore crucial for governments if they want to stay in the confidence game.

However, the problem in financial markets is that exit options are (nearly) always available. Because capital controls are not easily perceived moves in the confidence game,[23] the omnipresence of exit options contributes also to the decreased usage of the voice option. Emerging market investors do have choices—contrary to what happened in the nineteenth century for example when financial assets were less mobile.[24] Investors can diversify their portfolio or, more abruptly, quit and put their money elsewhere. The ability and willingness of investors to take up the voice option might then be lower in financial markets than elsewhere precisely because of the speed of financial movements and adjustments. Their propensity to voice, and then to postpone exit, will be constrained by the fact that in financial markets speed is as crucial as timing. Slower players are frequently the losers. That explains why, in financial markets, exit is frequently used as a *reaction of last resort*, simply because one does not have time to wait for the failure of the voice option (assuming there are incentives to use the voice option). At the same time, as voice requires group action it is also constrained by difficulties related to coordination and free riding, whereas exit does not require any kind of coordination with others. Financial coordination is difficult and it contributes to the atrophy of the use of voice.

Another aspect of financial markets is loyalty, which is problematic and contributes to making exit a more likely option than voice. In Hirschman's analyses loyalty holds exit at bay and activates voice. It also raises the cost of exit as loyalty means stronger attachment, intricate links and more involvement. Nothing comparable is available in the emerging market financial worlds. There is little incentive to remain loyal. There are no mechanisms helping to reinforce loyalty or to enforce high penalties for exit. This does not imply that loyalty should not be observed. To pull out of an investment from a country or to break relationships with a company or a sovereign issuer is painful, as it takes time to reconstruct the client relationship and even more time later for rebuilding.

Loyalty is directly linked with credibility. The propensity to remain loyal depends on the confidence attached to the actions of government officials. This propensity will tend to increase if, for example, during the past, investors observed that commitments were honored. In the international debt games, for example, past behaviors are taken into account. However this backward looking and retrospective view is limited, as financial markets seem to have a selective memory. In their impressive study of sovereign debt since the 1850s, Lindert and Morton conclude, "investors seem to pay little attention to the past repayment record of borrowing governments. They do not punish governments with a prior default history, undercutting the belief in a penalty that compels faithful repayment."[25]

In history the Great Depression is proof that creditors have a short-term and selective memory.[26] However more recent research, based on two centuries of international financial history in emerging markets, underlined that reputation and credibility is taken into account by creditors. In particular a government that faces economic recession, a war or any adverse shock and still honors its commitments increases its credibility in the eyes of investors. "By the same logic, a government that defaults under favourable conditions will see its reputation sink. But creditors will not deprecate a borrower that defaults under duress, nor will they esteem a government paying when the yoke is light. Credit history does affect reputation, but only under certain conditions."[27] What creditors dislike above all are unexpected defaulters. There is therefore a temporal dimension to the credibility issue. Another temporal dimension pertains to the past. As stressed by a Brazilian economist, credibility is an intertemporal issue: "I do not mean credibility in the normal use of the term, i.e., an almost ineffable quality that some individuals and institutions possess, which makes others believe that they will carry out their promises. I mean it in the precise sense of factors that force an individual or institution to act against their short-term objectives to preserve long-term strategy. The traditional example is, of course, Odysseus (Ulysses) tied to his ship's mast, so that he could listen to the Sirens, but would not jump towards certain death. The ropes that tied Odysseus are what lend credibility to his long-term objective (return home), despite the short-term temptations."[28]

The use and abuse of exit options is certainly characteristic of financial markets. However, although exits accelerate financial crises, if we consider it to be an act of leaving for a better good, service or benefit believed to be provided by another, indirectly or unintentionally exit can also improve performance. Thus exit and crises can have "unintended consequences" and involve some "blessings in disguise" as it is argued regarding the way crises can work as accelerators of reforms or even breakdown of regimes. Reforms and regime breakdown are obviously open options even without crises.[29] It is also true that crises create economic distortions widening the spectrum of possibilities. They enable societies to enact costly reforms that would be impossible to execute in less critical junctures. For example, the heavy cost of extremely high inflation in several Latin American countries has provided a powerful reason to enforce and hasten the adoption of stabilization plans and of painful fiscal adjustments.[30]

2.2   Economic Reforms as Strategic Labels

Building or maintaining investor confidence is a subtle and complex exercise in which policy-makers try to curb the negative expectations of asset managers, strategists and economists. They move money, write reports and voice in global arenas such as the international newspapers, Bloomberg or Reuters screens or world conferences (or simply exit in silence, pulling their money out of the country).

However, as pointed out by Krugman, the strategies followed by policy-makers can lead to unintended consequences: "Because speculative attacks can be self-justifying, following an economic policy that makes sense in terms of the fundamentals is not enough to assure market confidence. In fact, the need to win that confidence can actually prevent a country from following otherwise sensible policies and force it to follow what would seem perverse." "Because crises can be self-fulfilling, sound economics is not enough to gain market confidence; one must cater to the perceptions, the prejudices, the whims of the market. Or, rather one must cater to what one hopes will be the perceptions of the market."[31]

Therefore market failures can be closely linked to political and economic failures and to policy making. As stressed by several studies, the Brazilian devaluation of 1999—the Mexican and Argentinian devaluations are discussed in subsequent chapters—can be partly explained by an "endogenous-failure" of the workings of financial markets operating with an overabundance of liquidity and overdependent on increasingly volatile capital flows.[32] But, as pointed out by one scholar, the "magical realism of Brazilian economics," was also involved: "the way in which the government dealt with the inevitable domestic fragility that (unstable) rates created, were at the heart of the process that led to Brazil's crisis (...) By struggling to avoid three types of financial crisis (a 'Kindlebergian' Mexican-type one, an external or internal shock creating an East-Asian-type sudden loss of confidence and panic-withdrawal of funds, and a domestic banking collapse), the Brazilian authorities ended up creating a different type of crisis—it seems that in Brazil solutions to difficult problems cannot be done without a magical realist hint."[33]

From this perspective, realizing liberalization policies, implementing deregulation or trade liberalization and strengthening central bank independence are ways of consolidating confidence. All these reforms, implemented during the 1990s, can be seen as highways to the promised high economic growth and to secure the support of local voters.[34] But above all these reforms can be seen as *strategic labels* providing visibility in the landscape of populous emerging markets and signaling credibility to investors. Enjoying credibility, or in other words playing the confidence game, means to signal to relevant actors (that can vary across time and space), such as domestic and foreign investors, that the announced economic reforms will be fully implemented.

In the 1990s many emerging markets chose the Washington Consensus highway, wearing more or less constraining clothes inspired by neoliberal fashion designers. The tightness of such self-imposed strait-jackets has been obviously highly dependent on the country's coalition games, economic conditions and needs for external funds. As stressed by many scholars, international capital mobility has not constrained emerging countries in a similar fashion.[35] Countries like Chile or Korea were liberalized in a much more selective way than countries like Mexico or Turkey whose opening has been quicker and deeper. Some, with more bargaining power and lesser need for external funds, adopted a gradualist opening of their financial markets whilst others, due to external debt burdens and financial needs, opted for a quicker liberalization of their current accounts.

The reform fever of the 1990s must thus be seen in the context of the urgent need for new capital inflows. These reforms helped one country to differentiate itself from others, to compete in attracting scarce foreign investment funds and, in the end, to catch the attention of friendly free-market investors. Sovereign governments, in order to consolidate their reputation in the eyes of investors, will then make international legal commitments. This propensity to signal commitment and compliance in the international monetary system will increase if other countries in the same region do so, suggesting that competitive market forces (and not only "imposed" IMF conditionality) acts also as an incentive and is a "likely enforcement mechanism."[36] The adoption of liberal economic ideas and the spread of liberalization reforms throughout the world during the 1990s are highly clustered both temporally and spatially. The liberalization of the current account and capital account or the shift toward unified exchange rates are highly concentrated in certain years suggesting a temporal clustering of foreign economic policies. The propensity to adopt (and adapt) these reforms is also driven by geographic clustering and emulation effects. Neighbors emulate neighbors, but the motivation to adopt reforms can also be explained by strategic and economic competition, information about the impact of reforms or even cultural proximities.[37]

The wave of privatization in emerging countries, for example, was a competitive emulation game with a mimetic dimension. The prior existence of privatization in a nation's peer group, defined in spatial (geographic proximity) or temporal terms (common legal heritage), was more likely to provoke other nations within the peer group to launch privatization.[38] It appears that one of the most important rules, to avoid being removed or erased from the game, is to continue participating in the confidence race. The pursuit of happiness then passes through an unlimited reform fervor and, for emerging market government officials, the recitation of the economic Decalogue. In the case of privatization reforms the most striking comparative fact is the scale, the speed and the scope of these reforms during the 1990s. They increase exponentially during the 1990s suggesting a large diffusion effect. Within a decade, 75 percent of Latin American countries initiated privatization programs. Whilst they might differ by the number of privatizations and total revenues, the ratio of privatization revenues and 1997 GDP is comparable at least for the biggest countries of the area. Brazil to all intents and purposes joined the race by the end of the 1990s; explaining the relatively modest levels measured by the end of 1997. The number of emerging countries engaged in the privatization process jumped from less than 20 on average by the end of the 1980s to over 60 in each year in the late 1990s (see graph 2.1).

The example of pension fund reforms also demonstrates the dynamics of emulation and competition. Economists emphasize that the shift toward funded private pension schemes became a necessary response to failures of public pay-as-you-go pension schemes. During the 1990s social security privatization became firmly established as a sign of credibility of emerging countries government's commitments to market reforms. Chile's economic success story was associated with pension privatization. All around the world, policy-makers and Wall Street brokers began to notice and associate the high levels of savings and the development of local stock market with this reform.[39] In Latin America, other governments, looking to send positive signals of credibility and to attract

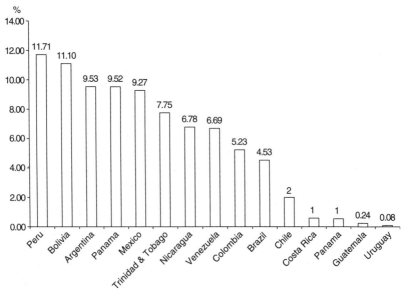

Graph 2.1   Latin American 1988–1997 privatization revenues/1997 GDP (%).
Source: Based on Brune and Garrett, Yale University Working Paper, 2000.

scarce foreign investments, followed the Chilean road. After Chile's 1981 reform, 17 countries implemented pension reforms, accelerating during the 1990s particularly among Latin American countries. Among the 17 countries 7, nearly half, were Latin American and all adopted the reform within a temporal horizon of six years. Peru, Argentina, Colombia, Uruguay, Bolivia, Mexico and El Salvador adopted the pension reforms between 1993 and 1998. The spread of pension reforms across Latin American countries suggest that the timing of privatization is directly linked with emulation and competition among emerging countries. The likelihood of adopting pension reforms increases with social and cultural ties across nations. A policy innovation, perceived as a "successful model" by international market actors, further increases the likehood of the adoption by local policy-makers of such reforms (see graph 2.2 and table 2.1).[40]

These reforms can be seen then as policy choices, delivering confidence shocks, lowering instability and restraining uncertainty, all the things that foreign investors dream of avoiding. In a world of increasing capital mobility and exploding short-term liabilities resulting from financial liberalization, to regain or to retain confidence becomes a strategic asset for emerging countries' economic development. Without confidence one is exposed to capital flight and money

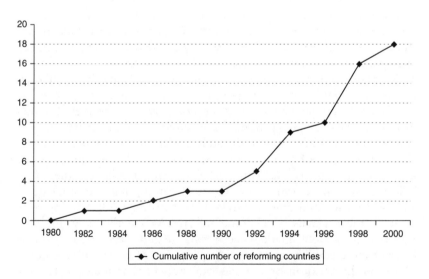

Graph 2.2   Diffusion of pension reforms around the world, 1980–2000.
Source: Based on Brooks, 2001 (unpublished paper).

Table 2.1 Timetable of pension reforms around the world

Country and year of pension reform implementation	
Chile	1981
Switzerland	1985
U.K.	1988
Australia	1992
Denmark	1992
Netherlands	1993
Peru	1993
Argentina	1994
Colombia	1994
Uruguay	1996
Bolivia	1997
Hungary	1997
Mexico	1997
El Salvador	1998
Kazakhstan	1998
Poland	1998
Croatia	2000
Sweden	2000

Source: Based on Brooks, 2001.

runs. Without confidence even domestic investors can exit the country. They can convert their short-term assets, bank deposits and government bills into currency and take them out of the country.

From this perspective, Mexico's integration into Nafta or the building process of Mercosur also corresponds to signals made in order to boost confidence.[41] Free trade areas indicate not only a pro-market commitment but are also a sign regarding the search for economic stability. In the case of Mexico, Nafta brought the additional promise of linking a Third World country to a First World one, boosting confidence among foreign investors. This international commercial agreement enhanced the credibility of Mexican reformers and reforms by mitigating two problems—adverse selection and time inconsistency—that frequently lead investors to doubt the longevity of economic reforms. As underlined by empirical research using stock market data from Mexico, Nafta trade reforms boosted the credibility of Mexico. Stock prices of labor intensive companies on the Mexican Bolsa rose as investors became increasingly confident of reforms implementation in Mexico. The day after the Nafta vote in the U.S. Senate, investors' portfolios experienced abnormal gains of more than 3.3 percent (4.5 times larger than its standard error[42]). In the same way the Mercosur promise has also materialized with increasing capital inflows, especially foreign direct investment (FDI), that reached a stock of more than US$100 bn. in 2000 for Brazil alone.

Whilst the net effect of democracy on growth remains uncertain, and the correlation between economic development and democratic propensities lacks empirical proof (even if the link seems more robust[43]), the unintended consequence of democratic transitions in the 1980s and 1990s appears to have been to boost international investor confidence. For fund managers and strategists, democracy is seen as a "positive asset." It is perceived as "bringing more stability" and "more transparency." The diffusion of "corporate governance rules into the economy is comparable to the diffusion of electoral rules into the political sphere. It increases the levels of checks and balances, brings more openness and secures the rule of law."[44] According to recent studies examining the potential links between democracy and economic stability (rather than on the—weak—impact of democracy on long-run growth rates), investors might be right in preferring to invest in participatory political regimes. These regimes, as underlined by Rodrik,[45] are associated with lower levels of economic instability. One explanation is the propensity of democracies to moderate social conflicts.[46] Empirical research confirms that private investors, portfolio fund managers or company managers tend to prefer political regimes that guarantee stability and lower uncertainty. Clearly they associate democracies with these qualities.[47] In a study based on 43 developing countries from 1981 and 1995, there is evidence that economic investment (both FDI and portfolio investment) and government respect for human rights and political liberties tend to be interlinked.[48]

Similarly, at the same time as the 1990s financial liberalization process, a wave of emerging countries reforms made the central bank independent. The purpose was not only to bring about more stability and avoid political interference on monetary policies but also to successfully signal creditworthiness to international investors.[49] Referring to the possible strengthening of the Brazilian central bank during the last years of the Cardoso administration, a major Wall Street operator affirmed that "in seeking Central Bank independence, local policymakers are simply expressing a desire to put Brazilian monetary policy practices in line with international norms. Together with the recently passed Law of Fiscal Responsibility, it would be a crucial move away from populist economic policies that have often plagued Brazil in the past."[50]

Argentina, like Brazil and many other emerging countries, also implemented impressive reforms in the 1990s including a profound

reorganization of its banking and financial system in order to establish
credible discipline and restore the confidence lost in monetary institutions during the high-inflation years of the previous decade.[51] When
Pedro Pou, Argentina's central bank chief, came under fire in 2001 after
the release of a report by the U.S. Senate about possible money
laundering in the financial system during his mandate, not surprisingly
the key issue for Wall Street and London was the interpretation of signals emitted regarding the commitment of the Argentinian government
to the central bank's sacred and beloved "independence." As put by
an ING Barings economist interviewed by the *Financial Times*, "it matters
very much whether this (respect of central bank independence) is done
according to the rules. If they were to show that they don't respect the
rules of the game, I don't think it would cause an immediate crisis, *but it
would be another negative signal for investors.*"[52]

   Throughout the twentieth century, the number of central banks and
ministries of finance increased with the number of emerging countries.
They became key players within the confidence game, in the front line
between states and markets. By the end of the century, 173 central banks
were competing to provide (or hide) the most accurate data to financial
markets. They increased their staff employing more economists and
fewer lawyers than their supervisory/financial stability wing to produce
a macro-approach (better adapted to the analysis of the financial crisis of
the 1990s, many of them micro-induced).[53] However despite the
increased number, employees remain under-utilized in comparison to
the developed countries. On average, in the year 2000, Euro area central
banks have nearly 20 staff per 100,000 population. This is twice as much
as countries like Venezuela or Colombia and four times more than
Argentina, Mexico or Brazil. With their increased level of independence
they also became relevant indicators of credibility. A change of governor
before end of term became an element of the confidence building
process much more than the timing of governors' nominations
(disconnected or not with presidential elections) and the length of their
mandates (see graph 2.3 and chart 2.1).

   In a world of liquid capital flows with increasing financial needs in
middle-income developing countries, the propensity of politicians to
seek creditworthiness and to give strong signals to international investors
is on the rise. With bondholders becoming more and more involved in
emerging market finance, the incentives for independent central banks
also increased and became one of the confidence game tools used during the 1990s to secure investor loyalty.[54] Regarded as highly desirable
by investors, central bank independence became one of the best moves

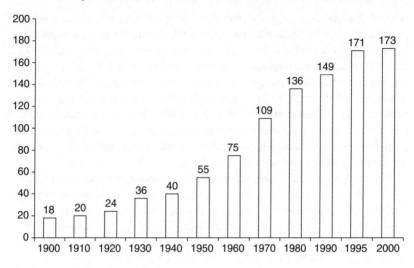

Graph 2.3   Number of central banks, 1900–2000.

Source: Santiso, 2001, based on Morgan Stanley Dean Witter, The Morgan Stanley Dean Witter Central Bank Directory, New York, Morgan Stanley, 2001.

Chart 2.1   Change of governors and terms of office

Change of governors	1997	1998	1999	2000	2001
At end of term	8	11	12	6	7
Before end of term	11	5	15	7	6
Indefinite term	2	5	5	2	3
Unknown term	4	8	5	8	9
Total	25	29	37	23	25

Terms of office	Number of banks
Indefinite	21
8 years	2
7 years	10
6 years	24
5 years	52
4 years	14
3 years or less	12
Not available	38

Source: Santiso, 2001, based on Morgan Stanley Dean Witter, The Morgan Stanley Dean Witter Central Bank Directory, New York, Morgan Stanley, 2001.

within the confidence game for emerging countries looking to signal greater stability. In Latin American countries, central banks, as with other institutions, reflected this instability with frequent removals of governors. Apart from a few countries like Mexico, where central bankers' turnover has been low with a change on average every five and a half years (5.7) between 1935 and 2000, Latin American countries show higher turnovers. In Brazil, between 1945 and 2000, the central bank governor has been removed almost every two years (1.72).[55] In Argentina the turnover was even higher, the central bank governor having changed nearly every year (1.30) between 1935 and 2000.

Market operators, policy-makers in emerging countries, U.S. Treasuries decision-makers, IMF economists, asset managers and brokers analysts, are all involved in this worldwide game whose name is confidence, the only game in the global financial village. As stressed by Dani Rodrik, "bankers and currency traders study economics in typically Northern American or British universities, they read *The Economist* and the *Financial Times*, look at reports by the IMF and the World Bank, listen to academics hired as consultants, call up their friends in international organizations, and generally imbue the economic zeitgeist of the time. In all this, the pronouncements of the official Washington community (the IMF and the Treasury in particular) play an important anchoring role."[56] They help to shape the conventional wisdom that contributes to frame the cognitive regimes not only of markets participants but also of emerging market policy-makers. They become "aware" of how they can be part of the game, which language, signals and policies trigger confidence. Or, on the contrary, with the loss of confidence can become a pariah or a renegade and be transformed in risky moves leading to withdrawal of foreign (and even local) investments.

In order to preserve investors' loyalty, the IMF will demand more structural reforms and, if needed, will supply more emergency lines. The IMF international assistance packages to Mexico, Asia, Russia, Brazil, Turkey and Argentina are the ultimate ways of restoring confidence or avoiding the use of exit options (contagion effects). One of the last IMF emergency loan innovations, namely the Supplemental Reserve Facility, was created in 1997 precisely to deal with the disruptive effects of a sudden loss of market confidence. In order to gain this confidence, policy-makers from emerging countries will need to multiply road shows and face-to-face interviews in the city centers of the global financial village (Wall Street and London) and, time allowing, in the suburbs, such as Paris, Madrid or Boston. Reuters and Bloomberg screens and international financial newspapers, such as the *Financial Times* or the *Wall Street Journal*, are being transformed into arenas of the confidence game.

They are veritable financial thermometers, indicating the amount of confidence or distrust that investors place on a country.

2.3 The Dollarization Game

In order to avoid a sudden loss of confidence one of the most radical move is the dollarization game. Abandoning one's currency and adopting the dollar became, by the end of the 1990s, the solution for a number of small Latin American economies facing currency pressures and economic crises. One after the other regional economies, such as Ecuador and El Salvador in 2000, are adopting the dollar in order to protect themselves against setbacks. In the case of Ecuador dollarization came as a last attempt to avoid economic explosion and restore confidence. Dollarization has also been contemplated by several larger economies in the region including Argentina and Peru.[57] Some economists insist on the virtues of dollarization citing its effect on trade where the sharing of a common currency with the United States can, in some cases, increase the volume of trade by a factor of two to three.[58]

However dollarization is also a tool to boost confidence. Dollarization implies avoiding the costs of investing heavily in policies and institutions to build market confidence in a local currency. It is above all a kind of institutional fast track, a way to "achieve instant credibility by hiring the respected Federal Reserve instead."[59] As stressed by Barry Eichengreen, "countries like Ecuador or Argentina have dollarized or installed currency boards not because they succeeded in pushing other reforms but precisely their economic problems have proven so intractable."[60] Dollarization can then also be seen as a means to achieve instant credibility, a kind of quick fix to deal with high inflation and to gain credibility speedily.[61] Also it makes the costs of turning back very high. It avoids any kind of exit, in other words, it's an irreversible institutional change. "Hence, as stressed by Alesina and Barro, these regimes are *much more credible* than customary (typically ephemeral) promises to peg the exchange rate."[62] The principal trade-off in the dollarization game is in the end between "credibility" and "competitiveness."

Above all it's a rapid move, a monetary adjustment that is also temporal. To dollarize is to achieve immediate results and to prevent a possible run or a coming financial spillover. As stressed by Walter Molano, a respected Wall Street economist, "it can provide *immediate results* to countries facing economic distress. A shift to the dollar allows a *rapid reduction* in the inflation rate, as well as a drop in nominal interest rates." "Proponents argue that dollorization *will buy the time needed* to implement the necessary reforms."[63] The cost of dollarization (and regaining confidence) is not little however. Dollarization eliminates the possibility of an independent monetary policy that can be used to stabilize the business cycle. It bars in particular the use of a national monetary policy. It is also followed by the loss of seignorage for the country. But above all the dollarization game is embedded in political and economic considerations. In the end, the ultimate decision about dollarization is made by politicians who are charged with assessing the pros and cons.[64] For policy-makers, the timing of dollarization matters as over a shorter time period they can face high political costs and so are likely to dollarize after elections rather than before.[65]

States are not always the losers and markets always the winners of the game. States can restore confidence and market loyalty with success. A good example is provided by Argentina when policy-makers responded to the spillover effects of the Mexican devaluation of December 20, 1994 and the Brazilian devaluation of January 13, 1999. They prevented a financial crash without abandoning the currency system by following an active announcement policy and sending the right signals to the markets. During the Mexican crisis, among the most positive signals received by the markets was the announcement of the IMF's agreement for the dollarization of deposits and Menem's reelection, to which stock and bond markets reacted positively.[66] During the Brazilian devaluation, when investors lost confidence and began pulling out of the country, Argentinian authorities began to "voice" officially saying that they were considering dollarization. The purpose was above all to distance themselves from Brazil and to buy time in order to avoid a drop of confidence just before major elections due by mid-1999. As stressed by a Wall Street economist, "faced with a time horizon of less than six months, Argentine officials understood that dollarization would buy them sufficient time to end the term."[67]

One can even argue that bringing the IMF back into the game, can be, for the state, not only a self-imposition of constraints in economic and political terms but can also be viewed as a strategic move. It helps to boost confidence and works like an "international insurance" as financial markets can—in some cases—react positively to the announcement of the package, as stressed by some operators after the IMF rescue packages to Argentina and Turkey in December 2000. In the case of Argentina, a political crisis in October and November 2000 led to an abrupt decline in international financial markets' confidence as to Argentina's debt repayment capacities, hindering access to foreign funding. Within a few days sovereign risk increased, as measured by the evolution of Argentinian spreads (that exceeded 1,100 basis points over U.S. Treasuries by early

November). Fund managers became increasingly risk averse regarding Argentina. As stressed in November by BAREP asset managers in their asset allocation monthly report "Argentina is obliged to roll its debt at higher spreads making its debt service more and more expensive." "This system is not sustainable anymore as investors begin to lose confidence on the country ability to access the market and we arrived at a point where we need a multilateral package to break these self-fulfilling anticipations before a more serious crisis happen."[68]

With the prospect of an aid package, whose expected size climbed within a few weeks from US$20 bn. to more than 30 bn., sovereign risk decreased. With the announcement in December 2000 of a package of nearly twice the expected amount (US$40 bn.), markets reacted very positively. From U.S.-based research teams Morgan Stanley and Santander Investment to Canadian-based Scotiabank or London-based WestLB and HSBC, the news came as a relief,[69] the package working as "global liquidity insurance" from the point of view of financial operators.[70] "There is no question about it, commented a fund manager, the packaging is impressive. You have had top international and national figures announcing headline figures of USD 40 billion (yes billions) in exceptional financial assistance for Argentina and over USD10 billion for Turkey. The packaging has had its desired impact in abruptly reversing the sense of panic that had gripped Argentine and Turkish financial markets."[71]

The good news was that the package covered more than the anticipated financial needs of Argentina in 2001. The confidence game could then proceed (even if it happens to be short-lived as shown by the February 2001 Turkish crisis and the new Argentinian crisis in March 2001). Nearly a few weeks after the package, in January 2001, most Latin American emerging markets, Mexico, Argentina and Colombia, were already making a come back in bond markets.[72] By the end of January, all the operators were expecting the rebirth of Argentina in the debt issuance game.[73] At the same time, Argentinian officials were roadshowing in New York, London and Paris. In less than one month, January 2001, bond issuance from emerging markets reached nearly US$7 bn. and the yield spreads between JP Morgan's Emerging Market Bond Index and U.S. Treasuries, the most accurate confidence barometer, tightened by nearly 100 points since the start of the year. Furthermore at the beginning of February, less than 60 days after the sudden confidence drop and less than one month after the announcement of the IMF package, Argentina carried out a US$4.2 bn. swap of existing dollar and peso bonds to readjust maturity profiles.

By the beginning of 2001, a new threat replaced the "old" Argentinian one on traders' screens: the specter of a U.S. hard landing for 2001. Within a few weeks, a complete set of new words and phrases replaced the Argentina-centered ones. Nearly all analysts changed the dominant perspective shifting their attention from the Southern Cone country to the northern U.S. economy. From CDC Ixis and Fortis Investment Management in Paris to BBVA Securities or UBS Warburg in London and Morgan Stanley in New York or Standard Chatered in Miami, the new name of the game became the U.S. hard landing.[74] Goldman Sachs emerging market economists started developing U.S. recession scenarios to foresee the impact in their investment universes. Discussions polarized on the speed and depth of the U.S. recession, Goldman Sachs predicting a slowdown scenario and HSBC a U.S. hard landing.[75] Equity teams started to predict how hard Latin American corporates would be hit by the U.S. economic slowdown.[76] Nearly all the research units polarized their energies in forecasting and projecting the impacts of the U.S. fast or slow landing on the emerging markets universe so that Argentina became an old—but unfinished—story. In March 2001, the convention changed once again and Argentina came back under the spotlights.

In less than a fortnight, Argentina changed its finance minister three times. Two of them, José Luis Machinea and Ricardo López Murphy, were forced to resign. By the second half of March a third man became the new economy minister: Domingo Cavallo, the father of the currency board implemented exactly ten years before.[77] For Argentina it meant that the game was not over but could continue. Analysts once again started working hard publishing papers on convertibility, currency baskets, dollarization and debt default[78] while rating agencies jumped on the bandwagon of downgrading Argentina's sovereign rating. Numbers (the announced Competitivity Law program) but above all individuals became the key to restoring confidence. Domingo Cavallo was by the time presented and perceived by analysts as a kind of White Knight and Argentina 2001 Odissey as a kind of quest of the Holy Graal—the Graal being in this case Growth.[79] "Argentina, wrote Walter Molano in his daily emerging markets review, is a high stakes poker game, with Domingo Cavallo as a steely-eyed card player. His deft gamesmanship is generating a return of confidence. Cavallo clearly has his grip on the reigns of power. He is managing the media. He is dictating terms to the Brazilians. He is in the driver's seat in his relationship with the IMF. Unlike previous economic teams, which sought approval from Washington before flinching, Cavallo's team informs the IMF through the press. He is a man of action."[80]

That said, it must be stressed that the issue of passing through was not only extremely important for Argentina but also for all emerging market analysts and fund managers. Argentina represented by the time the bulk of emerging bond markets with more than 35 percent of Latin American bond issues and nearly a quarter of all emerging bond markets issues in 2000.[81] Within a matter of weeks, markets started speculating on Argentina's possible exit out of the woods and the return to business as usual[82] while Cavallo was starting his one-to-one meetings with U.S. officials and Wall Street operators.[83] Others still remained skeptical regarding Argentinian political instability and its ability to maintain authority.[84] The parliamentary elections of October 2001 helped in fact to maintain the uncertainty that has dominated the political climate since President de la Rúa assumed power. From the date that democracy was reintroduced on December 1983 until March 2001, Argentina has seen a ministerial change every 2.2 months. Under the de la Rúa government instability has been greater than average with a change every 0.6 months. Between 1991 and 2000, the finance portfolio changed every 17 months on average, but every 5 months under de la Rúa. The return of Cavallo represented the promise of a more stable governance as he had held, under the Menem presidency, the long-term service record as head of the finance ministry, a post he filled for 85 months, from July 8, 1989 to July 26, 1996. This promise was however short-lived: by the end of 2001, the political equilibrium collapsed. In less than two weeks, Argentina changed presidents five times. By the beginning of 2002, Duhalde was sworn in, becoming the fifth president since December 20, 2001 when Fernando de la Rúa resigned.[85] (See table 2.2.)

Other studies confirm the high level of turnover within the legislative branch in Argentinian history. Between 1983 and 1999, for example, less than 17 percent of the representatives had been reelected. During this same period the rates of turnover in congress have been above 40 percent in average with deputies only staying in office for less than four years.[86] This instability is present in the provincial and national levels, the probability of staying in the national congress decreasing with the passage of time and the ability to survive in office being constrained by the disproportional power held by local party leaders vis-à-vis incumbent legislators.[87] It is also present in the supreme court where judges, since the 1960s, stayed 3.7 years in office in Argentina as against 12.5 years in the United States, 9.2 in Chile, 6.5 in France, 5.7 in Brazil and 4.4 in Colombia.[88] Likewise since 1958 only three Argentinian presidents had completed their alloted terms.

Table 2.2   Argentina's political speed: ministerial changes between 1983 and 2001

Portfolios	Alfonsín (67 months)	Menem (125 months)	De la Rúa (15 months)	Total
Labor	5	6	2	13
Defense	4	6	2	12
Economy	4	5	3	12
Health	3	7	1	11
Interior	3	6	2	11
Education	3	4	3	10
Justice	0	5	2	7
Infrastructures	3	1	2	6
External affairs	2	2	1	5
Cabinet chief	0	2	2	4
Social	0	0	3	3
Total	27	44	23	94
Ratio ministers/ months	2.5 months	2.8 months	0.6 months	2.2 months

Source: Santiso, 2002; based on Nueva Mayoria database.

2.4   Speed is the Rule of the Game

This Argentinian episode leads us to the central charateristic of the confidence game: the high speed of the moves in financial markets. Speed, as stressed by the high turnover in Argentinian politics, is not the privilege of economics or finance. That being said, one can observe that in financial and emerging markets in particular, conventions change very quickly and with high frequencies. Reversals of capital flows and confidence crises occur very rapidly, in a matter of hours, days or months. The financial exit of the crisis (i.e., the return of an emerging country to international capital markets) accelerated during the last two decades. It took, for example, seven years for Mexico to return to capital markets after the 1982 debt crisis but it took only seven months for Mexico to revert to sovereign bond markets after the December 1994 devaluation. In the same way, domestic debt exchange, after a crisis, has commenced speedily when they involved very few local players. When foreign investors are involved however the situation is very different. It took two years for Russia, one year for Ecuador and just a few months for Ukraine for example to complete their respective debt restructuring after the declaration of default.

Not only was the financial aid involved large but above all it was made available very speedily. If a lesson has been learnt from Mexican, Asian and Russian crises, it has been the need for timely rescue operations. Time and speed became strategic assets to restore market confidence. For this purpose, one of the actors, the IMF, established new tools in order to prevent financial crises. In early December 1997 the so-called Supplemental Reserve Facility (SRF) was established by the IMF to help emerging countries confront abrupt and disruptive losses of market confidence. Another new facility called Contingency Credit Lines (CCL) was set up in April 1999, designed as a precautionary line of defense. Large aid packages are then made available not only in a short-term decision process but also ex-ante, the timing and the speed of the aid being as relevant as the amount itself. These new instruments are made available with an interest surcharge. Repayment terms for SRF and CCL are 2–2.5 years as against 3.25–5 years for the standby programs and 4.5–10 years for the Extended Facility Fund (EFF). This is to encourage early repayments. It has framed, one can argue, the confidence game within shorter time horizons, the speedy and accelerated cognitive regime of the markets having been adopted (and adapted) by the states and international agencies (see chart 2.2).

In some cases, governments can enter into an IMF agreement not only because they need loans and are urged to avoid a liquidity crisis, but because they want to pass unpopular and costly reforms. Furthermore, the bringing in of the IMF can be a strategic resource, a blessing in disguise, tying one's hands, and helping governments to ensure the approval of unpopular reforms that had been delayed because they were perceived as being too costly by domestic opposition players. It played a smaller role in the structural adjustment of the 1990s, frequently imposing reforms, labeled "neoliberal."

The best example is Argentina that, in order to resist the lure of inflationary and fiscal spending, tied itself to the mast of its convertibility plan. In other words Argentina followed an approach that recalls the "Ulysses strategy" described by the philosopher Jon Elster.[89] Another example was the IMF loan for Brazil secured at the end of 1998. As with

Chart 2.2   IMF facilities: shortening temporal horizons of the confidence game

Facility	Charge	Repayment
Stand-by	Basic	Between 3.25 and 5
Extended Fund Facility	Basic	Between 4.5 and 10
Supplement Reserve Facility	Surcharge of 300–500	Between 2 and 2.5
Contingent Credit Lines	Surcharge of 300–500	Between 2 and 2.5

Source: Santiso, 2002 (based on IMF data).

any IMF package, Brazil was expected to conduct some drastic reforms including a fiscal adjustment program. The measures included large cuts in overall federal expenditures and federal infrastructure projects, and also a long-delayed reform of the social security system. Without these reforms, the government was expected to register a fiscal deficit in 1999. However with them it was able to achieve a primary surplus. Above all with the IMF package and the Russian crisis looming, the Brazilian president was able to push through reforms for which he had been trying to get approved for many years without success given strong opposition both inside the congress and inside his own ruling coalition. Immediately after his team negotiated the IMF straitjacket, Cardoso won approval in the Lower House for the pension system reform. This specific reform had been impossible to reach even after many years of painful negotiations. Thus the IMF's involvement, and the threat of a foreign reserve crisis, acted as accelerators, speeding the pace of hitherto hampered reforms.[90] The Brazilian government and the IMF shared, in a sense, the political cost of unpopular policies. Countries, like Brazil, may in fact enter into agreements with the IMF not only because they need loans and liquidity but also because governments can utilize IMF conditions to push through unpopular economic reforms. As stressed by the empirical work of James Vreeland, this desire for IMF "imposed" conditions can help explain why countries like Uruguay in 1990, a country with little need for an IMF loan, and why others, like Tanzania in 1983, with the strongest need for an IMF loan, did not participate in an IMF agreement.[91] The propensity of governments to enter into IMF agreements may also increase with the institutional resistance to policy change and with veto players' power to block key economic reforms.[92]

2.5   The Conflicting Cognitive Regimes of an Open Society

Even within the same side, visions of the game can be remarkably different. Not all the players inside markets behave or react in the same way or as a lonely crowd. A microeconomic sociological perspective can throw light on one of the most important aspects of the confidence game—the diversity of the players. For many observers financial operators are the usual suspects. They are seen as the culprits of the emerging market financial crisis as they provoke uncontrolled swirling and gyrations of capital flows. Critics of capital mobility, deeply rooted in the dependency tradition, insist that unstable financial flows can work against emerging democracies. They argue that the actions of financial investors effectively undermine the range of policy choices available and shape the policy preferences and autonomy of elected governments.[93] However, when we take a closer look at the wide spectrum of financial actors participating in the confidence game, the picture is in fact more colored, offering more *clairs obscurs* than the sharp glare of the spotlights.

In fact, investors have differing, if not conflicting, demands regarding governments' economic policy choices. Some, like bondholders, will be unhappy with expansionary fiscal policies. They will punish a Keynesian expansionary policy because their first preference is for high interest-rate, growth-oriented policies. On the contrary, foreign direct investors and stockholders will seek countries with high growth levels rather than with high interest rates. Most of them will be appraising the engines of growth not only in a country as a whole but also within sectors and industries. As stressed by Chase Fleming Asset Management emerging markets team, "our traditional answer has been to say that we like to invest in companies where the drivers of growth are as specific to the company as possible. That means they don't just depend on a booming economy; they exist within a growing industry, and can grow their share of it too."[94] Unlike investors who buy bonds, stockholders and direct investors' returns will depend mainly on such engines of growth. Only growth will boost the earnings of the companies in which they have invested or the sectors in which firms are operating. Investors present a large variety of preferences. These preferences can be conflicting, converging or diverging from democratic governments' most desired policies. This microeconomic view focuses on an understanding of the cognitive regimes, preferences and incentives of investors.

Even within the same category of investors, bondholders for example, the range of preferences can be very large and conflicting, preventing classification. As stressed by Sylvia Maxfield, it is also necessary that "before we rush to portray villainous bondholders in a global economy supply contraction champing at the bit to punish signs of growth in emerging market countries because it could signal inflation, lower interest rates and falling central bank reserves, we should note important differences among bondholders."[95] These actors can diverge in their moneymaking strategies and the temporal horizons of their investments. Some will express concerns about economic slowdown because it will dampen enthusiasm for emerging market debt or because only restored growth will restore confidence, decrease investor risk aversion and prevent debt spirals in emerging markets.[96]

In the same way, the temporal horizons of portfolio investors tend to be shorter than those of foreign direct investors.[97] Even within the same category investors' temporal horizons can also differ. Some (few) portfolio fund managers will prefer long-term strategies. "Dedicated" investors such as mutual funds or institutional investors such as pension funds, insurance companies or corporate treasuries, can make long-term decisions to allocate funds to emerging market asset class while others can prefer short-term and tactical allocations for their portfolios.[98] For asset manager Mark Mobius patience is the watchword of his (declared) investment style: "on a short-term basis, stocks may over-react to news and noise. On a more long term basis, we believe markets are efficient and may reward patient investors who have identified undervalued stocks."[99] Used as marketing arguments, long-term strategies will correspond to beliefs or strategies. But more pragmatically speaking they correspond also to considerations of financial returns as the frequency of stock purchase or sale is also a cost (transactions fees charged by brokers). Others will be oriented toward rapid returns and focused on short-term horizons and arbitrages will punish growth-oriented policies because they will involve lower interest rates.[100] These short-term preferences are explained by the set of constraints these investors face, that is their performance depending on quarterly temporal horizons. In the case of mutual funds for example, investment behavior is strongly constrained by the fact that they can face immediate redemptions if performance falls below the average of their tracking indexes and competitors.[101]

They thus face constraints that are hardly comparable to those of the hedge funds, another kind of investor. Hedge funds' strategies can be implemented with long-term horizons as their assets under management are committed for a relatively longer time (in the case of the famous LTCM it was nearly three years). As they do not face quarterly redemptions they can deploy long-term strategies. If we add that the investor universe is completed by other players such as pensions funds, insurance companies and commercial banks, who might have either long- or short-term strategies and horizons, we can argue against the current and dominant view that financial actors play against emerging democracies. While some short-term bondholders, focused on interest rates, may play against emerging democracies, others on the contrary may even help to strengthen democratic rules. They can act to boost bond and equity markets, to dismantle rent-seeking behavior and expensive public oligopolies or to consolidate corporate governance rules resulting in less corruption, less cronyism and more transparency and reliability of information for minority shareholders.

Even within governments, as shown by the Mexican, Brazilian or Argentinian examples, discrepancies can be important. Ministers can differ on the choices of options and responses to a confidence crash or on the way to restore credibility. Given their political interests, local actors can diverge in their policy choices. Exchange rate strategies and interest rate policies can be conflicting. Further governments acting as market operators can have different temporal horizons. In some cases governments can be more short-termists than markets. For short-term political reasons, governments intent on securing their tenure in office (or the tenure of their party), will tend to delay exchange rate adjustments in the run-up to elections. Their election secured, they will raise the probability of an immediate devaluation making the adjustment more painful.

This short-term strategic horizon has been frequently witnessed in Latin America. Witness the painful episodes of electorally motivated delayed devaluations seen in Mexico in 1976, 1982, 1988 and 1994, as well as in Brazil in 1986 and 1999.[102] In the last financial crisis in Mexico in late 1994, for example, the huge capital inflows and real appreciation of the peso promised high rewards for some politically important segments of Mexican society. By that time, the PRI was fighting the hotly contested 1994 presidential election. So the government and PRI officials could not risk alienating potential electoral supporters. A sudden depreciation would have a tremendous impact on middle-class purchasing power and more particularly upon urban consumers, both pivotal supports for an election victory.[103] So despite divergences among policymakers (presidency, Central Bank, Minister of Finance), the Mexican government finally opted for a postponed depreciation strategy, the consequences of which we already know.

The political economy of exchange rate regimes requires political actors and government institutions to make conflicting arbitrages. Options range from a complete free float to managed floats and fixed, pegged or dollarized regimes, each one involving specific tradeoffs and different distributions of gains and costs throughout society and the economy. Depending on their political, economic and social support, actors and institutions inside the state are unlikely to have a homogeneous or unique policy orientation but rather a different and varied set of preferences. In the same way, as reported by Joseph Stiglitz in an account of his own three-year tenure as a World Bank Chief Economist, the so-called Washington Consensus was more a façade than reality. The Washingtonian trinity (IMF, World Bank and U.S. Treasury) differed markedly on how to manage the financial crisis in Asia and Russia given the differences in their own preferences and strategies.[104]

CHAPTER THREE

Capital Flows to Emerging Markets: Goodbye the Golden 1990s?[1]

During the 1990s, emerging countries enjoyed dramatic inflows, which boosted their financial resources but also increased their vulnerability to financial turbulence. However capital flows to emerging markets have steadily declined since their peak of nearly US$240 bn. in 1995 according to the IMF. A key issue is whether these changes, both the sharp declines and changes in composition of the flows, are cyclical rather than structural, long term or short term.

Latin America was the first to receive massive capital inflows during the early 1990s. By 2000, the total amount of capital flows in the region represented nearly 1.3 percent of Latin American GDP (against less than 1 percent at the beginning of the 1970s and negative inflows during most of the 1980s).[2] But, as for nearly all emerging markets, since 2000, capital inflows to Latin America declined. By 2002, the expected inflows of foreign direct investment (FDI) were expected to fall to a low of US$35 bn. (compared to US$75 bn. two years before and US$60 bn. in 2001). The composition of private capital flows changed also with an increase in the amount of debt issuance. During the 1990s Latin American countries became particularly active in bond markets. In 2001 alone, just before the Argentina debt default, Latin American debt issuance accounted for more than 60 percent of all emerging market debt issuance according to JP Morgan.[3]

Stock market liberalization around the world led to a private investment boom as investors rebalanced their portfolios. Therefore the 1990s have been a period of ups and downs of capital inflows, high turbulences and have witnessed several acute currency crises among emerging markets that invariably spread to other nearby at-risk countries. Speculative foreign investments and high-volume movements of capital in and out of those countries exacerbated all these episodes—in Mexico, Thailand, South Korea, Russia, Brazil and Argentina.[4]

Through opening their markets, emerging countries experienced dramatic increases in private investment. As shown by Peter Blair Henry: in a sample of eleven emerging countries that liberalized their stock markets at the end of the twentieth century, nine experienced impressive growth rates of private investment.[5] In the year that developing countries opened their stock markets to foreign investors and in each of the next three years, the average growth of capital stock for the 370 firms studied, exceeds its pre-liberalization mean by 4.1 and 6.1 points respectively.[6] Other authors showed that equity market liberalizations lead on average to a 1 percent increase in annual real economic growth over a five-year period.[7] Liberalization of the capital account then seems associated with higher domestic growth and investment in emerging countries. However a brief review of the literature suggests that liberalization is at best mildly beneficial for growth as stressed by the IMF in a summary review of the related academic studies.[8]

The flip side of more open emerging capital markets has been an increased vulnerability to financial crises caused by a pattern of lending booms and busts, massive capital inflows and outflows. This had been a problem during the previous golden age of globalized capital markets, before 1914.[9] But, unlike in previous eras, modern-day crises are slightly worse on average, as measured by recurrence and output costs. The incidence of emerging market crises nowadays is considerably higher than in earlier periods, at 11.5 percent a year per country versus 4.3 percent previously. The effects of such crises on output have proved somewhat more severe in the recent period than in the pre-1914 era. Banking and currency crises have been far more disruptive since 1973, with an average 5 percent decline in the growth rate, as against 2 percent in the pre-1914 era.[10] In general terms, volatility of capital flows lower growth dynamics in emerging economies. This pattern is even more pronounced when countries have weak institutions, such as weak financial supervision and regulation.[11]

Other studies on crisis frequency and length partly confirm these findings.[12] If all types of crisis (banking crisis, currency crisis and twin crisis) are aggregate in nature, the frequency of disruptions in emerging nations climbed during the twentieth century. For emerging countries the frequency jumped from 6 to 26.8 percent during the periods

1880–1913 to 1973–1997. In total, crisis frequency since 1973 has been double that in the Bretton Woods period. However, there is little evidence that crises have grown longer or output losses have been larger according to other empirical research. The duration of crises (i.e. their recovery time defined as "the number of years until GDP growth returns to its pre-crisis trend, including the year when it returns to that trend") remained stable reaching 2.3 and 2.4 years on average for emerging markets during the 1880–1913 and 1973–1997 periods. In a revised version, the authors find similar results supporting the notion that recovery from currency crises were not faster before 1913. For the 21 emerging markets analyzed, it took on average 2.5 years for growth to resume before 1914 but only 2 years after 1972.[13]

Regarding the depth of crises they remained comparable reaching 10.4 and 9.2 percent of GDP during those same periods. In other words, crises have grown more frequent but they have not grown more severe in emerging markets. Another observable pattern has been, at least for Latin American countries during the 1990s, high financial volatility episodes that are short-lived, lasting from two to twelve weeks.[14] (See graph 3.1 and table 3.1.)

Crises are therefore growing more frequent rather than more severe. Relative to the pre-1914 period, crises are twice as prevalent today. At the same time contagion effects are also increasing. Understanding the

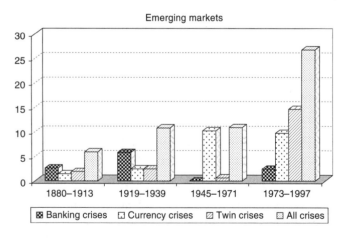

Graph 3.1   Crisis frequency in emerging markets (percent probability per year).

Source: Bordo, Eichengreen, Klingebiel and Martinez-Peria, "Is the Crisis Problem Growing More Severe?" *Economic Policy*, vol. 16, no. 32, April 2001.

Table 3.1 Frequency of crises in emerging markets 1880–1997

| Period | Crisis frequency by crisis type, 1880–1997 | | | |
	Banking crises (%)	Currency crises (%)	Twin crises (%)	All crises (%)
Industrial nations				
1880–1913	2	1	0.5	3.5
1919–1939	3.7	4.3	4	12
1945–1971	0	5.4	0	5.4
1971–1997	2.5	8.1	1.7	12.2
Emerging nations				
1880–1913	2.6	1.4	1.9	6
1919–1939	5.8	2.5	2.5	10.8
1945–1971	0	10.3	0.6	10.9
1971–1997	2.4	9.8	14.6	26.8

Source: Santiso, 2002; based on Bordo, Eichengreen, Klingebiel and Martinez-Peria, "Is the Crisis Problem Growing More Severe?" *Economic Policy*, vol. 16, no. 32, April 2001.

changing dynamics in capital flows can thus be very helpful as increasing manias and panics has largely been associated with international bank lending and portfolio investment flows. Since the 1618 Dutch Tulips crisis, there have been a total of 46 episodes of manias and panics, according to Charles Kindleberger's classic count.[15] Around ten involved a currency fluctuation component, indicating that capital flows were part of the problem. But, most important, of those ten episodes, six were twentieth-century events. An examination of Kindleberger's data from a different angle also suggests that the international repercussions of twentieth-century crises proved to be more significant. Over the three centuries from 1600 to 1900, only seven of the 31 manias and panics had major international dimensions, while during the twentieth century the proportion has been far higher, with 9 out of 15 episodes recorded showing significant international repercussions and spreading effects.

3.1 The Democratization of Capital Markets

Capital inflows to emerging countries are not new. Although capital mobility is widely regarded as an unprecedented phenomenon, this process began during the closing decades of the nineteenth century during the first wave of globalization.[16]

By that time, capital flows to emerging economies were in fact a few thousand wealthy British families financing a large share of infrastructure spending of the "emerging countries," that is the United States, Argentina, Canada and other dominions of the British Empire.[17] In the years prior to the World War I, Britain's external assets represented 140 percent of GDP, compared to a 9 percent peak for the United States in 1981. The earlier period of globalization, that lasted from around 1840 to 1914, led to a backlash that stemmed from the cross-border flow of goods, people and money, a backlash that that has been, in some respects, far more dramatic than the integration of world markets. Transport costs and trade barriers fell faster; international capital flows as a share of national output were far larger; and cross-border immigration was far greater. In 1894, America's net foreign debts totaled 26 percent of its GDP, while Brazil's in 1980, prior to the Latin America debt crisis, was a mere 19 percent of its GDP.[18] Data from Latin America's twentieth-century FDI history also offer clear evidence of the extent of emerging markets' integration into world capital markets in the last century.[19] Prior to 1914, Latin America was receiving nearly 20 percent of British foreign investment, more than 16 percent of German foreign investment and more than 13 percent of French foreign investment.[20] (See table 3.2 and graph 3.2.)

Yet capital flows today are far more diverse than in the pre-1914 era, which saw the predominance of securitized capital flows. While in the nineteenth century, the world's surplus savings were controlled by a small number of wealthy families, in the modern era, the concentration of capital, although still important, has been limited by the growth of pension

Table 3.2   European investments in emerging countries before World War I

Distribution of European foreign investment 1931–1941 (in %)

Destination	Britain	France	Germany
Eastern Europe	3.6	35.5	27.7
Western Europe	1.7	14.9	12.7
Europe (not specified)	0.5	3.3	5.1
Total Europe	53.8	45.5	
Latin America	20.1	13.3	16.2
North America and Australia	44.8	4.4	15.7
Other New World (not specified)	2.8	17.7	34
Asia and Africa	26.5	28.4	20.5
Total New World	67.7	17.7	34

Source: Santiso, 2002; based on Michael A. Clemens and Jeffrey Williamson, "Wealth Bias in the First Global Capital Market Boom, 1870–1913," *Harvard University Working Paper*, July 2001 (unpublished).

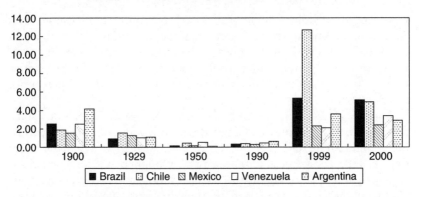

Graph 3.2   Foreign direct investments in Latin America, 1900–2000 (in % of GDP).

Sources: Santiso, 2002; calculations based on Angus Maddison, *The World Economy. A Millennial Perspective*, Paris, OECD, 2001; CEPAL, *La inversión extranjera en América Latina y el Caribe*, Santiago de Chile, CEPAL, 2002; UNCTAD, *World Investment Report 2001. Promoting Linkages*, Geneva, UNCTAD, 2001; Banco Central do Brasil, Banco de Mexico, 2001; Chilean Foreign Investment Committee, 2001.

funds, mutual funds and other financial intermediaries. All these institutions have paved the way for an increasing number of financial institutions dedicated to encouraging middle-class wealth accumulation. Additionally, there has been a "democratization" of wealth in OECD countries. When the U.S. stock market crashed in 1929, there were only 3 mn. Americans out of 120 mn. who owned equities. Today it is estimated that almost 45 percent of Americans own equities, either directly or through defined contributions to pension plans, compared with fewer than 5 percent in the 1950s. In 2000, the U.S. mutual fund industry had more than US$5.5 tn. in assets, compared to US$4.7 tn. in the banking system.

The growth of this industry has helped to promote an unprecedented process of international diversification of household equity portfolio, with more than 600 funds offering international equity investment (compared to less than 30 in 1984) and managing assets over US$215 bn. (compared to less than US$37 bn. in 1992). A closer examination of a database on emerging markets, eMergingPortfolio.com, covering geographic asset allocation of equity funds, can also give an idea of the rapid growth during the 1990s of emerging market asset class. At the beginning of the period covered by the database (1996), it contained 382 emerging market equity funds with assets reaching US$117 bn. Four years later, by the end of 2000, the number of equity emerging market funds reached 639 (they managed quite the same amount of assets, US$120 bn.).[21] Parallel to these trends is the development of institutional investors in Latin American countries. As of December 1998, there were approximately US$300 bn. in assets in the ten largest Latin American countries, half of the total held by pension funds, another half by mutual funds and smaller amounts by insurance companies. In 2001, Latin American pension funds assets alone reached US$170 bn., representing in some countries like Chile 55 percent of GDP (20 percent of Latin American GDP).[22]

Another major trend has been the shift from public to private capital flows in emerging countries. Coupled with the boom of portfolio investments and FDI, private capital flows became, during the 1990s, the major source of foreign financial resources for developing countries. These flows accelerated sharply in the early 1990s after a moderate increase during the 1980s.[23] Market sentiment and reversals in capital flows such as bank lending, foreign direct and portfolio flows became then key issues in understanding the dynamics of emerging markets. In 2000 net capital flows to emerging countries reached nearly US$170 bn. according to the Institute of International Finance (against less than US$3 bn. in 1970 and US$67 bn. at the beginning of the 1990s).[24] Over the same period, net official flows fell sharply representing nearly 50 percent of all net capital flows to emerging countries at the beginning of the 1970s and becoming nearly nonexistent by the end of the twentieth century.

Not all areas have been enjoying this boom in private capital flow. For developing countries the bulk of capital flows has been concentrated in Asia and Latin America. According to the IMF, the largest users of FDI have been on an average, for the period 1970–2000, China (with more than 33 percent of all FDI flows to emerging countries), Brazil (11 percent) and Mexico (10 percent). Portfolio flows have also been heavily concentrated in a few counties with Brazil (20 percent of total), Mexico (16 percent), Korea and Argentina (14 percent each) receiving the bulk of portfolio investments during the last 30 years of the twentieth century. At a more aggregate level, since the Asian crisis, the major region receiving capital flows in 2000 was Latin America (37 percent of total private flows to emerging markets), followed by emerging Asia (36 percent) and Eastern Europe (24 percent) according to IIF data. In fact, an entire region, Africa and Middle East, has been out of the map of private investors, this region receiving, in 2000, less than 3 percent of total private flows to emerging markets (the exception is however South Africa, which received on average nearly 7 percent of all portfolio investments to emerging countries during the period 1970–2000).

The analysis at the country level confirms the fact that private capital flows became increasingly concentrated in a few major emerging countries. In 2000, the two leading recipients of FDI in emerging countries,

China and Brazil, received 31 and 15 percent of total FDI to emerging economies.[25] In Latin America, for example, net capital flows reached US$61 bn. in 2000 but remain concentrated in the three major economies of the region (Argentina, Brazil and Mexico). However as underlined by the UNCTAD, the number of countries receiving capital flows also increased. By the end of 2000, 51 developing countries were reporting FDI stocks of more than US$10 bn. (against 17 in 1985). More importantly, and even if the smallest economies remain out of the map of foreign investors, the investment received by some small developing countries relative to the size of their economies, increased in a significant way. In Latin America, for example, while a country like Bolivia was suffering FDI outflows by the end of the 1980s, the amount of FDI by the end of 1990s jumped to more than 7 percent in 1997.[26] (See graphs 3.3 and 3.4.)

Another major issue, within the composition of private capital flows, has been the declining trend of bank lending. Since the mid-1990s, net flows from banks to emerging countries has declined, falling from US$117 bn. in 1996, or about one-third of total private inflows, to US$43.5 bn. in 1997, or about 10 percent of private inflows, subsequently becoming negative. By 1998, net bank inflows had turned into net outflows of nearly US$55 bn. As the IIF pointed out, the breakdown of bank lending by country for the 29 emerging countries covered shows that bank lending declined not only in the five East Asian economies (Indonesia, South Korea, Thailand, Malaysia and the

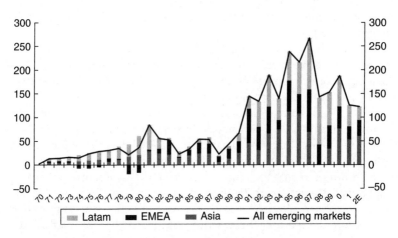

Graph 3.3   Net capital flows to emerging markets by region (US$bn.).

Sources: Santiso, 2002; based on databases of IIF (International Finance Institution) and IMF (International Monetary Fund), 2002.

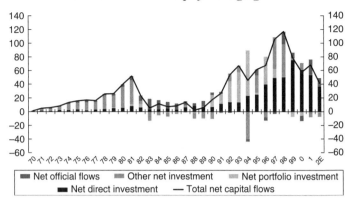

■ Net official flows   ■ Other net investment   ■ Net portfolio investment
■ Net direct investment   — Total net capital flows

Graph 3.4   Net capital flows to Latin American countries (US$bn.).

Sources: Santiso, 2002, based IIF and IMF data, 2002.

Philippines), Russia and Brazil, but also in noncrisis countries. Large-scale net bank lending has been inhibited not only by changing patterns of finance in emerging countries but also by the structural changes in financial risk management procedures and BIS rules[27] and the escalation in perceived higher risk, which produces a stronger impact on highly leveraged lenders like banks.[28] One major implication of these combined trends is that the decline in net bank lending to emerging markets may very well become a persistent phenomenon over the medium term as confirmed by 2000 and 2001 data, in which net commercial bank lending remained negative (US$−6 bn. and US$−22 bn. respectively). (See graph 3.5.)

However this trend might not be such bad news for emerging markets for two main reasons. First, under the current BIS plans to link regulatory capital to sovereign rating agencies, the new rules might help destabilize private flows to developing countries as sovereign ratings lag rather than lead the markets, and they are mainly pro-cyclical, reinforcing boom–bust cycles.[29] Second, as stressed by empirical research, most of the hot-money driven financial crises resulted from bank lending and herding behavior, not from nonbank investments such as pension funds, mutual funds or even hedge funds.[30] During the 1990s, quarterly swings in aggregate foreign bank lending to emerging markets have, in fact, been far more volatile than changes in bond and equity portfolio investments. Over this period, the volatility (measured by the coefficient of variation, or the standard deviation of flows divided by the average size of capital flows for the entire world) of bank loan flows was 82 percent, against 50 percent for portfolio flows. From 1992 to 1997, the average

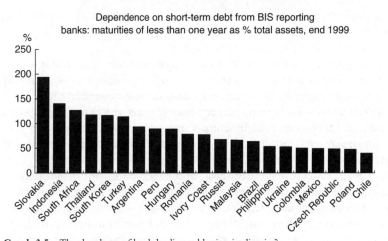

Dependence on short-term debt from BIS reporting banks: maturities of less than one year as % total assets, end 1999

Graph 3.5 The slowdown of bank leading: a blessing in disguise?

Source: Santiso, 2001; based on ING Barings, June 2000, based on BIS-reporting banks data, 2000.

volatility of annual foreign bank lending to individual countries was 239 percent versus 176 percent for bond flows and 150 percent for equity flows. During the Asian crisis, the behavior of foreign banks appeared to play a role in spreading the crisis. This applied especially to the actions of U.S. and Japanese banks, which began to curtail drastically their lending to affected Asian countries after the devaluation in Thailand, with cuts of more than 30 percent by U.S. banks and 23 percent by Japanese banks in less than one year.[31] Bank credit outflows from the four East Asian countries most affected by the crisis represented more than 92 percent of total outflow.

3.2 The Boom in Foreign Direct Investments to Emerging Markets

In fact, the lion's share of private flows have been in the form of FDI—more than US$130 bn. in 2000, or nearly 80 percent of total net private flows to emerging countries. This trend confirms that FDI became a reliable source of financing for major emerging countries. This is a big change from previous years, because while securities markets have grown explosively in recent years, more than a half of all capital flowing to emerging markets has been on average in the form of FDI during most of the 1990s. Above all, the nature of FDI has also changed.

While it is true that these flows continue to be related to privatization and liberalization processes, they have also become increasingly sustained by corporate global investment strategies.

If we place this trend in historical perspective, once again, the difference in the nature of FDI is even more striking. Before 1914, FDI was mainly undertaken by free-standing companies. Conversely, today, most FDI comes from multinational corporations that are expanding abroad and are spreading not only financial capital across borders, but also pre-existing managerial and productive capabilities. According to the last *Templeton Global Performance Index 2000* report, which covers 214 companies from 15 countries, European and U.S. multinationals are playing a critical role in the global economy, as they are increasing their exposure in foreign markets, including emerging markets. These companies now maintain an average of 36 percent of their assets in foreign markets. These foreign assets continue to generate a disproportionate share of total revenues (39 percent). (See graph 3.6.)

The majority of these companies are based in the triad—109 in North America, 55 in Europe and 46 in Japan. They are reallocating their operations toward emerging markets and integrating them into global production schemes. This trend is directly correlated to the increasing openness of emerging markets, except for certain countries like China and Uzbekistan, which rank at the bottom of the *Emerging Market Access*

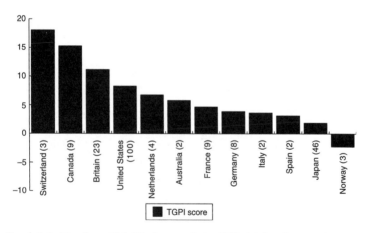

Graph 3.6   Templeton Global Performance Index 2000: global performance by country (number of companies).

Source: Based on Templeton College, Templeton Global Performance Index 2000, Oxford, Oxford University Templeton College, 2000.

Index (EMAI) produced by the Tuck School of Business at Dartmouth University.[32]

One major trend related to FDI is the increasing total value of international mergers and acquisitions. According to the *2000 World Investment Report* from the UN Conference on Trade and Development, M&A activity reached US$720 bn. and in 2000 foreign inflows are set to top US$1 tn. Most of the deals involved developed countries, but M&A activity is also gaining importance in flows to emerging countries. Argentina, Brazil and South Korea were among the biggest emerging net sellers. In these countries, foreign companies made net purchases of over US$25 bn. Another interesting trend is that emerging countries are now also involved in buying activity. South African firms led the pace, with more than US$4 bn. in net foreign purchases.

According to United Nations data, the world's 60,000 multinational companies account in 2000 for about one-quarter of world output, with sales of their overseas affiliates accounting for more than US$13 tn. compared to global exports of US$7 tn. In 1999, FDI surged by 25 percent, reaching a record US$827 bn. worldwide. This increase follows a jump of 41 percent in 1998 to US$660 bn. and represents a near doubling of international investment flows in just two years. This is mainly attributable to the growth in cross-border mergers and acquisitions, rather than to greenfield investment in new factories and so forth. Also, international investors, after the 1998 Asian crisis, regained their enthusiasm for direct investment in emerging economies.

In 1999, for the first time since 1986, Latin America and the Caribbean overtook Asia as the most attractive developing region for FDI. According to IIF, Latin America raked in an estimated US$75 bn. in FDI, one-third of which went to Brazil, while US$55 bn. went to developing Asia, half of which went to China, the largest developing-country recipient of FDI. During the 1996–1999 period, Latin America became the region with the highest ratio of FDI-to-GDP, with a ratio of 1.7 percent of regional GDP, compared with an average of 1.3 percent of GDP for East Asia and Eastern Europe and less than 1 percent of GDP for Africa. The surge in Latin America FDI—a jump of 33 percent compared to just 1 percent for Asian emerging markets, dampened by the impact of the region's financial crisis—was largely due to a four-fold increase in FDI flows to Brazil, Mexico and Argentina.

According to UNCTAD and CEPAL data, FDI flows to Argentina jumped to US$25 bn. in 1999, from US$6 bn. in 1998. This upturn mainly reflects a single, huge company takeover (the US$17 bn. purchase of YPF, Argentina's largest oil company, by the Spanish oil company

Repsol) and will not be sustainable in the forthcoming years. Brazil again took the lion's share of inflows into Latin America. Its FDI skyrocketed to US$33 bn. in 1999, up from US$28 bn. in 1998, and reached US$23 bn. in 2001. Another major recipient of capital inflows has been Mexico, which drew in a steady US$10 bn. in FDI per year between 1994 and 2000. The 2000 upratings by Moody's and S&P of Mexico's sovereign debt to an investment-grade status help to boost FDI in the near future improving the country risk and thereby the conditions of lending to these countries. In 2001, Mexico nearly doubled the total amount of FDI, which reached a record of more than US$27 bn. with only one operation (the US$12.5 bn. acquisition by Citicorp of Banamex representing the same amount of FDI received in the past year).

However once again in 2002, overall capital flows to Latin American countries were hindered by tougher global and regional conditions. FDI flows in particular were forecasted to plunge to less than US$38 bn. in 2002 from US$62 bn. in 2001, according to JP Morgan estimations.[33] CEPAL estimations also point to a decline from the top reached in 1999 (US$105 bn.) to lower amounts of FDI flows for the years 2001 (US$80 bn.) and 2002 (US$55 bn.).[34] Due to October's 2002 presidential elections, FDI into Brazil was expected to slide while in Argentina, due to acute economic and political uncertainties, it was expected to plummet, and Mexico (because of the size of Citibank's purchase of Banacci Group the previous year) was also expected to be down by almost half.

By the end of the twentieth century, European investors were challenging the dominance of U.S. companies in Latin America. In the region the United States is still the leading investor in terms of book value of accumulated assets and total corporate sales. But while the United States remains the single most important investor in the region, European corporates, especially Spanish companies, have also been actively buying stakes in the electricity, oil and gas, telecommunications industries and in the financial sector. In 1998 the flow of investment from Europe surpassed that from the United States. Moreover, according to CEPAL, out of the 25 largest foreign companies in Latin America, 14 were European and 11 were American in terms of consolidated sales. For both European and U.S. companies, the biggest prize is Brazil, that is Latin America's largest market, U.S. companies being more involved in Mexico than European ones who are more heavily invested in Mercosur's countries.[35] Rather than being scared off by the currency devaluation in January 1999, foreign investors took it as an entry opportunity to snap up cheap prime assets.

This rise of FDI is profoundly transforming financial systems in several emerging countries. After having restricted foreign investment into their financial systems for years, many developing countries have opened the door to foreign participation. In 2000, foreign-owned banks control over half the domestic bank assets of Latin America, 60 percent of Poland, 80 percent of Hungary and 90 percent of Estonia. In Argentina, for example, foreign banks now control more than 55 percent of total banking assets and nearly 47 percent of total deposits, contributing to the increasing concentration of the banking sector (70 percent of the deposits and loans are in the hands of the top ten banks). This has several consequences on emerging countries' macroeconomic stability and prospects.

FDI indeed is usually considered as the most desirable form of capital inflow because it brings with it technology and management expertise. Above all it brings more stability, since it is not volatile, being in particular much more costly to reverse than portfolio flows. FDI is also less sensitive to international interest rates and is driven more by strategic firms' considerations of long-term profitability. In particular, the volatility of FDI flows is significantly lower than that of other types of flows of private capital. Net capital flows into emerging countries are sensitive to U.S. cycles, running twice as high during U.S. expansion phases as during recessions.[36] But the pattern also depends on the type of capital flow, with FDI flows proving to be more stable than portfolio investment flows. From 1975 to 2000, in 90 percent of emerging countries, FDI flows were less variable than other net flows (with a coefficient of variation of 0.79 for FDI flows versus 2.35 for other types of net flows).[37] Robert Lipsey's work confirms this point, underlining in particular the very low ratio of volatility of FDI for Latin America (0.59 for the emerging Latin American economies from 1969 through 1993, compared to 0.74 for Southeast Asia).[38] There is however a tendency for countries with lower credit worthiness to attract larger shares of FDI flows and the benefits for developing countries in terms of growth of FDI inflows depends on the existence of sound institutions like, for example, a well developed local financial market.[39]

Another consequence is on stock markets. The case of Argentina is particularly relevant as delisting by foreign companies of their Argentine subsidiaries is accelerating in 2000. The consequence of this is a drastic downsizing of Argentina's stock market: the stock market capitalization to GDP ratio has fallen from 16 percent to a paltry 8 percent (in comparison Brazil has market capitalization of 43 percent of GDP while the United States has 159 percent of GDP).[40] (See graph 3.7.)

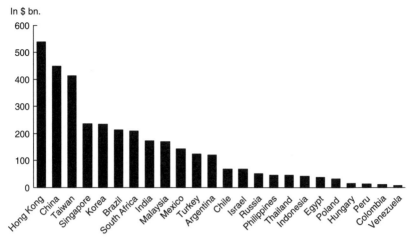

Graph 3.7   Global emerging market capitalizations in 2000.

Sources: Santiso 2001; based on data from IFC & IMF, 2000.

And there are more delistings in the pipeline. BSCH and Telefónica are planning to delist Banco Rio and Telefónica de Argentina from Argentina and offer BSCH and Telefónica shares instead, a model already used by Spanish oil company Repsol after the takeover of Argentina oil company YPF (this company accounting then for about 15 percent of the index). As in Argentina, Telefónica of Spain is also buying the remaining stakes in TelespPar and Telesudeste Celular of Brazil and Telefónica del Perú. Given the importance of the two telecom carriers in Argentina and Peru and the forthcoming delistings in Argentina, Lima and above all Buenos Aires will see a reduction in their liquid stocks. (See graph 3.8.)

Recent empirical research has borne out the strong growth-enhancing properties of equity-related inflows, indicating that emerging countries should strengthen their domestic financial system in order to benefit from financial integration. Sarno and Taylor, among others, have estimated the relative importance of temporary and permanent components of broad categories of capital flowing from the United States into a large sample of developing countries.[41] Their analysis confirms that FDI has permanent components only, while equity flows, bond flows and official flows consist mainly of temporary components.

In one of their last reports, IADB economists also substantiated that FDI in Latin America involves more long-term commitment and does not present the U-turns characteristic of other private capital flows,

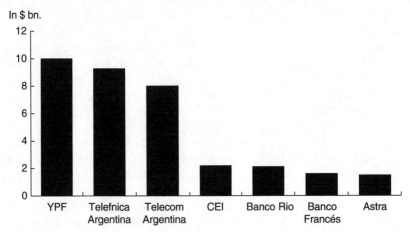

Graph 3.8   The slow death of an emerging stock market? Major delistings of Argentina's Bolsa in 2000.

Source: Euromoney, 2000.

arguing also that FDI, as opposed to debt liabilities, involves neither currency nor maturity mismatches.[42] Another OECD econometric study based on a dynamic panel of 44 developing countries, with yearly observations running from 1986 to 1997,[43] concluded that FDI and portfolio equity flows present a positive, significant and robust correlation with developing countries' income growth. Another finding of this study was that portfolio bond inflows and short-term debt display a negative correlation. Additionally, short-term and long-term bank-related inflows display a significant negative correlation with growth, this negative link being retained only when domestic banks present low capitalization ratios (when bank capitalization is large enough bank-related inflows may even be growth-enhancing).

Private capital inflows are key to boosting economic growth by increasing investment and consumption in developing countries. In the short term, they help emerging countries cover their current account deficits. This is notably the case of Latin American countries where in 2000 the projected higher net private capital inflows has been largely compensated by the projected higher current account deficit. However, those large capital inflows are not an unmitigated blessing. They can lead to monetary expansion, exchange-rate appreciation, inflationary pressures and dramatic swings in the current account. In addition, as the experience of the 1990s financial crises in Mexico, Asia, Russia and Brazil have shown, financial integration can lead to greater volatility. In some cases, it can be accompanied by sudden stops in capital inflows, entailing a dramatic loss of access to external finance. Indeed, the crises experienced in the 1990s by many heavily indebted emerging countries were preceded by a surge of capital inflows and, when the crises broke, there was an abrupt loss of confidence and market access. Spillover effects to other similar economies have usually developed, with the magnitude of the reversals in capital flows (i.e. the sum of inflows and outflows) being impressive in many episodes. The extent or occurrence of these effects depends on the composition of liabilities of developing countries, with the ratio of FDI-to-debt having a positive effect on the probability of avoiding a crisis in emerging markets.

In other words, it means that FDI offers a safer form of financing than debt or other forms of non-FDI obligations. If this is true, monitoring the flows of FDI to emerging countries during the years after the Argentina crisis of 2002 is relevant. One of the specificities of the Argentina debacle is the high involvement of foreign operators in the exit of the crisis process. Unlike the previous Mexican and Brazilian crises, the alteration of property rights, through redenomination and pesification of contracts, could have some negative implications for the value of property rights not only in Argentina but in other countries, "implying, as underlined by some analysts, in particular a slowing of the rate of foreign direct investment and banking activity."[44] In the same way, the Argentina debt default, as underlined by the IIF could "erode investors' attitude toward emerging market bonds as an asset class."[45]

3.3   Portfolio Investments and Market Sentiments

That being said, a need is felt for instruments to track investors' appetite for emerging markets, such as the one utilized by Merrill Lynch. Each quarter, since 1989, Merrill Lynch has conducted a quarterly survey of Global Fixed Income Fund Managers, asking them how their portfolios are weighted vis-à-vis their benchmarks of the world's major currencies and fixed-income markets.[46] Deutsche Bank has also been conducting a survey designed to track the sentiment of a selected group of top institutional equity portfolio managers and analysts. But here once again the polls are limited to U.S. institutional equity investors (15 to 75 each time, depending on the monthly poll) and to expectations concerning mainly the U.S. stock market. Several important researches have been conducted in the past years to track the trading behavior of foreign portfolio investors in emerging countries before and during a crisis. Other banks, like Crédit Lyonnais Securities Americas, Morgan Stanley or UBS Warburg have also dedicated research teams to track flows using AMG Data Services or S&P databases, two leading providers of fund flows data.[47]

By analyzing portfolio flows, some World Bank[48] and Harvard[49] research groups find that emerging market funds use positive momentum strategies systematically buying winners and selling losers. These strategies tend to be stronger in a crises rather than noncrisis period. Further they report that contagion strategies are used for selling assets from one country when a crisis hits another. Other researches revealed that contagion effects are more important when shocks originate in the center (i.e. U.S., Japan or European financial centers) than when they originate in the periphery. They underline therefore that it's possible to discriminate, focusing on investors behavior and market making, between shocks transmitted from one periphery to another periphery from shocks transmitted from one periphery to another through a central country.[50]

All these studies point to the same idea. We need, as one of the leading authorities on financial markets and economic professor at Yale pointed out in his last book, Robert Shiller,[51] a better understanding of how markets think. In other words, we need better socioeconomic knowledge of investors' behavior. Such a perspective, if important for developed markets, is even more relevant in emerging markets where herd behavior, asymmetric information and market failures seem to be more salient than anywhere else. Tracking investors' appetites and forecasts for emerging markets is a key issue.

Focusing on investors' behavior has become particularly relevent because portfolio flows from U.S. markets have been playing an increasing role in emerging markets. BIS studies furthermore reveal that the impact of institutional investors' portfolio reallocations on local markets' capitalization are significant: a 1 percent reallocation of U.S. institutional investors is likely to provoke a 35 percent impact on Latin American market capitalization and 14 percent on Asia (on industrial countries the impact is less than 1 percent). (See graph 3.9.)

During the Asian crisis they represented nearly 30 percent of the reversal of flows and during the Mexican peso crisis, they were the main source of the reversals. Recent studies, based on quarterly holdings of 13 dedicated Latin America mutual funds, find that contagion effects could be linked to these shifts in fund flows. For example, Latin American mutual funds had extremely large outflows both during the

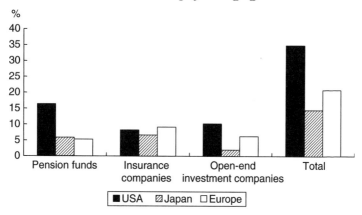

Graph 3.9   Impact of investors' portfolio reallocation on Latin American stock markets.

Source: Based on Stephany Griffith-Jones, "The Role of Mutual Funds and Other International Investors in Currency Crises," *Institute of Development Studies Working Paper*, University of Sussex, February 2000 (unpublished).

Mexican peso crisis and during the Asian and Russian crises. Mutual funds pulled out in a major way from Mexico and Argentina—but not from more illiquid markets as in Colombia—during the crisis in the former and in a broader way during the crisis in the latter, with heavy sales reaching even the most illiquid Latin American markets. The largest outflows were from Brazil, Venezuela, Peru and Argentina.[52]

Other studies, based on a detailed analysis of international portfolio flow data from State Street Bank, confirmed these findings. Looking at net equity flows by institutional investors (not only mutual funds but also pension fund and hedge funds), they confirmed significant outflows from Latin America during the Russian and LTCM crisis. This data reveals that international investors did not abandon emerging markets during the Asian crisis, but on the contrary remained net buyers (at a reduced rate) of emerging markets equities between July 1997 and July 1998.[53] It must also be stressed that the sizes of portfolio outflows were clearly never as large as the reversal of bank loans, particularly during the Asian crisis.[54]

The largest sources of portfolio inflows come in fact from non–global emerging market dedicated funds, which are very risk sensitive. However, data on emerging markets equity flows suffers from a number of problems. Available sources show considerable differences that are explained by differences of methodology and coverage. In a very detailed analysis, Goldman Sachs has estimated global emerging market flows in

2000 at US$38 bn.[55] The main conclusion of this chapter is that the largest sources of portfolio inflows come from nonglobal emerging market dedicated funds. Global emerging market dedicated funds accounted for less than one-quarter of flows into emerging markets, the bulk coming from international, global and domestic U.S. funds, offshore accounts, hedge funds and insurance companies. International, global and domestic equity funds allocate respectively 6.5, 11.7 and 6.5 percent of their assets, these funds being far more important in terms of total assets than dedicated emerging markets funds. (See graph 3.10.)

In 2000 portfolio flows to emerging markets are estimated to be mainly intermediate through fund managers (90 percent of total portfolio flows). Equity funds account for about 90 percent of emerging market funds, the other 10 percent being invested through bond funds. In 2001, according to IIF, emerging market portfolio equity investment reached US$42 bn. Portfolio equity flows to Latin America and Asia might reach US$11 and US$24 bn. respectively this year. But they are likely to be sensitive, as mentioned previously, to developments in industrial country equity markets. Even if on average the correlations between the U.S. S&P 500 equity index and emerging market equity index has been modest since 1992 (a 1 percent increase in the United States tended to provoke a 0.30 percent change in global emerging markets), this correlation increased sharply during periods of volatility. Above all,

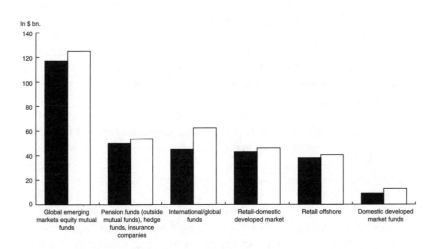

Graph 3.10   Global equity emerging market holdings, 1999 and 2000.

Source: Santiso, 2000; based on Goldman Sachs, 1999 and 2000.

the good years for emerging markets might be over with a retrenchment continuing on the investment side where assets dwindled from their 1997 peak. According to fund flow analysis from AMG Data Services, investors yanked nearly US$400 mn. out of Latin America mutual funds in 2000, representing nearly 75 percent of their 1997 apex US$5.6 bn.

3.4   Emerging Bond Markets: The Latin American Ivy League

On a micro-level focusing on equity funds and benchmarks games is particularly helpful to understand the behavior of international investors and therefore the dynamics of financial crises. Contagion and financial spillover, as it is generally accepted, are not fully explained by economic and domestic fundamentals. Most of the financial crises of the past decades (48 out 58) have been temporally and geographically clustered.[56] While there are fundamental economic reasons behind this clustering, related to trade links and common external shocks, there are also factors related to investors' behavior in international capital markets.

As underlined by Avinash Persaud, one of the most respected emerging market strategist, "the agent of contagion is not only and perhaps not even mainly, local and international economic factors or risks, but a reduction in investors appetite for risk."[57] A shift in investors' appetite for or aversion for risk will induce them to reduce their exposure to risky assets immediately, which consequently, will tend to fall in a synchronized manner. A crisis in one country may lead investors to reduce their exposure to other risky assets and rebalance their portfolios in terms of liquidity and risk requirements and they will tend to avoid similar risks in other countries.

As argued by some observers, herding behavior among investors played a crucial role in explaining financial contagion during the 1990s. The fact that investor performance is measured against specific benchmarks (MSCI or IFC/S&P for equity funds and EMBI for bond funds) is also frequently mentioned as an incentive to herd.[58] These widely used indexes go a long way in explaining asset allocations of country funds. As noted by some observers, the simple correlations of benchmark weights of the MSCI EMF indices range from 0.49 for funds invested worldwide to 0.89 for Latin American funds.[59] But in emerging markets the propensity to replicate benchmarks tends to be greater simply because the number of big liquid stocks is limited.[60] At 2000 levels, Latin

America's total equity capitalization is less than US$190 bn. (excluding small caps and privately held stocks). From a comparative perspective this market capitalization is less that that of General Electric Co. "With so little liquidity, global investors and regional funds tend to focus on less than two half of dozen Latin stocks."[61]

However, fund managers remain quite active and try not to simply replicate the benchmark but to beat it. Fund managers use in fact indexes as a benchmark for their portfolio allocation as clients ask (by contract) for it. By mid-2000 an estimated US$8 bn. were tracking the S&P/IFC family of emerging market indexes. Approximately US$30 bn. were tracking indexes actively, which means that portfolio managers do not simply follow the indexes weights but rather choose their own weights to try to beat the index.[62] However the incentives to have a portfolio that is not too different are "huge" as underlined by fund managers as "it's always better to be wrong with market that wrong against it."[63]

The index and portfolio rebalancing became particularly significant during the 1990s with the development of emerging bond markets. Latin American economies have been among the most dependent on international bond markets. By 2000, Latin American countries totaled close to 55 percent of all emerging market issues, with one country (Argentina) concentrating nearly 23 percent of the total.[64] Morover, according to JP Morgan, Latin American sovereign bonds had a weight of more than 70 percent in the EMBI, which makes them the perfect market movers in emerging bond markets.[65]

Latin American sovereign bonds have therefore considerably shaped the dynamics of this market during the past decade. Most importantly, the 1990s have been the first time, since World War I, to see a large return of private investors toward emerging markets in the form of bonds. This wave of bond issues started with the Brady bond market and the first restructuring of Mexico's defaulted sovereign loans into Brady bonds in 1990 (with a 35 percent debt forgiveness[66]).

Following the implementation of Brady agreements, emerging bond market issues grew significantly in the years 1995–1997. Later bond issuance decreased but the Latin American dominance of issuance continued to increase. In 2001, according to IIF, and even with the absence of Argentina, the largest emerging market issuer, Latin American borrowers still concentrated three-quarters of the emerging market issuances. Argentina was among the most active Latin American countries in tapping international capital markets during the 1990s. The country experienced a dramatic increase of its total external debt and public external debt, mostly composed of bonds. Mid-2001, for example, bonds represented 70 percent of Argentinian public debt.[67] From 1994 to 2001, Argentina's external debt jumped from 33 percent to nearly 55 percent of GDP. These trends reflect the growing importance of international bond markets in the refinancing of Argentina's economy and more generally on Latin American economies during the 1990s.

At the same time, the currency composition of bond issuances continued to be dominated and denominated in dollars although it slowly started to weaken (56 percent of all emerging market issuances in 2000 against 51 percent in 2001). One of the novelties of the late 1990s was precisely the increasing issuances denominated in Euros (34 percent in 2001 compared to 31 percent in 2000 according to IIF), reflecting greater appetite for emerging market issuances in Europe. Here again, Latin American countries lead the trend with Argentina multiplying euro-bond issuances by the end of the 1990s (nearly 50 percent of all, private and sovereign, bond issuances in 2000 compared to 10 percent in 1994).[68] By mid-2001, nearly 20 percent of Argentina's public debt was euro-denominated. (See graphs 3.11 and 3.12.)

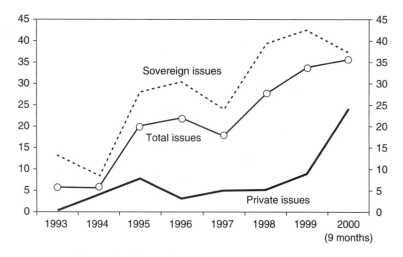

Graph 3.11   Euro share growth in Latin American bond issues (in % of total issues by type).

Source: Miotti, Plihon & Quenan, "The Euro and Financial Relations Between Latin America and Europe: Medium- and Long-Term Implications," presented at seminar on *L'euro et son impact en Amérique Latine*, Paris, CDC Ixis, September 25, 2001.

	Argentina (%)	Brazil (%)	Chile (%)	Colombia (%)	Mexico (%)	Venezuela (%)
In private obligations issues						
1993	0.0	0.0	0.0	0.0	1.0	0.0
1994	0.0	12.9	0.0	0.0	0.0	0.0
1995	21.0	6.5	0.0	0.0	0.0	0.0
1996	7.5	2.2	0.0	0.0	0.0	0.0
1997	8.6	3.9	0.0	0.0	0.0	0.0
1998	5.8	3.6	0.0	0.0	5.4	0.0
1999	29.2	4.5	18.5	0.0	0.0	0.0
2000	20.9	16.8	0.0	0.0	40.1	0.0
In government obligations issues						
1993	28.2	0.0	0.0	0.0	4.5	14.4
1994	22.4	0.0	0.0	0.0	0.0	0.0
1995	37.8	34.7	0.0	21.1	12.8	48.8
1996	47.2	30.5	0.0	11.0	18.7	68.6
1997	28.4	29.1	0.0	0.0	33.1	0.0
1998	57.0	32.5	0.0	16.0	16.1	26.0
1999	56.1	58.3	0.0	0.0	13.9	54.3
2000	51.7	25.3	0.0	36.1	19.9	68.5
In total obligations (private and government)						
1993	10.7	0.0	0.0	0.0	2.3	13.8
1994	9.9	11.5	0.0	0.0	0.0	0.0
1995	33.3	15.7	0.0	8.8	11.1	48.8
1996	39.2	13.6	0.0	9.7	15.7	68.6
1997	22.8	16.6	0.0	0.0	22.5	0.0
1998	44.3	17.7	0.0	16.0	11.9	26.0
1999	52.9	43.2	12.7	0.0	8.3	54.3
2000	47.7	24.4	0.0	36.1	23.7	68.5

Graph 3.12 Growth of euro-denominated bond issues in Latin America.
Source: CDC Ixis, Studies Department, Country Risk, Bondware, 2001; and Miotti, Plihon and Quenan, "The Euro and Financial Relations Between Latin America and Europe: Medium- and Long-Term Implications," presented at seminar on *L'euro et son impact en Amérique Latine*, Paris, CDC Ixis, September 25, 2001.

During the 1990s the Latin American debt market grew in volume, types of instruments traded and number of investors. Compared to previous periods, the 1990s emerging bond markets, dominated by Latin American issuers, presented some specificities. In particular the co-movement of spreads, as stressed by Paolo Mauro et al., across all emerging markets tend to be higher than during the previous phase of bond trading activity in emerging markets, the so-called 1870–1913 golden era for international capital markets.[69] This empirical research suggests that world integration became greater than during the earlier period, co-movements being stronger and mainly driven by economic fundamentals and also investors lack of attention to country-specific events. Because "all of the emerging market countries in the modern sample had defaulted prior to the period considered," "emerging markets today might be viewed by investors as a relatively higher-risk group than emerging markets in the past."[70] Among other things, the 1990s experienced the debt crisis of the 1980s and had to work out a solution. By contrast, during 1870–1913, solutions to financial crises were in fact facilitated by the less-dispersed universe of investors and a limited number of operators, most creditors being organized through a Corporation of Foreign Bondholders as underlined by Albert Fishlow.[71]

During the 1990s the Latin American debt market grew in volume, types of instruments traded and number of investors. At the same time, the volatility of spreads on Brady bonds and eurobonds differed significantly across countries. This fact leads one to question the drivers of these sometimes abrupt changes in market fundamentals.[72] Other scholars have been insisting more on external factors such as international interest rates or investors sentiments. Eichengreen and Mody underlined in particular that changes in fundamentals are only part of the story.[73] Based on an analysis of 1,000 developing bonds issued during the first half of the 1990s, they show that market participants distinguish between emerging countries on the basis of economic fundamentals but insist also that changes in spread seemed to be explained by market sentiments.

CHAPTER FOUR

The Usual Suspects: Timescales, Strategies and Constraints of Emerging Market Asset Managers

Professional investment may be likened to those newspaper competitions in which the competitors have to pick out the six prettiest faces from a hundred photographs, the prize being awarded to the competitor whose choice most nearly corresponds to the average preferences of the competitors as a whole; so that each competitor has to pick, not those faces which he himself find prettiest, but those which he thinks likeliest to catch the fancy of other competitors, all of whom are looking at the problem from the same point of view.

John Maynard Keynes

Fund managers play a fundamental role in the confidence game. They allocate assets around the world, investing in firms' stocks or countries' bonds. In this confidence game with its financial crises, they are the usual suspects, frequently accused of being short-termist. By the time of the Asian crisis, for example, concerns arose about offshore funds (the so-called hedge funds) and their impact on financial market volatility.[1] In fact the results of research are mixed, underlining above all that offshore funds are not especially worrisome monsters herding more than onshore funds during a crisis.[2] In the same way, as underlined by previous researches, using large sample data on closed end country funds, foreign investors don't tend to move out of a country when there is imminent crisis ahead before domestic fund managers.[3] Because they are better informed, local investors tend infact to move quicker than foreign investors. Different types of investors tend to behave differently. This is the case for individual versus institutional investors or local versus international. It is therefore misleading to lump all investors, or even all foreign investors, into one single basket. Individual foreign investors, due to lack of information, tend to herd more than institutional foreign investors, and nonresident investors tend to herd more than resident ones.[4]

As argued by Avinash Persaud, conventional wisdom regarding the greater volatility of portfolio capital flows versus FDI, can also be discussed. Bond portfolio or equity portfolio managers do not always employ short-term strategies in their investment decisions. Based on empirical evidence he underlines that the popular perception that M&A is less volatile than bond or equity flows and might be a partially misleading perception.[5] On the other hand FDI flows are not always long term. The treasury operations of a multinational subsidiary for example or the occasional hedging operations of the balance sheets of local subsidiaries can add great volatility to financial markets.[6]

Financial institutions, and fund management in particular, became in fact central to several researches conducted over the past years. One of the major purposes has been to track trading behavior of foreign portfolio investors in emerging countries before and during crises. By analyzing portfolio flows, some World Bank[7] and Harvard[8] research groups, for example, find that emerging market funds use positive momentum strategies systematically buying winners and selling losers. These strategies tend to be more relevant during crises rather than non-crisis periods. They use also "contagion strategies" selling assets from one country when a crisis hits another. Other researches revealed that the contagion effects are stronger when shocks originate in the center (i.e. in the United States, Japan or European financial centers) than when they originate in the periphery, and that we could discriminate, focusing on investors behavior and market making, between shocks transmitted from one periphery to another and from shocks transmitted from one periphery to another through a center country.[9]

These works stress the diversity of actors, their cognitive regimes, temporal horizons and strategies or constraints. Such actors are obviously at the center of the confidence game and it is now widely accepted that contagion and spill-over effects are not fully explained by domestic economics alone. It is related also to the financial behavior, risk aversion or risk appetite of investors. As stressed by Avinash Persaud, a strategist from State Street Bank, a key issue has been temporal and spatial clustering, "crisis like company" (48 of the 58 crises identified over the 1990s occurred in a cluster of two or more). This clustering is partly related to trading links but also to the financial dynamics of confidence games, such as reduction in investors' appetite for risk.[10] Other agendas of research try to focus on the changing patterns of market sentiments, emphasizing for example the social transmission of conventional wisdom or underlining the psychological dimensions of financial confidence games.[11] There are even some sudies that stressed phenomena such as the effects of sunshine and sunlight on stock markets, providing an attractive means of testing whether psychological biases can affect stock returns.[12]

In fact there are many types of funds and asset management strategies. Some are open-end funds other closed-end, some are regional or global emerging market funds. Some have contrarian or momentum strategies, different investment styles and research teams. Some travel extensively and have an in-depth knowledge of the assets they buy or sell—others do not. The archetype of the emerging market fund manager is probably Mark Mobius from Franklin Templeton. He is constantly on the move, visiting clients or targets and meeting companies and officials all around the world—a perfect icon of a globetrotter. Between January and June 2002, in a brief period of six months, he visited at least 46 cities in 20 countries.[13]

But it's not only spatial mobility that characterizes some of the leading fund managers. The density of the use of time is another component of fund managers as stressed by Mohamed El-Erian: "I wake up at 3.15 a.m. and check in with London offices for an update of overnight events. They provide a summary of major developments and levels at which different key instruments are trading. After I walk my dog Che, I leave for the office in Newport Beach. I'm there by 4.30 a.m., at which time emerging market team prepares a daily note on market developments. We typically begin trading around 6.00 a.m. and wrap up the bulk of the day by 4.00 p.m. Of course, there are always analyst calls to listen to, press interviews to schedule, meetings to attend and e-mails to return."[14]

One interesting classification is based on the spatial dimension of investments with four broad categories: global/international; emerging markets (well diversified, regional and country funds); regional; and country. This classification helps to underline the major trends of the industry, that is the dramatic development of global/international funds in terms of total assets under management and number of funds. The other trend is the development of (U.S.-based) emerging market funds during the 1990s with overall emerging market assets jumping from a level estimated at US$105 mn. by the beginning of the decade to 21 bn. by the end of the decade.[15]

In terms of research resources, asset managers can rely on brokers. But they also tend to develop their own research in order to reduce agency problems, asymmetries of information or simply to improve their investment decisions. One of the most important research teams (and also emerging market funds in terms of size of assets under management) was Capital Group in 2000. The investment team in emerging markets comprises 9 portfolio managers supported by 19 equity analysts, 3 emerging markets debt analysts, 8 private equity analysts and 10 dedicated traders, according to S&P. This is by far one of the most important teams within the emerging market funds industry. On comparison with European asset managers, the resources devoted to emerging markets are much more (and also linked with the size of the assets managed in emerging markets). Ashmore, Cazenove, Colonial First State or Gartmore, for example have emerging market teams of five, six, eight and nine respectively according to our survey. There are however other big research teams in the emerging markets asset industry even in Europe, such as Baring (12 investment managers and 9 research analysts), Genesis (16) and above all Schroder, which has for Latin America alone a team of 14 fund managers, according to data released by S&P.

Although different in their structures, strategies or size of assets under management and different in their cognitive regimes, fund management corporations, portfolio equity or bond investors, tend to be regarded as the culprits during financial crises. They are, for example, frequently accused of being short-termist. As confessed by Mohammed El-Erian, who has prior experience at the IMF, "in the public sector, you tend to take a longer term view, driven primarily by policy considerations. When I was at the IMF, we looked at what made a country sustainable over three years. When I moved to Salomon Smith Barney, we focused on what happened over the next three days! PIMCO is in the middle. We have a long-term approach orientation, but we also take short-term market developments into account."[16]

In fact, as we would like to stress, the issue of timescales and temporal horizons of fund managers is related to the political economy of the fund management industry itself. Fund managers' timescales are locked by the benchmarks used to assess their performance and the monitoring process of their own clients. Time horizons for asset managers are mostly constrained by the monitoring systems (related to client demand) that focus strongly on quarterly or even monthly performance. Each quarter or each month fund managers deliver newsletters, monthly or quarterly reports and data on their portfolio performance according to the mandates negotiated with clients. Even if, according to the interviews realized both in Europe and the United States, institutional clients do not generally ask for strategic shifts in allocations during a single quarter, fund managers tend to perceive their clients as concerned by quarterly performances and tend to adopt strategies dominated by short-term horizons.[17] Therefore it is not London or Wall Street asset managers that tend to favor short-term strategies but rather the mandates imposed on them that curb their vision. In order to understand the dynamics of financial markets it's important to focus on the trends and constraints experienced by the asset management industry. There are at least two powerful trends in the fund management industry.

4.1   The Mimetic Game: To be or Not to be in the Index

The first trend is related to the index game. While temporal horizons of emerging market operators are limited to short-term options, the universe of investment of asset managers is spatially limited. Their vision of the world is technically constrained, in a way they are myopic not only from a temporal point of view but also from a spatial point of view. This defective and restricted vision is not the result of fund managers' inabilities but mainly explained by the imposed prisms through which they can watch the world that is the index. As underlined by an asset manager, commenting on the index games during the Argentina debt swap operation of mid-2001, "because of these index games (in this case bond index game led by JP Morgan), de facto, investors like myself that on a macro-economic base would have not invest in Argentina, have been forced to."[18] Why therefore do fund managers follow the indices? "Because, as argued by a leading firm, many of us have to. The contracts of clients frequently specify such benchmarks." As underlined by several leading scholars, index games and benchmark imperatives contribute to the herding behavior in financial markets. They boost incentives to herd and play a crucial role in explaining contagion effects.[19]

Each investor has a specific prism. For most emerging market equity fund managers the name of the prism is the Morgan Stanley Capital International MSCI EMF (Emerging Market Free).[20] For emerging bond markets it's the JP Morgan EMBI. The inclusion or exclusion on one index can have direct financial impacts on the stocks or countries included or excluded or more frequently rebalanced. Such widely used benchmarks go a long way in explaining emerging market funds' country allocation. As underlined by an IMF study, the correlations of funds' weightings with that of benchmarks (for the MSCI EMF index) range from 0.49 for funds investing worldwide to 0.89 for Latin American funds.[21]

As pointed out by one asset manager, the inclusion in the MSCI Hong Kong index of Henderson Land in 2001 boosted the stock value by 8 percent in less than three days while at the same time the exclusion of Cheung Kong provoked a slump of 10 percent. As underlined by PIMCO's emerging market fund manager, "the asset class remains hostage to industry-wide indices that, by construction, accentuate systemic risks. While some effort has been made to introduce more diversified indices, that remains insufficient. Recognizing this, some fund managers have shifted to customized indices that better capture the heterogeneous nature and underlying economic characteristics of the asset class. But, pending further changes, the risk of adverse (and from the outside, seemingly irrational) contagion remains an almost unavoidable feature of the asset class."[22]

The world vision of asset managers is in fact limited to a happy few chosen countries. For most emerging market bond managers the world is limited to the JP Morgan EMBI+ leading index. According to JP Morgan, this index is followed by at least US$33 bn. worth of funds. In 2002, the universe of investment was limited to no more than 21 countries. JP Morgan publishes a total of five emerging market bond indices. They have similar objectives (they are indicators of benchmark returns) but differ in the class of assets included, the poll of issuing countries and also the country weights. The number of countries covered for example ranged from 21 (EMBI+) to 33 (EMBI Global and EMBI Global constrained) in 2002. Latin America is the most represented area in the indexes, accounting for more than half in the former. The EMBI, which tracks exclusively Brady bonds, concentrates the greatest weights on Latin American countries, specifically Argentina, Brazil and Mexico.

The name of the game is not only to be or not to be in the index, weight is also very relevant. In fact, the index is concentrated in a few countries. Before the weighting changes in EMBI+ in Argentina by the end of 2001, just four countries weighted 70 percent of the index.[23] Each rebalancing makes waves, boosting some countries or reducing the weights of others and therefore the appetite of investors for the country. In 2001, the biggest country move in the index was Argentina, the weighting of the country dropping from more than 20 percent at the beginning of the year to less than 3 percent by the end of the year provoking large rebalancing in the asset class at the peak of the crisis.

For equity fund managers the spatial horizon of investments is limited by the MSCI indexes. Being the index chosen by nearly 90 percent of U.S. investors, the MSCI imposes itself during the 1990s in the global investing market with about US$3,500 bn. benchmarked against its indices (compared to US$2,500 benchmarked to FTSE another leading index provider from the United Kingdom). The world according to the MSCI is composed of 49 developed and emerging markets, that is 25 percent of all existing countries. Developed and emerging countries are not equals. According to the MSCI, in the new All Country World Index of the company, rebased in May 2001, the U.S. Index weight is nearly 55 percent, well above the 0.69 percent for Taiwan or the 0.59 percent for Mexico. As for bond indexes, not only do country weights differ but some countries simply don't exist for fund managers. The so-called emerging countries are less represented than developed countries: only 26 to 15 percent of all developing countries are included in the index as against 23 countries for the developed world, that is nearly 100 percent of OECD countries. If we take for example Latin America, the universe of equity fund managers is limited to only seven countries. This means that only a little more than 25 percent of the Western Hemisphere exists in the screens of equity investors.[24] If we take a closer look at the MSCI index, not only is the number of countries included limited but also inside each country the entire stock market universe is not present. The number of securities by country is limited to a very happy few.

The same applies for the other major equity emerging markets provider, S&P/IFCI, where the tendency has been to concentrate on a few Latin American markets. In October 2001, for example, the indexer announced that Venezuela and Colombia would be dropped from its investable series. Venezuela was dropped mainly because the country did not have five stocks that traded enough to be eligible for the series. Colombia was dropped because its market capitalization was too low rather than the traded volumes of eligible shares.[25] The market capitalization of Colombia and Venezuela, in IFCI tables, are less than US$2 bn. each in 2001 (each weighting 1 percent of the IFCI) compared to US$74 bn. for Brazil or US$60 bn. for Mexico. Given that the IFCI index is a benchmark for many institutional investors, the removal of both countries at the end of 2001 will mean that investors will have even less incentives to invest in these tiny markets; Peru remaining the only Andean country available. This index game is accentuated with the development of the so-called tracker funds, that is indexed funds that follow the indexes more closely. While active fund managers may have a tracking error of 2 percent or more (i.e. deviation from a chosen benchmark index) index trackers have a much narrower tracking error of 0.5 percent.

For equity markets, the main index providers are the FTSE (jointly owned by the *Financial Times* and the London Stock Exchange), the Dow Jones Stoxx and the MSCI. The MSCI dominates the index industry. It is the most widely used benchmark by global portfolio managers, particularly by emerging market managers. About US$3,500 bn. of investments around the world are benchmarked against the MSCI and nearly 1,500 fund management companies worldwide use the index as a benchmark for gauging their portfolio's performance. In North America and Asia, the index is the choice of nearly 90 percent of institutional international equity investors, according to the estimates of the MSCI. In Europe also, the MSCI dominates the index industry providing benchmarks for nearly two-thirds of continental European fund managers, according to Merrill Lynch/Gallup and Primark Extel surveys. The MSCI is clearly the choice of emerging market fund managers, increasing its market share since the launch of the Emerging Market Series in 1987 to well above the former IFC World Bank index, introduced in the late 1990s by Standard & Poor's.

It is interesting to note that the MSCI index company was created by a broker and an asset manager: Morgan Stanley and Capital International.[26] Today the company is still controlled by what has become Morgan Stanley Dean Witter, one of the leading securities firms, and the Los Angeles–based (and the world's biggest asset manager) Capital International. According to the MSCI, Morgan Stanley Dean Witter (MSDW), which is both a global financial services firm and a market leader in securities, asset management and credit services, is the majority shareholder of the MSCI while The Capital Group Companies (Capital), remain a minority shareholder. The key point is that both companies operate from both sides of the so-called Chinese Wall, sell-side and buy-side, that theoretically divide the worlds of brokers and asset managers. Morgan Stanley has its own asset management firm, Morgan Stanley Asset Management (MSAM), which happens to be one of the top five players in emerging markets with US$4.5 bn. in global emerging market accounts, according to S&P. The Capital Group Companies is a global asset manager founded in 1931 in Los Angeles with a keen interest in emerging markets.[27] The Capital Group investment team manages more than US$26 bn. in global emerging markets. The MSCI therefore is an exotic bird born from the strange yoking of a leading operator of the so-called sell-side industry (Morgan Stanley) and a leading operator of the buy-side (Capital Group). Both companies are from both sides of the Wall and both are also market markers in global emerging markets. The MSCI represents an unusual "moral hazard" located inside the financial market.

When the MSCI revamps its indices the impact in equity markets is huge. Active fund managers, passive fund managers and hedge funds are all affected by the changes in the investment criteria determined by the MSCI.[28] Most of them are obliged to wait until the official start dates of MSCI revamps because of the terms of their mandates from pension funds or other institutional clients. Others, for example hedge funds, can alter their portfolio's compositions before the MSCI's revamps hoping they have successfully guessed what the changes will be. In the forward-looking world of financial markets, index companies are playing an even greater role as the so-called index tracking funds are increasing. These "passive" fund managers, who simply replicate the index[29] are becoming big players. In 2001, index-tracking specialists were estimated to be running more than US$2,300 bn. worth of assets around the world.[30] In the United Kingdom, about 25 percent of the assets under management in 2001 are indexed funds while in the United States, where the indexing was developed in the early 1970s, the figure is about 35 percent. In Japan around 12 percent of the funds are passive and in continental countries consultants like William M Mercer and Watson Wyatt calculate that between 4 and 13 percent of funds are indexed, the trend showing an increase since the late 1990s for all countries. The rationalization trend of managers ending in a greater proportion of index managers is combining with the concentration trend in the asset management industry. Both trends point to the fact that in the future portfolio rebalancing might become even more mimetic and more abrupt because of the increasing consolidation within the asset management industry.[31]

Above all the game is a mimetic one. Passive or active, fund managers have incentives to follow the crowd. They carefully scrutinize index games and rebalancings, anticipating moves to increase its gains.[32] Active fund managers have clearly more latitude in their strategic asset allocation but as their performance is measured with reference to the relevant peer group, it's rational for them not to stray too far from the index path.[33] As stressed by the U.K. Myners Report in 2001, this peer group benchmark has distorting effects the major one being the incentives to reproduce investment decisions based on what other funds are doing. Passive fund managers simply follow the path receiving specific instructions from their clients to invest in one or more asset classes and to stick to the relevant index as a benchmark. The mimetic games are accentuated by the process of investment for institutional investors. In the United Kingdom for example, a leading and highly successful institutional investment country, most pensions are organized on a trust basis with a board of trustees responsible for the determination of how their assets are invested. A survey conducted for the Myners Report of 2001 revealed however that the analytical and monitoring capacities of this board of trustees were highly limited as 62 percent of the 226 trustees interviewed have no specific professional qualification in finance or in investment and 77 percent of them have no inhouse staff or professionals to assist them (23 percent of trustees even confessed that they did not know what their benchmark was).

In May 2001, the MSCI rebalanced its major indexes provoking a huge wave of changes in the financial universe of asset managers, the new percentage weightings being key to investors who manage US$3.5 tn. and try to mimic the indexes, which track more than 2,200 stocks around the word. Some emerging countries decreased by more than 3 percent (India) or by 2 percent (Mexico) while others became winners without any kind of macroeconomic or microeconomic deterioration or improvement but simply for technical reasons: the new MSCI indexes were calculated to reflect the percentage of companies' shares available for trading (known as free float) against the previous weights based on their market value, including shares that do not trade (see graph 4.1).

The rebalancing game can create significant fund flows in or out of a country or a stock. ING Barings calculated in 2000 that the impacts of index rebalancing of the Dow Jones, FTSE and MSCI following the "free-float adjustment" process would move in total US$120 bn. out of Japan. The United Kingdom was expected to be one of the major winners in this rebalancing while Latin America would be losing US$1.1 bn. and emerging Asia more than US$33 bn. The same index rebalancing game, with the MSCI and EMBI changes in end 2001, due in part to the free float for the first one and to the swap operation and then the default of Argentina for the second one, implied rebalancing in the Latin American region. Argentina nearly disappeared in both indexes while Mexico and Brazil increased their weights (see table 4.1).

In the end, deciding to remove a stock, to change a country weight or to play the index game is a political economic issue. The original idea of indices was to reflect the "mood" of the market with an approach that was impressionistic rather than scientific. Later, tools and teams were strengthened. Indices came to be used more and more as a performance

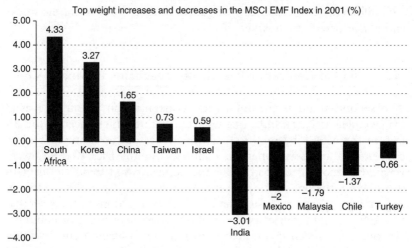

Graph 4.1   The index game in 2001: MSCI emerging market rebalancings.

Source: Based on Morgan Stanley Capital International, 2001.

Table 4.1   Effects in terms of fund flows of free float adjustments (% weight change)

	MSCI	FTSE	Dow Jones	Estimated net flow ($bn.)
United States	8.7	6	7.2	59.2
Europe (not Britain)	−6.3	−5.8	−7.6	−17.1
Japan	−19.7	−16.4	−15.9	−122.1
Britain	11.2	6.7	11.5	115.9
Asia Pacific (not Japan)	−21.1	−11.9	−22.9	−33.8
EMEA	−7.1	1	15.1	−0.2
Latin America	−11	−4.5	−10.2	−1.1

Source: Based on ING Barings, 2000.

benchmark for investors. With the success of tracking funds, the industry has been obliged to adapt and adopt more and more indices. In a way most of the fund managers have been forced to use these indices with the generalization of the "tracking error" measurement, obliging fund managers to follow the index as closely as possible. The effect of these trends in the industry is that many fund managers are nearly obliged to mimic the indexes and to pick up the heavily weighted stocks whether they believe the investment is good or bad. "Simply if we do not own the stocks, if we underperformed the index, we simply loose the business."[34] "One of the dimensions of the herding behavior in financial markets lies precisely in the index game. With index-tracking a blindfolded chimpanzee throwing dices or darts could select the stocks and perform with the market."[35]

4.2   The Concentration Trend: Big Elephants in Small Ponds

The second trend is the increasing concentration within the asset management industry. Index games contribute to this concentration. In fact, in the MSCI, by mid-2001 almost three-fourths of the index was concentrated in just six emerging countries (South Africa, Korea, Taiwan, Brazil, Mexico and China).[36] But the concentration trend we want to stress here is the one in the asset management industry itself. The role of large trader operators or large and highly leveraged institutions such as hedge funds and proprietary desks of big investment banks or commercial ones, have been questioned regarding the contagion and volatility issues in financial markets. It has been underlined that the presence of large players is deemed to increase a country's vulnerability to a crisis, amplifying phenomena such as herding or momentum trading. Some operators are more efficient market makers than others because of their reputation or more simply because of their ability to leverage and the size of their assets under management. As underlined by Corsetti, Pesenti and Roubini, the presence of some actors with market power increases the vulnerability of a country, both size and reputation of those market markers being major explanations of their impact.[37]

The industry is dominated by U.S. and U.K. operators. It is also developing speedily in other European and emerging countries. London is the world's largest center for equity management, just ahead of New York, Tokyo and Boston. But whatever the country, the funds are getting larger. Fidelity, Boston's largest fund manager group, is roughly twice as big as Scotland's entire fund management industry, and is ranked fifteenth in the world's equity fund management center. Over a quarter of asset managers were involved in merger activities in 2000. The top five managers' worldwide assets totaled US$4,000 bn., which is more than the GDP of France and Germany together.[38] The Myners Report in the United Kingdom revealed that the Herfindahl–Hirschman index, which provides a measure of market concentration, gives U.K. fund management a figure of 650. By any standards this is the highest figure for the global fund management industry (below the 1,000 level that causes anti-competition authorities to take notice).[39]

In fact, only a few big players can make or move the markets. The concentration trend is widely spread over all asset classes but it is particularly striking in the narrow emerging markets asset class dominated by a few players. At an aggregate level, the share of assets held by the five largest money managers jumped from less than 14 percent of total assets to more than 18 percent between 1993 and 1998. Retail money is increasingly flowing into broad international funds rather than to region-specific funds. International and global funds dominate the confidence game, representing respectively 57 and 38 percent of all funds (against 5 percent for emerging equity market funds).[40] One consequence of this is that money managers tend to concentrate their investments in a manageable number of large liquid stocks. Foreign flows between January 2000 and June 2001 have been concentrated in a few global sectors and large countries, 42 percent of the US$67 bn. in flows to global emerging markets going to only 11 offerings representing 66 percent of total offerings. The concentration increased during 2001 following the rebalancing of the MSCI indices with the seven largest markets (Taiwan, Mexico, Korea, South Africa, Brazil, India and China) accounting for a cumulative 72 percent of the MSCI emerging markets index up from 64 percent.[41]

The United States and the United Kingdom have respectively US$18.5 tn. and US$4.1 tn. assets under management, well above Switzerland (US$2 tn.) and France (US$1.5 tn.). These numbers are hardly comparable with that in Latin America. In Latin America, the total amount of assets held by institutional investors in the ten largest countries is approximately US$0.35 tn., one-half held by pension funds and the other half by mutual funds.[42] By the end of 2001, Latin American pension and mutual funds held nearly US$300 bn. in assets with Brazil alone holding over 65 percent of the managed assets in the region (45 percent of pension funds market share and 78 percent of mutual funds market share). In Latin America, Previ from Brazil and Provida from Chile with respectively US$17 bn. and US$11 bn. have under management the two biggest pension funds. The three biggest mutual funds are all Brazilian (Banco do Brasil, ITAU and Bradesco). There are 32 pension fund asset managers and 33 mutual fund asset managers each holding more than US$1 bn. in Latin America.[43]

In the United Kingdom, London is the home of most fund managers operating in emerging markets. However there is also a thriving investment management industry located in Scotland, Edinburgh and Glasgow being the sixth biggest management center in Europe in 2001. U.K. pension fund assets alone represent 40 percent of Europe's total pension fund assets and 90 percent of U.K. GDP in 2000.[44] In the last few years, the industry has been engaged in several mergers and acquisitions, some leading and biggest U.K. asset managers being bought by foreign operators some of them American. Many firms, which once were independent boutiques, are now part of wider financial organizations. Mercury Asset Management, once a leading U.K. independent fund manager, became Merrill Lynch Investment Managers; Morgan Grenfell was acquired by Deutsche Bank and became Deutsche Asset Management; Gartmore, another leading independent U.K. boutique, is now owned by U.S. Nationwide Mutual; Scudder a leading U.S. asset manager in emerging markets was merged with Deutsche Asset Management units; and so on.

The industry is heavily concentrated. In the United Kingdom for example the five biggest players (Schroders Investment Management, Merrill Lynch Mercury Asset Management, Barclays Global Investors, Phillips & Drew and Hermes Pension Management) controlled 50 percent of the market share of U.K. pension assets. In smaller countries like Spain for example, only two players, BBVA and BSCH controlled the bulk of the market share. At the same time, the size of institutional assets has grown exponentially all around Europe and mainly in northern countries like Netherlands or Sweden. The two other biggest markets in Europe are Switzerland and France, both half the size of the United Kingdom. The total pension fund market in Europe is at an estimated value of nearly US$4 tn. in 2000 and the entire fund management industry is estimated to have more than US$10 tn. assets under management. Assets in emerging market equity funds were around US$175 bn.

This concentration is also important in emerging markets. Emerging market bond stocks represented more than US$500 bn. by mid-2001 according to CDC Ixis.[45] The biggest players among emerging market debt fund managers are a very selective club formed by Alliance Capital, PIMCO, Prudential, GMO, Templeton, Scudder Kemper, Merrill Lynch, Salomon Smith Barney and Morgan Stanley Dean Witter. According to our estimates, based on Bloomberg data, the two biggest emerging bond funds are PIMCO, with US$7.5 bn. under asset management in emerging markets, nearly 30 percent of all assets under management in emerging bond funds, and Alliance (US$6 bn.). Only four other asset managers have more than US$1 bn. under management in emerging bond markets (Prudential, GMO, Merrill Lynch and Templeton). Though JP Morgan runs the most widely followed emerging bond markets index, it only has US$130 mn. under management in emerging bond markets, according to Bloomberg data.

For a closer view of the concentration and dispersion of the asset management industry in equity emerging markets we used a single database, one of the most complete on emerging market funds, emerging-portfolio.com. According to this database, equity emerging market funds totaled US$133,315 mios in June 2000. The bulk (55 percent of total assets) is managed by global emerging market funds. Asian funds (20 percent), Latin American funds (6 percent) and Eastern Europe funds (4 percent) come after. In countries like China, India, South Korea, Russia, Mexico and Brazil there are some equity funds of more than US$1 bn. of assets under management (see table 4.2).

Most of the funds are located in developing countries. If we classify funds according to their country of registration (which is only a very rough indication regarding their location), we can have a first approximation of the location of asset management teams. Not surprisingly most of them are located in the United States but not in New York. Boston is in fact the predominant financial center regarding emerging market fund managers' locations. London is the other important financial platform. Los Angeles is host to the biggest equity emerging market fund managers, which distorts the location map. Los Angeles is home of

Table 4.2   Emerging market equity funds in 2000

	US$ mios
Global Emerging Markets Funds	70,173
Asia ex-Japan regional Funds	25,313
Latin American Regional	7,523
Central and East Europe Regional Funds	5,550
India Country Funds	3,770
Greater China Country Funds	3,383
Korea Country Funds	3,003
Russia/CIS Country Funds	1,239
Mexico Country Funds	1,126
Taiwan Country Funds	1,072
Brazil Country Funds	852
Asia ex-Japan Smaller Country Funds	792
Chile Country Funds	767
Hong Kong Country Funds	731
Asean Funds	702
China Country Funds	631
Indian Sub-Continent Funds	576
South Africa Country Funds	492
Africa Regional Funds	345
Malaysia Country Funds	315
Egypt Country Funds	248
Turkey Country Funds	172

Source: Santiso, 2001; based on emergingportfolio.com.

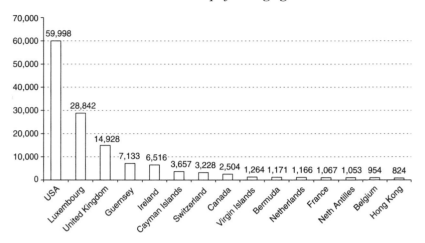

Graph 4.2   Top 15 fund assets ranked by country of registration, July 2000 (in US$ mios).
Source: Santiso, 2001; based on emergingportfolio.com.

Capital International, which alone manages nearly US$30 bn. in emerging markets. Edinburgh is also an important financial center for emerging market funds as are Milan and Paris (see graph 4.2).

If we consider Latin American funds alone, the most important assets under management are located in London, in particular Schroder and Scudder Threadeneedle. Among the 20 most important funds operating in Latin America, 40 percent are based in London (8), 30 percent in Boston (6) and 20 percent in New York (4). France and Switzerland ranked one each in the top 20. Among these funds, interviews and questionnaires were obtained with more than 60 percent of them. In table 4.3 there is a micro-picture of the asset management industry operating with Latin American funds (only funds of over US$100 mios were taken into account).

Less than 20 funds were holding more than US$1 bn. in assets in equity emerging markets. Only one fund, the largest one, Capital International's Emerging Markets Growth, had more than US$26 bn. in assets by the end of 2000, twice the assets of the entire emerging market bond fund industry. Emerging market equity funds represent however only the tip of the iceberg as they totaled only 5 percent of all equity assets managed by mutual funds, according to AMG Data and MSDW, while international equity concentrated 57 percent and global equity 38 percent. However focusing on global emerging market funds can give an idea of the concentration/dispersion of the asset

Table 4.3 Latin American emerging market equity funds, July 2000

Fund name	Assets (US$ mios)	Fund manager	Domicile
Schroder Latin American Fund	902.18	Schroder Investment Management	U.K.
Threadneedle Latin American growth Fund CI 1	557.7	Threadneedle Investment Managers	U.K.
Scudder Latin American Fund	494.3	Scudder Kemper Investments	U.S.
Fidelity Latin America Fund*	357.2	Fidelity	U.S.
Morgan Stanley SICAV Latin American Fund I	232.22	MSDW Investment Management	U.S.
F&C Latin America Investment Trust	218.07	Foreign & Colonial Emerging Markets	U.K.
Fleming Latin American Fund	201.3	Fleming Asset Management	U.K.
AAF Latin American Equity Fund*	198.43	ABN Amro Asset Management	U.S.
Fidelity Funds Latin America*	168.06	Fidelity	U.S.
Mercury ST Latin America Fund	165.07	Mercury Asset Management	U.K.
Latin American Discovery Fund	162.59	MSDW Investment Management	U.S.
Latinvest Fund*	155.41	Globalvest Management Corporation	U.S.
BG Latin American Fund*	149.37	Baillie Gifford	U.K.
Lion Fortune CL Latin America Equity C	145.6	Crédit Lyonnais Asset Management	France
Morgan Stanley SICAV Latin American Fund A	139.81	MSDW Investment Management	U.S.
UBS Equity Fund Latin America*	119.44	UBS Asset Management	Suisse
Latin America Equity Investment Fund	112.96	Credit Suisse Asset Management	U.S.
Scottish Widows Latin America Trust*	111.9	Scottish Widows Investment MGT	U.K.
Latin America Equity Fund	107.46	Credit Suisse Asset Management	U.S.
Baring Puma Fund Ltd*	100.99	Baring Asset Management	U.S.
Gestinova Latin America*	97.25	BBVA Gestinova	Espagne
CS Equity Fund Latin America	86.75	Credit Suisse Asset Management	U.S.
Morgan Grenfell Latin American Companies	79.7	Morgan Grenfell Asset Management	U.K.
Invesco GT Latin American Fund	71.09	Invesco Asset Management	U.K.
AIM Latin America Growth Fund A	58.81	Invesco Asset Management	U.K.
CI Latin American Fund	56.07	Credit Suisse Asset Management	U.S.
AIM Latin America Growth Fund B	49.86	Invesco Asset Management	U.K.

Table 4.3 (*Contd.*)

Fund name	Assets (US$ mios)	Fund manager	Domicile
Fleming Select Latin American Fund	45.52	Fleming Asset Management	U.K.
Sogeux Fund Equities Latin America	43.74	Société Generale Asset Management	France
Groupe Indosuez Fund Latin America	42.92	Gartmore Investment	U.K.
AIM Latin America Growth Fund C	37.86	Invesco Asset Management	U.K.
Invesco Latin America Growth Fund	27.84	Invesco Asset Management	U.K.
Green Line Latin American Growth Fund	27.23	MSDW Investment Management	U.S.
F&C Latin American Exempt Fund	26.61	Foreign & Colonial Emerging Markets	U.K.
Schroder ISF Latin American Fund C Dis	24.79	Schroder Investment Management	U.K.
Deutsche Latin American Fund	20.7	Morgan Grenfell Asset Management	U.K.
CDC Emerging Latin America	19.08	CDC Asset Management	France
JPM Latin American Equity Fund A	18.1	JP Morgan Investment Management	U.S.
Schroder ISF Latin American Fund A Dis	17.92	Schroder Investment Management	U.K.
Gartmore CSF Latin America Fund	15.64	Gartmore Investment	U.K.
MSDW IF Latin America Portfolio A	13.68	MSDW Investment Management	U.S.
JPM Latin American Equity Fund C	12.45	JP Morgan Investment Management	U.S.
S&P Latin American Fund	10.7	Fleming Asset Management	U.K.
State Street Amerique latine	10.22	State Street Global Advisors	France
AIM Latin America Growth Class	9.98	Invesco Asset Management	U.K.
Schroder ISF Latin American Fund C Acc	8.11	Schroder Investment Management	U.K.
CI Sector Fund Latin American Shares	7.06	Credit Suisse Asset Management	U.S.
Pictet IF Latin America	6.91	Pictet Asset Management	U.K.
Schroder ISF Latin American Fund B Dis	6.67	Schroder Investment Management	U.K.
Atlas Latin American Value Fund	5.23	Pictet Asset Management	U.K.
JPM Latin American Equity Fund X	2.94	JP Morgan Investment Management	U.S.
Nestor Lateinamerika Fonds	2.1	Pictet Asset Management	U.K.
JPM Latin American Equity Fund B	0.86	JP Morgan Investment Management	U.S.

* Funds with more than (or nearly) US$ 100 mios assets under management not interviewed (located in Boston, Madrid, Edinburgh and Zurich).

Source: Santiso, 2001; based on emergingportfolio.com.

management industry. In fact, there are a lot of small funds sharing a market with some big asset managers that dominate (see table 4.4).

The emerging markets equity industry presents a high Herfindahl–Hirschman index.[46] We calculated the concentration index according to the criteria of assets under management of the total emerging market equity funds and focusing also on the top 100 funds. The concentration index obtained is respectively 6.93 and 7.99 percent (see tables 4.5 and 4.6).[47]

De facto, the most important funds, in terms of being market markers, are not the top performer in terms of returns. In the year 2000, for example, there were some top performers in emerging market funds like Carmignac Gestion in Paris and Genesis in London. These small funds weren't even referenced in the league tables of Lipper Analytical, a ranking company based in the United States. Based on our survey and on a large sample of 145 questionnaires, those funds were never mentioned. Instead, the most frequently quoted funds as a "top 3 leading and best informed fund manager" were Capital, Templeton, Scudder, Fidelity, Schroder or Fleming, all of them were also leading funds in terms of volume. In other terms, the perceived market markers by the industry are precisely the biggest asset managers. Most of them now have data available from the Internet but otherwise it is quite difficult to collect the data. One of the paradoxes of emerging markets confidence game is that while states became increasingly open and transparent, releasing more and more data, the fund management industry remains more closed regarding data on assets under management and the distribution of their portfolio investments country by country. Some firms however, even through the Internet, are releasing more and more data. In total we were able to construct a database of 47 global emerging market funds, 41 Asian regional emerging markets, 27 Latin American regional emerging market funds and 22 Eastern European funds, realizing data through the Internet (see table 4.7).

4.3   Timescales and Temporal Myopia

We have also tried to specify fund managers' temporal horizons through a questionnaire and direct interviews. Timescales locked by quarterly trustee meetings are usually quoted by fund managers as one of their major constraints.[48] This trend is widespread in the industry as suggested by the Myners report referring to pension funds, where fund managers tend to look at the quarterly results.[49] But most of the fund managers believe however (true or not is another issue) that their clients are quite

Table 4.4 Global emerging market equity funds, sample of interviews, July 2000

Fund name	Assets (US$ mios)	Fund manager	Domicile
Emerging Markets Growth Fund*	22,638.65	Capital International	U.S.
Capital International Emerging Markets*	4,310.35	Capital International	U.S.
Schroder Emerging Markets Fund	2,781.77	Schroder Investment Management	U.K.
Templeton Developing Markets Trust*	2,733.49	Templeton Investment Management	U.S.
Templeton IF Emerging Markets Series*	2,242.67	Templeton Investment Management	U.S.
Genesis Emerging Markets Fund*	2,180.29	Genesis Investment Management	U.K.
MSWD Emerging Markets Portfolio A	1,417.58	Morgan Stanley Dean Witter Investments	U.S.
SEI Emerging Markets Equity Fund*	1,378.88	SEI Investments	U.S.
UBS Equity Fund Emerging Markets*	1,227.36	UBS Asset Management	CH
Templeton Emerging Markets Inv. Trust*	1,136.47	Templeton Investment Management	U.S.
Vanguard Emerging Markets Stock*	1,102.41	Vanguard Group	U.S.
GMO Emerging Markets Fund*	1,101.66	Grantham, Mayo, van Otterloo	U.S.
Deutsche GSF Emerging Markets Fund A	1,073.60	Deutsche Morgan Grenfell Asset MGT	U.K.
Batterymarch Global Emerging Markets*	1,063.31	Batterymarch Financial Management	U.S.
Emerging Markets Trust*	931.49	Capital International	U.S.
Investdion Emergents	723.03	Crédit Lyonnais Asset Management	France
Berstein Emerging Markets Fund	661.89	Sanford C. Bernstein	U.S.
Quantum Emerging Market Fund*	660.04	Soros Fund Management	U.S.
AAF Global Emerging Markets Equity*	610.72	ABN Amro Asset Management	U.S.
Mercury ST Emerging Markets Fund	549.42	Mercury Asset Management	U.K.
Franklin Templeton IF Emerging Markets*	505.67	Templeton Investment Management	U.S.
Baring EMUF Global Emerging Markets*	459	Baring Asset Management	U.S.
Frank Russell Investment EM Fund S	427.35	Frank Russell Investment Management	U.S.
Pictet targeted Fund Emerging Markets	421.62	Pictet Asset Management	U.K.
Fidelity Institutional Emerging Markets*	418.28	Fidelity	U.S.
Morgan Stanley Dean Witter EM Fund	407.07	Morgan Stanley Dean Witter Investments	U.S.
Schroder Global Emerging Markets Fund	391.56	Schroder Investment Management	U.K.
Ssga Emerging Markets Fund	378.59	State Street Global Advisors	U.S.

Fund	Manager	Country
Schroder Emerging Markets Fund	Schroder Investment Management	U.K.
Fleming Emerging Markets Fund	Fleming Asset Management	U.K.
JPM Emerging Markets Equity Fund A	JP Morgan Investment Management	U.S.
Mercury Emerging Markets Fund	Mercury Asset Management	U.K.
Fleming Emerging Markets Investment T	Fleming Asset Management	U.K.
F&C Emerging Markets Investment Trust	Foreign & Colonial Emerging Markets	U.K.
CS Equity Fund Emerging Markets Fund	Credit Suisse Asset Management	U.S.
Axa Sun Life Emerging Markets Fund	Axa Sun Life Investment Management	France
Morgan Stanley SICAV EM Fund A	Morgan Stanley Dean Witter Investments	U.S.
Global Emerging Markets Country Fund	City of London Investment Management	U.K.
Morgan Stanley SICAV EM Fund I	Morgan Stanley Dean Witter Investments	U.S.
Gartmore PSF Emerging Markets Strat.	Gartmore Investments	U.K.
JPM Emerging Markets Equity Fund X	JP Morgan Investment Management	U.S.
Deutsche GSF Emerging Markets Fund B	Deutsche Morgan Grenfell Asset Management	U.K.
AIM Developing Markets Fund A	Invesco Asset Management	U.K.
Invesco GT Developing Markets Fund A	Invesco Asset Management	U.K.
Deutsche Emerging Markets Equity Fund	Deutsche Morgan Grenfell Asset Management	U.K.
MP Emerging Markets Country Fund	City of London Investment Management	U.K.
Emerging Markets Infrastructure Fund	Credit Suisse Asset Management	U.S.
State Street Emerging Markets Fund	State Street Banque	France
Schroder Emerging Countries Investment	Schroder Investment Management	U.K.
CI Emerging Markets Fund	Credit Suisse Asset Management	U.S.
Schroder ISF Emerging Markets Fund C	Schroder Investment Management	U.K.
JPM Emerging Markets Equity	JP Morgan Investment Management	U.S.
Emerging Markets Telecom Fund	Credit Suisse Asset Management	U.S.
SG Extentiel	Société Generale Asset Management	France
JPM Emerging Markets Equity Fund C	JP Morgan Investment Management	U.S.
AIM Developing Markets Fund B	Invesco Asset Management	U.K.
Schroder ISF Emerging Markets Fund A	Schroder Investment Management	U.K.
Investable Emerging Markets Fund	City of London Investment Management	U.K.

Table 4.4 (*Contd.*)

Fund name	Assets (US$ mios)	Fund manager	Domicile
Van Kampen Emerging Markets Fund A	104.88	Morgan Stanley Dean Witter Investments	U.S.
Pace International Emerging Markets	86.34	Schroder Investment Management	U.K.
Carmignac Marché Emergents	83.09	Carmignac Gestion	France
Gartmore CSF Emerging Markets Fund	82.28	Gartmore Investments	U.K.
Green Line Emerging Markets Fund	77.5	Morgan Stanley Dean Witter Investments	U.S.
Indocam Marchés Emergents	72.16	Indocam Asset management	France
Cazenove Global Emerging Markets	71.95	Cazenove Fund Management	U.K.
F&C Global Emerging Markets ex-Pacific	70.09	Foreign & Colonial Emerging Markets	U.K.
WestLB Compass Fund Global EM	65.88	WestLB Asset Management	U.K.
Van Kampen Emerging Markets Fund B	62.74	Morgan Stanley Dean Witter Investments	U.S.
Gartmore Emerging Markets Fund	58.61	Gartmore Investments	U.K.
Nations Emerging Markets Fund	58.21	Gartmore Investments	U.K.
ACM GI Developing Regional Fund A	56.65	Alliance Capital Management	U.S.
ACM GI Developing Regional Fund A	56.65	Alliance Capital Management	U.S.
Invesco GT Global Emerging Markets	50.93	Invesco Asset Management	U.K.
ACM GI Developing Regional Fund I	44.82	Alliance Capital Management	U.S.
Schroder ISF Emerging Markets Fund Acc	42.72	Schroder Investment Management	U.K.
Schroder ISF Emerging Markets Fund Ccc	41.43	Schroder Investment Management	U.K.
Martin Currie Emerging Markets Fund	40.2	Martin Currie Investment Managers	U.K.
City of London Emerging Markets CT	39.39	City of London Investment Management	U.K.
Indocam Mosais Global EM IA	37.79	Indocam Asset Management	France
Henderson HF Global Emerging Markets	37.21	Henderson Investment Management	U.K.
Saint Honoré Marché Emergents	37.17	Cie Financière Rothschild	France
Invesco GT Emerging Markets Country	35.55	Invesco Asset Management	U.K.
Van Kampen Emerging Markets C	33.37	Morgan Stanley Dean Witter Investments	U.S.
Global Emerging Markets Investment C	31.46	Foreign & Colonial Emerging Markets	U.K.
Magellan	30.15	Comgest	France
GFM Inist. EM Country Fund	27.23	City of London Investment Management	U.K.

Fairbairn Emerging Market Equity Fund	23.48	Old Mutual International Asset Managers	U.K.
State Street GAF Emerging Markets Fund	22.65	State Street Banque	France
GIF Developing Market	18.8	Indocam Asset Management	France
Morgan Stanley SICAV EM Fund B	17.92	Morgan Stanley Dean Witter Investments	U.S.
Sinopia EMF World Emerging Eq.	16.53	Sinopia Asset Management	France
CDC Global Emerging Markets	16.06	CDC Asset Management	France
Valeurs Emergentes	14.21	Fortis Investment Managers	France
City of London World Emerging Fund	12.34	City of London Investment Management	U.K.
Delaware Emerging Markets Fund A	8.72	Delaware International Advisers	U.K. / U.S.
Berenberg Universal Emerging Markets Fund	7.87	Martin Currie Investment Managers	U.K.
CG Pays Emergents	6.87	Comgest	France
Actions Sud	6.01	Crédit Lyonnais Asset Management	France
Vivemergent	6.01	ING Ferri	France
Delaware Emerging Markets Fund B	3.99	Delaware International Advisers	U.K. / U.S.
Total interviews	16,303.59		

* Funds with more than (or nearly) US$ 500 mios assets under management not interviewed (located in Boston, Los Angeles, Madrid, Edinburgh and Zurich).

Table 4.5 Herfindahl–Hirschman concentration index of emerging market equity funds: money managers ranked by total net assets, July 2000

	Assets under management	Rank, July 2000	Assets under management	Participation	Participation^2
Capital International	27,955	1	27,955	0.22077332	0.048740859
Templeton Investment Management	9,115	2	9,115	0.071985291	0.005181882
Schroder Investment Management	7,636	3	7,636	0.060304957	0.003636688
Fidelity Investments	7,130	4	7,130	0.056308845	0.003170686
Morgan Stanley Dean Witter Investment Management	5,176	5	5,176	0.040877221	0.001670947
Jardine Fleming Investment Management	3,193	6	3,193	0.02521657	0.000635875
Genesis Fund Managers	3,041	7	3,041	0.024016157	0.000576776
Morgan Grenfell Asset Management	3,027	8	3,027	0.023905593	0.000571477
Scudder Kemper Investments	2,776	9	2,776	0.021923332	0.000480632
Fleming Investment Management	2,750	10	2,750	0.021717998	0.000471671
Invesco Asset Management	2,537	11	2,537	0.02003584	0.000401435
UBS Asset Management	2,531	12	2,531	0.019988456	0.000399538
Credit Suisse Asset Management	2,521	13	2,521	0.019909481	0.000396387
Baring Asset Management	2,438	14	2,438	0.019253992	0.000370716
HSBC Asset Management	1,913	15	1,913	0.015107829	0.000228246
ABN Amro Asset Management	1,839	16	1,839	0.014523417	0.0002109
T Rowe Price Fleming International	1,655	17	1,655	0.013070286	0.000170832
Mercury Asset Management	1,466	18	1,466	0.011577667	0.000134042
SEI Investments	1,377	19	1,377	0.010874794	0.000118261
Foreign & Colonial Emerging Markets	1,272	20	1,272	0.010045561	0.000100913
Grantham, Mayo, van Otterloo	1,259	21	1,259	0.009942894	9.88611E-05
Frank Russell Investment Management	1,256	22	1,256	0.009919202	9.83906E-05
Batterymarch Financial Management	1,225	23	1,225	0.009674381	9.35936E-05
Dresdner RCM Global Advisors	1,151	24	1,151	0.009089969	8.26275E-05
Newport Pacific Management	1,146	25	1,146	0.009050482	8.19112E-05
Deutsche Bank Investment Management	1,144	26	1,144	0.009034687	8.16256E-05
Impulsora del Fondo Mexico	1,105	27	1,105	0.008726686	7.61551E-05

Vanguard Group	1,102	28	1,102	0.008702994	7.57421E-05
Merryl Lynch Asset Management	1,058	29	1,058	0.008355506	6.98145E-05
JP Morgan Investment Management	973	30	973	0.007684223	5.90473E-05
Credit Lyonnais Asset Management	950	31	950	0.007502581	5.62887E-05
Advantage Advisers	931	32	931	0.007352529	5.40597E-05
Aberdeen Asset Managers	926	33	926	0.007313042	5.34806E-05
Threadneedle Investment Managers	792	34	792	0.006254783	3.91223E-05
Soros Fund Management	725	35	725	0.005725654	3.27831E-05
Sanford Bernstein	662	36	662	0.005228114	2.73332E-05
Unit Trust of India	610	37	610	0.004817447	2.32078E-05
City of London Management	598	38	598	0.004722677	2.23307E-05
Gartmore Investment	597	39	597	0.00471478	2.22291E-05
Lloyd George Management	595	40	595	0.004698985	2.20805E-05
Pictet Asset Management	591	41	591	0.004667395	2.17846E-05
State Street Global Advisors	587	42	587	0.004635805	2.14907E-05
Edinburgh Fund Managers	556	43	556	0.004390984	1.92807E-05
Henderson Investment Management	529	44	529	0.004177753	1.74536E-05
Bank Brussels Lambert	522	45	522	0.004122471	1.69948E-05
American Express Asset Management	517	46	517	0.004082984	1.66708E-05
Hill Samuel Asset Management	502	47	502	0.003964522	1.57174E-05
Alliance Capital Management	498	50	498	0.003932932	1.5468E-05
Indocam Asset Management	490	51	490	0.003869752	1.4975E-05
KBC Bank	478	52	478	0.003774983	1.42505E-05
Citibank Global Asset Management	469	53	469	0.003703906	1.37189E-05
Axa Investment Managers	455	54	455	0.003593341	1.29121E-05
Montgomery Asset Management	425	55	425	0.003356418	1.12655E-05
Arisaig Partners	416	56	416	0.003285341	1.07935E-05
Royal & Sun Alliance Funds Management	408	57	408	0.003222161	1.03823E-05
Lazard Asset Management	407	58	407	0.003214264	1.03315E-05
ING Investment Management	407	59	407	0.003214264	1.03315E-05
SEB Investment Management	403	60	403	0.003182674	1.01294E-05
Investec Guinness Flight Global Asset Management	390	61	390	0.003080007	9.48644E-06

Table 4.5 (*Contd.*)

	Assets under management	Rank, July 2000	Assets under management	Participation	Participation^2
Union Investment	389	62	389	0.00307211	9.43786E-06
China Securities Investment Trust	384	63	384	0.003032622	9.1968E-06
Martin Currie Investment Management	372	64	372	0.002937853	8.63098E-06
CMG First State	370	65	370	0.002922058	8.53842E-06
Sofaer Capital	355	66	355	0.002803596	7.86015E-06
Perpetual Portfolio Management	353	67	353	0.002787801	7.77184E-06
International Investment Trust	347	68	347	0.002740416	7.50988E-06
Hermitage Capital Management	345	69	345	0.002724622	7.42356E-06
AIB Govett Asset Management	341	70	341	0.002693032	7.25242E-06
Old Mutual International Asset Managers	340	71	340	0.002685134	7.20995E-06
Société Générale Asset Management	338	72	338	0.002669339	7.12537E-06
Framlington Asset Management	332	73	332	0.002621955	6.87465E-06
Nicolas–Applegate Capital Management	328	74	338	0.002590365	6.70999E-06
Hansberger Global Advisors	323	75	323	0.002550878	6.50698E-06
Commercial Union Investment Management	319	76	319	0.002519288	6.34681E-06
Stewart Ivory Company	307	77	307	0.002424518	5.87829E-06
Globalvest Management Corporation	297	78	297	0.002345544	5.50158E-06
BNP Asset Management	286	79	286	0.002258672	5.1016E-06
Matthews International Capital Management	285	80	285	0.002250774	5.06599E-06
Baillie Gifford	276	81	276	0.002179697	4.75108E-06
WestLB Asset Management	170	106	170	0.001342567	1.80249E-06
Barclays Global Investors	153	111	153	0.00120831	1.46001E-06
Fortis Asset Management	133	119	133	0.001050361	1.10326E-06
Cazenove Fund Management	101	135	101	0.000797643	6.36234E-07
Carmignac Gestion	83.09	no	83.09	0.000656199	4.30598E-07
CDC Gestion	51	166	51	0.00040277	1.62224E-07
Congest	42	176	42	0.000331693	1.1002E-07
Total			126,623	1.0000	6.93%

Source: Santiso, 2001; based on web research.

Table 4.6 100 largest emerging market equity funds concentration index, July 2000

Name	Assets (US$ mios)	Ranking	Assets (US$ mios)	Participation	Participation^2
Emerging Markets Growth Fund	22,638	1	22,638	0.263401012	0.069380093
Capital International Emerging Markets Fund	4,310	2	4,310	0.050148351	0.002514857
Schroder Emerging Markets Fund	2,781	3	2,781	0.032357903	0.001047034
Templeton developing Markets Trust	2,733	4	2,733	0.031799407	0.001011202
Templeton IF Emerging Markets Series	2,424	5	2,424	0.028204084	0.00079547
Genesis Emerging Markets	2,180	6	2,180	0.025365059	0.000643386
MSDW IF Emerging Markets Portfolio A	1,417	7	1,417	0.016487288	0.000271831
SEI Emerging Markets Equity Fund	1,377	8	1,377	0.016021874	0.0002567
UBS (Ch) Equity Fund Emerging Markets	1,227	9	1,227	0.014276572	0.000203821
T Rowe Price New Asia Fund	1,205	10	1,205	0.014020595	0.000196577
Templeton Emerging Markets Investment Trust	1,136	11	1,136	0.013217756	0.000174709
Mexico Fund	1,105	12	1,105	0.0128576706	0.000165304
Vanguard Emerging Markets Stock Index Fund	1,102	13	1,102	0.012822154	0.000164408
GMO Emerging Markets Fund III	1,101	14	1,101	0.012810518	0.000164109
Deutsche GSF Global Emerging Markets Fund A	1,073	15	1,073	0.012484729	0.000155868
Batterymarch Global Emerging Markets Fund	1,063	16	1,063	0.012368375	0.000152977
Deutsche Profunds Pacific Fund A	1,007	17	1,007	0.0011716796	0.000137283
Korea Fund	1,002	18	1,002	0.011658619	0.000135923
Fidelity Funds South East Asia	955	19	955	0.01111758	0.000123471
Emerging Markets Trust	931	20	931	0.010832509	0.000117343
Schroder Latin American Fund	902	21	902	0.010495084	0.000110147
Crédit Lyonnais Investlion Emergents	723	22	723	0.008412357	7.07677E-05
FF Fleming Asian Opportunities Fund	721	23	721	0.00838986086	7.03768E-05
India Fund	676	24	676	0.007865495	6.1866E-05
Fidelity Institutional South East Asia Fund	666	25	666	0.007749142	6.00492E-05
Berstein Emerging Markets Value Fund	662	26	662	0.007702601	5.93301E-05
Quantum Emerging Growth Fund	660	27	660	0.00767933	5.89721E-05

Table 4.6 (*Contd.*)

Name	Assets (US$ mios)	Ranking	Assets (US$ mios)	Participation	Participation^2
AAF Global Emerging Markets Equity Fund	610	28	610	0.007097562	5.03754E-05
Fidelity Far East Fund	609	29	609	0.007085927	5.02104E-05
Fidelity South East Asia Fund	605	30	605	0.007039386	4.9553E-05
Templeton Dragon Fund	587	31	587	0.006829949	4.66482E-05
Asian Tigers Fund NV	584	32	584	0.006795043	4.61726E-05
FF Fleming Eastern European Fund	577	33	577	0.006713596	4.50724E-05
Morgan Stanley Dean Witter India Inv. Fund	563	34	563	0.006550701	4.29117E-05
Threadneedle Latin America Growth Fund	557	35	557	0.006480889	4.20019E-05
Mercury ST Emerging Markets Fund A	549	36	549	0.006387806	4.08041E-05
Baring GUF Eastern Europe Fund	538	37	538	0.006259817	3.91853E-05
Franklin Templeton IF Emerging Markets Fund A	505	38	505	0.005875851	3.45256E-05
Scudder Latin America Fund	494	39	494	0.005747862	3.30379E-05
Frank Russell Trust Co Emerging Markets Fund	480	40	480	0.005584967	3.11919E-05
Fidelity Emerging Markets Fund	473	41	473	0.00550352	3.02887E-05
Baring EMUF Global Emerging Markets Fund	459	42	459	0.005340625	2.85223E-05
Templeton Emerging Markets Fund	453	43	453	0.005270813	2.77815E-05
Fidelity Southeast Asia Fund	442	44	442	0.005142824	2.64486E-05
CS Equity Fund Tiger	432	45	432	0.00502647	2.52654E-05
Frank Russell Investment Co. Emerging Markets	427	46	427	0.004968294	2.46839E-05
Pictet targeted Fund Emerging Markets	421	47	421	0.004898482	2.39951E-05
Fidelity Institutional Emerging Markets Fund	418	48	418	0.004863576	2.36544E-05
Royal & Sun Alliance Emerging Markets Trust	408	49	408	0.004747222	2.25361E-05
Morgan Stanley Emerging Markets Fund	407	50	407	0.004735587	2.24258E-05
Henderson TR Pacific Investment Trust	403	51	403	0.004689045	2.19871E-05
JF Eastern Trust	396	52	396	0.004607598	2.123E-05
Brazil Fund	395	53	395	0.004595963	2.11229E-05
Lazard Emerging Markets Portfolio Instl	393	54	393	0.004572692	2.09095E-05
Schroder Global Emerging Markets Fund	391	55	391	0.004549421	2.06972E-05

Fidelity Hong-Kong China Fund	386	56	386	0.004491244	2.01713E-05
Taiwan Fund	384	57	384	0.004467974	1.99628E-05
Edinburgh Dragon Trust	383	58	383	0.004456338	1.9859E-05
Invesco GT Asia Entreprise Fund	382	59	382	0.004444703	1.97554E-05
Schroder Pacific Growth Fund	380	60	380	0.004421432	1.95491E-05
SSgA Emerging Markets Fund	378	61	378	0.004398162	1.93438E-05
Schroder Emerging Markets Fund (Australia)	372	62	372	0.00432835	1.87346E-05
Genesis Chile Fund	371	63	371	0.004316714	1.8634E-05
Lulius Baer Pacific Stock Fund	365	64	365	0.004246902	1.80362E-05
Newport Tiger Fund A	360	65	360	0.004188725	1.75554E-05
FF-Fleming Emerging Markets Fund	359	66	359	0.00417709	1.74481E-05
Newport Tiger Fund B	359	67	359	0.00417709	1.74481E-05
Fidelity Latin America Fund	357	68	357	0.004153819	1.72542E-05
SCI Asian Hedge Fund	355	69	355	0.004130549	1.70614E-05
Baring Emerging Europe Trust plc	354	70	354	0.004118913	1.69654E-05
India IT Fund Ltd	353	71	353	0.004107278	1.68697E-05
ROC Taiwan Fund	346	72	346	0.00402583	1.62073E-05
Hermitage Fund	345	73	345	0.004014195	1.61138E-05
Korea Asia Fund Ltd	331	74	331	0.0038513	1.48325E-05
UBS (CH) Equity Fund Emerging Asia	326	75	326	0.003793124	1.43878E-05
JPM Invest Emerging Markets Equity Fund A	324	76	324	0.003769853	1.42118E-05
Hansberger Institutional Emerging Markets Fund	324	77	324	0.003769853	1.42118E-05
Korea Europe Fund Ltd	321	78	321	0.003734947	1.39498E-05
Fleming Asian Investment Trust	320	79	320	0.003723311	1.3863E-05
Perpetual Asian Smaller Markets Fund	315	80	315	0.003665135	1.34332E-05
UBS (CH) Equity Fund Asia	314	81	314	0.003653499	1.33481E-05
FF Fleming China Fund	308	82	308	0.003583687	1.28428E-05
Frank Russell Emerging Markets Equity Fund A	305	83	305	0.003548781	1.25938E-05
Mercury Emerging Markets Fund	304	84	304	0.003537146	1.25114E-05
AXP Emerging Markets Fund	304	85	304	0.003537146	1.25114E-05
Citimarkets Global Emerging Markets Fund	301	86	301	0.00350224	1.22657E-05

Table 4.6 (*Contd.*)

Name	Assets (US$ mios)	Ranking	Assets (US$ mios)	Participation	Participation^2
Fidelity Funds Thailand Fund	299	87	299	0.003478969	1.21032E-05
Schroder India Fund	296	88	296	0.003444063	1.18616E-05
DBIM Mandarin Funds	295	89	295	0.003432428	1.17816E-05
Montgomery Emerging Markets Fund R	291	90	291	0.003385886	1.14642E-05
Indocam Himalayan Fund	290	91	290	0.003374251	1.13856E-05
Fidelity Funds ASEAN Fund	288	92	288	0.0033535098	1.12291E-05
Nicolas Applegate Emerging Countries Fund I	280	93	280	0.003257897	1.06139E-05
Hill Samuel Global Emerging Markets Trust	279	94	279	0.003246262	1.05382E-05
Fleming Emerging Markets Investment Trust plc	273	95	273	0.00317645	1.00898E-05
HSBC GIF Asian Equity Fund	267	96	267	0.003106638	9.6512E-06
Arisaig Asian Small Companies Fund	263	97	263	0.003060097	9.36419E-06
F&C Emerging Markets Investment Trust	263	98	263	0.003060097	9.36419E-06
T Rowe Price Latin America Fund	261	99	261	0.003036826	9.22231E-06
CS Equity Fund Emerging Markets Fund	261	100	261	0.003036826	9.22231E-06
Total			85,945	1.0000	7.987%

Source: Santiso, 2001; based on web research; for the asset data see emergingportfolio.com.

Table 4.7 Emerging market equity funds ranked by assets and websites, July 2000

	Assets under management	Rank, July 2000	Website
Capital International	27,955	1	http://www.capgroup.com/
Templeton Investment Management	9,115	2	http://www.franklintempleton.com/
Schroder Investment Management	7,636	3	http://www.schroder.co.uk/
Fidelity Investments	7,130	4	http://www100.fidelity.com/
Morgan Stanley Dean Witter Investment Management	5,176	5	http://www.msdw.com/institutional/investmentmanagement/
Jardine Fleming Investment Management	3,193	6	http://www.jffunds.com/
Genesis Fund Managers	3,041	7	http://www.giml.uk.com/
Morgan Grenfell Asset Management	3,027	8	http://www.deam-us.com/dam/
Scudder Kemper Investments	2,776	9	http://www.scudder.com/t/index.jhtml
Fleming Investment Management	2,750	10	http://www.flemingfunds.co.uk/
Invesco Asset Management	2,537	11	http://www.invescofunds.com/
UBS Asset Management	2,531	12	http://www.ubsbrinson.com/
Credit Suisse Asset Management	2,521	13	http://www.csam.com/
Baring Asset Management	2,438	14	http://www.baring-asset.com/flash.htm
HSBC Asset Management	1,913	15	http://www.hkbc.com/english/
ABN Amro Asset Management	1,839	16	http://www.abnamrofunds-usa.com/
T. Rowe Price Fleming International	1,655	17	http://www.troweprice.com/index.html
Mercury Asset Management	1,466	18	http://www.mam.com/uksite/index.htm
SEI Investments	1,377	19	http://www.seic.com/
Foreign & Colonial Emerging Markets	1,272	20	http://www.fandc.co.uk/
Grantham, Mayo, van Otterloo	1,259	21	http://www.gmo.com/
Frank Russell Investment Management	1,256	22	http://www.russell.com/us/home/
Batterymarch Financial Management	1,225	23	http://www.batterymarch.com/
Dresdner RCM Global Advisors	1,151	24	http://www.drcm.co.uk/
Newport Pacific Management	1,146	25	http://www.lib.com/newport.html
Deutsche Bank Investment Management	1,144	26	http://www.deam.co.uk/
Impulsora del Fondo Mexico	1,105	27	
Vanguard Group	1,102	28	http://www.vanguard.com/

Table 4.7 *(Contd.)*

	Assets under management	Rank, July 2000	Website
Merryl Lynch Asset Management	1,058	29	http://www.merrilllynch.com/mutual_funds.htm
JP Morgan Investment Management	973	30	http://www.jpmorgan.com/mutualfunds/
Credit Lyonnais Asset Management	950	31	http://www.clamdirect.com/
Advantage Advisers	931	32	
Aberdeen Asset Managers	926	33	http://www.aberdeen-asset.com/
Threadneedle Investment Managers	792	34	http://www.threadneedle.co.uk/
Soros Fund Management	725	35	http://www.aminter.com/Pages/soros.html
Sanford Bernstein	662	36	http://www.bernstein.com/
Unit Trust of India	610	37	http://www.unittrustofindia.com/
City of London Management	598	38	http://www.citlon.co.uk/
Gartmore Investment	597	39	http://www.gartmore.com/
Lloyd George Management	595	40	http://www.lloydgeorge.com/
Pictet Asset Management	591	41	http://www.pictet.com/en/services/mutual
State Street Global Advisors	587	42	http://www.ssga.com/
Edinburgh Fund Managers	556	43	http://www.edfd.com/
Henderson Investment Management	529	44	http://www.henderson.co.uk/
Bank Brussels Lambert	522	45	http://www.bbl.be/
American Express Asset Management	517	46	http://finance.americanexpress.com/finance/fishub.asp
Hill Samuel Asset Management	502	47	http://www.hillsamuel.co.uk/
Alliance Capital Management	498	50	http://www.alliancecapital.com/
Indocam Asset Management	490	51	http://www.ca-indocam.fr/
KBC Bank	478	52	http://www.kbc.be/
Citibank Global Asset Management	469	53	http://www.ssbciti.com/
Axa Investment Managers	455	54	http://www.axaworldfunds.com/
Montgomery Asset Management	425	55	http://www.montgomeryfunds.com/
Arisaig Partners	416	56	http://www.arisaig.com.sg/
Royal & Sun Alliance Funds Management	408	57	http://www.rsa-investments.co.uk/

Lazard Asset Management	58	http://www.lazardnet.com/lam/us/index.html
ING Investment Management	59	http://www.ingfunds.com/
SEB Investment Management	60	http://swp4.vv.sebank.se/cgi-bin/pts3/pow/index_fond.asp
Investec Guinness Flight Global Asset MGT	61	http://www.gffunds.com/
Union Investment	62	http://www.union-investment.com/
China Securities Investment Trust	63	http://www.thetaiwanfund.com/
Martin Currie Investment Management	64	http://www.martincurrie.com/
CMG First State	65	http://www.cmgfirststate.com.hk/
Sofaer Capital	66	http://www.sofaer.com/
Perpetual Portfolio Management	67	http://www.perpetual.co.uk/
International Investment Trust	68	
Hermitage Capital Management	69	
AIB Govett Asset Management	70	http://www.aibgovett.com/
Old Mutual International Asset Managers	71	http://www.omam.com/
Société Générale Asset Management	72	http://www.sgam.fr/
Framlington Asset Management	73	http://www.framlington.co.uk/
Nicolas-Applegate Capital Management	74	http://www.nacm.com/
Hansberger Global Advisors	75	http://www.juliusbaer.com/inv__funds/rhesf_e.html
Commercial Union Investment Management	76	http://www.cgugroup.com/
Stewart Ivory Company	77	http://www.stewartivory.co.uk/index.asp
Globalvest Management Corporation	78	http://www.globalvest.com/
BNP Asset Management	79	http://www.bnpparibas.com/
Matthews International Capital Management	80	http://www.matthewsfunds.com/
Baillie Gifford	81	http://www.bailliegifford.co.uk/
WestLB Asset Management	106	http://www.westlb.com/
Barclays Global Investors	111	http://www.barclaysglobal.com/
Fortis Asset Management	119	http://www.fortisimf.fr/
Cazenove Fund Management	135	http://www.cazenove.com/
Carmignac Gestion	nc	http://www.carmignac.com/
CDC Gestion	166	http://www.cdc-assetmanagement.com/
Comgest	176	http://www.comgest.com/

Source: Santiso, 2001; based on web research; for the assest data see emergingportfolio.com.

concerned by short-term performance not to talk about their own direct management.[50]

Surveys are frequently used by the industry in order to acquire information, for example, on how fund managers foresee future developments or on how firms foresee their future FDI in emerging countries. The samples, methodologies and results are very diverse. Regarding the samples they can range from 20 fund managers to nearly 200.[51] The Deutsche Bundesbank conducted a survey on institutional investors in 2000 soliciting fund manager's basic views and information on their evaluation methods, data sources, time horizons and decision-making processes.[52] The major advantage of such a methodology, as underlined by this research, is that it can shed light on institutional investment otherwise it would approach the market as a black box. There are of course methodological limitations in such an approach, it can be very time consuming and can have a selection bias or distorted responses. However the use of surveys as a tool to approach capital markets research and issues remains very useful, above all if linked with conventional empirical analysis and statistical approaches.

The survey results of the Deutsche Bundesbank reveal some characteristics of the industry in Germany. The fund managers tend to be young (35 years on average). Their professional experience is on average five years in the asset management industry. Nearly 60 percent are trained economists, with a university degree in economics or business administration. The survey indicates that fund managers tend to consider conversations and exchange of views with company executives or professional colleagues as their major and most important source of information before media publications, external analysts research and economic forecasts by research institutes. A less-considered source information—but not irrelevant—are the economic forecasts prepared by investment companies or the portfolio investments by other market players. The frequency of performance evaluation tends to be quite high, explaining in part their propensity to limit the time-horizon of analysis, investments and tactics. On average for 42 percent the evaluation is made on a monthly basis or less (44 percent declare that the evaluation is at most yearly and 14 percent twice a year).

Another survey, conducted by the French SBF Bourse de Paris confirmed these temporal horizons. While the temporal horizon of holding assets (in this case French equities by some 52 operators) tends to be more than three years on average, the performance of the fund is evaluated over a shorter period of time, on average on a yearly base. But nearly all fund managers' performances are monitored on a weekly or monthly basis. Financial operations (i.e. buying and selling) are hardly realized in less than a daily or weekly period of time. On the contrary, 64 percent of the fund managers who participated in this survey maintain their holding for a period on average of more than a year, for nearly half of their total holdings. Interestingly, nearly all the orders (63 percent) are transmitted before midday (12 noon) and most of them in the hour that follows the opening of the market.[53]

According to our own survey questionnaires and direct interviews conducted with fund managers in 2000 and 2001 in Europe and in the United States (87 answers received and treated), the short-term temporalities were confirmed and even more pronounced. Most of the fund managers, whether they are based in London, Edinburgh, Madrid, Paris, New York or Boston, tend to be evaluated by their own management and the fund clients on a "monthly" basis (more than 86 percent of the fund managers). Some even declared that they had an evaluation taking place "every day" (three of them) or on a "weekly" basis (one).[54] Only two declared that their evaluation was "yearly" and one on a "semester" basis (see table 4.8).[55]

The short-term horizon of investors is therefore closely related to the way their performance is measured by clients. For fund managers performing in accordance with the benchmarks is crucial if they want to keep their clients and therefore their jobs. As underlined by empirical research the probability that managers are likely to be fired or demoted is negatively associated with fund's current and past performances and the promotion probability will increase with funds performance, current and past. The performance measures on quarterly bases strongly constrained the temporal horizons of fund managers and the timing of their

Table 4.8 Frequency of the evaluation of fund managers' performance

	Total answers	In % of total
Every day	3	3.45
Every week	1	1.15
Every month	75	86.20
Every quarter	5	5.75
Every semester	1	1.15
Every year	2	2.30
Total	87	100

Source: Santiso, 2001; based on the survey questionnaire and direct interviews, 2000 and 2001.

tactical moves or strategic investments.[56] At the same time, during the 1990s there is evidence that portfolio turnover ratios have increased suggesting more accountability and also more quarterly evaluation constraints on fund managers. During the 1976–1996 period the replacement rate of fund managers tended to increase (see table 4.9). There were 307 management changes for a sample of 216 mutual growth funds during this period. The number of changes increase with the number of funds; but interestingly during the 1990s the ratio of changes per fund tend to be higher than during the previous decades.[57] At the same time, the asset management industry faced increasing pressure to consider changes to the disclosure requirements for the semiannual and annual reports provided by mutual funds to their shareholders, once again shortening funds' temporal horizons.[58]

In emerging markets in particular, different classes of investors will have different temporal horizons. Since the rise in private portfolio investment by the late 1980s, investors have diversified from mutual

Table 4.9 Fund managerial replacement, 1976–1996

Year	Number of funds	Number of changes	Changes per fund
1976	87	2	0.023
1977	91	3	0.033
1978	94	1	0.011
1979	96	5	0.052
1980	97	8	0.082
1981	103	5	0.049
1982	108	5	0.046
1983	115	8	0.07
1984	128	6	0.047
1985	141	4	0.028
1986	159	14	0.088
1987	178	17	0.096
1988	201	17	0.085
1989	214	23	0.107
1990	214	30	0.14
1991	215	24	0.112
1992	215	29	0.135
1993	216	31	0.144
1994	216	34	0.157
1995	216	29	0.134
1996	216	12	0.056

Source: Santiso, 2001; based on Hu, Hall and Harvey, "Promotion or Demotion? An Empirical Investigation of the Determinants of Top Mutual Fund Manager Change," *Duke University Fuqua School of Business Working Paper*, September 2000.

funds to hedge funds. As underlined by Sylvia Maxfield, "these investors tend to be yield-oriented and respond to short-term changes in yield rather than signals of a fundamental change in the host country's political economy. They have short time horizons because investors in mutual or hedge funds can redeem their funds if any particular money managers' return fails to perform as well as or better than the industry average."[59] International portfolio investors in emerging markets can also be classified according to their temporal horizons. Some investors, with short-term horizons, will be pushed into emerging markets by low yields and less risky investments. Others will be focusing more on prices than relative yields. Others, on the contrary, the so-called patient investors will be pushed by international conditions or pulled into the host country allowing time to policy-makers to correct errors and impacting on governments policy choices in many different ways.[60] Portfolio investors will be concerned with inflation rates, government indebtedness and fiscal issues, while other types of investors, such as foreign direct investors, will tend to take more into account the longer-term implications of governments' policy making, as their fixed investment tends to be more physical.[61] There are also some fund managers who develop long-term strategies with investment horizons of 3–5 years. They will keep the stocks in their books because, as stressed by a leading London-based emerging market fund manager, it "is simply too costly to buy and sell stocks with high frequencies. The fees charged by the brokers are high and we implemented studies that show us that we were frequently leaving the market too early or too late. So we decided to focus on rather long-term temporal horizons more for pragmatic reasons that for let's say ethic motivations or whatever else."[62]

The length of time that investors own shares in a fund is an indicator of temporal short-term confidence games. The redemption rate, which expresses annual equity fund redemptions as a percentage of average assets, is a useful tool for approaching investors' temporalities. For mutual fund investors, the redemption rates tend in fact to be quite long (seven years on average according to a survey of the *Investment Company Institute*[63]). Another study finds that at least 25 percent of the 31,000 households with mutual fund accounts at large U.S. discount brokers never sold shares during a period of more than five years.[64]

4.4   The Bonus Game and the Timing of Financial Crises

In the financial industry in Wall Street and London, fund managers are relatively well paid. However there are differences that are important in terms of base salary and median bonus from one category to another and also from one trading place to another. Systems of remuneration in London, Wall Street, Frankfurt or Paris tend to converge but still there are differences in levels and structure of remunerations. One important point, at least in London and Wall Street, the two leading emerging market platforms, is the importance of bonuses in paid salaries. To give an idea of their relevance we used data from Monks Partnership in London.[65] In this financial center the median bonus ranges from 18 percent of the salary to more than 100 percent of the salary for equity trading head or corporate finance head. Fund managers are among the best paid in London, a fund management director getting one of the highest bonuses in the industry, the median bonus on average being more than 66 percent of the salary (see table 4.10).

The data collected during the survey, combined with numbers derived from polls realized by the *Association for Investment Management Research, Russell Reynolds Associates* and *Robert Half France*, can help to underline the importance of the bonus and also some differences among the financial centers. In the United States, as in the United Kingdom,

Table 4.10   Salaries and bonuses in fund management and investment banks, London (in pounds per 1000)

Position	Base salary		Average salary	Median bonus in % of salary
	Median quartile	*Upper quartile*		
Credit Head	106	125	120.6	21.3
Private Banking Head	139.8	150	144.7	35
Chief FX Dealer	100	120	101.7	24
Money Market Head	80	90	81.6	35.9
Future & Options Head	100	109.3	100.7	52.3
Capital Markets Head	161.5	168.8	152.8	62
Eurobond Trading Head	104	133.8	45.9	45.9
Bond Sales Head	102.5	122.5	110.4	55
Equity Trading Head	107.5	125	114.2	100
Fund Management Director	150	196.7	159.5	66.3
Corporate Finance Head	—	—	151.2	105.2
Head of Risk	105	120	107.2	23.5
Head of Research	87.5	120	99.1	18
Legal Services Head	77	95	83.4	18
Financial Director	92.5	115	104.2	20.4
Operations Director	90	100.5	93.8	20.2
IT Director	85	110.8	90.9	20.8
Personnel Director	86.2	91.3	86.5	25.2

Source: Santiso, 2001; based on Monks Partnership, 2000.

remunerations tend to be higher and structured around the bonus game.[66] Based on a large study screening systems of remuneration, the *AIMR–Russell Reynolds Associates* poll, aggregate data was obtained from 27 percent of the 8,500 U.S. operators contacted. As in the United Kingdom, the heads of bond and equity fund management are among the best paid within the industry. For a ten-year-old fund manager in the industry salaries can range from US$200,000 to 800,000 or more per year. At the same time, bonuses also tend to be important ranging from more than 50 to 65 percent of their salary base.[67] In Paris, the salary base is nearly half of that in New York and the maximum bonuses reached are 80 percent of the salary base (when in New York they can reach double the levels) (see table 4.11).[68]

The important point to underline however is not the levels of the salaries but the importance of the bonus, that is the part of the remuneration based on performance and therefore on risk-taking behavior as underlined by the fund managers themselves.[69] They tend to focus attention (and intentions) on short-term gains with a maximum temporal horizon of one year (bonuses are given in a yearly base). Clear evidence of the transformation of the financial industry is the episode in 2000 of

Table 4.11   Salaries and bonuses in the United States

	Salary median US$ 1999	Bonus median US$ 1999	Other (slock options) 1999	Total remuneration	First quartile
Managing Director	150,000	100,000	20,000	253,500	1,250,000
Head of Strategy	125,000	45,000	18,000	188,000	794,419
Head of Fund Management Equity	143,000	75,000	25,000	257,000	1,165,000
Head of Fund Management Bonds	135,000	75,000	20,000	230,500	1,035,000
Fund Managers Equity U.S.	100,000	40,000	10,000	153,000	533,571
Fund Managers Equity Int.	135,000	70,000	15,000	211,000	672,500
Fund Manager Bonds U.S.	100,500	42,350	7,000	158,000	484,231
Fund Manager Bonds Int.	120,000	55,000	7,000	185,000	526,000
Strategist	100,000	35,000	10,000	155,000	492,500
Head of Research	120,000	50,000	10,000	180,000	588,000
Analyst Equities U.S.	87,400	50,000	4,500	140,250	490,000
Analyst Equities Int.	90,000	40,000	1,000	150,000	394,444
Sales	95,000	50,000	10,000	168,000	515,417
Trader	65,000	25,000	400	97,467	395,000

Source: Santiso, 2001; based on Association for Investment Management & Research and Russell Reynolds Associates, 2000.

Cazenove, the London's last big stockbroker partnership that broke by the end of the century to become a public company. Cazenove's decision to remove its partnership structure was in fact necessary for its survival. In the past, Cazenove partners were loyal to the firm simply because they had many of their own capital tied up in the company so they hardly left the company. This structure helped the firm to build long-term relationships with the clients, as the management was quite stable. But the partnership became unattractive during the 1980s and 1990s for young talent who wanted a quick fix under the form of bonuses and share options rather than the remote perspective of becoming a partner after ten years. The ethos of partnership was an example in a way of loyalty building processes. The strength of the Cazenove structure was that it encouraged long-termism in the service of clients and the hope of becoming a partner for employees, which was a powerful inducement to loyalty. In a way, the decision of Cazenove to remove its partnership structure in 2000 (followed by Lazard in 2001) is symptomatic of a profound transformation in an industry driven by short-term performance pressures (to which fund managers, as all other financial operators have to adapt and have to adopt if they want survive). "People's time horizons have change in the new financial industry. Several decades is too long to wait, remaining loyal is too costly for individuals, they wanted quick-fix, huge gains in the shortest period of time."[70] "Our ethos is not driven by trust or loyalty—too expensive—but rather by the pursuit of annual bonuses."[71]

This trend driven in part by changes in the structure of remunerations is obviously not specific to the financial industry. During the past 20 years, executive stock options have grown significantly. One of the driving forces behind this trend was the attempt to mitigate the agency problem by linking the fortunes of managers and owners. Recent studies however underlined that such options increased also risk-taking behavior. Risk-averse managers who hold large amounts of their own money in the firm are likely to take fewer risks than are optimal. But, as underlined by a Harvard Business research team, executive stock options provide managers with incentives to take actions that increase firm risk exposure. "There is in particular a statistically significant correlation between increases in option holdings by executives and subsequent increases in the firm risk."[72]

In the specific case of the asset management industry, the impact of incentive fees on performance has become an increasingly important issue in financial economics. However there are still very few empirical studies trying to assess this impact on financial behavior. One research underlines that mutual funds with incentive fees tend to attract superior managers with more involvement. But incentives fees also seem to impact on average returns and performance with a larger impact on risk taking. "Funds with incentives fees have a higher risk than funds without incentive fees. Whether risk taking is measured in terms of tracking error or total risk, incentive fees cause risk taking. Managers using incentives fees often pursue non-benchmark strategies in an attempt to earn excess returns and higher fees."[73] As underlined by other research, incentive fees and the structure of package remuneration is far from neutral in terms of risk-taking behavior and risk seeking. Managers who have been performing poorly in the past and are low in the compensation schedule will have an incentive to take high risks.[74] When managers are sufficiently high on the compensation schedule, they will however have a tendency to overinvest in the index and have a lower tracking error being in a way more risk averse.[75]

What is definite is that the bonus incentives are important for fund managers. When, during the interviews, we asked fund managers to what extent they are motivated by the bonus nearly 90 percent said they were "highly" motivated and all said that they were "highly" or "somewhat" motivated. In most of the cases (70 percent) bonuses represented between 30 and 60 percent of their total reward package and in some cases (25 percent) even more than 60 percent. But more interestingly, systems of remuneration and evaluation are more or less standardized around the world. According to our survey, and out of 145 answers received and treated, there is no significant difference between fund managers, analysts and economists: nearly all received their bonuses based on months of the calendar year. This temporal pattern is the same in Paris, Madrid, London, Edinburgh, Boston and New York, that is in all the financial centers where we conducted the interviews and from where we received questionnaires. If we refer to the timing of the bonus game in particular, the buy-side and sell-side industry is evaluated by the end of the calendar year in Q4 (60 percent) or the very beginning of the calendar year in Q1 (32 percent). According to our survey questionnaire and direct interviews, the payment is primarily done (79 percent) during the first quarter of each calendar year in Q1 (see table 4.12).

It is therefore interesting to underline that negotiations and payments of bonuses take place around the end and beginning of the calendar year, exactly when financial crises take place in Latin America. There is obviously no possible demonstration of a direct link but at least one can infer strange overlapping temporalities. In fact many of fund managers,

Table 4.12   Timing of bonus negotiation
and payment (in % of total sample: 145)

	Timing of bonus evaluation	Timing of bonus payment
Q1	32	79
Q2	5	7
Q3	3	5
Q4	60	9

Source: Santiso, 2001; based on the survey
questionnaire and direct interviews, 2000 and
2001.

confirmed that the year is "done" mostly during the very first months,
if they can get good results they will tend to become more risk averse,
risk aversion increasing with the timing of bonus negotiations.[76]
The crisis in Brazil was a "no event" because it occurred at the very
beginning of the calendar year (January 13, 1999).[77] The bonuses of the
previous year were already negotiated (and safe). The crisis in Mexico
occurred at the end of 1994 (with the devaluation of the peso taking
place on December 20) but the overreaction of the market only took
place during the firsts weeks of 1995, after the end of the 1994-year
evaluation.[78]

CHAPTER FIVE

A Small Embedded World: Technopols, Arenas and Trespassers

The language of the confidence game is economics. Nearly all the key players are professional trained economists and when not—fund managers for example—they adopt economic language. In a world of probabilities and projections, economics is the highway to financial heavens and a powerful interpretative method in a forward-looking world. They earn M.B.A.s, B.A.s or Ph.D.s in economics from the most prestigious universities. Be it in governments, in international organizations, in rating agencies or in investment houses, they speak fiscal deficits and liquidity ratios. Although they share a common vocabulary they might however differ in their phrasing and conjugation. Economic rhetoric brings powerful tools, assumptions and views of the world. It brings a common technical language shared not only by Wall Street and London actors but also, increasingly, during the past decades, by the emerging market actors, ministers, debt negotiators and central bankers who became free-market believers.

This is particularly true for the Americas during the 1990s. By then, in Latin America, the "technopols," well educated, with Harvard or MIT credentials, followed the path of the Chilean Chicago Boys.[1] They became increasingly influential, removing the old guard, the "dinosaurs," from office. In addition to papers and books on specific issues, they began to analyze the performance of their economies, most of them during the 1960s and 1970s. In Argentina the Instituto de Desarrollo Económico y Social (IDES) started to produce a quarterly analysis of the Argentinian economy till the end of 1964 and on a monthly basis from 1965. It was followed by the Fundación Mediterránea (Domingo Cavallo think tank) on a monthly basis from 1978 while during the 1980s the Fundación de Investigaciones Económicas Latinoamericanas (FIEL), started also to multiply encounters on economies with a broad audience.

They explained, and some times implemented with success, how free-market reforms and the liberalization of the capital account would change developing countries. By the early 1990s, all central bankers and ministries of economy in Argentina had Ph.D.s in major U.S. universities. In Mexico, the shift toward more trust in free-market reforms paralleled the rise of a new generation of young foreign-educated professional economists such as the Salinas Finance Minister Pedro Aspe (1950; Ph.D. MIT, 1978), Minister of Commerce Jaime Serra Puche (1951; Ph.D. Yale, 1979), Nafta's chief negotiator Herminio Blanco Mendoza (1950; Ph.D. University of Chicago, 1978) and the Minister of Programming and Budget Ernesto Zedillo (1951; Ph.D. Yale) who would succeed President Carlos Salinas de Gortari (Ph.D. Harvard, 1978) (see table 5.1).[2]

It must be stressed that these reforms were embedded in local political worlds. Market reforms were not only a way to bring in more "efficiency" but also a way of creating political assets and buying off elites. In the case of Mexico, for example, not only did finance policy reforms provide rent-seeking opportunities for the private sector, but it also brought political support to President Carlos Salinas de Gortari who, in spite of his promotion of free-market policies, decided to insulate banks from competition and maintain an artificial overvaluation of the peso through exchange rate intervention.[3] Finance policy is not only imposed from outside, an inevitable outcome embedded in global ideological shifts, but it can be a resource that governments are able to manipulate in order to secure internal political and economic support among local interest groups.

For this generation of reformers Cambridge, Mass. played a pivotal role. There, Pedro Aspe, for example, connected with other promising Latin American students, among them Domingo Cavallo (1946, Ph.D. Harvard, 1977) and Alejandro Foxley (1939; then a visiting scholar at MIT). It was Cavallo, as Argentinian economist minister, and Foxley, as Chilean finance minister, who would lead the reforms of the 1990s. In Cambridge, they met some of the prominent economics scholars who would play a prominent role in the emerging market confidence games of the 1990s. Among others, they met academics such as Stanley Fisher, who years later would become the IMF's second in command, or

Table 5.1 Top and medium economic policy-making positions in Mexico, October 1994

Name	Position/year	Undergraduate degree	Graduate degree
Carlos Salinas de Gortari	President	UNAM Economics, 1969	Ph.D. Political Economy and Government, Harvard, 1978
Pedro Aspe Armella	Minister of Finance	ITAM Economics, 1974	Ph.D. Economics, MIT, 1978
Guillermo Ortíz Martínez	Deputy Minister of Credit (Finance Ministry)	UNAM Economics, 1972	Ph.D. Economics, Stanford, 1977
Francisco Gil Díaz	Deputy Minister of Revenues (Finance Ministry)	ITAM Economics, 1966	Ph.D. Economics, the University of Chicago, 1972
Carlos Ruiz Sacristán	Deputy Minister of Budget Control (Finance Ministry)	Anáhuac Economics, 1972	Ph.D. Economics, Northwestern University, 1974
Antonio Sánchez Gochicoa	Oficialía Mayor (Finance Ministry)	ITAM Economics, 1974	M.A. Economics, Cambridge University, 1977
Carlos Jarque	Director of National Bureau of Statistics (INEGI—Finance Ministry)	Anáhuac Accounting, 1976	M.S. and M.A. in Statistics, London School of Economics, 1977, 1978; M.A. Economics, Australian National University, 1981
Jaime Serra Puche	Minister of Commerce	UNAM Political Science, 1973	Ph.D. Economics, Yale, 1979
Pedro Noyola de Garagorri	Deputy Minister of Foreign Trade (Commerce Ministry)	No information available	No information available
Fernando Sánchez Ugarte	Deputy Minister of Industry and Foreign Investment (Commerce Ministry)	ITAM Economics, 1973	Ph.D. Economics, University of Chicago, 1977
Eugenio P. Carrión Rodríguez	Deputy Minister of Domestic Trade and Foodstuffs (Commerce Ministry)	UNAM Business Administration, 1972	M.A. Economics, Colegio de México, 1975; Ph.D. Economics, University of Grenoble, France, 1980

Table 5.1 (*Contd.*)

Name	Position/year	Undergraduate degree	Graduate degree
Miguel Mancera Aguayo	Central Bank Director	ITAM Economics, 1956	M.A. Economics, Yale, 1960
Ariel Buira Seira	Director of International Organisms and Agreements (central bank)	B.A. Economics, University of Manchester, England, 1963	Ph.D. Economics, University of Manchester, England, 1966
Agustín Carstens Carstens	Assistant to the Director (central bank)	ITAM Economics	Ph.D. Economics, University of Chicago
Marín Maydón Garza	Director of Development Credit (central bank)	Autonomous University of Nuevo León (UANL) Economics, 1965	Ph.D. Economics, MIT, 1967
Angel Palomino Hasbach	Director of Monetary Programming and Financial Systems Analysis (central bank)	UNAM Economics, 1966	M.A. Economics, Colegio de México, 1971
José Julian Sidaoui Dib	Director of Central Bank Operations (central bank)	University of the Americas, Economics, 1973	M.A. Economics, UPenn, 1974 Ph.D. Economics, George Washington University, 1978

Source: Sarah Babb, *Managing Mexico: Economists from Nationalism to Liberalism*, Princeton, Princeton University Press, 2001. Top positions include president, finance minister, commerce minister and central bank director.

Rudiger Dornbusch, who would become a prominent *voice* both before and during the Mexican and Brazilian crises (Dornbusch became a clever advisor of the Boston-based custodian State Street Bank). In some cases, after the return to their birthplaces, they maintained close contacts with Cambridge's alma mater. Pedro Aspe, for example, became head of ITAM's Economic Department in Mexico and there reshaped the economics curriculum, raised academic standards and continued to send young promising students to U.S. universities. Most of these "technocrats" colonized the Mexican ministries when Aspe took charge of the financial portfolio during the Salinas presidency, filling senior posts in the central bank, education and agriculture.

In the case of Domingo Cavallo, he founded his own think-tank, the *Instituto de Estudios Económicos sobre la Realidad Argentina y Latino-Americana*, or IEERAL, and gained a strong backing from the *Fundación Mediterranea*. When he became minister, he appointed nearly all the staff of IEERAL to key senior positions in order to boost a "technocratic reforming shock."[4] Under Cavallo as minister of the economy (1991–1996) Argentina reached a peak in technical capacity with its executive branch concerning attributes shared by some of the former ministers but none to the same extent as Cavallo.[5] Likewise, in 1970 Alejandro Foxley founded the economic think-tank CIEPLAN, an institution that played a pivotal role during the Pinochet regime, as it gave a technical voice to the opposition. With the return of democracy in 1990, as in the case of Aspe and Cavallo, the CIEPLAN boys colonized major government agencies.[6]

At the same time, in Wall Street and London, there was more involvement in a new asset class called emerging markets, a notion "invented" by financial marketers to present these new developing nations as potential gold mines.[7] In Washington, former teachers and colleagues were in the process of creating a new Decalogue, a new "Global Brand" labeled the Washington Consensus.[8] The involvement of academics ranges over a wide spectrum. Their works diffuse within and without the academic community. They can advise governments or international organizations. They can also advise or even trespass upon Wall Street firms and the spheres of involvements can easily overlap. They can be, at the same time, scholars and advisors to the central bank or investment houses. As stressed by Michael Walzer, all selves are self-divided and academics, as any others, are self-divided among different interests, roles, identities and values, playing many parts not only during their lifetime but also during a week or even a single day.[9] These actors are not "above" the confidence game but "within" it, in some cases, even for those few who assume multiple roles.

5.1   Academics' Shifting Involvements

The first mode of involvement is through research activities. Academic research can help in understanding financial crises and dynamics of contagion. It can bring very useful and new analytical tools or theoretical understandings with empirical applications on financial crises. One of the best examples of this is the "early warning signals" approach developed by IMF economists and U.S.-based academic scholars. Starting in the mid-1990s there has been an explosion in studies of "early warning signals." These approaches have been discussed and used by many actors, ranging from international organizations such as the BIS in Basle, government institutions such as the Bank of England, Banque de France, Federal Reserve Board in the United States, and investment houses such as Crédit Agricole Indosuez or Goldman Sachs.[10]

.   Early warning signals are based on the precise definition of a crisis and are intended to build a framework for generating predictions of crises using the "signal extraction" approach, which follows the works of Kaminsky, Lizondo and Reinhart published in 1998 and the works of Goldstein, Kaminsky and Reinhart and Berg and Patillo of 1999 and 2000.[11] Basically the system involves monitoring the evolution of several economic indicators that behave differently prior to a crisis. These policy-oriented works develop on the previous literature on currency crisis pioneered by academics such as Eichengreen, Rose and Wyplosz in a series of papers dating back to 1994 (focused mainly on industrialized countries) and those of Frankel, Rose and Sachs and Tornell and Velasco that shifted the focus just after the Mexican crisis, in 1996, toward modelling currency crises in developing countries.[12] Following the Mexican crisis, several scholars, namely Kaminsky and Reihnart, developed warning system models in order to increase their predictive power of banking and currency crises. They find that prior to a crisis in developing countries (roughly 20 analyzed using monthly data from 1970 to 1997), emerging markets experienced economic slowdowns, overvalued exchange rate, loss of international reserves and high ratios of broad money to international reserves. These findings helped them to construct an early warning system. Later other researchers, namely Berg and Patillo in 1999 and Masson, Borensztein, Milesi-Ferretti and Patillo in 2000, evaluated and developed improved early warning systems for the use of the IMF.[13] Most of them are based on qualitative comparisons comparing economic fundamentals, econometric regression analysis and nonparametric estimations.

In addition to these academic studies and IMF research, other institutions have been involved in building their own early warning systems, the aim being to remedy their own record of crisis prediction in a context of their increasing incidence, financial operators being notoriously poor at predicting crises. In Europe, for example, the Banque de France, the Bank of International Settlements and, in the private sector, Crédit Agricole Indosuez investment house, have been constructing such models of crisis in 2000.[14] In the United States, many institutions, among them the Federal Reserve Board or investment houses such as JP Morgan, Credit Suisse First Boston or Citircorp Securities, have been inspired by early warning approaches that try to forecast the probability of large currency depreciations.[15] Morgan Stanley, in an attempt to build a composite indicator of currency pressure within a quantitative predictive framework, introduced such approaches and questions around these issues in mid-July 2001.[16] Other firms like ABN Amro, more cautious regarding early warning signals and other traditional indicators of near-term financial vulnerability of sovereigns (like debt service and import–coverage ratios), tried to build near-term sovereign default risk indicators using BIS reporting data like the amount of all liabilities to commercial and investment banks reported.[17]

A model developed by Goldman Sachs received considerable attention combining previous approaches with the early warning signal of Kaminsky, Lizondo and Reihnart and other econometric modelling developed by Eichengreen, Frankel and Rose. By the end of 1998, this Wall Street house replaced its previous model, the Short Term Market Pressure Indicators by a new one the GS-Watch. The explicit task was to move from "subjective assessment of qualitative variables" to more objective and quantitative indicators.[18] The predictive power of this last approach gave some positive results signalling crises within a time horizon of less than three months for countries like Brazil, Ecuador and Turkey but failed to predict, for example, the Colombian currency depreciation. In nearly all the studies some economic variables provided better signal than others, namely a high ratio of short-term debt to reserves or a high ratio of M2 to reserves, substantial losses of foreign exchange reserves, and so on but they also stress the relevance of more in-depth specific analysis to prevent false alarms.

Built as new tools for their clients—Credit Suisse Suisse "Emerging Markets Risk Indicator," JP Morgan "Event Risk Indicator" or Lehman Brothers "Currency Jump Probability"—they all deliver the same promise: to predict currency crises. They all face the same perils of prediction. As pointed out by many of their defenders, even if there is some consensus based on econometric evidence, there are substantial disagreements about the relevant indicators and their respective weights. But the key question is whether these models have predictive power for crises that occur after the period from which the equations are derived, that is their ex ante and not ex post predictive power. In order to evaluate the performance of several leading indicators, two IMF economists, Berg and Patillo, asked the question "if we had been using these models in late 1996, how well armed would we have been to predict the Asian crisis?"[19] The results would have been mixed as only one model provides some useful though still not reliable information while the two others evaluated failed to give useful forecasts. They mainly looked at three models created by academic economists before the Asian crisis and find a low predictive power.

In other comparative evaluations, made by economists of the Board of Governors of the Federal Reserve System, the IMF in the United States and by Banque de France or Bank of England in Europe, the results demonstrate the same temporal horizons of prediction. Above all they demonstrate a low percentage of correctly predicted crises and a high percentage of false alarms.[20] IMF economists, for example, point out that "the predictions from the most promising models contain substantial information about the risks of crisis, but they often provide false alarms." In about 50 percent of the cases they signaled a crisis (i.e. they issue a warning signal in about 12 of the 24 months). "The warnings issued by the typical early warning system model are not very reliable: about 60% of the times that the typical model issued a warning, no crisis occurred during the following two years."[21]

It is not necessary to draw on Karl Popper's insights on the epistemological problems intrinsic to attempts to see in the future,[22] in order to recognize that one of the problems of these approaches is that they are running after the numbers and the crisis. Accurate data is part of the difficulty but, crisis after crisis, surprises arise. The variables that seemed to be pertinent in the past become less so in the present. Indicators that seemed to explain a past crisis fail to catch in their fillets the next. Open Asian economies were mainly facing competitiveness problems while Latin American economies were facing internal monetary problems and a slump in commodity prices. The Mexican crisis was mainly a public finance issue embedded in short-term debt problems while the Asian crisis was more linked with bank lending and private sector finance. In their own evaluation of early warning systems, Goldstein, Kaminsky and Reinhart don't hesitate to warn and prevent the readers against too much enthusiasm: "while we would not place much confidence in the precise estimated ordering of vulnerability across countries, we think the signals approach looks promising for making distinctions between the vulnerability of countries near the top of the list and those near the bottom—that is, it may be useful as a first screen which can then be followed by more in-depth country analysis."[23]

In the same way some strategists of investment houses argued that "in a world of herding, tighter market-sensitive risk management regulations and improved transparency can, perversely, turn events from bad to worse, creating volatility, reducing diversification and trigging contagion." As stressed by Avinash Persaud, State Street Bank currency strategist, the move toward more quantitative and market-sensitive approaches tend to exacerbate mimetic behavior, banks switching at the same time out of the same countries, according to the "signals" sent by management risk units using DEAR models (Daily Earnings at Risk). "Banks and investors like to buy what others are buying, sell what others are selling, and own what others own." This herding behavior is explainable by three major drivers. "First in a world of uncertainty, the best way of exploiting the information of others is by copying what they are doing. Second, bankers and investors are often measured and rewarded by relative performance, so it literally does not pay for a risk-averse player to stray too far from the pack. Third investors and bankers are more likely to be sacked for being wrong and alone than for being wrong and in company."[24] "To be very different form the benchmark increases risk against that benchmark enormously. Emerging markets are largely driven by economic and not corporate fundamentals. Therefore, unlike in developed equity markets, fund managers are all working with the same data, interpreted by the same experts, disseminated through the same media above all Bloomberg screens. It would be a brave, and perhaps a foolish person, a truly highlander, the person who believed he can beat the market and differ from the crowding trend."[25]

5.2   World Forums as Financial Alephs

But economists can also play an indirect role and contribute to the configuration of cognitive regimes with their presence in international arenas. They can participate in world forums such as international conferences or in newspapers. Economist tribes meet and voice during annual professional congresses, "pure player" scholars mixing with the other players of the game, be they in the government, international organizations or in Wall Street. These channels are powerful amplifiers of their voice, no longer limited to a cohort of specialists (through professional reviews and professional world congress associations), but toward the financial community, governments, investors and so on. From this point of views, for example, LACEA meetings bring the opportunity for all the players to exchange points of view, discuss rumors, share views on current issues, Argentina dollarization or external debt management, the meetings being transformed into world brainstorming and confidence arenas. The spectrum of LACEA Rio 2000 speakers, for example, ranged from world renowned academics from U.S. universities to senior officers from international organizations, governors of central banks, ministers of finance from emerging countries and, last but not least, international bankers, strategists and economists from Wall Street firms such as Goldman Sachs, J P Morgan.

IMF, IADB and World Bank meetings[26] and, for more discrete encounters the ones organized for example by the Federal Reserve of Dallas,[27] are good examples of voice enlargers. In this small-embedded world scholars, central bankers, ministers, investors and bankers exchange formal and informal views. They can try to curb others' perceptions, anticipate next moves, interpret what they say and what they choose to remain silent about or simply be abreast of the current *air du temps* in the world confidence game arena.[28] As stressed by one emerging market's debt manager, referring to IMF/World Bank meetings, "the Annual Meeting provides a unique opportunity to exchange views on both country-specific issues and systemic trends. After all, where else do you get ministers of finance and central bank governors from over 180 countries gathered under one roof, participating in roundtables and willing/able to hold frank one-on-one meetings with investors? Our specific aim in going to Prague (the 2000 annual meeting took place in this city) is to obtain further input for the day-to-day management of structural and tactical strategies impacting our emerging market portfolio (see table 5.2)."[29]

The IADB and the World Bank/IMF annual meetings are an opportunity for security houses to organize their own encounters such as the ones organized by Deutsche Bank. In the IADB 2000 meeting, an encounter was organized with leading speakers including William Cline (from the Institute of International Finance), Liliana Rojas Suárez (then Deutsche Bank chief economist for Latin America), Sebastian Edwards (UCLA economist), Guillermo Calvo (Maryland University economist), Daniel Marx (Argentinian vice minister of finance), José Angel Gurria (Mexican minister of finance), José Suarez (Venezuelan minister of finance), Ricardo Hausmann (then IADB chief economist) and Moisés Naim (foreign policy editor). During the 1999 World Bank/IMF meeting, among the speakers of the Deutsche Bank emerging markets conference were also, for the Latin American panel, Guillermo Ortiz and

Table 5.2   World confidence game arenas, annual meetings in 2000

LACEA Rio 2000 Sample of Speakers, Rio, October 12–13, 2000
IMF/World Bank Annual Meeting, Prague, September 19–28, 2000
Federal Reserve Bank of Dallas, Dallas, March 6–7, 2000

International organizations	*Governments*
Stanley Fisher (IMF, First Managing Director)	Pedro Malan (Brazil, Finance Minister)
	Norman Loayza (Chile, Banco Central)
Eduardo Borensztein (IMF)	Alexander Foffmaister (Costa Rica, Banco Central)
Olivier Jeanne (IMF)	Luiz Miguel Trevino (Peru, Min. of Economy)
Gaston Gelos (IMF)	José de Gregorio (Chile, Min. of Planning)
Ernesto Stein (IADB)	Edward Amadeo (Brazil, Min. of Finance)
Nora Lustig (IADB)	Carlos Winograd (Argentina, Min. of Economy)
Carmen Pagés (IADB)	Fabio Ghironi (USA, Reserve Federal Bank of NY)
Nicholas Stern (World Bank)	Fernando Aportela (Mexico, Banco Central)
Guillermo Perry (World Bank)	Rodrigo Valdés (Chile, Min. of Finance)
Ariel Fizbein (World Bank)	Klaus Schmidt-Hebel (Chile, Banco Central)
Martin Ravallion (World Bank)	Andrew Powell (Argentina, Banco Central)
Luis Servén (World Bank)	Arminio Fraga (Brazil, Banco Central)
Banks	*Universities*
Paulo Leme (Goldman Sachs)	Graciela Kaminsky (George Washington University)
Luis Carranza (BBVA)	Guillermo Calvo (University of Maryland)
Walter Molano (BCP Securities)	Ricardo Hausmann (Harvard University)
John Welch (Barclays Capital)	Roland Bénabou (Princeton University)
Paulo Vieira da Cunha (Lehman Brothers)	Raquel Fernández (NYU)
Mohamed El-Erian (PIMCO)	Andrés Velasco (Harvard University)
Russell Cheetham (Frank Russell Company)	Ricardo Caballero (MIT)
Wolfgan Wendt (Deutsche Bank)	Rudiger Dornbusch (MIT)
Michael Gavin (UBS Warburg)	Dani Rodrik (Harvard University)
	Sebastián Edwards (UCLA)
	Andrew Rose (Berkeley)

Sources: http://www.puc-rio.br/lacea-rio-2000/; http://www.dallasfed.org/htm/dallas/archives.html; http://www.imf.org/external/am/2000/prague.htm.

Arminio Fraga, governors of the Mexican and Brazilian central banks respectively.[30] Organized for their clients, these parallel meetings were among the myriad possible encounters offered, bringing all the players the opportunity "to meet during this global financial mass, exchange vanities, worlds and silences, in a corridor, after a speech, during a dinner or any other social informal event."[31] Forum investors are helpful for exchanging ideas, impressions and analysis, offering a large range of social interaction opportunities (from dinners with Domingo Cavallo's minister of economy, Argentina or even nights of partying with the Gipsy Kings[32]). They are the tip of the iceberg in global confidence arenas, bringing a unique opportunity to meet in a very brief time and within the same space—a kind of Aleph of the financial community as the Argentinian writer J. L. Borges would have said—all the "big guns" of the confidence game.

They bring for the governments a unique opportunity to reassure investors that their economies remain stable and transparent. In Prague, for example, within the Chase four-day program organized parallelly with the IMF/World Bank annual meetings, an impressive army of officials and private sector analysts filed past. Among them were the chief economists of multilateral institutions like Nicholas Stern of the World Bank or Willem Buiter of the European Bank for Reconstruction and Development and all Latin American Ministry of Finance and central banks officials. From Mexico came José Angel Gurria, Ministry of Finance; Carlos Garcia Moreno, Director of Public Credit, Ministry of Finance; Guillermo Ortiz, Governor of the Central Bank; Armando Baquero, director of economic research and Javier Guzmán, director of external affairs, both from Banco de Mexico; Luis Ernesto Derbez, economic advisor for president elect Vicente Fox. From Argentina, were present Daniel Marx, secretary of finance; Guillermo Mondino, chief economist of Fundación Mediterránea and Miguel Kiguel, director of Banco Hipotecario.[33]

IADB meetings provide also a clear indication of the dominant conventional wisdom prevailing among Latin American emerging market financial communities. In the IADB meetings special issue of March 2001, Deustche Bank synthesized the dominant conventions prevailing among Wall Street and Latin American financial communities. For the bank the U.S. downturn was identified as the main external risk by the time.[34] Also the lack of growth in Argentina was ranked as the main internal risk in Latin America as well as the slowdown in confidence and reforms among Latin American emerging countries. The political factor was presented as the major explanation with presidential election in Peru and legislative elections in Argentina in 2001 and October 2002 elections in Brazil coming closer.[35] Such programs give an idea of the precise "geography of money" of the global confidence game. Hardly any of the participants of emerging countries in these meetings arranged by brokers come from "lost countries" (for international investors) like Bolivia, Costa Rica or Cuba, too small and too local to be included even in the suburbs of the global village. Some countries are simply drawn out of the world map of international investors and brokers. In the Chase

IMF/World Bank 2000 annual meetings program, for example, the cohorts of Mexican and Argentinian officials were impressive (six presentations for Mexico and three for Argentina) as compared to other countries like Venezuela and Colombia (two). These numbers reflect in a way the respective economic weight of the countries and international investors' interest in them. In table 5.3 we can see another example of these meetings with the distribution of speakers at the JP Morgan Chase program held during the Inter-American Development Bank annual meetings in March 2001 in Santiago de Chile. Focused exclusively on Latin America, it shows also the openness to small countries such as Ecuador, Panama and above all Uruguay. The classification of speakers by countries indicates the good representation of large Latin American emerging market countries' officials with Argentina, Chile and Mexico leading. Because of its southern location countries like Uruguay have been very well represented.

For a broader view on nonofficial financial meetings organized by brokers, we also compare the "who's who" of IADB 2001 forum participants for three major investors: JP Morgan Chase, Crédit Suisse First Boston and Salomon Smith Barney. Organized for their clients, these forums indicate also the dominance of large-country speakers. Within the confidence game, all countries are not equals. Officials from big emerging markets have obviously greater opportunities to be heard and at least to "voice" within the confidence game global arena. During the IADB 2001 forums investors from Argentina, for example, were under the spotlight and therefore had exceptional exposure to express their views. They represented nearly 16 percent of the 92 speakers at CSFB, Salomon Smith Barney and JP Morgan Chase investor forums. Venezuela, Mexico, Colombia, Chile and Brazil followed Argentina. Among the smaller economies, only Panama, Ecuador, Uruguay and Peru were represented. In total Latin American officials comprised more than 60 percent of all speakers, rating agencies (12 percent) and economists from international rating organizations (6.50 percent) ranking second and third. Among the participants leading academics were also quite well represented comprising more than 5 percent of the speakers— mainly academics from major U.S. universities such as Harvard, Columbia and John Hopkins (see tables 5.4 (a) and (b)).

5.3   Newspapers as Global Confidence Game Arenas

International meetings are not the only global arenas where—among others—academics, brokers and government officials can *voice*, they can

Table 5.3 JP Morgan Chase program speakers during the IADB 2001 annual meetings, Santiago de Chile, March 17–20, 2001

U.S. and Latam officials	Country	Number	%
Robert Zoellick, U.S. Trade Representative	U.S.	3	7.00
John Taylor, Undersecretary for International Affairs, U.S. Treasury	U.S.		
John Maistro, Special Assistant to the President, U.S. Security Council	U.S.		
Daniel Marx, Secretary of Finance	Argentina	4	9.00
José Luis Machinea, Minsiter of Economy	Argentina		
Pedro Pou, Governor Central Bank	Argentina		
Carlos Menem, Former President of Argentina	Argentina		
Daniel Gleizer, Deputy Governor for International Affairs, Central Bank	Brazil	2	4.50
Martus Tavares, Minister of Planning	Brazil		
Jorge Marsh, Deputy Governor, Central Bank	Chile	4	9.00
Heinz Rudolph, Director of International Finance	Chile		
Rodrigo Valdés, Director of Economic Policy	Chile		
Raul Saez, International Coordinator	Chile		
Salomon Kalmanovitz, Board of Directors, Central Bank	Colombia	3	4.50
Juan Manuel Santos, Minister of Finance	Colombia		
Juan Mario Laserna, Director of Public Credit	Colombia		
Jorge Gardo, Minister of Finance	Ecuador	1	2.00
Alonso Garcia, General Director for Public Credit	Mexico	3	7.00
Francisco Gil Diaz, Minister of Finance	Mexico		
Guillermo Ortiz, Governor Central Bank	Mexico		
Norberto Delgado, Minister of Economy and Finance	Panama	2	4.50
Domingo Latorraca, Deputy Minister of Economy and Finance	Panama		
Javier Silva Ruete, Minister of Finance	Peru	1	2.00
Alberto Bension, Minister of Finance	Uruguay	3	7.00
César Rodriguez Batlle, President of Central Bank	Uruguay		
Umberto della Mea, Director of Economic Research Central Bank	Uruguay		
José Rojas, Minister of Finance	Venezuela	2	4.50
Jorge Giordani, Minister of Planning	Venezuela		
IMF and World Bank representatives	*Institution*	4	9.00
Claudio Loser, Western Hemisphere Department	IMF		
Miguel Bonangelino, Deputy Director, Western Hemisphere Department	IMF		
Thomas Reichmann, Deputy Director, Western Hemisphere Department	IMF		
Guillermo Perry, Chief Economist for Latin America	World Bank		
Scholars		2	4.50
Ricardo Hausmann, Professor JFK School of Government	Harvard		
Sebastian Edwards, Professor UCLA	UCLA		
Rating agencies		7	16
Vincent Truglia, Managing Director	Moody's		
Ernesto Martinez, Senior Latin American Analyst	Moody's		

Table 5.3   (*Contd.*)

U.S. and Latam officials	Country	Number	%
Mauro Leos, Senior Latin American Analyst	Moody's		
John Chambers, Deputy Director	S&P		
Laura Feinland Katz, Managing Director	S&P		
Bruno Boccara, Director	S&P		
Graciana del Castillo, Director	S&P		
Brokers and banks		2	5
John Lipsky, Chief Economist	JP Morgan Sec.		
Miguel Kiguel, President	Hipotecario		
Total		44	

Source: Santiso, 2001, based on JP Morgan Chase, March 2001.

Table 5.4(a)   Speakers at the IADB 2001 investor forums, number of speakers by country

	CSFB forum	SSB forum	JPM Chase forum	Total	%
U.S. and int. org.	2	11	17	30	33
Argentina	7	3	5	15	16
Venezuela	2	4	2	8	9
Mexico	4	1	3	8	9
Chile	1	2	4	7	7.50
Colombia	3	1	3	7	7.50
Brazil	1	2	2	5	5.50
Panama	0	2	2	4	4
Uruguay	0	0	3	3	3
Ecuador	0	1	1	2	2
Peru	0	1	1	2	2
Total	20	28	44	92	

Sources: Santiso, 2001; based on Crédit Suisse First Boston (CSFB); Salomon Smith Barney (SSB); and JP Morgan Chase (JPM Chase), 2001.

Table 5.4(b)   Speakers at the IADB 2001 investor forums, number of speakers by profession

	CSFB forum	SSB forum	JPM Chase forum	Total	%
Latam government officials	11	19	26	56	61
Rating agencies	1	3	7	11	12
International organizations	0	2	4	6	6.50
Brokers/banks/funds	2	1	2	5	5.50
Academics	2	1	2	5	5.50
U.S. officials	0	1	3	4	4
Corporates	3	0	0	3	3
Think-tanks	1	1	0	2	2
Total	20	28	44	92	

Sources: Santiso, 2001; based on Crédit Suisse First Boston (CSFB); Salomon Smith Barney (SSB); and JP Morgan Chase (JPM Chase), 2001.

also do so in international newspapers. The countries and issues coverage, wordings, columns, the media, Bloomberg screens, Reuters news or international newspapers such as the *Wall Street Journal* or the *Financial Times*, participate in the confidence game as global confidence arenas, where voices are expressed. Wall Street analysts, mainly through Bloomberg screens, pay a lot of attention to these information flows. Some even developed an unusual interest in monitoring the wording of newspapers. In particular *The Economist* magazine, for example, developed an "R-word index" that counts the number of times the word "recession" is mentioned in the written media.[36]

As underlined by Robert Shiller, in fact "news media play a prominent role in generating our conventional wisdom, more so among professionals, but among investment professionals as well." "The news media are generators of attention cascades, as one focus of attention in public thinking leads to a related focus of attention, and then in turn to yet another focus attention."[37] They participate in the creative process of generation and destruction of conventional wisdom, help in the shaping of investors' world visions and cognitive regimes. An empirical analysis based on a comprehensive search of all articles published on Russian transition, using keywords and phrases such as "shock therapy," "gradualism," "reform" and "capital controls" in leading U.S. and U.K. newspapers, corroborates the importance of the narrative of financial press in establishing conventional wisdom and shaping cognitive regimes, even reinforcing the adoption of government policies and the widespread support for conventional wisdom (until its crisis).[38]

The newspaper most read by financial communities around the world is the *Financial Times*. It is instrumental in shaping public attention and categories of thought, contributing to creating the cognitive environment within which financial market events are played out. Unlike other leading economic and financial newspapers in the United Kingdom, the *Financial Times* has a global circulation with more than 50 percent of sales being derived from overseas (Europe, North America and the Far East). Once little more than a stock-market organ, heavily focused on the affairs of London, by the 1950s the newspaper started to expand, covering industry and politics. By the 1970s it had transformed its coverage becoming more international. In terms of net circulation the *Financial Times* sold more than 400,000 copies in 2000 distributed mainly in the United Kingdom (42 percent), Europe (31 percent) and North America (20 percent). In 2001, the *Financial Times* reached more than 500,000 worldwide sales for the first time, three-fifths outside the United Kingdom (compared with 290,000 sales in 1990, two-third of which was in the United Kingdom). In Europe it dominates other leading financial journals such as the *Wall Street Journal Europe* and in turn is dominated by the *Wall Street Journal* in North America. But even among the Wall Street financial community, at least for professionals working in emerging markets, the *Financial Times* is considered the major source of information. When we asked what are the most reliable and useful sources of information on Latin American emerging markets, a vast majority of fund managers, economists and strategists considered the international newspapers (93 percent, out of a total of 145 interviews) as a relevant source. And when asked to mention the leading source within this category, the *Financial Times* was ranked at the top. It's the most referenced international newspaper by financial market operators (75 percent), far ahead of the *Wall Street Journal* (46 percent) or the *New York Times* (20 percent). It is ranked first among the international newspapers by 60 percent of the operators (11 percent preferring the *Wall Street Journal* to any other international newspaper as a source of information). International newspaper preference is given in graph 5.1. Graph 5.2 ranks reliability and usefulness of international newspapers as sources of information.

The most surprising results were related to Wall Street and Boston operators: as in London, Paris, Madrid and Edinburgh, the *Financial Times*

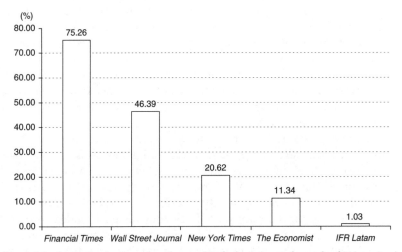

Graph 5.1   International newspaper preferences (% of references out of a sample of 14 interviews).

Source: Santiso, 2001; based on interviews (145) conducted in New York, Paris, London, Boston, Edinburgh and Madrid, 2000.

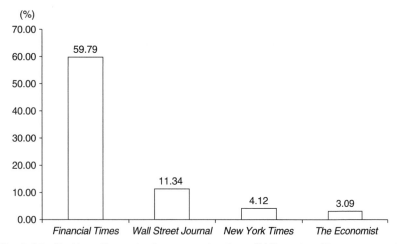

Graph 5.2   Ranking of international newspapers based on reliability and usefulness as sources of information (in %; size of the sample: $N = 145$).

Source: Santiso, 2001; based on interviews (145) conducted in New York, Paris, London, Boston, Edinburgh and Madrid, 2000.

ranked far ahead of the *Wall Street Journal* even in the U.S. financial centers. In New York, for example, the *Financial Times* is ranked 3.5 more times as the first newspaper source of information rather than the *Wall Street Journal*. As expected in London the numbers are even more contrasting: the *Financial Times* is ranked eight times more as the first newspaper source of information, by financial operators in emerging markets in London. When the numbers are compared for brokers and fund managers, the former appeared to rely more on international newspapers than the latter. More than 90 percent of brokers' analysts mention them as a source of information compared to less than 65 percent for fund managers (see graph 5.3).

Newspapers contribute then in a major way to the cognitive regimes of financial communities. During the Asian crisis, London was dominated by homogenous risk-adverse expectations best characterized as pessimistic compared to Wall Street. In a study relying upon material provided by the *Financial Times*, two researchers of Oxford University try to understand this pessimism.[39] They constructed an index based on a close analysis of one of the leading *Financial Times'* senior columnists Barry Riley, a 30-year-old professional, recognized as one of the best-informed financial reporters. Throughout the Asian crisis, London operators focused upon leading independent journalists like Barry Riley,

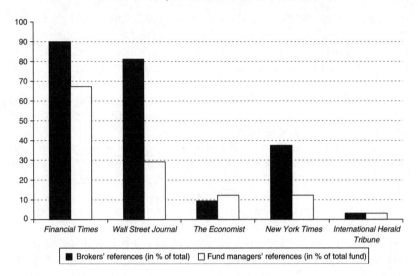

Graph 5.3   Brokers versus fund managers reliance on international newspapers (in % *N* = 145).

Source: Santiso, 2001; based on interviews (145) conducted in New York, Paris, London, Boston, Edinburgh and Madrid, 2000.

which represented the pessimistic view on Asia. During a crisis as market data is discounted by many market participants, there was a "flight to quality" to the sources of information believed to be the most accurate, independent and credible. The focus of attention on Riley's *Financial Times*' columns was in the end a rational way to manage uncertainty for investors unease about data integrity. Even in the global village, local knowledge seemed to survive as suggested by this study carried out by two geographers.

During the Argentina crisis and debt default of November 2001, the *Financial Times* became a major catalyst of shifting opinion among leading economists. In a matter of few weeks, leading economists backed exchange rate flexibilization—in other words devaluation—as part of the cure for Argentina. The first one, signed by Ricardo Hausmann, the former chief economist of the IADB who became a Harvard scholar by the end of 2000, explicitly dismisses dollarization—a former solution— as an appropriate exit option for Argentina.[40] Instead he advocated a re-denomination of dollar assets and liabilities into domestic currency and the adoption of a floating exchange rate regime. A few days later, another prominent voice of international finance, Michael Mussa, ex–chief economist at the IMF, argued in the same way that the currency board was no longer viable.[41] Both comments, with others by Joseph Stiglitz, were carefully quoted by the financial community. As underlined by a broker, "the comments of Mussa and Stiglitz carry unusual weight. If their opinions reflect the majority (but, for obvious reasons, unstated) view both in the Fund and World Bank, I will have major implications for the policy advice and conditionality attached to further official support for Argentina."[42] The *Financial Times'* articles participating in the increasing negative voices (some of them U-Turns) surrounding Argentina were channeled also by major players in Wall Street.[43]

The *Financial Times* provides then a unique global and powerful confidence game arena as it is the most widely read newspaper by financial communities in New York, not to mention London or other European financial centers. Being referenced or published by the *Financial Times* brings a unique strength to your "voice." From this point of view the most published scholars are Paul Krugman (MIT) and Jeffrey Sachs (Harvard University). However being mentioned by the *Financial Times* does not mean that your voice will be taken into account. A good example of this is the Cassandra-like warnings of Rudiger Dornbusch, on several occasions, about the looming economic crises in Mexico and Brazil. This gained little attention in spite of the accuracy of the prediction. In early April 1994, Rudiger Dornbusch with Alejandro Werner presented a paper to the Brookings Panel on Economic Activity where they advocated a 20 percent devaluation of the peso. Their main conclusion was that the currency was overvalued. But no one seemed to pay attention, even some former Mexican students who were in charge of finance in Mexico by then.[44]

A closer study, based on the analysis of all the references made in the *Financial Times*, from November 1995 to November 2000, shows that the coverage of information is not equally distributed. As expected major Latin American economies received the largest news coverage with countries like Mexico, Brazil and Argentina leading. The references to Mexico during this five-year period amounted close to 9,000 (30 times more than the total references to El Salvador). The Mexican coverage represents however half of the Chinese coverage and it is comparable to South Korea coverage for the period if we make some Asian comparisons (see graph 5.4).

The analysis of references by individual actors gives an indication of who is participating in the confidence game. Brokers, economists or strategists are not the major voices within this global arena. Their exposure within an international newspaper can be risky and, even for those authorized to communicate, they may not want to be visible in the

Number of references

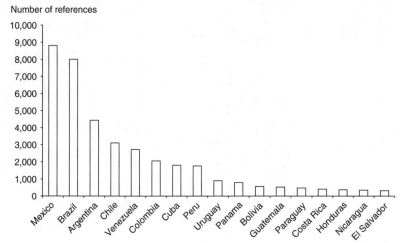

Graph 5.4   The *Financial Times* as a confidence game arena: number of references between 1995 and 2000.

Source: Santiso, 2001; based on the *Financial Times* and FT.com web databases, 2000. The data has been processed for a period of 5 years between November 1995 and November 2000.

media. Among the most referenced by the *Financial Times'* journalists are however some leading analysts such as Geoffrey Dennis of Salomon Smith Barney and Peter West from BBVA Securities (see table 5.5). It is interesting to note that both are British citizens, the first based in New York and the second based in London. Of the 20 most-quoted financial economists in the *Financial Times*, 70 percent are New York-based and 30 percent London-based. The most quoted financial professional is Georges Soros who is ten times more quoted than any other emerging markets financial analyst. Among Washington officials and academics, the rankings prevailing are also indicators of the distribution of powers between financial official institutions, the Federal Reserve (Alan Greenspan) ranking well before the IMF (Michel Camdessus) and the U.S. Treasury (Larry Summers). Among academics the top confidence game players referenced by the *Financial Times* are Jeffrey Sachs and Paul Krugman whose "voice" is five times more present that the IADB chief economist for example. For Latin American policy-makers, the rankings don't follow the weights of the economies, the top player in this category being the Cuban leader Fidel Castro (however the mandate periods of Latin American leaders are quite different).

Table 5.5 The *Financial Times* confidence game arena

	Number of references		Number of references		Number of references
Washington and Academia		*Wall Street and London*		*Latin American Policy-makers*	
Alan Greenspan (Federal Reserve)	3,058	Georges Soros (Soros)	907	Fidel Castro (Cuba)	753
Michel Camdessus (IMF)	558	Geoffrey Dennis (SSMB)	83	FH Cardoso (Brazil)	636
Larry Summers (U.S. Treasury)	431	Peter West (BBVA)	70	Hugo Chavez (Venezuela)	617
Jeffrey Sachs (Harvard)	149	Walter Molano (BCP Secutiries)	46	Ernesto Zedillo (Mexico)	508
Paul Krugman (MT)	102	William Rhodes (Citigroup)	38	Alberto Fujimori (Peru)	478
Joseph Stiglitz (World Bank)	88	Paulo Leme (Goldman Sachs)	33	Carlos Menem (Argentina)	438
Enrique Iglesias (IADB)	44	Arturo Porzecanski (ABN Amro)	32	Fernando de la Rua (Argentina)	179
Ricardo Hausmann (IADB)	28	Joyce Chang (Chase)	17	Domingo Cavallo (Argentina)	170
Guillermo Perry (World Bank)	18	Francis Freisinger (Merrill Lynch)	17	Guillermo Ortiz (Argentina)	127
Sebastian Edwards (UCLA)	17	Jorge Mariscal (Goldman Sachs)	15	Pedro Malan (Brazil)	111
Claudio Loser (IMF)	15	Damian Fraser (UBS Warburg)	13	Roque Fernandez (Argentina)	87
Rudiger Dombusch (MT)	14	Tim Love (SG)	11	José Angel Gurria (Mexico)	72
Victor Bulmer-Thomas (ILAS)	6	Neil Dougall (DkB)	10	Arminio Fraga (Brazil)	67
Guillermo Calvo (Maryland)	3	Ernest Brown (Santander)	8	José Luis Machinea (Argentina)	54
Ricardo Ffrench-Davis (ECLAC)	3	Jay Pelosky (MSDW)	8	Daniel Marx (Argentina)	17
José Antonio Ocampo (ECLAC)	0	Philip Suttle (JP Morgan)	3	Francisco Gros (Brazil)	8
		Michael Hood (JP Morgan)	3		
		Mark Precious (UBS Warburg)	3		
		Michael Gavin (UBS Warburg)	3		
		Tom Trebat (SSIVB)	2		
		Vladimir Werning (JP Morgan)	1		

Note: Five years November 1995–November 2000; *Financial Times* references only.
Source: Santiso, 2001; based on the *Financial Times* and FT.com; Reuters Business Briefings.

5.4   The Trespassing Game

Academics can take part in the confidence game in many other ways. They can themselves be investors or advisors of investment houses.[45] One of the best examples in emerging markets is Steve Hanke, not only a leading professor of economics at Baltimore's Johns Hopkins University, but also the well-known pope of currency boards and (less) well-known chairman of an asset management company. He is not only a "pure player" "voicing" from academia, but one playing for both sides in the game, as the advisor of governments around the world and also as a financial operator. He is not only a chairman of the Friedberg Mercantile Group in New York and president of the Toronto Trust in Buenos Aires,[46] a mutual fund, but also an advisor to emerging market governments on currency reforms, privatization and capital market developments, in several countries such as Lithuania, Indonesia and Argentina.

The most recent and famous example of academics trespassing into Wall Street, is probably the one of LTCM's partners. Among them were prestigious figures such as 1997 Nobel laureates in economics, Robert Merton and Myron Scholes, responsible (with their colleague, the late Fischer Black) in the early 1970s for one of the single most important breakthroughs in the modern mathematical theory of finance. They provided a new way of thinking about risk, suggesting a method that has become fundamental to modern finance for pricing risk. During the 1990s, as partners of LTCM a U.S. investment boutique, these financial theorists became part of what they were accustomed to be examining.

The involvement of academics in Wall Street and London is in any case not new and, is in a way, a continuing trend.[47] In the past decade, many high-profile academics streamed into Wall Street, putting their theories to test, and contributing to the increasing merging of academic and applied professional research in finance. Eugene Fama, for example, a University of Chicago scholar, is also the research director of an asset management company, Dimensional Funds Advisors.[48] This company has also other leading scholars like Merton Miller, 1990 Nobel Prize recipient, and Kenneth French, an MIT economist, among other distinguished academic theorists as members of the board. In Europe, Bruno Solnik, a well-known professor of finance at HEC School of Management, is also member of the board of Sinopia Asset Management. Other examples included Steve Kealhofer, a Ph.D. in economics from Princeton, who taught finance at both Columbia and Berkeley universities, founded KMV,[49] a leading financial boutique specializing in credit risk analysis. Rudiger Dornbusch from MIT and Kenneth Froot from Harvard, initiated with other academics, a joint venture with State Street Bank in 2000 to analyze fund flow data and participate as partners in an investment management corporation State Street Associates. Joseph Stiglitz and Albert Fishlow, two prominent academics, joined Wall Street in 2000. After leaving the World Bank, the former became a board member of Brookdale, a Manhattan hedge fund, and later professor at Columbia University where in 2001 he received the Nobel Prize in economics. The latter became the chief economist for Latin America of the financial boutique Violey, Byorum and Partners (in 2002 he went back to the academy to head the newly created Centre for Brazilian Studies at Columbia University).[50]

The trespassing game of academics is particularly interesting when, as in the case of Rudiger Dornsbusch or many others mentioned earlier, they have full access to global confidence arenas such as the *Financial Times*. One could argue that when they write in the newspaper they are taking more than a "neutral" view from the top of the academic hill. They are, at the same time, playing in the Wall Street valley. For example, it's just a few weeks before the Argentine crisis by the end of 2001, leading to a devaluation and a debt default amid riots and presidential resignations, that Ricardo Hausmann published his previously mentioned paper. He was arguing for Argentina's need to devalue after having defended Latin America's need for dollarization.[51] Such a U-turn caught the attention of many people.

As a leading economist on Latin American issues and as a former chief economist at the IADB, Hausmann achieved a high reputation and visibility, being respected for his provocative and refreshing views. After the IADB he moved to Harvard University. So the *Financial Times* article was signed as a professor at Harvard. But as underlined by a Wall Street broker, Hausmann was also by the time involved in advising a leading New York Wall Street firm very much involved in Argentina. "Ricardo, wrote by the time Walter Molano commenting on the multilateral officials advocating for a devaluation in Argentina, the former Chief Economist of the IADB, is the most perplexing. Hausmann went on the record countless of times, claiming that dollarization was a 'no brainier' for Argentina. Now he is calling for devaluation. Hausmann openly recommended institutional investors to buy Argentine bonds when he was invited to speak at a 1999 seminar in Argentina, foregoing any notion of 'conflict of interest' or the impartiality of the multilateral agencies. Now he is sitting at Harvard University, and working as a paid consultant for a New York investment bank, calling for default. While his position may cast doubts about the quality of the Ivy League education, it also shows one the inherent problems with the multilaterals. They have no accountability."[52]

Crossing boundaries into the real world and becoming key players in the emerging markets confidence game, can be a good move for economists as suggested by the case of Larry Summers, America's Treasury secretary and a leading "voice" regarding global emerging markets. It can however be a painful one as Andrei Shleifer, a Harvard economist and Russian expert, discovered in 2000.[53] Andrei Shleifer became, in the 1990s, a leading advisor of the Russian government. From 1991 to 1997, he advised on privatization and other reforms, while working at the Harvard Institute for International Development (HIID), a think-tank run at the time by Jeffrey Sachs, another Harvard scholar. Later the American government launched a US$120 mn. lawsuit against Shleifer alleging that he helped foreign investors (amongst them an investment banker who at that time was his wife) make investments in Russia that were prohibited by the terms of the contract received from the American government. This case is interesting in that we are talking about a leading economist who won the 1999 John Bates Clark Medal of the American Economic Association for the best American economist under 40 (an indicator of a potential Nobel Prize winner). He is also in the global village of international finance, as he runs, with two other academics (among them Robert Vishny from the University of Chicago), a Chicago-based investment management firm since 1994.[54]

Meanwhile leading IMF, World Bank and IADB economists have also been crossing boundaries, trespassing from international organizations into investment banks or asset management companies.[55] For example, leading JP Morgan Latin American economists such as Philip Suttle, Michael Hood, Marcelo Carvalho and Alfredo Thorne were previously at the Bank of England in London, The Federal Reserve Bank of New York, or, in the case of the last two, at the World Bank in Washington. Among one of the most respected emerging market economists is Paulo Leme, managing director emerging markets economic research at Goldman Sachs & Co. in New York, a Brazilian economist who joined Goldman Sachs in 1993 after working as a senior economist at the IMF for nine years. There he gained broad experience with stabilization reforms and debt restructuring programs and was responsible with Paris Club creditors for some Brady-bond with countries like Venezuela or Ecuador among others. His emerging markets colleague Federico Kaune, a Peruvian-born economist trained at Chicago University, left the IMF, where he spent three years, before jumping to Wall Street in 1997.

Probably one of the best examples of the attractiveness of Wall Street boutiques is given by Deutsche Bank were you can find several former high-profile individuals coming from the IMF, the academy or former central banks. Among the most significant trespassers to Deutsche Bank are David Folkerts-Landau, a former senior IMF economist,[56] and Peter Garber, a well-known scholar who before joining Wall Street spent the previous 15 years as a professor of economics at Brown University. Another high-profile scholar who joined Deutsche Bank was Robin Lumsdaine, appointed in 2001, as quantitative strategist after being a consultant for Deutsche Bank and professor at Brown University.[57] From the Inter-American Development Bank, Michael Gavin joined UBS Warburg, and Liliana Rojas-Suarez also made a (briefly) move from Washington to New York to join Deutsche Bank (see table 5.6).

Table 5.6 The trespassing game: the example of New York-based Deutsche Bank securities

Name	Position held at DB (year joining)	Previous position	Academic background
Leonardo Leiderman	Chief economist Latam (2000)	Central Bank of Israel	Ph.D. in economics, University of Chicago
Gustavo Canonero	Economist, Latin America (1998)	Salomon Brothers	Ph.D. in economics, MIT
José Carlos de Faria	Economist, Latin America (1999)	/	Ph.D. in economics, MIT
Piero Ghezzi	Economist, Latin America (1999)	Johns Hopkins University	Ph.D. in economics, Berkeley
Michael Spencer	Chief economist Asia (1997)	International Monetary Fund	Ph.D. in economics, Queens University
Peter Hooper	Global Economics and U.S. (1999)	Federal Reserve Board	Ph.D. in economics, University of Michigan
Nicholas Boorks	Economist, Asia (1999)	Santander Investment/ Peregrine	M.A. in Economics, Columbia University
Sanjeev Sanyal	Economist, Asia (1997)	Société Générale	M.Sc. in economics, Oxford University
Marcel Cassard	Chief economist, Emerging Europe (1997)	International Monetary Fund	Ph.D. in economics, Columbia University
Tefvik Aksoy	Economist, Emerging Europe (2000)	Bank Ekspres (Turkey)	Ph.D. in economics, University of Delaware
Natalia Gurushina	Economist, Emerging Europe (1999)	Bankers Trust (Russia)	Degree in Philosophy, Oxford University
Peter Garber	Global Strategist (1998)	Brown University	Ph.D. in economics, University of Chicago

Source: Santiso, 2001; based on Deutsche Bank, 2000.

Not only is the brokerage "sell–side" involved in these trespassing games, but also asset managers' "buy side." A good example is Mr. El–Erian, PIMCO emerging bond market portfolio manager, who after 15 years with the IMF (where he worked on debt and emerging market country issues) joined Salomon Smith Barney and then PIMCO in 1999. A further example is Nicholas Brady, currently chairman of Darby Overseas Investments, a Washington-based investment company he established in 1994,[58] after serving as U.S. Treasury secretary where he designed and implemented a strategy known as the Brady Plan to solve emerging market debt problems. Note that prior to this government appointment, he had a 34-year career in investment banking at Dillon Read. One of the last high-level IMF officials who moved from Washington to Wall Street, has been Stanley Fischer, former deputy managing director of the IMF, who joined Citigroup as a vice chairman and who will report to Robert Rubin, formerly from the U.S. Treasury that flew also from Washington to Wall Street.

Inside the game then, the players can change positions and even trespass into the opposing party, the trespassing game being another way to continue playing. Trespassers are particularly interesting players as they bring with them not only expertise but also a far-reaching network that takes root inside governments and international organizations. Even if the links with their former employer are severed, the connections remain.[59] Friendships are preserved and also interesting (weak or strong) ties.[60] "For strategic reasons one can be interested in delivering information to a former IMF director or senior member that crossed to Wall Street. Who knows, he could be your next (and wealthy) employer?"[61] "In any case previous IMF economists can return to the IMF to another management position. Then it can be in your own interest not to stop (at least in an obvious way) to transmit some kind of information, even (and above all) if your interlocutor is a senior banker and former IMF staff member. He can simply be back and become your next boss, as the institution preserve this kind of privilege to their previous employees."[62] Even without discussing inside information, one can only wonder if such trespassing and shifting involvement would be included in the agenda of "international finance architecture" and "moral hazard" debates. Is this shifting involvement changing the asymmetries of information among Wall Street firms? Isn't there a comparative advantage when you know how IMF rescue packages are negotiated and which are the inside processes and cognitive regimes of IMF decision-makers?

5.5 The Seduction Game

Even more spectacular, from the point of view of the confidence game is the trespass of some high-profile economists from Wall Street to emerging market governments. The most significant example is that of Arminio Fraga, a former Soros Fund Management executive, nominated in 1999 to head Brazil's central bank. After the devaluation of the real on January 15, 2000, Brazil hired the then hedge fund poacher as its economic gamekeeper. A *fin connaisseur* of the confidence game, Fraga, as a former fund manager, was well versed in making currency devaluations and other macroeconomic bets in emerging markets. The move was clearly a double play. Mr. Fraga brought with him very useful expertise at a time when the country was forced to let the currency float, after nearly 50 years of fixed exchange rates. He had been brought in with the aim of neutralizing new speculative pressures and, above all, of rebuilding central bank credibility.

Another kind of involvement is the one of legendary Bill Rhodes, Citigroup vice chairman, who had been involved in nearly all problem solving related to financial crises in Latin America over the past two decades. In 2000, he helped Ecuador to restructure its sovereign debt, being involved as an international advisor with the Latin American country at the request of the IMF's first deputy managing director, Stanley Fischer (a former distinguished MIT professor), who wanted to avoid an IMF bailout of the country's private sector. It seems as though the *New Money Doctors*, instead of coming from the Academia, were once again from Wall Street. This situation is not new—when compared with J. Pierpont Morgan's involvement in rescuing and becoming the central banker of what was then, by the end of the nineteenth and beginning of the twentieth century, an emerging country, United States.[63] But it supports the idea that bringing the state back into the game make market experts into government bureaucracies.

In many Latin American countries, an analysis of the curriculum vitae of top officials in technical ministries and central banks confirms this point. This strategy of seduction is at work more directly with the multiplication of investment agencies. Built with the purpose to seduce foreign investors, these agencies provide useful and timely information, competing with each other to catch investors' attention. Most Latin American countries now have official web portals. Transformed into information brokers they provide high quality and frequently updated data, some of them, such as the Central Bank of Brazil, on a daily basis. If there is one thing that some Latin American governments understood it's that markets don't like to be kept in the dark. They aren't birds of the night. They like light and transparency above all, and must be fed with massive, coherent and timely flows of information. The confidence game is then transformed into a circular game. Markets watch states and vice versa. States monitor the pulse of the markets in order to proceed with (or cancel) planned bond emissions. From Peru and Colombia down to Chile, many governments are publishing reports on the pulse and sentiments of markets (see table 5.7). Started in 1993 with the explicit aim of promoting an attractive image of the country abroad, PromPeru, for example, decided in 1998 to published quarterly reports of analysts' view on the Peruvian economy.[64]

Table 5.7 A circular game: analysts' views in Latin American national investment agency reports

Brokers and raters	Chile	Colombia	Peru (2000)	Peru (1999)
ABN Amro		x	x	
BCP Securities		x		
ING Barings		x		
JP Morgan	x	x	x	x
Merrill Lynch	x	x		x
UBS Warburg	x	x		
SG Cowen Sec.		x		
Standard NY Sec.		x		
Bear Stearns			x	x
CSFB	x		x	
Goldman Sachs	x		x	x
Salomon Smith Barney	x		x	
BSCH Investment	x		x	x
BBVA	x		x	x
Chase Sec.	x		x	x
Dresdner Bank			x	x
Deutsche Bank Sec.	x			x
Scotiabank				x
Morgan Stanley				x
Lehman Brothers				x
BNP Paribas	x			
DLJ	x			
HSBC	x			
Duff & Phelps (Fitch)		x	x	x
Standard & Poor's	x	x	x	
Moody's	x	x		x
Number of analysts: 26	15	11	12	14

Sources: Santiso, 2001; based on PromPeru, December 2000 and December 1999; Coinvertir, December 1999; Chile Foreign Investment Committee, August 2000.

In a similar way Coinvertir, the Colombian investment agency, started publishing on a regular basis a comparative analysis of government and analyst forecasts, taking a detailed look at economic aggregates and projections made by Wall Street operators.[65] By mid-2000, the Chilean Foreign Investment Committee started to reproduce what Wall Street rating agencies and investment banks have been writing about the Chilean economy.[66] Used as marketing publications, these governments are then regularly publishing Wall Street analysts, views on their economies, editing reports and analysis made by brokers—being interested in courting emerging countries in order to win their lucrative sovereign bond issue.

5.6   The Democratic Dilemma of the Confidence Game

Hence the confidence game involves a democratic dilemma. Governments may be caught between choosing to implement the socially friendly policies preferred by their *local voters* (citizens) and capital friendly measures demanded by *global voters* (investors). The art of government involves pleasing internal voters, who can exit, voice or remain loyal. But it also involves keeping the support of global voters, who can also exit, voice and remains loyal. For them the most visible exit option is simply voting with their screens and pulling money out of the country or stopping investing. The positive side of capital market openness is in a way that it not only provides (financial) support and greater access to capital, but subjects governments to a strong discipline, governments being obliged to sell their policies not only to voters but also to investors. The dark side of this double imperative is the conflicting arbitrage that governments may face.

Markets may impose costs and constraints on governments that limit democratic games as illustrated by Rodrik's "political trilemma." Arguing by analogy to the Mundell–Flemming conditions for open economies, he contends that, given the pace and scope of global market integration, emerging countries have to choose between a "golden straight jacket" that limits government room for maneuver.[67] Regarding exchange rate policy choices, emerging countries face severe limitations, an "impossible trinity" that can be summarized in the impossible task countries face to reconcile capital mobility needs, independent and sound monetary policy and fixed exchange rates all at the same time.[68] Andrés Velasco adds, following the analysis of the 1990s emerging market crises: "you cannot enjoy free capital movements and a counter-cycle monetary policy, regardless of your exchange rate regime."[69]

One basic rule of the confidence game is then to be very careful when nominating the official government voicer. For investors it is mainly the ministry of economics or finance or the governor of the central bank. He will be chosen not only for his or her political and technical abilities but also for his capacities to play the game, that is to ensure market confidence and strengthen market loyalty. Backed with strong skills and analytical tools, fluent in English, most of them are introduced via their old-school ties or previous professional experiences with foreign banks and international institutions. They were able to deal with the world of international finance, be it New York or Washington and with epistemic communities, fund managers or multilateral staff economists. In other words they were the perfect players for the confidence game, adopting and adapting the totems and taboos, language and rituals of foreign investors.[70]

This technocratization of elites in emerging countries followed years of continuous economic crises, which impel states to raise their technocratic capacities. The need to solve the complex problems that followed the debt crisis in 1982 encouraged the appointment of technician reformers. Known as "technopols" these technocrats were also the perfect interlocutors for the much-needed potential providers of liquidity, the international financial community, public or private operators, multilateral and—more and more—private financial markets.[71]

This technocratization of the confidence game within Latin American bureaucracies deserves many examples. Chilean newly elected President Ricardo Lagos, a socialist, pledged his commitment to free-market reforms. He quickly secured investors confidence by appointing a former IMF director and Harvard graduate Nicolás Eyzaguirre as finance minister while José de Gregorio, a well-respected scholar and MIT-trained economist, was named minister of the economy.

In a much more dramatic move, by the end of Fujimori's reign, in November 2000, the Peruvian authorities were looking to restore national and international confidence. One of the answers was naming Javier Perez de Cuellar (a former UN secretary general with strong democratic credentials) as the new prime minister (later under Toledo's new government he became minister of foreign affairs). For the same reasons, Javier Silva, a former minister, central banker and former representative to the World Bank, IMF and Inter-American Development Bank, has been named the new finance minister. When in 2001, the newly elected president of Peru, Alejandro Toledo, a Stanford-trained Ph.D. and former World Bank consultant, had to choose his minister of finance he did not hesitate. In a drive to beef up Peru's international credibility, he appointed Pablo Kuczynski, a Miami-based fund manager as economy minister and Roberto Danino, a Harvard-trained corporate lawyer as prime minister. Immediately after the announcements Peruvian bonds rallied while securities houses were nearly euphoric with what was by the time labelled the Peruvian economic "dream team."[72]

In Mexico in 2000, the newly elected President Vicente Fox (from PAN, the former opposition) appointed well-known pro-market economists from the previous two PRI governments. The most prominent figure was Francisco Gil Diaz, the new minister of finance and former deputy finance minister in Carlos Salinas' administration, who (confidence game obliged) holds a doctorate from Chicago University. Mr. Gil's love of fiscal austerity, his reputation as "a tough, honest reformer and fiscal disciplinarian" (quoted from *The Economist*), were strong signals to the market. These confidence boosters and stabilizers came a few weeks after declarations from some of Fox's advisors that sent confusing signals to the markets regarding fiscal discipline and fears of overheating.

From the perspective of the confidence game, central bank and ministry of finance appointments became the most sensitive decisions during the 1990s for emerging market governments. Both central banks and the ministry of finance have found themselves in the front line. Much more analysis would be needed in order to understand, this time from the perspective of the states, how to manage the relations with Wall Street and London and how to play the game. But one clear answer has been to hire the brightest people, that is, those with the highest credentials from the point of view of international finance communities, those most capable of playing the confidence game.

The homogeneity of background and training obviously doesn't mean homogeneity of cognitive regimes and ways of thinking. However it tends to consolidate a common language, a more or less technical and economic Esperanto, shared by emerging country officials, Wall Street brokers and IMF economists. English-speaking analysts, trained in the north—and above all if they come from southern countries in the U.S. centers—are then the beloved fellows of these confidence game institutions. A clear example is the IMF, an institution at the center of the game. There, according to data for 1999, 47 percent of department heads came from English-speaking industrialized countries. IMF recruitment presents a clear homogeneity of training: no recruits of the IMF EP Program in 1999 were trained outside industrial countries. All were recruited from the top (and also leading) universities of the north (and United States above all).[73]

As underlined by Barro and Jong-Wha Lee,[74] the IMF responds to economic and financial conditions, but they are also very sensitive to political-economy variables. The sizes and frequencies of loan programs are influenced by a country's presence at the IMF and by its share of quotas and professional staff. In 2002, among the nearly 2,300 staff members of the IMF, 29 percent were from the United States and 33 percent from Western Europe. Among developing countries, Argentina, for example, a country that has been under an IMF agreement nearly every year from 1973 to 2002, had relatively large numbers of professional staff (note that until 2002, the head of the Western Hemisphere was an Argentinian). The share of own national IMF economists raises the probability and size of IMF lending. In the same way a member country's political proximity to the IMF's major shareholders, and particularly to the United States, is also important.

The small-embedded world confidence game one can argue has positive sides. When faced with a crisis, close ties and confidence-building processes are easier to achieve when every one knows each other and share a common cognitive regime. A good example of this is the way Argentina dealt with its banking crisis in 2002 after the default, the devaluation and the pesification of the loans (and not the deposits, causing mismatches between assets and liabilities in the banking sector). By end June 2002, the Argentinian government assembled a team of high-profile economists, all involved in the ups and downs of confidence games of the 1990s. Stanley Fischer, the former IMF managing director, Miguel Mancera, Mexico's central banker during the 1994 currency crisis, Arminio Fraga, Brazil's central bank chief, who managed the impact of the devaluation of the real in 1999 and other influential economists such as Adam Lerrick and Allan Meltzer, who have been offering their services to Argentina. A direct link between Buenos Aires and the IMF was established with the arrival of Mario Bléjer, a former IMF official until 2001, as the head of the Argentinian central bank.

CHAPTER SIX

The Timing Game: Wall Street, Mexico and Argentina. A Temporal Analysis

There is no hard rule about the timing of crises. It is surprising how long basically unsustainable situations can be given extra lives, notably if an election is in sight. With an election on the horizon, creditors are willing to believe that much or anything will be done to hold off a crisis or a corrective devaluation. Governments will do anything, including high interest rates or preferably a shortening of maturities and re-denomination into foreign exchange of claims. As a result, crises happen after elections, not before. This is akin myopic political business cycle but no less real.

Rudiger Dornbusch[1]

The interaction between politics and economics is central to an understanding of financial crises in Latin American emerging markets. The paradox is that, in spite of the evidence, very few studies have been devoted to an analysis of the links with, and importance of, political variables in the empirical literature on currency and financial crises. One of the reasons might have been the difficulty in formalizing political variables. But whatever the reasons behind this lack of integration of political variables, they are indeed significant explanatory factors of emerging market crises. As underlined by a recent study, structural political variables are significantly correlated to currency crises. Left-wing governments seemed more conducive to currency crises, democracies were in general less vulnerable than nondemocratic regimes and strong governments with legislative majorities and fragmented oppositions tend to be less vulnerable.[2]

Among the three latest and largest financial crises in the area, Mexico in 1994, Brazil in 1999 and Argentina in 2001, financial crises took place within presidential or parliamentary electoral years.[3] The same is true also for other emerging markets as nine of the emerging market financial crises of the 1990s happened during periods of political elections or political transitions.[4] Moreover, among the three types or risk—financial risk, political risk and policy risk—political risk appears to be the major driver behind capital flight from emerging markets.[5] Elections in emerging countries are associated with significant effects on market spreads and sovereign rating agencies. As underlined by an empirical test, on average elections in emerging markets tend to be associated with a decline of one rating level on a 17 (0–16) point scale. Similarly spreads on emerging market sovereign debt over the U.S. Treasuries Bills tend to increase by 21 percentage points two months after a major election compared to the same period without an election. "Together, underlines Steven Block in his stimulating study, these results suggest that at least two key actors in international credit transactions, agencies and bond-holders, view elections in developing countries negatively and exact a substantial premium on developing sovereigns and sub-sovereign individual seeking capital."[6] Together also these results question the apparent cost that democracy and elections entail for developing countries.

In fact, for countries with already weak economic fundamentals, political instability tends to have a stronger impact on financial vulnerability.[7] This is particularly relevant in emerging countries where political institutional instability tends to be higher. As measured by Philippe Aghion, Alberto Alesina and Francesco Trebbi,[8] the total number of institutional political changes in a 20-year period for a large sample of 177 countries is concentrated in emerging countries. Of a total of 294 significant changes (almost two per country on average), Africa and Latin America concentrated the highest degree of politico-institutional instability with respectively 138 and 59 institutional changes (compared with 15 for industrial countries). In other terms, Africa alone concentrated nearly half of all the politico-institutional changes that occurred over the period and Latin America 20 percent.

Obviously, the fact that democratic politics affect currency or bond markets is not specific to emerging markets. Expectations and uncertainty about electoral outcomes and government survival affects the financial markets of OECD countries where political processes, elections, polls, cabinet formation and dissolutions, make it more difficult for traders to forecast exchange rates resulting in exchange rate volatility.[9] However the impact of electoral outcomes is particularly significant for emerging markets. Financial markets tend to behave with increasing nervousness because of the uncertain political outcomes involved in election years. In emerging markets in particular the levels of uncertainties are higher reflecting the changeability of currency or bond traders' expectations about the stability of governments, and their policy-making capabilities are more uncertain. During election times, the propensity of governments to increase their public spending in order to win political support tends to increase hurting investors' interests.[10] Whilst this is not specific to emerging countries, fiscal deficits tend however to be more critical given these countries' financial needs and their difficulty in accumulating capital.[11]

These propensities must however be analyzed more carefully as not all election years can be associated with financial disruptions. Empirical investigation provides considerable evidence of fiscal policy distortions during election years in emerging countries. In a study that analyzes 17 Latin American countries over a time period (1947–1982), the panel regression shows an increase of more than 6 percent in the preelection year of public expenditure and a decrease of more then 7.5 percent in the postelection year.[12] A more recent study, testing 69 countries, confirms the evidence of electorally motivated changes in the composition of public expenditure in emerging countries. The election-year public expenditure tends to shift toward more short-term (and visible) current consumption away from public investment goods. Typically, current expenditure shares show an increase of as much as 2.3 percentage points during election years while long-term expenditure like capital investment tends to decline by as much as 1.55 percentage points. However, countries with non-competitive systems exhibit no election-year effect on public spending consumption.[13] In the same way, political institutions that limit discretionary behavior of policy-makers will tend to reduce the volatility of government expenditures and revenues prior and after elections.[14]

The response of financial markets to electoral and partisan changes examined in another study, based on a sample of 78 developing countries using monthly data from 1975 to 1998, confirms that speculative attacks are more likely just after an election as compared to all periods.[15] The reactions of global financial markets to politics in new democracies within a same region may also differ depending on democratic degree of the polity and transparency (or perceived transparency) of its policy-making process, the temporal depth of democratic institutions or the size of government's legislative majority and political cohesion.[16]

The interactions between economic and political sequences have been confirmed in other studies, particularly in the case of Mexico between 1965 and 1985 or more generally for Latin American countries in more recent periods of time.[17] In fact, the political budget cycle tends to be directly correlated with degree of democracy: in more democratic countries, opportunistic cycles in macroeconomic policy tend to be of smaller magnitudes and highly irregular over time as underlined by recent studies.[18] The opposite is also true, that is in imperfect democracies opportunistic election cycles tend to be stronger and more regular. Another study, relating the level of democracy and the strength of the political cycle for a sample of 43 countries in Asia, the Americas and Europe in the years 1950–1997, further confirms also that countries with intermediate democratic levels tend to have higher electoral effects than those of emerging economies located in countries at the tailend of the democracy indices.[19]

Politics is then not neutral regarding financial markets. As suggested by recent research, there is a clear evidence for taking into account political events. The returns of certain stocks can clearly be affected by expectations of political outcomes[20] and those stock price movements occur in the weeks immediately prior to elections.[21] The monitoring of political events by financial emerging market analysts is also underlined by the analysis of research products of investment boutiques that continuously take into account uncertain political outcomes as in elections. Some firms, such as Lehman Brothers even created specific joint ventures in order to incorporate in their analysis political and social factors in their fixed income research,[22] while others as CDC Ixis for example have specific political analysts to cover political issues in emerging markets.[23] Obviously this monitoring of politics intensifies during crises as underlined by the coverage of political issues during the meltdown of Argentina by the end of 2001, a collapse analyzed by some financial operators as a clear evidence of a political governance, representation and legitimacy crisis.[24]

There are also linkages between lack of transparency, political uncertainty and financial crises.[25] Rational contagion in emerging markets can in part be driven by political considerations. Because of their opaque policy processes, less-democratic countries can suffer more from contagion in international financial markets. At the same time, because political rumors float freely in the global arena regardless of emerging market political regimes, all countries, be they democratic or authoritarian, suffer some costs.

Regarding creditworthiness, there is also a lack of "democratic advantage": even if democracies are supposed to pay lower interest rates than authoritarian regimes because they can make credible commitments to repay their debts, the evidence shows that this expectation is unfounded. Empirical research, using a large sample of data on sovereign loans for 132 countries during the period 1970–1990, suggests not only that dictatorships are less likely to reschedule their debts but that the major source of better borrowing conditions for emerging democracies is due to the behavior of multilateral agencies. They tend to bail out democracies rather than any enhanced capacity of these emerging democracies to make credible commitments.[26]

6.1   The Political Economy of the Mexican Financial Crisis

Among the 1990s emerging market crises, the Mexican crisis presents clear evidence of the interaction between politics and economics. Every six years, during every presidential election, Mexico was caught up in major economic and financial disruption.[27] As noted by an observer commenting on Mexico, "every six years, with surprising regularity, the currency collapsed every six years, shortly after each new president took office. Invariably, the exchange rate had been used to bring down inflation only to collapse again and open yet another cycle."[28]

Elections are crucial in both political and economic timing. They define both the pace and path toward democracy and the speed and depth of economic reforms with timely stabilizations *prior* to elections (but not after) resulting from opportunistic calculations. Policy-makers, particularly risk-averse to electoral uncertainty, adopted policy choices prior to the elections trying to anticipate the preferences of voters in order to maximize the chances of reelection of the ruling party. The survival strategy of the PRI (70 years in power) was partly built on a variety of policy instruments moving according to the election calendar. As stressed by Beatriz Magaloni, populist administrations during the past decades tended to increase the monetary supply in order to stimulate aggregate demand *just before* elections in order to boost consumption and to benefit the Mexican middle class. Later, during the 1980s and 1990s, the technocratic elite was similarly uninsulated from electoral processes and likewise framed policy that attempted to anticipate electoral preferences. In particular, Mexican "neoliberal" governments tried to fight macroeconomic instability by reducing inflation *just before* elections to signal technical competence against what turned out to be unpopular levels of inflation.[29]

At the same time, during the 1990s and in just a few years, Mexico has visited the greater part of the garden of delights offered by international finance. Lost in the maze-like U-turns of Wall Street expectations, the country has passed successively through the financial markets' heaven and hell. The optimism prevailing in the early 1990s was replaced in 1995 by an equally intense distrust, which in turn gave way to renewed respectability, as agents' expectations made another about-turn. If it is true, as one analyst has stated, that the financial markets are fond of stories rich with intrigues and twists of fate, the Mexican fairy tale must be among their favorites.[30]

In the 1990s, Mexico became the darling of financial markets and the shining star of Latin America in the eyes of foreign investors. Despite the collapse of the "Mexican miracle" at the end of 1994, the country remained in the glare of the camera lights of foreign investors.[31] In 2000, Mexico was awarded the precious label of investment grade by Moody's. Mexico was the only Latin American country that did not receive such a recognition during the 1980s. Within less than a decade Mexico became a land led by a young generation of technocrats, U.S.-trained economists who were free trade–oriented and decision-makers speaking and sharing the same language as their former roommates in Boston, Palo Alto or New Haven, by that time running government offices in Washington or major investment boutiques or firms in the United States.[32] During this decade, Mexico became the only Latin American country to join the closed OECD club, concluding at the same time a North American Free Trade Agreement (NAFTA) with the world's most powerful economy.

In the early 1990s Mexico emerged as the new El Dorado of international finance. Like the rest of the continent, the country was in the process of implementing far-reaching economic reforms under the guidance of a vanguard of brilliant economists. In the eyes of Wall Street, the Mexican technocratic revolution seemed irreversible. Privatizations were speeding up, generating tremendous business opportunities for investors. Above all, the country of the "plumed serpent" was about to slough its skin and undergo one of the most spectacular metamorphoses in its history. By signing the free trade agreement with yesterday's arch-fiend, the United States, Mexico seemed to have finally mended its old ways of macroeconomic populism. In Mexico City, NAFTA was seen as the magic word that would open the door from the Third World to the First World.[33] In New York it was seen as the ultimate pledge of good behavior and gave rise to a veritable Mexican gold rush. Capital inflows were in the tens of billions of dollars. In the eyes of the world, of Wall Street in particular, Mexico embodied the quintessence of the exotic new worlds that New York's financial agents were discovering, namely the emerging markets.

Yet these markets were not really novelties. Most of the emerging markets came into being at the end of the nineteenth century: Argentina in 1872, Brazil in 1877, Mexico in 1894. In fact, these markets tend to appear and to disappear along a life cycle that allows several births and deaths.[34] In this sense, the 1990s are nothing more than their latest and most spectacular resurrection. Compared with previous decades, there are nonetheless striking differences regarding both the volume of transactions and the players and investors involved. Since 1990, the emerging markets have been attracting ever-increasing capital volumes, which grew from US$40 bn. in 1990 to 113 bn. in 1993. In 1993, Mexico alone received US$30 bn.[35] In spite of all this, on December 20, 1994, the Mexican authorities announced a devaluation of the peso, which took investors by surprise and unleashed a vast wave of panic. Within a few days the capital ebbed away from the country, leaving it sucked into a major crisis. Meanwhile, the other emerging markets were swept by the undertow of the retreating floodwaters.

The 1994 Mexican crisis was not the first, nor will it be the last. Nor is it, contrary to widely held belief, the "first crisis of the twenty-first century." Kindleberger's studies clearly remind us that the history of international finance is littered with crises, panic and speculative bubbles, all equally spectacular and unexpected. A survey conducted by Barry Eichengreen reveals a singular resemblance between the Mexican crisis and the Baring crisis of 1890, so that it could more accurately be described as the "last financial crisis of the nineteenth century."[36] There is no need to go back as far as that. The Chilean monetary crisis of the early 1980s actually constitutes a notable precedent, a fact that led economist Sebastian Edwards to declare that what was most astonishing was that so many observers had been caught unawares by the turn of events in Mexico.[37] And what is more, in the short memory of the financial markets the Mexican crisis has already been relegated to history, forgotten in the turmoil buffeting Southeast Asia today and possibly Brazil tomorrow.

The purpose of this chapter is to demonstrate that the Mexican episode actually provides an excellent laboratory for exposing the interactions between political and economic timescales. The events in Mexico invite us to take a closer look at what has become a crucial factor in world affairs, namely the mechanisms driving the financial markets and their interactions with the international system. The latter, led by the United States, was forced to adjust its own reaction time to that of the financial markets. States that had long been the unquestioned masters of time are now confronted with a driving force whose scope and paroxysms are major challenges as the twentieth century draws to a close.

6.2   Mexico's New El Dorado: The Golden Decade of the 1990s

The Mexican crisis belongs to the current economic history, which changed course during the 1980s before flowing into the sea of liberalism. In the early 1980s Mexico managed to unburden itself of several decades of populist macroeconomic policies and import substitution. Across the entire continent, the winds of change began to blow in the direction of market economy. Mexico, after Chile but before Argentina, jumped on the bandwagon of reform. The country, eager to climb out of the rut of indebtedness and underdevelopment began to implement a series of deregulation measures and a privatization program, slowly at first during the presidency of Miguel de la Madrid (1982–1988), then faster starting in 1989 with the new team set in place by Carlos Salinas de Gortari (1988–1994). It took only a few years for economic growth to recover, peaking at 4 percent in 1990 before falling back again. Between 1989 and 1992 the public deficit decreased from 5.6 to 3.4 percent of GNP. Exports diversified beyond oil and registered a spectacular surge between 1980 and 1995, when their volume was multiplied by 6.4 and their value by 5.2, outstripping by far the performance of the Chilean jaguar (3 and 3.4 respectively) and almost equalling the results posted by the Asian tigers.

The acceleration of the privatization program, a single-digit inflation rate and the liberalization of international trade and the financial sector, all suggested that the country was heading for the new Cape of Good Hope represented by economic liberalism.[38] On Wall Street, Mexico's technocratic revolution was greeted with increasing enthusiasm. The Mexican economists, most of them graduates from the most prestigious North American universities, proved equal to their task and gained the confidence of the financial community.

Impatient to be admitted into the First World, the Mexican authorities embarked on a large-scale exercise in seduction, at which two ministers were particularly adept: Pedro Aspe and Jaime Serra Puche, ministers of finance and foreign trade respectively, both with doctorates from U.S. universities: Aspe from MIT and Puche from Yale.[39] They succeeded in charming the business and financial circles, which were once again eyeing Latin America in search of new opportunities, gambles and businesses. Attention became all the more focused on Mexico as, for the first time in its history and in the history of developing countries in general, the country was about to anchor its economy to the world's most advanced nation, the United States, through NAFTA. Beyond the economic impact (marginal for the United States, much larger for Mexico), NAFTA's most immediate consequence was to propel Mexico into the limelight of the media and American congressional debates.

In New York, the analysts at investment banks such as Morgan Stanley, JP Morgan and Goldman Sachs showed growing interest in these negotiations, which took on an official nature in 1992. Within a few months the New York–based financial institutions were expanding their teams of Latin America specialists. A striking example was the Salomon Brothers investment bank where John Purcell, the discoverer of South American bonanzas in general and the Mexican nugget in particular, had raised the number of analysts in his research department from one (himself) to over twenty-five.

One of the factors that triggered this strong revival of favorable expectations and the subsequent euphoria regarding Mexico on Wall Street was the privatization program launched by President Salinas de Gortari. Rumors about the privatization of Telmex, the Mexican telecommunications giant, were confirmed by the official announcement in 1989. This proved to be the starting-gun that sent investors off in the race to the Americas, which took place during the early 1990s. Privatization whetted the appetites of the New York–based investment banks. As one analyst put it, "From that moment we could not take our eyes off Mexico. We were transfixed by what was happening south of the Rio Grande. Most of us rediscovered the Americas (or, in some cases, discovered them for the first time). Privatizations were being launched throughout the whole continent. The results inspired confidence. So we went ahead and jumped in. It was a real gold rush."[40]

In addition, even though clouds were continuing to build up, in particular with regard to the ailing banking system, observers were impressed by the performances achieved. Analysts focused on the upward-headed indicators. Inflation fell sharply, from 180 in 1988 to 7 percent in 1994. Foreign currency reserves increased five-fold, rising from US$5 bn. in 1989 to 26 bn. in 1994. Finally, foreign debt was reduced considerably, declining between 1986 and 1994 from 400 to 200 percent of exports. The new-found confidence in Mexico had a direct impact on the financial markets: the country risk (spread between U.S. Treasury bills and Tesobonos) and the exchange risk (spread between Cetes and Tesobonos)[41] recorded by New York investment banks declined simultaneously, while the Mexican stock market was caught in an unprecedented flurry of activity.

In the space of a few years, huge capital flows worth tens of billions of dollars entered the country. During the "lost decade" net capital flows had abruptly dried up as a result of the debt crisis, tumbling from a level of 6 percent of overall Latin American GNP to close to zero in 1983. By 1994 investment flows had resumed, even surpassing the former level of 6 percent of combined GNP. Of all the countries then listed on the prompter screens in New York dealing rooms Mexico emerged as the uncontested champion in its category. Between 1987 and the peak year of 1994, the performance index measured by the *Financial Times* and Standard & Poor's, the barometer of international investors' enthusiasm, reached all-time highs, soaring from US$100 to 2,500. All told, between 1990 and 1994 Mexico attracted a total of over US$100 bn., over 30 bn. of which was invested in a single year (1993), an amount corresponding to 8 percent of that year's GDP. For example, Salomon Brothers alone invested over US$15 bn. in Mexico.

6.3   Chronicle of a Crisis Foretold: Financial Markets Forward-Looking Myopia

The resumption of capital flows to Mexico and Latin America was nonetheless proving problematic. New players, seeking increasingly short-term returns, entered the arena.

In the early 1990s a significant shift in the nature of investment flows to the emerging countries was taking place.[42] Capital flows of public origin were drying up while private capital movements were increasing. Given the low level of American interest rates and the sluggish growth in the OECD countries, nonbank institutional investors, seeking more profitable investment opportunities on the bond and equity markets, were rushing into the new emerging markets.[43] In 1994, the number of equity funds dealing in Latin America exceeded 150. These equity portfolio flows alone represented 40 percent of overall foreign investment. After a period of net capital withdrawals, Latin America again experienced net portfolio investment inflows, which, between 1990 and 1994, reached an annual average of US$26 bn., while between 1983 and 1989 net outflows had amounted to an annual average of US$1.2 bn. For

Mexico, these massive capital inflows were all the more necessary as the low domestic savings ratio was not sufficient to boost economic development. The downside of such substantial inflows was a widening current-account deficit fuelled by dangerously reversible and volatile portfolio investments. During 1994 public short-term debt was rising, and not only was 70 to 80 percent of this debt held by nonresidents, but a substantial share was scheduled to be indexed on the dollar within the year. These were the famous Tesobonos dubbed *"malditos bonos"*[44] by Arturo Porzecanski, ING Barings Latin America economist.

Thus all the elements of a currency crisis were brought together. In late 1994 Wall Street analysts suddenly became aware that the fundamentals had seriously deteriorated: the 1994 current-account deficit was close to 8 percent of GDP (against 3 percent in 1990), foreign currency reserves had fallen sharply, from US$29 bn. in February to 7 bn. in December.[45] Above all, as a number of economists had repeatedly been warning since March, the peso appeared to be dangerously overvalued. But their voices, not in harmony with the rest, were immediately drowned out in the general chorus of praise. In an article published in spring 1994, Rudiger Dornbusch and Alejandro Werner called attention to the fact that Mexico was suffering from sluggish economic growth for which the only plausible explanation was the appreciation of the real effective exchange rate by 20–25 percent between 1990 and 1994.[46] Devaluation was inevitable. When it finally occurred it was far too late: on December 20, 1994 the Mexican government announced a devaluation of 15 percent. But, far from reassuring investors, this decision heightened their anxiety and unleashed a wave of distrust, which spread through all the emerging markets. This phenomenon was called the Tequila effect. The currency crisis was rapidly turning into a liquidity crisis. In the Mexican Treasury bill market, over US$13 bn. came to maturity early in 1995, including the equivalent of some US$10 bn. in Tesobonos, the peso value of which was increasing steadily as the Mexican currency depreciated. Despite support from the United States, announced as early as January 11, 1995, doubts spread across the whole of Latin America (e.g., the Brazilian stock market registered a 25 percent decline between January and February 1995). All in all the peso lost more than 40 percent of its value between December 1994 and February 1995.

6.4   The Interactions Between Economic and Political Timescales

The Mexican crisis of 1994 occurred at a point in time when political and economic currents flowed together and mingled to cause trouble.[47]

For Mexico, 1994 was a paradoxical year. With NAFTA coming into force on January 1 and the outbreak of the crisis on December 20, it was a year marked by the country's long-desired entry into the First World— and by its equally sudden exit. It illustrates the extreme volatility of the financial markets, and even more the speed and frequency with which country-risk assessments can reverse. The chronology of events in that "crazy year" is especially revealing of the extent to which the interactions of economic and political trends had contributed to generate the crisis.

In February, the increase in the U.S. Fed Funds rate sparked a drop in the bond market. For Mexico, the consequences were instantaneous: the service on its foreign debt rose, while its capital holdings dwindled. The Chiapas unrest and the reversal of American monetary policy provoked the first about-turn in Mexico's country-risk assessment. The bond market plunged by 15 percent and the stock market by 20 percent. The assassination on March 23 of presidential candidate Luis Donaldo Colosio added to the already prevailing distrust surrounding the Mexican currency. In New York, analysts and investors alike discovered to their consternation that the events in the Americas were still unpredictable. Capital flight accelerated, intensifying pressure on the peso, which at that point had depreciated by almost 10 percent compared with the beginning of the year.

In a context of increasing political uncertainty, the Mexican authorities chose to support their currency and delved deeply into the reserves that had been carefully built up during the years of euphoria. As a result, reserves shrank over the course of the year by some US$19 bn. In President Salinas' view devaluation was out of the question as the Mexican government had made monetary stability the cornerstone of its macroeconomic policy's credibility. Moreover, NAFTA appeared to be providing all-in insurance coverage after Mexico's partners had granted the country a swap agreement worth nearly US$7 bn. So what was there to be alarmed about? After all, just a few days earlier, Mexico had made its entry into the closed circle of industrialized countries by becoming a member of the prestigious, liberal OECD.

However, the political calendar again put an end to this slightly undermined confidence. In Mexico, the timing of the presidential elections imposes a syncopated rhythm on the country's politics. For not only do these elections drag the political system along in their wake, they also generate most of the heart attacks that regularly strike the Mexican economy. Presidential elections often coincide with periods of high monetary instability, as evidenced by the devaluations in the 1970s and 1980s—that still linger in the minds of the Mexican leaders. Thus the prospect of extremely tough elections on August 21 explains the contradiction between the different authorities and the growing tensions among the president, the central bank and the ministry of finance regarding the strategy to adopt. President Salinas rejected an over-stringent monetary policy that would have throttled growth. The government chose to issue short-term Treasury notes indexed on the dollar but payable in pesos (Tesobonos) to refinance its peso-denominated short-term debts (Cetes). With Ernesto Zedillo's victory in August the country breathed a sigh of relief. Portfolio investments, in the form of massive purchases of Tesebonos by nonresidents, intensified to such an extent that by July the value outstanding exceeded the country's foreign currency reserves.

Autumn brought a new wave of concern to Wall Street fuelled by the assassination of Ruiz Massieu, the secretary general of the ruling party (PRI), and the resignation of his brother, incumbent minister of justice. At the same time, the Chiapas unrest gained ground, while a further tightening of U.S. monetary policy decided on November 15 raised the Fed Funds target rate by another 75 basis points. Moreover, until the outbreak of the crisis, the contraction of the currency reserves had been deliberately concealed from New York–based investors. The Mexican Central Bank tried to buy time by delaying the publication of its key figures, in an attempt to prevent a speculative attack during the preelection period. Currency reserves, which still amounted to US$17 bn. in autumn, continued to dwindle, and in the period from December 10–15 they shrank from 12 to 8 bn. dollars. It became clear that devaluation was inevitable. On December 19, an initial devaluation of 15 percent was announced. The following day the peso came under attack, triggering a further fall in reserves of 5 bn. dollars. On December 22, the central bank had to admit that the situation was critical. The peso was allowed to float freely, which led to a rapid decline. Wall Street's Mexican dream turned into a nightmare in the space of a few weeks. The rating agencies downgraded Mexico's long- and short-term debt.

With a few notable exceptions, Wall Street investors were caught unawares. But, after all, surprise is at the heart of all financial crises, which are unpredictable in essence, subject to contingencies and what economist Charles Kindleberger has described as the irrationality of the markets, whose movements are always jerky, marked by sudden fits and starts, which give them a see-saw pattern, with each vertical ascent followed by an equally steep descent. Shortly after the emergence of the Mexican crisis, Kindleberger described it in the following terms: "like pretty women: hard to define, but recognizable when encountered."[48]

Certain analysts, like Arturo Porzecanski from ING Barings, earned considerable glory for having expressed concern about the sustainability of Mexico's exchange rate policy early in December 1994.[49] On December 15, five days before the devaluation, Stefano Natella, the person in charge of emerging markets with Crédit Suisse First Boston, advised his clients to transfer their Mexican investments to Brazil.[50] But the mainstream surveys continued to express an unbridled optimism, like that of John Pelosky of Morgan Stanley & Co. who, in a note dated December 2, asserted, "of all the Latin American markets, Mexico is still the favourite." As the *Wall Street Journal* reported, whether it was Bankers Trust, Bear Stearns, Chase Manhattan, Goldman Sachs or Smith Barney, the great majority of analysts and banks described the Mexican situation throughout 1994 in rose-colored terms. Some were even urging for a credit rating upgrade less than a few weeks before the crisis, for example JP Morgan, Chemical Bank or Swiss Bank Corporation in October, November and December 1994 respectively.[51] As stressed by a Bear Stearns report of November 1994, "we expect a strengthening of the peso in the coming months, creating very high dollar returns on Cetes." Just a few weeks earlier JP Morgan stated also in an enthusiastic report "we view Mexico as investment-grade risk. We do not regard Mexico debt to have predominantly speculative characteristics."[52]

After the Madrid meeting of the IMF and the World Bank in September, the Mexican authorities, led by Pedro Aspe, scheduled an increasing number of meetings to reassure investors, occasionally meeting them one-on-one, as in the case of the portfolio managers of Fidelity, Morgan Stanley Asset Management, Scudder Stevens and Clark and Oppenheimer & Co.[53] For the majority of the experts, a devaluation appeared all the more unlikely as the cost was seen as extremely high and, in any case, unsustainable for Mexico.

A few analysts suffered unenviable fates, like John Purcell, a star of the New York financial scene, who had been in charge of Latin America for Salomon Brothers but was asked to retire shortly after the crisis.[54] In one of his last reports, dated November 22, 1994, he emphasized, "the probability of a devaluation [was] practically nil." He had, in fact, gone to Mexico in November to confirm his expectations and had been reassured by the Mexican authorities. Moreover, projections based on the information and data provided by the Mexicans gave no cause for alarm. The figure disclosed for currency reserves seemed sufficient to withstand any speculative attacks. However, tremendous losses accumulated in just a few hours, climbing rapidly to US$10 bn. in the first few days and finally exceeding 32 bn.

As Sachs, Tornell and Velasco have emphasized, there can be no single explanation for the crisis. Neither can it be ascribed to a mere market correction reacting to poor economic fundamentals, nor is it possible to assert that it represents nothing more than a purely speculative attack on an overvalued currency. Both these hypotheses fail to adequately account for the forces behind the crisis. Economic fundamentals were not wholly unsustainable. The country was conducting a tight fiscal policy and its debt ratios were relatively low by international standards. The explanation of the crisis as a mere speculative attack is also insufficient. In particular it shrugs off the fact that economic agents were not expecting the crisis and therefore did not charge a higher risk premium or raise interest rates before December 1994. This point is confirmed by an analysis of the interest rates on Cetes and Tesobonos, the differential between the two rates being an excellent indicator of an expected devaluation. The spread increased after the assassination in March 1994, then shrank again after Zedillo's victory in August, before remaining more or less constant until December.

International media coverage also confirms that operators were not expecting a peso crisis. Before December 1994, hardly any articles published in the *Financial Times*, the *Wall Street Journal*, or the *New York Times* mentioned the Tesobonos problem. The number of articles expressing concern about the situation climbed from six to forty-six between December and January, whereas throughout 1994 the press had generally reflected an optimistic outlook for Mexico. Over the course of that year financial institutions in New York had continued to give Mexico's macro-economic policy positive ratings: a balanced budget, disinflation and a reduction in the debt interest payments/export earnings ratio. Likewise, governments and international monetary authorities, including the IMF, the Fed, the French Finance Ministry and the American Treasury Department, had remained surprisingly placid in their assessment of Mexico's sovereign risk. The IMF internal report clearly evidences IMF's shortcomings in the follow-up of the Mexican crisis. A number of other reports, including those of the Senate Banking Committee and, in February 1996, the House Finance Committee highlight the conciliatory attitude adopted by the U.S. authorities toward Mexico, at a time when the situation required a firmer stance. The explanation and reasons put forward retrospectively for the inadequate assessment of Mexican risk were: the desire not to endanger NAFTA, the fragility of a partner in the midst of an election period and the lack of reliable statistics.[55]

The case of Mexico shows the importance of managing the time factor. In finance (as in politics), knowing when to enter and exit and recognizing the right moment for engagement and disengagement are the beginning and end of wisdom. "Timing," says one Parisian economist, "is essential. There are two ways to make money: either you are better informed and get in before everyone else, or you position yourself in the trough of the wave just after a turnaround."[56]

The way the Mexican authorities handled the crisis is particularly revealing of the difficulty of managing the time factor when dealing with swiftly reacting markets. It is worth recalling that the crisis struck at a politically sensitive moment: December 1994 was the month of presidential changeover. Zedillo's new team was gradually taking office while Salinas and Aspe were packing their bags. The situation was much like the period after Lloyd Bentsen's departure as secretary of the U.S. Treasury and his effective replacement by Robert Rubin (a former Wall Street financier), which left a temporary void at the helm of the country's monetary management. Meanwhile Zedillo had just appointed Serra Puche, the architect of NAFTA and former trade minister, to succeed Pedro Aspe as finance minister. The new team undertook an audit of the country's financial situation in November. When they took over the reins in December, they had hardly had any time to assess the gravity of the situation. "When we arrived," explained Antonio Argulles, the then head of Serra Puche's cabinet, to the *Wall Street Journal*, "six of the ministry's principal directors had already left office. We spent the first few weeks looking for the light switches and the toilets." Thus precious time was lost during the transfer of power from a team who had great experience in dealing with investors to one more acquainted with the dynamics of international trade.

In addition, the date chosen to announce the devaluation—early in the week (a Tuesday) and on the eve of the Christmas holidays—was ill-timed. The announcement took everyone by surprise, as the majority of Wall Street financiers were either on vacation or preparing to leave. By devaluing on a Tuesday (rather than a Friday), the markets had three days to overreact without the possibility of closing the stock exchange. By comparison, when Colosio was assassinated on March 23 (a Wednesday), Pedro Aspe, the incumbent minister of finance who had great experience in dealing with investors, immediately ordered that a national day of mourning be observed the following day so as to stifle rumors and freeze transactions. At the same time his team, headed by Jose Angel Gurria, hastened to counter any overreaction by negotiating a US$6 bn. swap deal with the U.S. Treasury, a measure that had an immediately calming effect on investors. Moreover, this gave Aspe more time to use his Wall Street connections over the weekend in order to restore credibility and confidence in his economic policy. Conversely, when tensions showed up on the market in December, a month marked by startling declarations by the Zapatistas, Jaime Serra Puche held discussions with Mexican businessmen on December 12 and with Wall Street investors on December 19. As a result, this approach triggered a two-fold wave of distrust. The loss of credibility and confidence in Mexican institutions was rapid as the asymmetries of information were perceived as relatively substantial by American investors.[57]

A further source of dysfunction was that several different authorities were interfering in the handling of the crisis, especially given the feud prevailing within the Mexican political *camarillas* and among the different authorities, including the presidency, the finance ministry and the central bank.[58] Even within a single ministry (finance) conflicts among the various directors concerning the minister's handling of the crisis— one of the directors, Guillermo Ortiz, who was later to become minister of finance, had been privately calling for a devaluation since late 1993—was a reflection of the political infighting within the government. In March 1995 the Mexicans put a stop to this deplorable discord and introduced a much stricter communications policy, making Alejandro Valenzuela the sole spokesman for the ministry, in charge of providing the international financial markets with regular press releases. As a result, for a year or so a statement was released by Valenzuela every Wednesday between 2 and 3 p.m. local time (Wall Street closing time). The choice of Wednesday allowed the Mexican authorities to keep an eye on the markets' behavior on Monday and Tuesday and to observe their reaction on Thursday and Friday.

One of the most striking features of the Mexican episode was the suddenness with which assets depreciated. Unlike what happened between 1982 and 1989, when a series of official negotiations with the creditors of the London Club had taken place following Mexico's declaration of default in 1982, this crisis precluded a negotiated settlement. In 1994–1995 both the speed with which this crisis unfolded and the way in which it was brought under control were incomparably faster: in less than three months, that is from the end of December to the beginning of March, the Mexican, American and international authorities had to take action to prevent contagion. Speed was of the essence, and primarily the speed with which the governments and international monetary authorities had to respond to a driving force whose development and speed were dictated by the financial markets.

Mexico and the United States immediately started negotiations aimed at stemming the crisis without the need of resorting to IMF therapy, at least in the early stages. However, as early as December 28–29, IMF officials arrived in Mexico to assess the situation. Another week went by before Mexico finally yielded to pressure from Wall Street investors and agreed to officially call on the IMF. Meanwhile the Mexican government, with the new Finance Minister Guillermo Ortiz in the lead as of January 5, made several trips to New York in order to reassure a financial community that had lost all confidence in the country, and a series of austerity programs were launched and highly publicized. The first measures announced on January 3 did not entirely convince Wall Street, but a second package including more drastic measures, disclosed on March 9, was accorded greater credibility.

An initial rescue plan, calling for US$40 bn. in U.S. aid, was prepared and announced by Clinton on January 13, less than a month after the beginning of the crisis. In the first stage, the plan met with favorable reactions from both Republicans and Democrats, but soon/rapidly an opposition movement began to build up, particularly among liberal Democrats with close ties to the unions and among Republicans who had supported Ross Perot's presidential campaign. This opposition was broadly identical to the coalition that had campaigned against the signature of NAFTA a few years earlier, and finally took the edge of the constant efforts of Robert Rubin and Alan Greenspan, the secretary of the treasury and chairman of the federal reserve, respectively. With Congressional hostility mounting,[59] Clinton was obliged to halve the amount so as to be able to push the rescue package through by mere presidential decree. Furthermore, in contrast to what had happened in 1982, commercial banks, which had been expected to come up with some US$3 bn., withdrew from the negotiations.[60]

Hence the necessity to find other sources of funding. An additional US$30 bn. in the form of special exceptional loans could be negotiated with the international monetary authorities, thus completing the safety net. The IMF in particular became fully involved and sent a second team of experts to Mexico City.[61] In less than two weeks the negotiations between IMF experts and the Mexican authorities resulted in a "turnkey" adjustment program that was ready at the beginning of February and adopted within barely three days by the Board of Directors hard pressed by the overreacting financial markets. Several countries, primarily European (Belgium, Germany, the Netherlands, Norway, Switzerland and the United Kingdom, which together account for 25 percent of IMF funds), showed their discontent at being presented with a *fait accompli* by the United States by abstaining at the board meeting on February 1. It was not until the G-7 summit in Toronto on

February 3–4 that the European finance ministers showed their solidarity with the United States, ostensibly at least. As one of the main negotiators stated, "we have been living with a gun to our heads for the last several weeks, keeping a close watch on the financial markets which continued to surge and which we were nevertheless supposed to outpace."[62]

At the end of these nonstop negotiations, Clinton finally announced the definitive rescue plan. All in all, some US$50 bn. were to be committed to rescuing Mexico. By comparison, the aid granted to Thailand in August 1997 by the IMF and the Asian countries, with Japan in the lead, amounted to 16 bn., that is only one-third.[63] The support given to Mexico was also more substantial than that granted to Indonesia in October 1997 (US$30 bn.). Out of the nearly US$50 bn., the American government secured over 20 bn. in the form of loans, guarantees and swaps, 18 bn. were supplied by the IMF and 10 bn. by the G-10 via the Bank for International Settlements. In its session held in June 1995 in Halifax, the IMF decided to double its liquid funds and to create an emergency fund in order to avoid such crises in the future. In the end, Mexico used only part of this aid (12.5 bn.) and reimbursed the whole amount three years ahead of schedule by raising funds on the international markets in January 1997.

One of the consequences of the Mexican crisis has been the introduction within the international monetary authorities of procedures that make it possible to speed up decision-making. Thus the IMF's decision-making process was significantly reshaped, and an emergency financing procedure aimed at reducing delays was established. On average the time between the conclusion of an IMF field mission and the submission of its report to the Board of Directors, the highest decision-making level of the IMF, ranged from 60 to 90 days. By the time of the Thai crisis, the lag had been reduced to less than 20 days.[64] However, the rapidity with which the crisis spread to the rest of Southeast Asia revealed the limits of the mechanisms put in place. Nevertheless this example illustrates the race that states and markets are having to run, with the former forced to adjust their reaction time to the speed at which turbulence can spread through the money market.

The Mexican crisis is still lingering on in the minds of many analysts and economists. It has become the yardstick by which future stock market digressions will be measured, as shown by the parallels—be they justified or not—drawn during the Asian currency crisis in the summer and autumn of 1997.

Much has been written about the Mexican crisis in an attempt to unravel the intricacies of its causes and consequences. These publications demonstrate the absolute necessity of keeping an increasingly watchful eye not only on the volume of the debt, but even more so on its structure, along with other factors and warning signals such as the increase in domestic lending or the rise in foreign interest rates.[65] They further underline the short-term investment approach prevailing in the emerging markets, as evidenced by the concentration of short-term debt in the form of Mexico's Cetes and Tesobonos, which came to maturity early in 1995. In total, 29 mn. dollar-indexed Tesobonos matured in 1995, including over 10 bn. during the first quarter, while the central bank saw its foreign currency reserves plummeting by 80 percent in just a few months. Through its own inaction Mexico thus found itself caught in the web of market expectations, with barely US$5 bn. in reserves while the maturities due at the beginning of 1995 alone were worth more than twice that amount. This situation led the international monetary authorities and economists to reconsider the famous Tobin tax on international transactions, in order to restrict and stem the seesaw movements on the financial markets especially on the foreign exchange markets, which are estimated at over US$1.2 tn. a day.

This crisis also confirms the existence of information asymmetries regarding the emerging markets: the IMF has pointed out that, from November 30 to December 19, that is during the three weeks preceding the peso's devaluation, withdrawals by foreign investors on the Mexican market amounted to only US$320 mn. out of total withdrawals of over US$2.8 bn.; moreover, withdrawals by foreign investors did not really reach major proportions until February 1995, over two months after the devaluation.[66] Following the IMF report, which presented incriminating evidence of the capital flight on the part of Mexican residents, econometric studies conducted by Jeffrey Frankel and Sergio Schmulker confirmed the existence of such asymmetries. Based on the figures of three Mexican investment funds, the studies clearly show that these funds withdrew relatively large sums even before the devaluation, a fact suggesting that they were better informed than anyone else.

According to later works published by the same authors outlining the prime causes of this mimetic crisis, the latter originated from the community of investors operating in Mexico and spread to Wall Street where the backlash was amplified, spreading to all the emerging markets. Moreover, the shock wave operated selectively, with a greater impact on countries showing fairly poor economic fundamentals and performances. This has meant that the Philippines' high debt/exports ratio made it a vulnerable prey, even though it is a great distance from Mexico, while a country such as Chile, although much closer to the epicenter of the crisis, was only marginally hit due to its good economic performance. Two channels of transmission are usually put forward by economists.[67] The first is foreign trade, but the analysis of the Mexican crisis puts this mechanism in quite a different light. True, it provides an explanation for the transmission to countries such as Brazil and Argentina, which have substantial trade with Mexico, but how can it be explained that countries such as Thailand or Malaysia that had only modest commercial ties with Mexico were shaken by the Mexican crisis? Attention, therefore, has also been paid to the second transmission mechanism, which finds its roots in macroeconomic similarities between countries: investors made their choice among the emerging economies and weighted their portfolios according to the economic fundamentals, seeking to pull out of the countries showing poor or unsustainable economic performance.[68]

The explanation of contagion via assessment of fundamentals can be coupled with another explanation putting forward the follow-my-leader behavior of operators, which can give rise to self-fulfilling prophecies. Given on the one hand the high cost of information and on the other the facility with which portfolios can be diversified, investors tend to bring about wide swings from one country to the other. This mimetic behavior was particularly visible in the case of Mexico, where noise traders and rational investors alike largely acted together, which does much to explain the selective contagion affecting Argentina, Brazil and Venezuela, rather than Chile or Colombia. In Asia, the First Philippine Fund saw its value fall by 28 percent, comparable to the drop that occurred in Argentina, while other countries such as Indonesia, Pakistan, Taiwan and Vietnam also had to bear the brunt of the shock wave. Such mechanisms of mimetic dissemination could be observed again several years later, when the Southeast Asian currencies came under attack in the summer of 1997.

This mimetic behavior is not irrational in itself. Operators individually tend to interpret other operators' purchase and sale orders as evidence of information held by the latter, which is presumed to be valid. This attitude can lead to problems when the mimetic behavior snowballs because operators instantaneously imitate the bullish or bearish conduct of those they are watching. In these circumstances, what is at stake is not the credibility or pertinence of the fundamental economic information as such but, as stated by a New York financier, the ability to forecast as well as possible, that is, earlier than anybody else, the long-term trend of the market and stick to it. In the Mexican case the loss of confidence had been quickly passed on to the market operators as a whole with the dynamics of suspicion spreading throughout the emerging markets. With regard to the forces behind prices, they are by no means reducible to a simple mechanical effect of the economic fundamentals' interaction. According to André Orléan price formation is not a mere reflection of objective scarcity, it also involves collective judgment on the part of the financial community in its quality as an instrumental entity, driven by interests and beliefs that are more or less justified.[69]

In this sense the Mexican crisis is a striking example of market failure: "Nobody saw the crisis coming, because nobody wanted to see it coming," commented a Wall Street economist.[70] In a report to the Group of Thirty; Kaufman noted that although it can be presumed that analysts had been aware that Mexico's fundamentals were deteriorating and, in particular, that the foreign currency reserves held by the central bank were melting away, there was no reversal of expectations. "Every company wants to do business in the emerging markets because of the high margins. Each analyst thus became a direct participant in the financial game. They proved to be remarkably restrained when it came to highlighting problems. Admittedly, they were also subjected to increased pressure from sales managers and corporate finance executives who encouraged them to come up with ideas for selling more rather than to interrupt the sales."[71]

A New York analyst adds that it was easy to convince many economists not to exhibit their skepticism publicly. At that time, expressing a negative opinion on Mexico was like wanting to kill the goose that lays the golden eggs. Who would have dared commit such an offence at a time when Wall Street's big shots, much more credible and heeded, were saying the exact opposite? "The wisest move, therefore, was to hold one's tongue and to drift along with the tide, even though it was clear to everyone that there was a precipitous fall in the offing."[72] As stressed by Sebastian Edwards, "in spite of the divergence between policy actions and economic results, the Mexican reforms were consistently praised by the media, financial experts, academics and the multilaterals—including the World Bank and the International Monetary Fund—as a major success."

Financial analysts among others played a key role in the invention of the Mexican miracle, their own optimistic beliefs helping to generate an asset price boom, reassuring in turn the believers in the accuracy of their analysis and the reality of the miracle. As argued by Paul Krugman, these optimistic beliefs, self-fulfilling and characteristic of financial bubbles, represented a "leap faith, rather than a conclusion based on hard evidence."[73]

The Mexican crisis induced investment banks and financial institutions to reassess their country-risk benchmarks. Traditionally two country-risk approaches have been used: the first, based on a qualitative assessment by a specialist on the specific country/economy; the second based on a rating according to a set scale, within which a grading is awarded to each of the emerging markets. In the wake of the Mexican crisis both methods were revised as they were sometimes regarded as being somewhat too subjective or biased depending on the criteria and correlations. Following the example set by New York investment banks such as JP Morgan or Santander, a New York–based Spanish bank that is currently one of the main operators in Latin America, European banks and credit insurance organizations, such as France's Caisse des Dépôts et Consignations and COFACE, strove to bolster their country-risk teams (in some cases by calling in Latin American consultants) and to reshape their methods and analysis criteria. The Caisse des Dépôts et Consignations (CDC) increased its country-risk/emerging markets team and readjusted its risk scale, while at the same time fine-tuning its classifications. Onsimilar lines, COFACE calculated a financial crisis index for the sixteen countries it was dealing with, taking into account a string of indices assessing structural vulnerability, market confidence and currency appreciation.

On an international level, efforts were made to define more suitable warning signs so as to prevent and be prepared for crises. Following the example set by the investment banks, the IMF launched in 1996 a series of indicators and a global standard—the Special Data Dissemination Standard (SDDS) that became operational in 1998—in the level of domestic and foreign reserves, real exchange rate, domestic lending (both private and public sector), inflation, trade balance, money supply growth, budget deficit and GDP growth, all indicators that are to be taken into account by economists in weighting and prospect models aimed at detecting the critical points. For their part, the Mexican authorities have made an effort to improve the communication of information and the reliability of their statistics, which the IMF and the international monetary authorities had recommended in the wake of the crisis. When the Mexican bubble burst in December 1994 the only figures available to investors and financial operators dated back to June, when Mexico still enjoyed a comfortable cushion of US$17 bn. (whereas in December only US$6 bn. remained). In 1995, *The Economist* carried out a rating of the reliability of statistics given out by governments.[74] In this rating, dated March 4, Mexico was rewarded for its efforts: whereas the previous December it had been among the last five, Mexico was now ranked sixth out of some forty emerging markets, just behind Taiwan,

South Korea, Argentina and Chile (placed first when the criteria include, apart from reliability, the precision of statistics).

Lack of transparency, being identified as one of the major causes of the Mexican crisis and contagion effect, the purpose of all IMF and Mexico efforts is to disseminate more timely and accurate data. With more high-quality information available, investors are expected to withdraw from some emerging countries sooner ending the speculative bubble risks and increasing the efficiency of their investments.[75] These attempts at better forecasting are also based on the postulate that crises can be explained first and foremost by economic fundamentals that are subjected to market corrections, but do not take into account the mimetic dissemination of self-fulfilling prophecies. In this case a reversal of expectations cannot be traced back or predicted through mere economic analysis: a better approach requires a combination of economic factors with the cognitive regimes of the financial markets.

Unfortunately, recent research suggests that these efforts to consolidate a global dissemination standard of economic data are associated with low benefits for the SDDS members and with quite high real and potential costs. Based on 61 surveys of fund managers between May and November 2000, research indicated that financial market respondents have a high concern for availability of information on emerging markets. The average score was 2.8 on a scale ranging from "extremely concerned" (=1) to "not at all concerned" (=5) when asked about the availability and quality of information. But when fund managers were asked to report and evaluate how IMF's SDDS improve their information access, 55 percent of the respondents indicated that they were "not at all aware" of the existence of the SDDS initiative and 29 percent labeled themselves as being "vaguely aware." Clearly SDDS efforts are not considered as major sources of information for fund managers, the most popular being brokerage houses like Merrill Lynch, Chase and Morgan Stanley ($n = 28$), the international financial press like the *Financial Times* and *The Economist* ($n = 20$), news providers like Bloomberg and Reuters ($n = 19$) and government agencies ($n = 16$), the IMF and the World Bank being mentioned not more than seven times out of 61 respondents.[76] (See table 6.1.)

6.5   From the Tequila Effect to the Sangrita Effect: The Speed of Financial Recoveries

In retrospect, the most striking aspect of the crisis is the remarkable recovery staged by Mexico in financial and economic terms.[77] Boosted

Table 6.1 IMF global standard efforts since Mexico: an empirical evaluation by fund managers (*n* = 61)

	Total number of respondents	Percentage of respondents
I use IMF's SDDS database as a key source of country-specific information	1	1.60
I use the IMF's SDDS database as a means of checking the accurary of country-specific information from other sources	2	3.30
I do not use the IMF's SDDS database directly, countries is of higher quality than nonsubscribers	6	9.80
All else equal, I would attach smaller risk premia to nations that are subscribers to the SDDS	4	6.60
The SDDS plays no role in my decisions	39	63.90
Not applicable/no response	9	14.80

Source: Based on Layna Mosley, *Global Capital and National Governments*, Cambridge, Mass., Cambridge University Press, 2003; and "Attempting Global Standards: National Governments, International Finance, and the IMF's Data Regime," *Review of International Political Economy*, May 2003 (forthcoming).

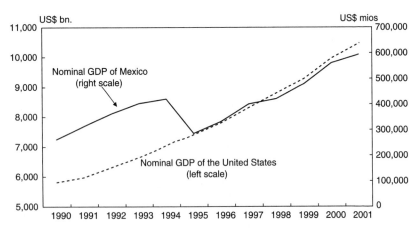

Graph 6.1 The synchronized economies: Mexico and the United States during the 1990s. *Source*: Datastream, 2001.

by U.S. growth, this recovery has been clearly driven by the increasing synchronization of U.S. and Mexico business cycles during the 1990s (see graph 6.1). Mexico's economy recovered quickly from the peso crisis and since 1996 the country experienced on average a 5.5 percent per year growth rate of GDP. This quick recovery is one of the main differences in comparison with the 1982 crisis, when the country was subsequently shunned by international investors for almost seven years. After the 1994 crisis, it took barely seven months for Mexico to integrate itself back into the financial markets, albeit at a very high cost.

During the 1990s, despite the mid-decade financial crisis, Mexico remained one of the most attractive countries for investors. Since 1994, the country has received nearly an annual average of US$12 bn. in FDI. Between 1994 and 2000, Mexico attracted a total amount of US$85 bn. in FDI, making it one of the top three FDI recipients among emerging markets. In 2001, because of the slowdown of FDI in Brazil and the amount paid by Citigroup for Banamex, Mexico overtook Brazil as the major FDI destination in Latin America. The interest of foreign investors in Mexico can also be underlined with a more micro focus. Each year, for example, the U.S. consulting firm AT Kearney conducts a large survey, the *Foreign Direct Investment Confidence Index*. The purpose is to measure the degree of emerging country attractiveness according to a qualitative questionnaire addressed to 1000 CEOs and CFOs from the world's largest institutions in 35 countries. In the 2001 survey, European managers were quite well represented, with 44 percent of total respondents (29 percent of other respondents were from U.S. companies). According to this survey, in 2001 Mexico is ranked number three as preferred emerging market, just behind China and Brazil. The absolute position of Mexico improved compared to the previous year as Mexico moved from the seventh to fifth rank as the world's most attractive country for investment.[78]

In fact as early as mid-August 1995 and throughout 1996, the banks in New York and London (Bankers Trust, Barings, Flemings, Salomon or Goldman Sachs, to mention just a few) trumpeted Mexico's return to the financial markets. Very quickly, the country was again in a position to issue Euro bonds for considerable amounts (US$4.8 bn. in 1995, 2.7 bn. for the first half of 1996 alone), and with increasingly longer maturities. Thus the Sangrita effect superseded the 1994 Tequilazo, softening the blow of the December 1994 fiasco. Although it did not completely restore the state of the Mexican economy, this revival still resulted in a return of foreign investors, wary at first, but increasingly confident as the country returned to economic growth (5.1 percent in 1996 against a fall in GDP of 6.2 percent in 1995). The *Financial Times*/Standard & Poor's index again doubled between 1995 and 1997, rising from US$700 to 1,500. Admittedly, it is still a long way from the record-high levels reached just before the 1994 crisis (over US$2,500, i.e. 25 times more than in 1987 when the index was introduced).

Nevertheless investors had renewed faith in this "Bravo New World" that Mexico had become once again in their view.[79]

In New York, many firms revised upwards their expectations, following the example of Deutsche Morgan Grenfell, Salomon Brothers, CS First Boston, Morgan Stanley and of rating agencies such as Standard & Poor's.[80] What is more, the recent acquisitions made by HSBC Holdings and Banco Santander in Brazil confirm the growing attraction exerted by the Latin American markets since the Mexican crisis. By purchasing Baremindus in May 1997 (for a price of almost US$1 bn.) and Banco Noroeste in August 1997 (US$500 mn.) respectively, these two banks bear out the increasing interest of foreign financial institutions in markets that are not yet over-banked. All in all, a group like Emilio Botin's Banco Santander has invested over US$3.7 bn. in this region, becoming in this way one of the main private banks not only in Spain but also in Argentina with its Latin American staff equalling its workforce in the Iberian Peninsula, in the same way as its Spanish competitor, Banco Bilbao Vizcaya. Apart from these acquisitions, the banks have further boosted their teams of analysts specializing in Latin America. In August 1997, for example, HSBC Markets recruited a new chief economist for Latin America in the person of Gary Newmann (originally from HSBC James Capel Mexico).

Another confirmation of Mexico's quick return to favor came at the annual meeting of the Inter-American Development Bank held in Barcelona in March 1997 where specialists from all over the world sang the praises of the country's performances, In a survey covering a panel of 1,000 investors, companies, financial institutions and banks, carried out by *Fortune* on behalf of the Bank of Boston,[81] over 80 percent of the managers questioned declared that they were more confident in and optimistic about the region than they had been five years earlier. Better still: 38 percent of these investors had particularly favorable expectations regarding Mexico, much better than for Brazil (19 percent), Argentina (13 percent) and even Chile (16 percent). The Institute of International Finance, a U.S. think-tank based in Washington, confirmed Mexico's returning strength: with FDI totaling US$7 bn. in 1996, Mexico was just behind Brazil (US$8 bn. FDI in 1996) but its progression was far more spectacular (almost 3 percent as a share of GDP between 1995 and 1996 against 1 percent for Brazil). Investors were even more convinced of this revival after the elections on July 6, 1997, when the Mexico stock exchange celebrated the country's entry into the era of democracy surging by more than 2 percent. The opposition was largely expected to win, but the moderation of the tone adopted after the election was in stark contrast to the rhetorical violence that had prevailed during the particularly bitter campaign. Still, the opposition's victory was unanimously greeted by all on all sides, ranging from the international financial community, the Mexican business circles and the employers' groupings.

On March 7, 2000, not suprisingly, Mexico reached the Moody's investment-grade status becoming, from a financial market point of view and rating agencies, a safe haven comparable to Chile, another Latin American investment-grade economy. The upgrade by Moody's of Mexican debt to investment grade, followed by Fitch and Standard & Poor's in the very beginning of 2002,[82] improved financial conditions in Mexico. Average yields came down almost immediately. Later in the year 2000, another good news came with the orderly elections of the new president that broke not only the monopolistic 70-year PRI rule but also the link between economic and political cycles, the presidential election year no longer being a financial and economic crisis year.[83]

As shown in table 6.2, the correlations between all other major Latin American countries and Mexican bonds dropped significantly after the March 7, 2001 investment grade date. Since, and in spite of the U.S. slowdown and the tremendous Mexican exposure to the U.S. economy underlined by almost all investment houses in 2001,[84] despite the emerging market crises in Turkey and Argentina, Mexico seemed almost immune. With this investment grade, Mexico changed financial category, the upgrade meaning also that a broader set of investors, because of regulatory restrictions, such as U.S. pension funds, big insurance companies and under certain conditions some mutual funds, can now hold Mexican debt.[85]

The reason for Mexico's return to favor can be found primarily in the implementation of an unprecedented US$50 bn. rescue plan under the

Table 6.2   Mexico investment grade: falling correlations between Mexico and other Latin American emerging markets (%)

	Mexico correlation with					
	Argentina	*Brazil*	*Colombia*	*Peru*	*Venezuela*	*EMBI+*
March 8, 1998–March 6, 2000	88.30	95.30	76.30	91.60	79.10	97
March 8, 1999–March 6, 2000	88.30	91.10	87.50	95	89.10	93.90
March 7, 2000–May 28, 2001	42.40	66.30	33.60	35.10	74.90	73.30

Source: Based on Roberto Rigobon, "The Curse of Non-Investment Grade Countries," NBER Working Paper, no. W8636, December 2001; published in *The Journal of Development Economics*, vol. 69, issue 2, December 2002, pp. 423–449.

auspices of the IMF and the United States. This aid functioned as a comprehensive insurance package and enabled Mexico to have a remarkably short period of convalescence. Officially, the intervention of the United States and the international community was justified on the grounds that there was a risk of contagion to all the emerging markets. In order to avoid the risk of a systemic crisis, as argued by Clinton and the international monetary authorities, a large-scale rescue plan was required.[86] Afterwards, with these new liquidities, Mexican policy-makers engaged also several key reforms, among them restrictive fiscal policy, banking system reforms and central bank autonomy. All these act as signals and reforms attempting also to stabilize the Mexican property rights regime and investors rights.[87]

Nevertheless, an alternative explanation can be put forward to explain the speed of the recovery. In particular the scope and speed of the plan may be explained by political considerations. The crisis was a test of the solidity and the internal solidarity of NAFTA. More important, the reasons behind the rescue plan can be found in the massive entry into the financial markets during the 1990s in general, and the emerging markets in particular of the famous North American pension funds, or so-called mutual funds through institutional investors. Unlike in 1982, this crisis affected not only a few large U.S. commercial banks, but also a great number of institutional investors, and hence millions of individual American savers, in other words voters.

The expansion of these funds is undoubtedly one of the most spectacular transformations that occurred on the financial markets in the past fifteen years. Since 1980, the asset volume managed by U.S. institutional investors increased five-fold. Mutual funds alone have shot up by 1,600 percent, while the volume of pension funds has grown from US$900 bn. in 1980 to more than 5,000 bn. in 1995. By the end of 1993, assets held by the 300 largest U.S. institutional investors amounted to US$7,200 bn., the equivalent of 110 percent of the American GDP, as against 30 percent of GDP in 1975. This development is having an impact on emerging markets as investment funds seek both higher returns and greater diversification of their portfolios. This has meant an increase in stock-market capitalization in the emerging markets from US$450 bn. to over 2,000 bn. over the course of the past six years, and these markets now represent 15 percent of global stock-market capitalization.

In this context, even slight shifts in the composition of portfolios can generate tremendous capital inflows or withdrawals. Modification of, say, two or three points in the multicurrency structure of institutional investors' portfolios can trigger capital movements, whose scope can exceed US$100 bn., whereas the amount of currency reserves held in 1993 by Mexico, for example, reached barely US$30 bn. These newcomers, who are mostly avid for renewable short-term investments and securities offering short-term capital gains, contributed to the mimetic rationale and the growing short-sightedness of the financial markets. As a result of this attitude the 1994 crisis hit hundreds of thousands of small investors: American workers and retirees who had put their savings into mutual funds managed by institutions like Fidelity Investments, Alliance Capital, Goldman Sachs, Salomon Brothers, or Scudder, Stevens & Clark. Some of these funds suffered substantial losses in 1994 such as Fidelity's Emerging Markets Fund when it lost 17.9 percent or Scudder's Latin America, which was down 9.4 percent. The Chemical Bank of New York alone lost more than US$70 mn. in a single day (January 3, 1995) exclusively on the peso/dollar exchange rate.

6.6   Are Financial Markets the New Masters of Time?

The Mexican crisis provides a good illustration of the time war being waged between states and financial markets. The official interpretation presents the crisis as a short-term liquidity problem, the markets having expected a devaluation of the peso, which was late in coming. This led to a race between markets overreacting and economic policy measures—the injection of nearly US$40 bn. by the United States and other international players with a view to hampering and putting a stop to capital flight and to restore exchange parities. In this particular case the various states reacted most swiftly to the emergency in order to prevent the financial crisis from spreading.

Why, then, did the Mexicans delay the devaluation that should have been decided as early as March 1994? Economists and politicians harped on the reasons that led Mexico to defer the adjustments, which were nevertheless seen as necessary. Fernández and Rodrik pointed out the existence of strong incentives for resisting the implementation of reforms: not only were costs and benefits unevenly distributed among the different segments of the population and social groups, but the uncertainty about the final distribution pushed the powers-that-be, if not to refrain from, at least to postpone the necessary alignment.[88] In the Mexican case, the electoral agenda heightened the government's reluctance to take firm action. The run-up to the presidential elections scheduled for August 1994, in which the government was involved, induced it to abstain from any steps that could harm its credibility and reputation.

There were other factors arguing against the devaluation of the currency, one of them external. In fact the arguments advanced by the American congressmen hostile to NAFTA was that once the agreement was signed, Mexico would devalue the peso, thereby "stealing" American jobs through disloyal means. Salinas, in an endeavor to prove his loyalty, had his hands tied throughout 1993 and during the first few months of 1994 since a devaluation would have been viewed as a betrayal of NAFTA. Other factors were of an internal nature. After 1988 the PRI had managed to regain the support of the middle class primarily by stabilizing exchange rates and prices. Given that a devaluation would have threatened the PRI with loss of support in this important segment of the population, such a move was politically inconceivable before the August presidential elections.

Finally there was the persistent memory of previous devaluations, generally linked to presidential elections. Indeed, in Mexico, devaluation was usually the consequence of a political defeat. In 1982 former president Lopez Portillo stated, "A president who devalues is a devalued president." Furthermore, a glance at the outgoing president Carlos Salinas de Gortari's personal ambitions helps to understand why any thoughts of devaluation were put off until December 1994. Since the beginning of the year, Salinas, whose mandate was to expire in November, had in fact since the beginning of the year started negotiations with the aim of becoming the head of the World Trade Organization. On the other hand, for Pedro Aspe, in charge of finance until the end of November 1994, a devaluation would have meant damage to both the credibility of his economic policies and his personal reputation with New York financial institutions. For this reason such a step was out of the question, in spite of the advice and recommendations of his mentor, MIT economist Rudiger Dornbusch.

The personal strategies and political agendas of the Mexican political leaders swayed on the decision-making process, since their main concern was to hold out for as long as possible. To this end, they adopted the policy begun in March of issuing the famous Tesobonos. This strategy gave the Mexican government some leeway throughout 1994. Meanwhile the share of Tesobonos in the total public debt increased from 6.5 in January 1994 to 63 percent in August 1994.[89] At the same time, the government resorted to massive volatile private financing. The monetary and financial assets held by nonresidents and the capital held by residents that was easily exportable totalled US$90 bn. with the risk that within a few weeks investors could ask for the conversion into hard currency of these sums, whereas in mid-1994 the country's foreign currency reserves amounted to only US$17 bn. Such a configuration could lead at any time to a foreign exchange crisis. The timebomb had been activated, and it exploded on December 20, when the central bank's peso intervention floor was lowered by 15 percent, and on December 22 when the currency was allowed to float freely.

6.7   Time, Politics and Finance: The Argentinian Crisis

The Mexican financial crisis underlines the importance of the time factor in emerging markets. Political calendars and election timings, because they can lead to major disruptions, are closely watched by Wall Street and London operators.[90] The temporal regimes of financial markets and policy-makers can be at odds but they can also overlap. As the financial operators, policy-makers can seek, as underlined by the Mexican episode, short-term gains and have short-term horizons. In the same way, the volatility and short-termism of financial markets is also possible within governments.

The Argentinian crisis is another example of these short-term horizons and volatility shared by governments. It confirmed the difficulties for emerging countries to ensure credibility through hard peg exchange regimes.[91] It confirmed also the timing game. As for the Mexican devaluation of December 20, 1994 or the Brazilian devaluation of January 13, 1999, the Argentinian devaluation occurred also at the turning point of the calendar year, on January 7, 2002. Latin American crises tend to be concentrated in the very end or very beginning of calendar years, precisely when the "bonus game" is the most important (i.e. the payment of bonus to financial operators).

The Argentinian episode involved not only "moral hazard trade" where "investors are not betting on Argentina's fundamentals", as underlined by a fund manager, "but they are betting on money being made available from the international community to meet Argentina's debt service obligations." If investors can be blamed, politicians also share part of the responsibility: "their lack of solidarity has been key in delaying the implementation of policies aimed at reversing the country's vicious cycle of economic contraction and deteriorating debt dynamics. The more the politicians have delayed, the less responsive the economy to corrective measures."[92]

Like Mexico, Argentina has been a darling of emerging markets, a star pupil, praised by officials all round the world during the 1990s. As for

Mexico during the first half of the 1990s, Argentina during the second half became the darling of bond investment bank teams and bond managers, after having fulfilling heavy deals for investment banks' divisions involved in the privatization of Argentinian assets. By the end of the 1990s, the country had the privilege, with Brazil and Mexico, to be one of the most indebted emerging countries in nominal terms. Above all, Argentina became one of the most indebted emerging countries in the international bond capital markets with nearly half of its total endebtedness being in bonds.[93] By the end of 2000, Latin America weighted nearly 65 percent of the JP Morgan EMBI Global and Argentina alone 21 percent (when the zone only weighted 28 percent of the MSCI emerging markets equity index and Argentina a mere 2 percent).[94]

However, and unlike the Mexican story, investors and analysts in this case were not surprised by the collapse. In fact as underlined by Walter Molano, everyone, from Washington officials to Wall Street investors had some interest, political or financial, in pursuing the Argentinian confidence game: "Argentina was Washington's star pupil, and Wall Street's best client. Every time there were any doubts about Argentina, IMF Deputy Managing Director Stan Fischer or U.S. Treasury Secretary Larry Summers jumped to the rescue. They immediately held press conferences voicing their support. They deployed billions of dollars in multilateral assistance. Multilateral officials openly exhorted investors to buy Argentine bonds. Most analysts and economists on the Sell side were troubled by the events in Argentina. They whispered their concerns privately, or disguised in technical jargon. Unfortunately, they could not openly voice their opinions. They were muzzled by their institutions. Argentina was the goose that laid the golden egg. The country had an enormous willingness to issue bonds, thus generating fat commissions for everyone. Therefore, why kill the goose?"[95]

At the same time, financial and technical mechanisms were pushing investors toward Argentina, even if most of them began to have their doubts about the soundness of policy implementation and the sustainability of the Argentine debt dynamic and the exchange rate. Again, as underlined by Walter Molano: "The Buy-side was not so convinced about the Argentine story. The Buy-side grew skeptical in the middle of 1999. Presidential elections and wanton disregard for proper fiscal restraint led many institutional investors to trim their Argentine positions. Asset managers who were EMBI-constrained were forced to maintain sizeable positions in Argentine bonds. Argentina represented a large percentage of the emerging bond indices. Nevertheless, intuitional investors began reducing positions in Argentinian bonds. Given the reduced appetite by institutional investors, the Sell side moved into the European retail market. Low interest rates, and the absence of a European high yield market, made the Euro market an easy target. More than EU30 billion in Argentine debt was raised in Europe. In the meantime, the IMF and U.S. Treasury downplayed Argentine risks. Argentina was a close friend of the U.S. It supported U.S. foreign relation initiatives around the world."

In 2001, Argentina's currency board was ten years old and in deep trouble.[96] In spite of an international aid plan worth almost US$40 bn. at the end of 2000, and a new one in September 2001 of US$8 bn., the financial markets have remained extremely nervous and skeptical.[97] Neither the ministerial re-shuffle of March 2001 nor the much-heralded arrival on the scene of the father of convertibility, Domingo Cavallo, has succeeded in restoring confidence. In total, in less than one year, six macroeconomic programs have been implemented and incidents have continued to pile up: the exchange-rate system has been altered twice, in April and June 2001, followed in early June by a huge debt swap operation for a record total of US$30 bn.

After the swap operation in mid-2001, the decisive factor, in a country where the unemployment rate was approaching 18 percent of the labor force (against 14.7 percent at the start of the year), was conclusive and quick results that could be achieved before the congress elections of mid-October 2001. With their eyes and minds fixed on the elections, politicians began to play the timing game. Wall Street and London analysts started to forecast the impact of elections. They were perceived once again as the leading temporal horizon in Argentina,[98] which would help or not to keep the political climate in the instability zone in which it has languished since the de la Rúa government came to power.[99]

Meanwhile, after July, Wall Street firms began to speculate and anticipate debt default or devaluation. Some leading firms issued cautious reports and warnings, their scenarios involving also the prospects for another IMF package and "too big to fail" discussions regarding the possible helping hand from international actors (the aid became effective in September with the second IMF package—US$8 bn.—in less than half a year).[100] With the terrorist attack of September 11, 2001, the accelerated slowdown of the United States and generalized risk-aversion, warning reports continue to proliferate regarding the situation in Argentina (and all around Latin America).[101] The last episode of the Argentina odyssey has been in the end a major debt restructuring in November 2001 modestly labelled as "selective default" by rating agencies, which led major investment banks and brokers to remember past crises in emerging markets, debt restructurings and debt games.[102] With the crisis intensifying Argentina was nearly all but eliminated from the emerging bond markets. By the very end of 2001 the interim government after the de la Rúa resignation officially announced a moratorium on debt payments and devalued the peso after the arrival of Duhalde as new president at the beginning of 2002. By end 2001, the country weight in the JP Morgan EMBI dropped to less than 3 percent of the bond index, a level comparable to the one of Colombia or Panama. Less than a year before, Argentina represented more than 23 percent. In less than a year, Argentina disappeared from the radar screens of bond investors.

The Argentina episode lacked contagion effects. Brazil and Argentina spreads remained decoupled in the last months of 2001 and in the very beginning of January 2002, the same day Argentina devalued the peso, Brazil launched with success a US$1 bn. bond issue, followed later by Mexico for the same amount. In fact, contrary to the Mexican crisis, the Argentine default (US$155 bn. of its external debt, the largest-ever sovereign default in dollar terms) hasn't been a surprise at all. The Argentina debacle was well anticipated by most of the analysts, economists and fund managers. Prominent academics already have been warning against the risks involved in Argentina and questioning both the exchange regime and the debt dynamics.[103] From within Wall Street, firms like JP Morgan, for example, also issued several reports months before the default and the devaluation warning against the risks and inviting their clients to be cautious. By mid-2001, the firm was already issuing strong warnings the risky and worsening situation in Argentina. "Argentina, wrote JP Morgan in the first days of December, five weeks before the devaluation, appears to be getting closer to an end game on the exchange rate regime—whether it be dollarization or depreciation of the currency."[104] The same applies for dozens of other Wall Street teams. In mid-November for example, Goldman Sachs openly stressed the public sector debt default in Argentina as their central scenario questioning the impact on Latin America of such an event: "given that a default on public sector debt has now become our central scenario for Argentina, we discuss the potential impact of such outcome on not only Argentina but the rest of the region from a macro-sector and stock specific standpoint," wrote Goldman Sachs analysts.[105]

Based on nearly 70 interviews and survey questionnaires with fund managers during the first half of 2000, our own survey confirms that European and U.S. mutual fund managers were already turning increasingly defensive regarding Argentina. By mid-2000, more than 75 percent of all the survey participants were mentioning Argentina as a major country risk in Latin America. This score is far above all other countries, Brazil (60 percent) and Mexico (54 percent) ranking second and third. It is interesting to note that Peru (13 percent) and Chile (21 percent) were by the time considered as the lowest country risk issues in the region (the case of Ecuador is particular as very few investors have this country in their holdings) (see graph 6.2).

If we look even closer at the responses received and take into account only the top number one risk, Argentina scored above all other perceived risks with nearly 30 percent of the participants referencing Argentina as the major country risk over the next 12 months in Latin America. Just behind lagged U.S. rates issue (25 percent) and Mexico (19 percent). For Argentina, as the peso was pegged to the U.S. dollar, higher U.S. interest rates were expected to constrain the Argentina market till the end of the year. But other major and endogenous reasons were prompting investors to reduce their holdings to lows on a yearly basis in Argentina. Slower economic growth and lack of competitiveness, related to the currency peg, were the major reasons for investors to remain cautious: 30 percent and 21 percent of all the respondents respectively were mentioning these risks as being among the most important for Argentina. It is also interesting to add that if we sum up all the issues related to financial needs (fiscal discipline; bailout/debt and impact of U.S. rates), 49 percent of all the respondents identified this issue as the major one in Argentina for the 12 forthcoming months (see graph 6.3).

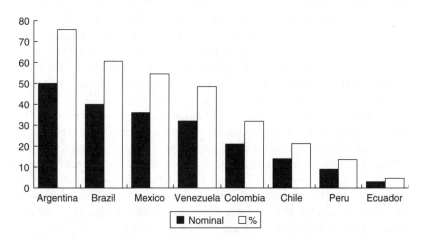

Graph 6.2   Major perceived country risks in Latin America by mid-2000: respondents referencing the country risk as a major concern over the next 12 months (66 responses).
Source: Santiso, July 2000; based on questionnaires and interviews, 2000.

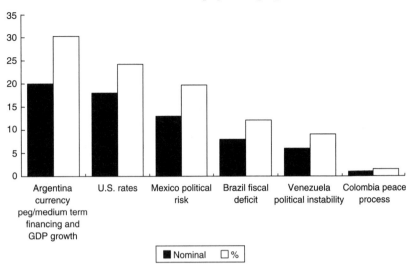

Graph 6.3   Top number one risks in Latin America; Q2 2000 (nominal responses and %; 66 interviews).
Source: Santiso, July 2000; based on questionnaires, 2000.

By mid-2000, always according to our own research, the Argentina currency peg was expected to hold for one more year. Even if mentioned as a major issue for Argentina by investors, the currency peg was not considered as relevant in the short term. Of those who expressed an opinion on expected devaluations (50), only 6 percent (3 respondents) were expecting a major change in currency regime over the next 12 months. They (74 percent, 37 respondents) considered that they won't be witnessing any major change regarding Argentina's currency regime over the next 12 months (see graph 6.4).

These findings and risk aversion in Argentina were confirmed by the Merrill Lynch Asset Allocation survey conducted in 2000. Both Latin and global emerging market fund managers were reducing their positions in Latam countries, Brazil and Mexico remaining the only countries that were overweighed. The most dramatic reduction took place in Argentina both for dedicated Latin American funds and global emerging market funds. By March, Latin American fund managers had already reduced their investments in Argentina by 21 percent.

Even rating agencies, so frequently criticized for their failure to issue early warnings, issued many reports warning against the unsustainability of the Argentina debt dynamic. Fitch Ibca, for example, even

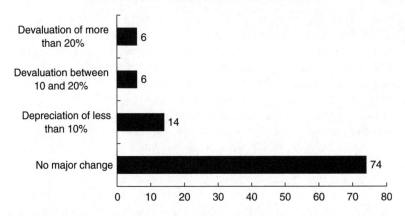

Graph 6.4   Argentina: expected currency change over the next 12 months by (mid-2000) (%, on a total of 50 expressed opinions, Q2 2000).
Source: Santiso, July 2000; based on questionnaires and interviews, 2000.

realized several months before the debt default, simulations testing the debt restructuring scenarios and issued publicly (available through their website) several reports on Argentina nearly half a year after the Argentina December debacle and the January 2002 debt default and devaluation.[106] On December 20, Cavallo resigned. The following days, a myriad presidents followed in the middle of riots and protests.[107] On January 7, 2002, the ten-year-old Convertibility Law was annulled and the two-tier exchange regime was adopted with a new "official" parity implying 30 percent devaluation.[108] Meanwhile, Argentina officially declared default, followed a few weeks later in January by the Buenos Aires province, by far the largest in Argentina; other provincial cross-defaults followed.[109] A few weeks later, on February 11, 2002, and after more than a decade of Convertibility Law, Argentina's peso began to float freely.

The measures adopted by Duhalde assured a return to the macro-economy of populism according to most Wall Street analysts. But probably one of the most interesting and accurate analyses of the situation came from Sao Paulo and from an economist who anticipated the crisis more than a year in advance. As underlined in his January 2002 report, Alex Schwartsman said:

> The great Argentine writer Jorge Luis Borges once described an infinite library (The Library of Babel), which comprised all the possible books. In fact, most of the books in the library did not

mean anything, consisting of a random selection of letters, but—amid this chaos—there was the book (or collection of books) that would contain the explanation for everything, from the meaning of life to the entire organization of the library itself. The image of logic attempting to emerge out of randomly selected elements came somehow to my mind while I was examining the latest measures announced by the Argentine government this weekend. There are elements that make sense, to be sure, but the program still seems to lack coherence, which shall prove the main obstacle to pushing Argentina out of the depths in which it has locked itself. Whereas the devaluation of the currency is a necessity, the program has not dealt with the entire range of consequences that should emerge from this change. For instance, balance sheets will have to suffer a major restructuring, which remains, so far, out of the program's reach.[110]

The direct financial contagion effects therefore have been limited, most of the investors being pulled out of Argentina since (or even before) mid-2001. According to client surveys realized by JP Morgan, at the end of November 2001, more than 80 percent of investors who manage US$133 bn. in emerging market debt were underweight in Argentina.[111] By the end of December, another JP Morgan survey based on responses received from a large sample of investors (171 investors managing an estimated US$122 bn. in emerging markets), revealed that more than 70 percent were underweight or significantly underweight, the number reaching 95 percent if "neutral" positions were included.[112] Since July 2001, some brokers were already starting to play with numbers and trying to quantify the levels of the cuts on foreign bond holdings, the guessing game becoming generalized by the end of the year while the crisis intensified.[113] At the same, the structural changes experienced in emerging markets helped to smooth the contagion effects. By the end of 2001, the level of leverage in emerging markets was very low and above all the markets investor base had substantially changed compared to the Russian crisis. At that time, hedge funds dominated the market while by the end of 2001 they accounted for less than 20 percent of investors while high-grade investors accounted for 25 percent of the market according to JP Morgan.

Another interesting comparison between Argentina and previous emerging market crises episodes lies in the political timing. By mid-2001, the major bet of politicians was to play against the clock and to avoid a major disruption before the October elections. In this sense, as for Mexico, the Argentina episode attempts to avoid as much as possible any disruption before elections and particularly a devaluation, which hurts the middle classes. A detailed study of the behavior of real and nominal exchange rates in Latin America confirms that changes of regime precisely coincide with elections.[114] To be even more precise, devaluations are, as much as possible, postponed until elections are held. In the months following elections (2, 3 and 4 months after), the average rate of nominal depreciation tends to be twice as high as in the months preceding elections. In the case of presidential elections, the average rate of nominal depreciation tends to be even higher: 4.5 percentage points higher than in the preceding months. Overall therefore, the probability of major devaluations increases in the run-up to elections, governments tending to put off the adjustment where possible until after the votes are cast. Similar behavior can be seen in the example of changes within a government (see graph 6.5).

Inversely, when governments embark upon programs to stabilize the exchange rate, these tend to occur in preelection periods, counting on the political effects of currency stability. For example, over the period 1970–2000, using a total of 18 Latin American countries (98 presidential elections and 108 legislative elections recorded over that period), involving in total 34 changes of currency regime aimed at greater stability (or fixing): in 26 of these cases, the change occurred ahead of

Graph 6.5   The currency game: the timing and political economy of exchange rates in Latin America (nominal exchange rate depreciation around elections (presidential + parlimentary)— 242 episodes).

Source: Jeffry Frieden, Piero Ghezzi and Ernerto Stein, "Politics and Exchange Rates: A Cross Country Approach to Latin America" in Jeffrey Freiden and Ernerto Stein, eds., *The Currency Game: Exchange Rate Politics in Latin America*, Baltimore, Johns Hopkins University Press, 2001.

major elections, in other words 76 percent of the cases occurred in the run-up to an electoral process.[115]

Overall, strategies for stabilizing the exchange rate are most frequently implemented ahead of presidential elections, with a probability three times higher at these times than at any other point in the political cycle. Another study, using a range of 88 speculative attacks on emerging market currencies between 1985 and 1999, highlighted also that the propensity of politicians to defend a currency regime is greatest in the months leading up to an election and falls drastically in the months that follow: the defence of the currency is 63 percent stronger in the four months preceding an election than in a normal period, this propensity collapsing to 19 percent in the three following months.[116]

Financial markets are not the only ones employing short-term strategies. Government officials can also seek short-term gains. This shared temporal propensity leads us to a more fundamental level. Looking beyond the individual strategies of government members, the financial crisis in emerging markets poses a broader issue, that is the problem of the transformation of policy-making: in the future states will have to adapt their responses to the speed of the markets, whose time-horizon is dominated by uncertainty and short-term constraints. After the so-called structural adjustment, today states are facing a new challenge: temporal adjustment.

CHAPTER SEVEN

Conclusion: Financial Markets and the Memory of the Future

> Once destiny was an honest game of cards which followed certain conventions, with a limited number of cards and values. Now the player realises in amazement that the hand of his future contains cards never seen before and that the rules of the game are modified by each play.
>
> Paul Valery

Emerging markets themselves are hardly new. Once countries like the United States, Japan and Argentina were emerging markets. Over the past century some changed status, reaching the financial nirvana of the investment grade, the economic paradise of the developing world. Others are still emerging, and from time to time, submerging. At the heart of the "emerging markets" notion is probably the one of a promise, a credible promise of a great transformation, a successful story that became a reality: a developed country.

From this point of view the emerging markets confidence game is above all a temporal game. As underlined by Richard Sylla, "becoming an emerging market implies that a nation convinces the world's investors that its economic promise is great and that it can be realized more quickly with infusions of capital from outside the country, to the mutual benefit of the country and the foreign investors. At its heart, the concept of an emerging market is tied with arbitraging the difference between a country's current economic reality and its future economic potential."[1] At the very heart of the political economy of the confidence game lies precisely this memory of the future. The confidence game is thus an intertemporal game where policy credibility and the future expectations of a nation are crucial.[2]

The decade 1991–2001 has seen both the rise and fall of the so-called emerging markets asset class. There was an unusual transformation compared to the previous decades with a rising share of capital no longer intermediated by states or commercial banks but instead by private investors, FDI and portfolio investments, opening what Barry Eichengreen and Albert Fishlow called a (new) "era of bond finance" and also an "era of equity" finance for emerging markets.[3] With capital flows moving in and out of emerging markets more easily, following the liberalization and financial openness of the past decade, nearly all emerging markets experienced an increase in the frequency of crashes following liberalization. When compared with developed countries, the frequency of crashes in developing countries tends to be much higher. The frequency of crashes for a closed emerging country is 25 percent as against less than 9 percent for a developed country according to a recent empirical test.[4] The frequency of crashes for an open emerging country is of nearly 62 percent compared to less than 10 percent for a developed country. These results confirm that emerging markets are much more prone to crashes than developed countries but also that open emerging countries are much more exposed to financial crashes than closed emerging markets.

The year 2001 can be seen as a turning point for financial emerging markets and Latin America in particular. The terrorist attacks of September 11 were clearly directed at the very core of U.S. power, the Manhattan financial district.[5] This incident underlined the fragility of the financial sphere—and at the same time its strength as the trading floors were quickly reorganized. The collapse of the Argentina economy a few months later and the massive US$155 bn. debt default, the largest-ever sovereign emerging markets default can also be seen as a critical juncture in the emerging markets confidence game. As underlined by Andrés Velasco, the Argentina default is not only a credit and financial default. "In defending the currency board and trying to avoid a default vis-à-vis those who hold pesos in their pockets, Argentina ended up defaulting against everyone else: her pubic employees, whose salaries were either never paid or arbitrarily cut; her own provinces, who have not received transfers accorded them by law: her depositors, who can no longer withdraw their funds from the bank; and, most crucially, her own democracy, with the mandate of a popularly elected president cut short by rioting and looting."[6]

Argentina, more than any other emerging country, followed the "Washington Consensus" of the 1990s, slashing regulations, privatizing state enterprises, promoting foreign multinational investments and welcoming Wall Street bond investors. As underlined by the Zurich Financial Services' chief global economist, "the Argentine crisis has not produced widespread financial contagion because it was widely discounted in the markets. But it could produce intellectual contagion in the form of reaction against market-oriented policies in the developing countries. Argentina was a star pupil of the so-called Washington consensus during much of the 1990s."[7] The model collapsed and with it much of neoliberal crusade rhetoric, at least in Latin American countries.

This ideological collapse might be a good news (even very painful) if it can lead to the consolidation of the aversion for blue-prints, paradigms and models that have been applied in Latin America too many times by spin-doctors, both foreign and local. But as suggested by Paul Krugman, in a *New York Times* column edited the first day of 2002, it might also end in a return to old-fashioned models, with Argentina leaders turning back the clock, imposing exchange controls and import quotas and defaulting in their external obligations. Populist rhetoric and nationalistic political economies are exemplify by the case of Venezuela, which intensified by the end of the 1990s and the beginning of the 2000s.

7.1   Ulysses and the Sirens

Whatever the outcome of this unending confidence game, several conclusions can be drawn from the research presented here. First, the timing of the Latin America crisis, studied in this book, is concentrated on a narrow temporal window. Mexico devaluated the peso on December 20, 1994. Brazil followed devaluating the real on January 13, 1999. The Argentina devaluation occurred also at the turning point of the calendar year, on January 7, 2002. Latin American crises tend to be concentrated in the very end or very beginning of calendar years. Precisely when the "bonus game" is the most important (i.e. the payment of bonuses to financial operators).

Crises tend also to be synchronized with major presidential and/or parliamentary elections. Depending on the timing of policy costs and benefits, policy-makers can (or not) play short-term games. In particular when long-term horizons and distant elections are in place, it tends to encourage more socially and fiscally responsible behaviors from policy-makers.[8] Above all, regarding political and economic timing issues, when countries, with already weak economic and financial fundamentals, face political uncertainty, they might enter a speculative tunnel. And the light at the end of the tunnel doesn't seemed to be the one of a bright and sunny day but rather the one of another train shock coming speedily from the opposite direction.

Second, to play the confidence game with success, that is to achieve this financial nirvana for emerging markets which is the "investment grade," is a matter of time, efforts and sound policies reiterated and implemented time after time. Markets tend to respond to reform policies in emerging markets by a gradual process of confidence building. The gradual impact of sustained and maintained reforms, liberalization and privatization policies for example during the 1980s and 1990s in emerging countries, contributed to this confidence building.[9] But it is not a quick fix a one-shot game. Rather it is a reiterated game in order to build, maintain and develop investors' confidence. It took nearly two decades for Chile to establish its status of sound economic management and reach a high level of confidence symbolized by the investment grade. In Latin America, there are a very (happy) few countries that have reached this status, Mexico being the last one to get it.

Argentina tried hard (and failed) to reach this financial nirvana but took the speed highway. As underlined by Dani Rodrik, "the Argentinean strategy was based on a simple idea: reduction of sovereign risk is the quickest and surest way to reach the income levels of the rich countries." One way of doing so was to play the confidence game in a spectacular manner by linking one-for-one to the U.S. dollar as in 1991, seeking to reverse nearly one century of monetary mismanagement. "Like Ulysses pimming himself to the mast of his ship to avoid the call of the sirens, Argentine policymakers gave up their policy tools lest they (or their successors be tempted to use them to repeat errors of the past."[10] The attempt failed after nearly 11 years of fixed exchange rates and finally Argentina had to devalue the peso.

One of the pending issues, corroborated by the crisis exit of Duhalde in Argentina or more unambiguously by the macro-populism policies implemented by Chavez in Venezuela, is the recurrence of populist episodes. The frequent repetition of such episodes in fact point to a dilemma, a tension in Latin American political economy (and not exclusive to the Americas obviously). The temporal policy-making style implemented is tactical rather than strategic, focusing on the short-term issues of the day and near-term demands rather than more long-term economic sustainable economics.[11] The shift toward democracy and the market-oriented reforms during the 1990s had not generated the expected results this in return boosted the populist leaders propensity to use crisis as a pretext to reverse market-oriented reforms instead of pushing more pragmatic-oriented adaptations in order to boost institutions. A bias for hope is however given by Chile, a country that appears to have broken the cycle of ups and downs. Some other countries (dare one hope, including Mexico) might be in the process of doing so too.

Third the debates on the international financial architecture, crisis prevention and crisis resolution, tend to focus on the macro-picture, leaving the micro-picture aside.[12] Much of the blame and criticism fall on the IMF. In fact, this actor only shares with others, governments, brokers and investors, the responsibility of crises. But as private actors, asset managers and brokers, the IMF can also become from time to time, caught in a trap. If the IMF decides to lend money, it will be criticized for boosting the moral hazard confidence game. If it decides to refuse support to a distress economy it will be blamed for the chaos that follows. But the crisis of Argentina in particular, because it involved not only a devaluation but also the most important and massive debt default from an emerging country since the debt crisis of 1982, exposed many other, more disturbing shortcomings of the international financial system. Before the crisis, nearly all the debates focused on the macro-picture, the IMF, private sector involvement or BIS rules, rather than focusing on the micro-picture. The mentioned issues are obviously important. But the Argentina crisis also underlined the lack of established and formalized procedures for dealing with sovereign default in the bond markets.[13] Because of the multiplicity and dispersion of the emerging bond market actors, the debt games nowadays look very different from the that of the 1980s. The crisis not only underlined the need for legally enforceable debt standstill to allow orderly workouts of insolvent sovereigns (a proposition that is much discussed by market operators) but also more understanding of the micro-picture. How does one negotiate with the invisible hand of the market when there are in fact many invisible hands, that is bondholders, brokers and other players with divergent strategies, interests and visions?

It is very difficult for a sovereign to identify who are the bondholders that bought, let's say, Argentina paper, and therefore to initiate any negotiation process with them. Many institutional investors, like pension and hedge funds, are not required to disclose their holdings or their portfolio changes. In the case of mutual funds, only U.S.-based ones have to report to the SEC and on a semiannual basis. Some private companies, investment firms or specialized firms such as Morningstar, AMG Data Services, Investment Company Institute, Lipper Analytical Services or

Bloomberg, provide mutual (partial) fund data with higher frequency, mainly quarterly, through qualitative surveys. The diversity of actors and institutions and the multiplication of emerging market funds (or global and international funds invested in emerging markets) make it difficult to see the whole picture. For mutual funds alone, for example, the number of sole emerging market funds registered in the United States jumped from 3 funds in 1991 to 165 in 1998.[14]

During the Argentina crisis, market participants started to organize themselves in order to voice more loudly. Interestingly an Emerging Markets Creditors Association and an Argentina Bondholder Committee were created as specific solutions to deal with the issue of the crisis. But it was by the time impossible to comprehend the concentration or dispersion of the Argentina bondholders making it impossible to attempt debt rescheduling or restructuring in a "voluntary" way. The paradox is that there is more and more transparency from the states (in terms of delivering data at least) but a strange opacity from the market: simply the data (fund per fund, bondholder per bondholder) of what and how much emerging bonds they hold is impossible to obtain. If the first stage of Argentina debt restructuring and negotiation process with domestic bondholders has been possible, in the last months of 2001, it has been precisely because the terms were not only acceptable but because the Argentina officials could get face-to-face meetings with in fact a very few number of actors. If we take into account the assets held by the local pension funds, mutual funds and local banks (all subsidiaries from the same holding company—most of them foreign operators), in fact less than ten private players concentrated more than 80 percent of total assets held by the local bondholders.[15] The issue (putting aside the terms of the restructuring "offered" to market participants) with the international bondholders was much more infinite; there were too many actors involving divergent strategies and interests, even conflicting, regarding the issue.

Argentina's slow burning debt crisis, which took three years of recession to blow up, raises a fundamental question not only regarding the costs and benefits of the emerging countries opening to capital markets, but instead, supposing that the benefits are greater than the costs, how to deal with the recurrent heart attacks faced by emerging countries when they loose the confidence game. During the 1990s, crisis after crisis led to the conclusion that sovereigns should avoid short-term debts or relying too heavily on cross-border bank flows. With the Argentina debacle, another issue arose: the difficulty in borrowing from bond markets (the issue of how to play the confidence game) and also the difficulty in dealing with the drawbacks. In the case of a default, it is an impossible task to get all the bondholders together to resolve the problem. Investment Goliaths such as large mutual funds only represented, according to estimates released by the *Wall Street Journal* mid-December 2001, a third of the roughly US$18 bn. of Argentina's dollar denominated bonds. About US$11 bn. of Argentina debt was estimated to be in the accounts of dispersed European institutional and individual investors (300 000 only in Italy for example).

This difficulty is linked with the speed of recovery that a country can expect (at least from a financial—not social—point of view) after a crisis. As a consequence of the dispersion or concentration of bondholders, domestic debt exchange, after a crisis, tends to be completed in very brief periods of time when they involved very few local players. Foreign investors being much more disseminated, the issue of international debt restructuring to exit crises looks starkly different. According to the experiences of the 1990s, it took two years for Russia, one year for Ecuador and just a few months for Ukraine to complete their respective debt restructuring after the declaration of default.

Emerging market operators became more and more informed, diversified and clever during the 1990s. We can argue that a learning process has taken place with emerging market operators differentiating more and more among borrowers of developing countries. However not all the problems of information have been solved and one important source of asymmetric information remains. Such asymmetries are still acute. From one side, buyers (some more than others) are not fully aware of the real conditions in borrowing countries. But, also the borrowers, when faced with a liquidity or solvency problem, are not aware of the real bondholder landscape. In the same perspective it is important to underline that the distribution of these asymmetries are variable depending on the type of actors and the category. Based on empirical studies of foreign portfolio investors during the Korean currency crises, scholars have underlined that foreign investors outside the country are more likely to engage in herding than subsidiaries of foreign institutions in Korea for example. Here again the difference of trading behavior suggests that financial markets are not a world of equals and that probably the difference is related above all to their levels of information.[16]

In fact when we talk of "financial markets" there is nothing like this. There are various types of investors, different actors, from brokers and rating agencies, involved in the confidence game but with divergent and frequently conflicting strategies. During the Argentina debt restructure operation of 2001, not everybody lost money. Some investors did but almost all the investment arms of leading Wall Street firms made lucrative deals. As underlined by the *Wall Street Journal*, "the high profile roster of investment banks hired by Argentina to restructure its crippling load of foreign debt includes many of the same that handled and profited from the original sales of Argentine bonds in the 1990s." "Though they don't break any rules by collecting fees on a country's boom and bust cycles, the banks' revolving role," added the *Wall Street Journal*, "in Argentinta's debt saga has heightened tensions between investment bankers and the investors that bought their product—Argentina—as a sound, long-term investment."[17] Among the banks hired to handle the US$30 bond swap for Argentina were banks like JP Morgan and Credit Suisse First Boston, two banks that managed big bond sales for Argentina during the previous years. Later during the year, it was the turn of Deutsche Bank, Merrill Lynch and Salomon Smith Barney, leading managers of Argentina's bond sales in previous years, to be hired by the Argentina government.[18]

7.2   Some Final Temporal Paradoxes

The speed of (financial) recoveries are quite impressive in the case of Mexico and Brazil. Argentina is probably another story if we take into account that events such as a debt default and the sovereign workouts that follow tend to take longer time and because the number of actors involved is very large, each bondholder being free to litigate separately because, in this case, of the lack of so-called "collective action clauses."

An indication of the acceleration of the pulse of world economy under financial pressure is the rapid reconfiguration of financial assets as a result of performance requirements imposed by institutional investors.[19] This search for performance also borders on tachycardia that leads to an ever-greater instability of capital. Capital that now flies from one investment to another and from one stock market to another, pausing for increasingly brief periods of time. Between 1980 and 1987, the rate of assets abandoned during the year (obtained through mergers and acquisitions) rose from 20 to 75 percent. The rate of stock rotation on the New York Stock Exchange jumped from 30 to 70 percent between 1979 and 1989.[20]

Throughout the 1980s and 1990s, international finance experimented with a series of major changes. The deregulation of the bond markets beginning in 1979 and then, with a certain delay, that of the stock markets in 1986, accompanied the craze in the financial sphere. Between 1980 and 1992, the annual growth rates of financial assets in OECD countries reached an average of six percent annually, or a growth rate

2.5 points higher than that of raw capital accumulation. A single figure is enough to indicate the (mis)dimension of the stakes involved. Each day, there are 40 times more financial transactions than commodity transactions in terms of volume. Pushed by new information technologies, the interconnection between the different financial centers takes place at a faster and more constraining pace for governments. The latter are not powerless, but their margin of action has been reduced. Sunk in the heart of what Susan Strange has called "casino capitalism," governments' grip and control has loosened.[21] They have especially been forced to face a formidable acceleration of financial movements. With the new information technologies, arbitration and adjustments are made in a matter of seconds. In one movement, financial investors can redo their asset portfolios (currencies, bonds, stocks and byproducts), undertake instantaneous arbitrations between the different financial instruments or compartments of the markets, choose the countries where they buy their currencies or hold their stocks.

This interconnection obviously varies from one market to the other, more developed in the currency and bond markets than in that of stocks. It is especially characterized by its pendulum swings, mimetism, and the ever-increasing speed of reactions with which the financial markets work. More than ever, these interactions warrant increasing attention on the part not only of those who live off the markets but also those whose lives are affected by them. By focusing on the time factor perhaps it is permissible, as we have tried to show, to bring to light what is happening at the end of this century: the formidable accelerations and contractions of time pushed by the accordion movements of the financial markets and the quest for speed of the national economies.

The imperative of speed comes in all shapes and sizes. Governments speak of a "rapid reaction force" in order to project themselves into foreign countries in a shorter period of time. International regulatory agencies such as the IMF evoke "emergency funds" to contain contagious financial crises. The speed of communications erases distances (think about the Concorde, CNN Television or Internet, e.g.) reducing the world to the size of a screen or a teleprompter. Not only have distances gone through a breathtaking contraction, but also telecommunications remove the hands from clocks by reducing transmission and connection time to a minimum. In a symbolic manner the switch from mechanical to quartz watches demonstrates this contraction of space and time.[22]

The important thing today is not mastering space but mastering time. When Paul Valery, in his *Regards sur le Monde Actuel*, evoked the idea of ended time that begins, he emphasized both the question of space and that of time. The end of world time that begins is above all the end of the cycle of discoveries, of virgin space. "The era of vacant lots, of free territories, of places that belong to no one, the era of expansion, is finished. There is not a single rock that does not carry a flag, no more empty spaces on maps, no more regions where customs check points and laws have no place."[23] Time no longer sanctions the end of the pre-eminence of space. "The great issue of politics was and still is for some the acquisition of a territory," Paul Valery underscored. Today politics focuses on a different challenge, no longer that of conquering space but of taming time. Or, more precisely, of dealing with the imperative of speed. The old tyranny of distance has been substituted by the tyranny of real time. The crushing of temporalities in the here and now imposes an omnipresence of the present, which the political arena must face. If politics consists above all in structuring time, in inscribing an event in time, in clearing a temporal horizon—a project that is also a projection into the future—one can understand that the shrinking of temporal horizons and the omnipresence of the present constitute one of the major challenges for politics.

"The further we go," adds Valery, "the less effects will be simple, the less they will be predictable, the less political actions and even military interventions—in a word, direct and obvious action—will be what we thought it would be." The perspective of real time in this way subjects politics to a level of greater unpredictability. In particular, it obligates governments to adjust the speed of their reactions to that of the markets. When states find themselves trapped in the net of financial turbulence, for example, they will try to contain the volatility of market flux by every possible means. Thus a country like Brazil spent more than 1 bn. per day during the first weeks of September 1998 in reserves so as to try and distance the specter of the crisis and gain time. At the same moment the Russian Central Bank, taken by surprise, threatened 11 Western banks by accusing them of channelling the Asian turbulence toward the Russian market. Among the banks cited by the Russians were JP Morgan, Crédit Suisse First Boston, Union Bank of Switzerland, Salomon Brothers, Société Générale, Crédit Agricole Indosuez, Bank of New York, Banque Nationale de Paris and Deutsche Morgan Grenfell.

7.3   *Il était une fois demain* (tomorrow never dies)

The temporal paradoxes inherent in how financial markets function are plenty. One of them is the speed of financial crisis, entrance and exit, compared to the social impact, from which it is to recover. Another one would involve bringing an unexpected response to the question of physicist Stephen Hawking, who, in the introduction to an essay, asked why one remembers the past and not the future.[24]

In many cases, financial markets, through the game of anticipation, remember the future. The rationality of market participants is forward looking rather than backward looking. As underlined by a market participant, a former chief economist of Paribas and Head of Research of Allianz Pimco Asset Management, "the eternal return of financial crises seems to suggest that in the best case we didn't learn anything from the past, and in the worst case we finish by forget everything."[25] The rationality of market participants is rather inductive than deductive.[26] They have the capacity to transform a hypothetical and far-off future into the present, crushing immediate temporal horizons, treating problems that were supposed to arise in a far-off future at the instant, in real time.

Financial markets are unique in their capacity to dismantle the most long-term anticipations, thus immediately dismantling present synchronizations. Nowhere else, underlined Lordon in his work, can anticipations be so immediately and radically put into action.[27] They run into one another, at a rhythm that is close to tachycardia, emerge and then disappear, replaced by new anticipations. Markets transform themselves into worlds without memory, which suffer from amnesia. "The market is a giant autism," underlines one analyst, "the games of opinion are as much deforming games of mirrors where rumors race at the speed of the humors of a handful of makers of the market who lose confidence, then lose their footing."[28] In this world, the speed of forgetting is extremely high. "Actors are faced with a tidal wave of interconnected relations that, by their reverberations, feed an enormous game of reflections that economists and analysts maintain by setting the tone of the times."

As an economist of a large Parisian investment bank stated, "the memory of the past" is overshadowed by "the memory of the future."[29] The most flagrant example is the issue of 100-year bonds by companies like Coca Cola or Disney, which commit themselves to pay investors the borrowed interest over the course of 100 years. In this case, the company gambles that the bonds will still be there in 100 years and the investor gambles that this promise for the future will be fulfilled.

Projecting into the future through the formation of anticipations is not particular to the financial world. It is, in fact, part of any human undertaking. However, it is not as much opening up to the future, as it is one's capacity to tear oneself away from the past that is in question. In a real world, an inert productive infrastructure requires longer adjustment periods that might be decades. A political project is equally confronted with the weight of institutional structures, constitutional synchronizations and the strain of social relations. The state, contrary to the market, imposes itself as the master of slowness and not of speed. The financial market, on the contrary, has the power to rapidly transform a far-off hypothetical future into an immediate present. The problems that could potentially arise from consolidation of the European Union, are brought into the present moment in order to be treated here and now. In addition, there is a large capacity for amnesia: a five-year worry that puts the market in a trance can be forgotten in half a day. Anticipation then has a short life expectancy, being inevitably pushed toward forgetfulness by another anticipation. The Mexican crisis has already been forgotten thanks to worries about the crisis in Thailand and acceleration of the Dow Jones, which passed the $7000 mark in February 1997 and then the $8000 mark in July the same year before establishing a new record in April 1998 by passing the $9000 mark. As stated by a former chief economist of Paribas' investment bank this "methodological zapping" is the essence of the financial markets: "at any moment, their (operators) behaviour always depends on what is regarded as the crucial variable, but this changes constantly over time, with, for example, the trade balance replacing money supply as the flavour of the month." "In this casino economy described by Keynes, each player becomes an elementary particle in a gaseaous mixture whose movements in space and in time he tries to anticipate(. . .) In order to survive, they will no need to examine with precision the evolution of the underlying factors. All they have to do is to make a correct prediction of the average opinion of the other speculators. The success—generally short-lived—of a few will make possible the permanent renewal of the speculator population."[30]

In general, the temporal regimes of financial markets are then singularly dominated by a short-term and immediate memory. The horizons of traders, for example, do not go beyond the square horizon of prompters and stock market floor screens, which continually display the highs and the lows, or the promises of gains and losses, in a world devoid of delays and antipodes, where tomorrow abolishes today and the distant confounds itself with the immediate.

The timing of financial operators can be equated to a world without memory where events pass by without leaving a trace unless to outline what may happen tomorrow. These operators are the lookouts, anticipators of the future. In a world without memory, an instantaneous history made of an unstoppable chronology dominates. Each event erases that which preceded it; a new crisis makes one forget the old. The worldview of financial operators could be best described using the metaphor employed by historian Fernand Braudel of a "firefly world" that glows for a few instants before being relegated to the realm of forgetfulness; he says: "I remember, one night, close to Bahia, I was enveloped by the pale fire of phosphorescent fireflies; their pale light shined, burned out, shined again, without truly piercing the clarity of night. In such a way, events, behind their glimmer, remain obscure."[31] The world of international finance operates in a similar way: once consumed, in a fraction of a second or several hours at most, the fireflies that are financial markets burn out and analysts move to other emerging markets where other fireflies shine just as brilliantly.

The Holy Graal of financial markets is prediction. The future remains an uncertain and unknown land that not only has to be explored but mastered. The evidence suggests however that financial institutions fail to predict changes in the probability of crises. Typically rating agencies downgrade occur during or after a crisis rather than before.[32] The Holy Graal remains out of reach.

7.4   An Invitation

The importance of time in economics and politics was amplified by the approach of the end of 2000 millenium. In the economic and financial sphere, time is more than ever the synonym of money. A study carried out by the New York investment bank JP Morgan estimated the potential increase in the volume of business after 2000 to be between $80,000 and $160,000 mn. The temporal analysis of financial markets merits more in-depth research. Economists in general are hesitant to integrate the time factor, even in light of abundant research on the subject. Numerous works, notably on political economy, focus on international arbitrations and the redistributive policies carried out by governments whose temporal horizons are relatively short because they are linked to the election cycle. Economists are particularly concerned with budgetary questions: the choice of financing through taxation, or through borrowing. The weight of these appeals to raise supplementary capital particularly interests economists in the United States.

The new classical macroeconomics has made serious efforts, under the influence of economists such as Lucas, Kydland, Prescott, Sargent and Wallace, to reintroduce a dynamic perspective into economics and to inscribe the economy in a temporal perspective. They focus their attention on the intertemporal expectations of economic agents, the existing asymmetries between the unlimited temporal horizon of the state and that limited by the lifespan of households, as well as on the problem of the credibility of political policy whose optimal short-term solutions often bring about long-term losses in well-being (the problem of temporal inconsistency).

A combined temporal and socioeconomic analysis furnishes equally precious analytical tools, which are still unexplored. There are too few empirical studies concerning reconfiguration of the temporal horizons of entrepreneurs. Managers of large companies, major actors on the international scene and important contributors to national economic development, should take into consideration the fluctuations of the international economy as well as the plans of representatives of institutional investors when developing strategies. What does the growing presence of pension funds and mutual funds within corporate governance structures signify for the governing of a company? What is the effect of eventual polarization on the results and quarterly distribution of dividends? Is the very hypothesis of the short-termism of pension funds and mutual funds empirically founded?

In all, American institutional investors manage more than $10,000 bn. and invest in other national markets where they buy stocks in local companies (such as Calpers, which has 20 percent of its resources outside the United States). Acquiring shares in these companies then allows them to impose their own management criteria and short-term profit objectives. A major consequence of this corporate governance system is to shorten the temporal horizons of companies that have become increasingly subject to management control procedures founded on the distribution of quarterly dividends. When the short-term profit objectives of institutional management organisms become the decisive parameter, companies are increasingly submitted to financial criteria. No country today can escape this tendency, as evidenced, for example, by the rise in power of foreign stockholders in French capitalism.[33]

The short-termism of investors who operate in financial markets deserves, to borrow Albert Hirshman's words, to undergo a certain "autosubversion." From financial wizard Georges Soros to billionaires and businessmen like Sir George Templeton, numerous actors have multiplied long-term actions by establishing permanent foundations that carry their names and also attack long-term problems. One of the most significant examples is donations made in the (long-termist) field of education. The funds collected from private operators by North American universities attest to this fact. Certain schools, such as Stanford University's Business School, raise up to 45 percent of their 44.2 mn.

annual budget in gifts and donations. These examples invite further segmentation of financial markets and differentiate more finely the temporal horizons of actors, depending on profession (even within the same profession) and reputational and institutional effects.

In addition, can we put forward the hypothesis that markets are essentially short-termist in opposition to states that are more long-termist? This question deserves to be explored. The Mexican example underlines how short-termism seems to be a prerogative of not only the market. The Mexican state, in issuing the famous *tesobonos*, or the "malditos bonos" as it was called by Arturo Porzecanski, not only sought to gain time, but also to prolong short-termist strategy in order to elude devaluation and correction of the economic trajectory before the deadline of December 1994. The immediate and brutal market correction, in fact, was a blessing in disguise, as a New York banker remarked: it immediately stopped the government's impulse to buy more time, forcing it to face the situation immediately. It could not relegate problems indefinitely to a more or less far-off future. By sanctioning Mexico and Thailand, financial markets ended the economic derivations of political leaders, who are occasionally squeezed by the short-term vice of the political calendar.

Much more research is still needed on the political economy of emerging markets. Underlining the political economy dimension is essential if one wants to understand the confidence game, a central issue to financial dynamics as well as to financial crises. As underlined by most of the research on international financial institutions, for example, the access to IMF programs is not only a matter of depth of financial distress and liquidity problems. Participation in IMF programs is influenced also by institutional, political and geographical dimensions. As underlined by Barro and Lee, for example, countries' political connections to the IMF, proximity or not to major IMF shareholding countries (and notably the United States), the quota of a country's national staff at the IMF, all these variables affect the probability of loan approvals. According to the authors a country that has more IMF staff, more IMF quota and voted more frequently with the United States in the UN is expected to have higher probabilities of getting IMF loan approvals by 9.6, 6.7 and 12 percentage points each respectively.[34] (See table 7.1.)

Futher steps would be needed. I only mention one that could lead to another research program in itself: the political economy dimension of the confidence game not from a market perspective but from the perspective of states and multilaterals. How states, central banks, ministries or promoting FDI agencies, play the confidence game, with which

Table 7.1 The power game: distribution of voting rights in the IMF by groups of countries

Groups of countries	% of votes
United States	17.29
G-5 (US, Germany, Japan, France, U.K.)	39.57
G-7 (G-5 + Italy, Canada)	45.84
G-10 (G-7 + Netherlands, Belgium, Sweden)	51.53
The North[1]	61.45
Emerging market countries[2]	9.00
HIPC countries[3]	2.29
Non-HIPC PRGF countries[4]	3.67
China and India	4.14
The rest of the South[5]	11.22
The South	30.32[6]
Transitional and other countries[7]	8.23

Notes

[1] "The North" includes 24 industrialized countries: the G-10 plus all remaining OECD members (Australia, Austria, Denmark, Finland, Greece, Iceland, Ireland, Luxembourg, New Zealand, Norway, Portugal, Spain, Switzerland, Turkey) except for Mexico and Korea (which are included under "emerging market countries") and transitional countries (Czech Republic, Hungary, Poland, Slovak Republic).

[2] Includes Argentina, Brazil, Chile, Korea, Malaysia, Mexico, Philippines, Singapore, South Africa, Thailand and Venezuela. Transitional emerging market countries, e.g. Czech Republic, Hungary, Poland, Slovak Republic, are included in the "transitional and other" category.

[3] See *2000 Annual Report* p. 50, table 5.1.

[4] See *2000 Annual Report* p. 58, table 5.3, excluding China and India. Includes, among others, Pakistan and Nigeria.

[5] Includes, among others, Colombia, Indonesia, Iran, Iraq, Morocco, Saudi Arabia, Costa Rica and Uruguay.

[6] An alternative measure of the South's voting power is to aggregate the votes of the "G-11" EDs, i.e. all those EDs whose constituencies are primarily countries from the South. This produces a total of 31.9% of the votes, but requires the cooperation of Spain and Australia who are also represented by G-11 EDs.

[7] Includes Russia, Czech Republic, Hungary, Poland, etc., as well as Israel.

Source: Peter Evans and Martha Finnemore, "Organizational Reform and the Expansion of the South's Voice at the Fund," prepared for the G-24 Technical Group Meeting, Washington D.C., April 17–18, 2001.

resources, which results and difficulties? It would be, for example, interesting to consider the number of ex-Wall Street analysts or ex–IMF staff economists and/or IADB and World Bank officials, who work in the governments of various countries and how they play the game. Several cases studies, the Paris Club debt games, the websites diffusion, the way central banks are organized or how treasuries in emerging countries interact with bond fund managers and fixed income teams, all could be part of this further research.

At least, as would have said Albert Hirschman, to whose memory this book is largely dedicated, there is a bias for hope: journeys toward international political economy research remain tremendously promising. The research agenda remains open and with it the horizons of investigations on what remain one of the most central issues of our century: the unfinished dialogue between states and markets.

NOTES

Chapter One   Introduction: Inside the Black Box.
A Journey Toward Emerging Markets

1. Quoted from the introduction of Charles Kindleberger, *Mania, Panics and Crashes: A History of Financial Crashes*, New York, John Wiley & Sons, 1989 and 2000. Dating the integration of emerging capital markets is a difficult task. The timing of *financial* integration can be different from the timing of regulatory integration as underlined by Geert Bekaert, Campbell Harvey and Robin Lumsdaine, "Dating the Integration of World Equity Markets," paper presented at the *28th Annual Meeting of the European Finance Association*, Universitat Pompeu Fabra, Barcelona, 22–25 August, 2001. The emergence of the so-called emerging markets can be dated previously to the 1980s and 1990s, emerging markets being in fact reemerging markets. Many of the contemporary emerging markets were already active in the 1920s and even before in the case of Latin America. See William Goetzmann and Phillippe Jorion, "Re-emerging Markets," *Journal of Financial and Quantitative Analysis*, vol. 34, no. 1, March 1999; and for an interesting article on China see also William Goetzmann and Andrey Ukhov, "China and the World Financial Markets 1870–1930: Modern Lessons from Historical Globalization," *The Wharton School, University of Pennsylvania, Financial Institutions Center Working Paper*, no. 01–30, July 2001.

2. On the first great global capital boom, both commercial and financial, see the essays of Barry Eichengreen, *Globalizing Capital: A History of the International Monetary System*, Princeton, Princeton University Press, 1996; Kevin O'Rourke and Jeffrey Williamson, *Globalization and History: The Evolution of a Nineteenth Century Atlantic Economy*, Cambridge, Mass., MIT Press, 2001.

3. Emerging markets refers in fact to developing countries screened by the IFC based on two major variables for classifying equity markets: income per capita and market capitalization relative to GNP. If a market resides in a low-income country and has a low ratio of investable market capitalization to GNP, then World Bank's IFC classifies the market as emerging. Several countries are however classified as "emerging markets" in spite of being members of the OCDE. This is the case e.g. in South Korea, Mexico, Czech Republic, Hungary and Poland. Greece, a member both of the OECD and the European Union, was also classified for a while as an emerging market. According to data based on World Bank, as of 1998, 75% of the countries of the globe (155 out of 206 countries) were considered as emerging markets. They represent the major world's population (85%) but a small share of world GNP (less than 22%) and a smaller share of equity market capitalization (8.5% of total equity market capitalization) and of bond market capitalization (4.7% of total). According to BIS data, in 1998, emerging markets accounted for around 15% of global foreign exchange trading activity. For a deeper analysis of

the data see Richard Levich, "The Importance of Emerging Markets," *New York University Stern School of Business Working Paper*, March 2001; published in the *Brookings Wharton Papers on Financial Services 2001*.

4. For a historical perspective on financial crisis, see Charles Kindleberger, *Mania, Panics and Crashes: A History of Financial Crashes*, New York, John Wiley & Sons, 1989 and 2000.

5. See Amartya Sen, "Rational Fools: A Critique of the Behavioural Foundations of Economic Theory," *Philosophy and Public Affairs*, vol. 6, no. 4, 1977, pp. 317–344.

6. For a general study on the financial community of Wall Street, see the socioeconomic analyses of Mitchel Abolafia, *Making Markets: Opportunities and Restraint on Wall Street*, Cambridge, Mass., Harvard University Press, 1997. Abolafia's approach is a socioeconomic analysis in the tradition of Max Weber, who wrote essays on the stock market as well as on the ethic of capitalism. The Bibliothèque du Citoyen translated both into French in 1894–1896. See Max Weber, *La Bourse*, Paris, Transition, 1999.

7. See e.g. the developments in economic sociology and approaches toward finance issues by *The Social Studies of Finance Workshop* held at Paris School of Mines, April 20–21, 2000 (http://homepage.altavista.com/ssfn/) and *The Society for Advancement of Socio-Economics SASE* (http://www.sase.org) that expounded the leading and seminal works of Mark Granovetter, "Economic Action and Social Structure: The Problem of Embeddedness," *American Journal of Sociology*, vol. 91, 1985, pp. 481–510; and Mark Granovetter, *Society and Economy: The Social Construction of Economic Institutions*, Cambridge, Mass., Harvard University Press, 2001.

8. The first models of balance of payments crisis were based on the seminal paper of Paul Krugman, "A Model of Balance-of-Payments Crisis," *Journal of Money, Credit and Banking*, no. 11, 1979, pp. 311–325; the "second generation models" were pioneered by Maurice Obtsfeld, "Rational and Self-fulfilling Balance of Payments Crises," *American Economic Review*, March 1986, pp. 72–81; and Maurice Obstfeld, "The Logic of Currency Crises," *Cahiers Economiques et Monétaires*, XLIII, 1994, pp. 189–213. For a discussion see Paul Krugman, "Are Currency Crises Self-Fulfilling?", *NBER Macroeconomics Annual*, Cambridge, Mass., MIT Press, 1996, pp. 345–378; and Robert Flood and Nancy Marion, "Self-Fulfilling Risk Predictions: An Application to Speculative Attacks," *Journal of International Economics*, vol. 50, no. 1, February 2000, pp. 245–268.

9. See (for a special analysis on international illiquidity issues and domestic banking system) Roberto Chang and Andrés Velasco, "A Model of Financial Crises in Emerging Markets," *The Quarterly Journal of Economics*, May 2001, pp. 489–517.

10. For a concise review of this literature, see Robert Shiller, "Human Behavior and the Efficiency of Financial System," *National Bureau of Economic Research Working Paper*, no. 6375, January 1998; and Robert Shiller, *Irrational Exuberance*, Princeton, Princeton University Press, 2000. The attraction of behavioral finance has not only been academic: in 2000 an estimate suggested that more than US$ 70 bn. was invested in the United States using behavioral finance theories. Chicago economist Richard Thaler (with Russ Fuller) founded an asset-management company making investments based on these heuristics discoveries. See http://www.fullerthaler.com

11. See for a synthesis André Orléan, "L'hypothèse autoréférentielle appliquée à la finance," paper presented at the *Third Annual Saint Gobain Meeting on Economic Research*, "Les transformations de la finance en Europe," November 8–9, 2001.

12. Financial actors live in a forward looking world whose pretention of mastering risk follows a long tradition as shown by Peter Berstein, *Against the Gods. The Remarkable History of Risk*, New York, John Wiley & Sons, 1996.

13. For prospect theory seminal papers, see Daniel Kahneman and Amos Tversky, "Prospect Theory: An Analysis of Decision Under Risk," *Econometrica*, 47(2), 1979, pp. 263–291; Daniel Kahneman and Amos Tversky, "Loss Aversion and Riskless Choice A Reference Dependent Model," *Quarterly Journal of Economics*, CVII, 1991, pp. 1039–1061; Richard Thaler, *Advances in*

Behavioral Finance, New York, Russell Sage Foundation, 1993; and Daniel Kahneman and Amos Tversky, *Choices, Values and Frames*, New York, Cambridge University Press, 2000.

14. See e.g. the anthropological works of Ellen Hertz on the Shangai Stock Exchange, Ellen Hertz, *The Trading Crowd: An Ethnography of the Shanghai Stock Market*, Cambridge, Cambridge University Press, 1998.

15. Womack's research, e.g., shows that the stock recommended by underwriters perform poorly when compared with the "buy" recommendations of unaffiliated agency brokers, thus proving the importance of conflict of interests and the biases they occasionally introduce into the recommendations made by brokerage. Most of the fund managers are aware of these conflicts and deal with them when they read brokerage research, "paying as much attention to what it is written than by whom and when" "because it's part of the confidence game." Interviews, London, June 22, 2000 and Paris, June 8, 2000, with emerging markets fund managers. See Kent Womack, "Do Brokerage Analysts' Recommendations Have Investment Value?", *The Journal of Finance*, vol. 51, no. 1, 1996, pp. 137–167.

16. For an evaluation of credit rating agencies after the Asian crisis, see Helmut Reisen, "Ratings Since the Asian Crisis," *WIDER United Nations University, Discussion Paper*, No. 2002/2, January 2002.

17. See Carmen Reinhart, "Default, Currency Crises and Sovereign Credit Ratings," *NBER Working Paper*, 8738, January 2002. See also, Deutsche Bank, "Sovereign Credit Ratings," *Deutsche Bank, Research Notes in Economics & Statistics*, January 29, 2002.

18. See in particular interviews in Paris, June 15, 2001; Edinburgh, November 17, 18 and 19, 2000; New York, November 5, 6 and 7, 2000; and Boston, November 19, 21 and 22, 2000.

19. Interviews in New York November 6 and 7, 2000; London, April 14, 2001; Edinburgh, November 17, 20 and 21, 2000; and Paris, June 14, 2001.

20. See BBVA Securities, "Mexico: Identifying the Catalysts," *BBVA Securities, Latin American Equities Strategy*, New York, January 17, 2002; and BBVA Bancomer Casa de Bolsa, "Se reconocen los esfuerzos económicos de Mexico; Fitch otorga grade de inversión," *BBVA Bancomer Casa de Bolsa, Estrategia Bancomer*, Mexico, January 21, 2002.

21. See Carmen Reinhart, "Sovereign Credit Ratings Before and After Financial Crises," paper presented at *The World Bank Group Conference on the Role of Credit Reporting Systems in the International Economy*, March 1–2, 2001 (unpublished); Guillermo Larrain, Helmut Reisen and Julia van Maltzen, "Emerging Market Risk and Sovereign Credit Ratings," *OECD Development Centre Technical Papers*, no. 124, Paris, OECD, 1997; and Richard Cantor and Frank Packer, "Determinants and Impacts of Sovereign Credit Ratings," *Federal Reserve Bank of New York Economic Policy Review*, October 1996, pp. 37–53.

22. The figure calculated by a group of Berkeley researchers include also around 610 bn. e-mails that are sent each year in America alone (e-mails are used by analysts and fund managers as the quickest way of diffusing or receiving research). See Peter Lyman and Hal Varian, "How Much Information?", *University of Berkeley Working Paper*, 2000 (unpublished), available through the net: http://www.sims.berkeley.edu/how-much-info/.

23. Thomson Financial is a provider of e-information services that owns leading units such as I/B/E/S (who provide asset managers and other professionals with forecasts and databases covering 18,000 companies in 60 countries, with estimates from 850 firms around the globe). First Call is another financial information provider for money managers; and the well known and popular Datastream which is a databases provider. See: http://www.ibes.com/; http://www.datastream.com/; http://www.firstcall.com/; and http://www.thomsonfinancial.com/.

24. Over the last years, the major operators increased acquisitions of smaller information companies as well as joint ventures. Reuters, e.g., acquired Lipper Analytical Services, a povider of mutual and global fund data, and in 2001 the company acquired assets of one of the major competitors Bridge Information Systems. Reuters also formed joint ventures with Multex.com Inc, a leading Internet online intermediary for the financial market place (they create Multex Investor Europe) and with Dow Jones & Co. to develop a web-based global service called

Factiva to provide corporate financial news and research data. For websites on financial windows see: http://www.reuters.com/; http://www.factiva.com/; http://www.lipperweb.com/.

25. With more than 18,000 employees and close to 2,150 journalists across 100 different countries in 2000, Reuters possesses the second most important satellite network in the world, after the Pentagon. The company, who marked its one hundred and fiftieth anniversary in 2001, was founded by Julius Reuter who began using pigeons to fly stock market prices between Brussels and Aachen. Later he moved to London to trasmit news and prices around Europe through the newly opened Dover–Calais submarine cable.

26. See "Calender of Events," *Emerging Debt Markets Biweekly*, New York, Goldman Sachs, Economic Research Department, February 4, 1997, p. 25.

27. For an empirical analysis of this crisis, based on a large survey and nearly 900 responses, see Robert Shiller, *Market Volatility*, Cambridge, Mass., MIT Press, 1991.

28. See André Orléan, *Le pouvoir de la finance*, Paris, Editions Odile Jacob, 1999.

29. For an analysis on the transformation of financial markets refer to the work of Frederic Mishkin, *The Economics of Money, Banking and Financial Markets*, New York, Addison Wesley, 1998; and Barry Eichengreen, *Globalizing Capital: A History of International Monetary System*, Princeton, Princeton University Press, 1996.

30. Philippe Delmas, *Le maître des horloges. Modernité de l'action publique*, Paris, Odile Jacob, 1991, p. 97.

31. See Paul Virilio, *La vitesse de libération*, Paris, Galilée, 1995.

32. See Javier Santiso, "The Fall into the Present: The Emergence of Limited Political Temporalities in Latin America," *Time & Society*, March 1998, 7(1), pp. 25–54.

33. Space has not disappeared, however: the localization of stock exchanges, determined according to time lags and the 24-hour service that they allow, are still pertinent. The end of geography actually designates the end of its monopoly or the quest for space as a vector of power. The main issue is no longer to expand a state's territory or to push frontiers further, it is rather to access, in record time, significant market shares and to increase the speed of the economy. For a discussion of the relation between space and time in international finance see Nigel Thrift, "A Phantom State? The De-Traditionalization of Money, the International Financial System and International Finance Centres," *Political Geography*, July 1994, 13(4), pp. 299–327; and Benjamin Cohen, *The Geography of Money*, Ithaca, Cornell University Press, 1998.

34. The goal of deregulation mechanisms is, first of all, to reduce transaction costs, which should be zero according to orthodox theory (zero transaction cost). The zero transaction-cost theory supports a hypothesis that has been proven by the facts, as Ronald Coase has pointed out concerning exchanges effectuated without delays in an instantaneous manner: "Another consequence of the assumption of zero transaction costs, not usually noticed, is that when there are no costs of making transactions, it costs nothing to speed them up so that eternity can be experienced in a split second." Ronald Coase, *The Firm, the Market and the Law*, Chicago, The University of Chicago Press, 1998, p. 15.

35. See Bruce Carruthers, *City of Capital: Politics and Markets in the English Revolution*, Princeton, Princeton University Press, 1996; and the essays published by Neil Fligstein, "Markets as Politics: A Political-Cultural Approach to Market Institutions," *American Sociological Review*, 1996, 61, pp. 656–673; and Neil Fligstein *The Architecture of Markets: An Economic Sociology of Capitalist Societies*, Princeton, Princeton University Press, 2001. As underlined by North and Weingast, Britain's performance, financial, economic and military after 1689, is closely linked with the establishment of the Bank of England, which provided the technological resources that improved the Crown's ability to borrow money. See Douglass North and Barry Weingast, "Constitutions and Commitment: The Evolution of Institutions Governing Public Choice in Seventeenth-Century England," *Journal of Economic History*, vol. 49, December 1989, pp. 803–832; and also, on the diffusion of credibility-enhancing institutions like central banks Lawrence Broz, "The Origins of Central Banking: Solutions to the Free-Rider Problem," *International Organization*, vol. 52, no. 2, 1998, pp. 231–268.

36. See the works of historians David Landes, *Revolution in Time: Clocks and the Making of Modern World*, Cambridge, Mass., 2000 (revised edition). More specifically on finance and politics during the Middle Age, see Jacques Le Goff, "La bourse et la vie: économie et religion au Moyen Age," in Le Goff, *Un autre Moyen Age*, Paris, Gallimard, 1999, pp. 1261–1337; and on the creation of modern stock markets in Amsterdam (1531) and in London (1571), Fernand Braudel, *Civilisation matérielle, économie et capitalisme*, Paris, Le Livre de Poche, II, 1979, pp. 99–101.
37. See Clifford Geertz, *After the Fact. Two Countries, Four Decades, One Anthropologist*, Cambridge, Mass., Harvard University Press, 1995.

Chapter Two The Confidence Game: Exit, Voice and Loyalty in Financial Markets

1. See Paul Krugman, "Dutch Tulips and Emerging Markets," *Foreign Affairs*, vol. 74, no. 4, 1995, pp. 28–44.
2. See Enrique Mendoza, "Why Should Emerging Economies Give Up National Currencies: A Case for Institutions Substitution," *NBER Working Paper*, No. 8950, May 2002.
3. See Ricardo Caballero and Rudi Dornbusch, "Argentina: A Rescue Plan that Works," MIT, http://web.mit.edu/caball/www/ARGENTINA22802.pdf.
4. Here, I refer to Albert Hirschman, *Exit, Voice and Loyalty: Responses to Decline in Firms, Organizations, and States*, Cambridge, Mass., Harvard University Press, 1970. Initially Hirschman's analysis was focused on consumers responses or members of organizations' (social and political included) contrasting responses to the deterioration in the quality of goods they buy or services they benefit from. In this sense "exit is simply the act of leaving, generally because a better good service or benefit is believed to be provided by another firm or organization. Indirectly and unintentionally exit can cause the deteriorating organization to improve its performance. Voice is the act of complaining, or of organizing to complain or to protest, with the intention of achieving directly a recuperation of the quality that has been impaired." See Albert Hirschman, "Exit, Voice and the Fate of the German Democratic Republic," in Hirschman, *A Propensity to Self-subversion*, Cambridge, Mass., Harvard University Press, 1995, p. 12.
5. Interviews with several fund managers and Latin American economists in Madrid, April 7 and 9, 2001; Paris, May 14, June 7 and 14, July 27, 2001; Washington, May 21, 2001; New York, May 8, 9 and 11, 2000 and January 15, 17 and 19, 2001; London, June 1 and 2, 2000.
6. See interviews with emerging markets fund managers, New York, May 8 and 10, 2000; and London. As pointed out by Mohamed El-Erian, a well-known emerging bond market fund manager, "judging from the behaviour of large Latin borrowers in particular, we are witnessing a sea of change in the way information is being communicated. Ad-hoc and sometime adversial relations are giving way to regular exchanges of information via non-deal road shows, conference calls, and even e-mails." "This provides investors with better access to more timely and comprehensive information, including regular e-mails from major borrowers." Mohamed El-Erian, *PIMCO Emerging Markets Watch*, PIMCO, October 2000 (http://www.pimco.com).
7. On asymmetric information and informational efficient markets, see the seminal paper of Sanford J. Grossman and Joseph Stiglitz, "On the Impossibility of Informationally Efficient Markets," *The American Economic Review*, vol. 70, no. 3, June 1980, pp. 393–408. Information asymmetries also played a substantial role during the early stages of financial globalization by the end of the nineteenth century when there was a clear dominance of railway bonds as underlined by Barry Eichengreen and Michael Bordo, "Crises Now and Then: What Lessons from Last Era of Financial Globalization," *NBER Working Paper*, No. 8716, January 2002; and Michael Bordo and Antu Panini Murshid, "Globalization and Changing Patterns in the International Transmission of Shocks in Financial Markets," *NBER Working Paper*, No. 9019,

June 2002. In fact according to Davis and Gallman, during this early stage of financial globalization, nine of every ten pounds of British investment between 1865 and 1890 went into railroad and government bonds. See Lance Davis and Robert Gallman, *Waves, Tides and Sandcastles: The Impact of Capital Flows on Evolving Financial Markets in the New World, 1865–1914*, Cambridge, Cambridge University Press, 2000.

8. On informational and normative mimetism in financial markets, see André Orléan, "Psychologie des marchés. Comprendre les foules spéculatives," in Jacques Gravereau and Jacques Trauman, eds., *Crises financières*, Paris, Economica, 2001, pp. 105–128; and André Orléan, "Informational influences and the ambivalence of imitation," in Jacques Lesourne and André Orléan, eds., *Advances in Self-Organization and Evolutionary Economics*, London, Paris, Geneva, Economica, 1998, pp. 39–56.

9. See Guillermo Calvo and Enrique Mendoza, "Rational Herding and the Globalization of Financial Markets," *Journal of International Economics*, vol. 51, 2000, pp. 79–114.

10. See Barry Eichengreen and Richard Portes, *Crisis? What Crisis. Orderly Workouts for Sovereign Debtors*, Washington, D.C., Brookings, 1995.

11. Interviews with EMTA's Starla Cohen, Paris, March 7, 2001; and with Starla Cohen and Jonathan Murno, Paris, April 19, 2001. See the Club de Paris website: http://www.club deparis.org/.

12. Interview with IIF's Ramón Aracena, Washington, June 21, 2001. See also the website: http://www.iif.com/.

13. See http://www.emta.org/ndevelop/emca.pdf. Among the leading firms that created EMCA were fund managers like MFS Investment Management, PIMCO, Western Asset Management, HBK Investments, Morgan Stanley Dean Witter, David Babson Mutual Financial Group and Metropolitan Life Insurance Company.

14. See Mohamed A. El-Erian, "The Long and Winding Road," *PIMCO Emerging Markets Watch*, October 2000.

15. See Jeremy Booth, "How to Keep Developing Countries in Their Place: Cut Them Off From Capital," London, *Ashmore Investment Management*, October 4, 2001 (short version published in Euromoney). See also http://www.emta.org/keyper/indusper.html.

16. Walter Molano, "Please, Don't Call the Lawyers," New York, *BCP Securities, The Latin American Adviser Daily*, November 9, 2001.

17. For a report, see "IMF Could Aid Argentina Debt Restructure Moves," *Financial Times*, November 7, 2001, p. 9; and *The Wall Street Journal* reproduced in spanish newspaper *Cinco Dias*, "Juguemos a una supuesta crisis en Argentina. Los principales actores se han visto las caras en un simulacro de suspension de pagos," *The Wall Street Journal/Cinco Dias*, November 8, 2001, p. 53. An analytical paper was later prepared by Adam Lerrick and Sanjav Srivastava, "Default Without Disruption: Simulation of a Sovereign Debt Restructuring," *Carnegie Mellon University*, Mimeo, June 2002 (unpublished).

18. See Anne Krueger, "International Financial Architecture for 2002: A New Approach to Sovereign Debt Restructuring," address at the *National Economists' Club Annual Member's Dinner American Enterprise Institute*, Washington, D.C., November 26, 2001.

19. See Nouriel Roubini, "Bail-Ins, Bailouts, Burden Sharing and Private Sector Involvement in Crisis Resolution: The G-7 Framework and Some Suggestions on the Open Unresolved Issues," New York, New York University, December 21, 2001; and Nouriel Roubini, "Should Argentina Dollarize or Float? The Pros and Cons of Alternative Exchange Rate Regimes for Domestic and Foreign Debt Restructuring/Reduction," New York, New York University, December 2, 2001.

20. See Merrill Lynch, "Reading the Washington Tea Leaves," *Merrill Lynch Emerging Markets Research*, July 30, 2001.

21. See e.g. the round trip organized by Schroder Salomon Smith Barney economists who held meetings in Buenos Aires on September 10–12, 2001 at a critical moment for Argentina, which was in the midst of a crisis, facing a congressional election on October 14, 2001; Schroder

Salomon Smith Barney, "Argentina: Trip Report," London and New York, *Schroder Salomon Smith Barney*, September 14, 2001.

22. See Hirschman, *Exit, Voice and Loyalty*, op. cit., p. 208 (footnote 4).

23. This doesn't mean that, within the game, marginal adjustments are not tolerated or even cele-brated as the Chilean example of *encaje* shows. Implemented in the early 1990s, these capital controls on exits have been widely discussed. See e.g. José de Gregorio, Sesbastian Edwards and Rodrigo Valdés, "Controls on Capital Inflows: Do They Work?" *Journal of Development Economics*, 63(1), 2000, pp. 85–114. There has also been an increased acceptance that capital controls could play a positive role as prudential measures preventing strong dependence on short-term liabil-ities. This is the case even within the IMF as stressed by Michael Mussa, "Factors Driving Global Economic Integration," paper presented in Jackson Hole, Wyoming at a symposium sponsored by the Federal Reserve Bank of Kansas City, August 25, 2000. On other capital controls such as Malaysian ones (much more discussed and critized), see for a balanced and nonorthodox view Ethan Kaplan and Dani Rodrik, "Did the Malaysian Capital Controls Work?" *John F. Fitzgerald School of Government, Harvard University, Working Paper*, December 2000 (unpublished); see also on the political economic dimension Stephen Haggard and Linda Low, "The Political Economy of Malaysian Controls," *University of California at San Diego*, 2000 (unpublished); and Stephen Haggard, *The Political Economy of the Asian Financial Crisis*, Washington, Institute for International Economics, 2000.

24. As noted by Daniel Verdier "the absence of a well-functioning security market denied investors the capacity to diversify their investment portfolio beyond the region in which they resided. Holders of securities were unable to exercise exit, but had to fall back voice, to use Albert Hirschman's terminology. Territorial specificity forced investors to join the political fray, both corporate and regulatory." See Daniel Verdier, "Capital Mobility and the Origins of Stock Markets," *International Organization*, vol. 55, no. 2, Spring 2001, pp. 327–356; and Daniel Verdier, *Moving Money: The Domestic Institutions of Capital Mobility*, Cambridge, Mass., Cambridge University Press, 2002.

25. Peter Lindert and Peter Morton, "How Sovereign Debt has Worked," in Jeffrey Sachs, ed., *Developing Country Debt and Economic Performance, vol. 1. The International Financial System*, Chicago, University of Chicago Press, 1989, pp. 39–106.

26. See Barry Eichengreen, "Historical Research on International Lending and Debt," *Journal of Economic Perspectives*, vol. 5, no. 2, 1991, pp. 149–169; Eliana Cardoso and Rudiger Dornbusch, "Brazilian Debt Crises: Past and Present," in Barry Eichengreen and Peter H. Lindert, eds., *The International Debt Crisis in Historical Perspective*, Cambridge, Mass., MIT Press, 1989, pp. 106–139.

27. See Michael Tomz, "How Do Reputations Form? New and Seasoned Borrowers in International Capital Markets," Stanford University, Department of Political Science, prepared for delivery at the *2001 Annual Meeting of the American Political Science Association*, San Francisco, August 30–September 2, 2001; and Michael Tomz, "Do Creditors Ignore History? Reputation in International Capital Markets," prepared for the *1998 Annual Meeting of the Latin American Studies Association*, Chicago, September 24–26 (draft updated in February 1999). See also on the intertemporal dimensions of debt games, Kenneth Kletzer and Brian Wright, "Sovereign Debt as Intertemporal Barter," *American Economic Review*, vol. 90, no. 3, 2000, pp. 621–639.

28. Quoted from Alexandre Schwartsman, "No Free Lunch: The Center, the Edge, and Everything in Between," *BBA Economic Research on Brazil*, September 28, 2001.

29. For a discussion on the "blessings in disguise" of economic crises regarding the collapse of authoritarian regimes and democratic transition, see Stephan Haggard and Robert Kaufman, *The Political Economy of Democratic Transitions*, Princeton, Princeton University Press, 1995; and Stephan Haggard and Robert Kaufman, *The Politics of Economic Reform Adjustment: International Constraints, Distributive Conflicts, and the State*, Princeton, Princeton University Press, 1992.

30. See e.g. Alberto Alesina and Allan Drazen, "Why are Stabilizations Delayed?" and Allan Drazen and Vittorio Grilli, "The Benefit of Crises for Economic Reforms," in Federico Sturzenegger and Mariano Tommasi, eds., *The Political Economy of Reform*, Cambridge, Mass., MIT Press, 1998, pp. 77–103 and pp. 127–141. For a discussion and an empirical test Allan Drazen and William Easterly, "Do Crises Induce Reform? Simple Empirical Tests of Conventional Wisdom," *Economics & Politics*, vol. 13, no. 2, July 2001, pp. 129–157.

31. Paul Krugman, "The Confidence Game," in Krugman, *The Return of Depression Economics*, London, Penguin Books, 2000, p. 113. See also the version published by The New Republic Online, http://www.thenewrepublic.com/archive/1098/100598/krugman100598.html.

32. See Ilan Goldfajn and Taimur Baig, "The Russian Default and the Contagion to Brazil," in Stijn Calessens and Kristin Forbes, eds., *International Financial Contagion*, Boston, Kluwer Academic Publishers, 2001; Ilan Goldfajn, "The Swings of Capital Flows and the Brazilian Crisis," in Stephany Griffith-Jones, Ricardo Gootschalk and Jacques Cailloux, eds., *Capital Flows in Calm and Turbulent Times*, Ann Arbor, Michigan University Press, 2001.

33. See Gabriel Palma, "The Magical Realism of Brazilian Economics: How to Create a Financial Crisis by Trying to Avoid One," *Center for Economic Policy Analysis, CEPA Working Paper Series III*, Working Paper No. 17, September 2000.

34. The public support for market reforms however remained questionable. The implementation of such reforms took place in some Latin American countries "by surprise," the presidents in Peru or Argentina, Fujimori and Menem, engaging market reforms after populist campaigns. See Susan Carol Stokes, *Markets, Mandates and Democracy: Neoliberalism by Surprise in Latin America*, Cambridge, Mass., Cambridge University Press, 2001; and Susan Carol Stokes, ed., *Public Support for Reforms in New Democracies*, Cambridge, Mass., Cambridge University Press, 2001.

35. See Arvid Lukauskas and Susan Minushkin, "Explaining Styles of Financial Markets Opening in Chile, Mexico, South Korea and Turkey," *International Studies Quarterly*, vol. 44, 2000, pp. 695–723; also underlined by Benjamin Cohen, *The Geography of Money*, Ithaca, N.Y., Cornell University Press, 1998. The globalization of finance made regulation costs higher and less effective while at the same time firms discovered new ways to evade controls and transfer funds and activities abroad, by exercising the exit option. See John Goodman and Louis Pauly, "The Obsolescence of Capital Controls? Economic Management in an Age of Global Markets," *World Politics*, vol. 46, no. 1, October 1993, pp. 50–82; Eric Helleiner, "Post-Globalization. Is the Financial Liberalization Trend Likely to be Reversed?" in Michael Loriaux et al., eds., *Capital Ungoverned. Liberalizing Finance in International States*, Ithaca, N.Y., Cornell University Press, 1997, pp. 193–224; and, on the transformation of world finance, Barry Eichengreen, *Globalizing Capital: A History International Monetary System*, Princeton, Princeton University Press, 1996.

36. For an empirical test of this argument see Beth A. Simmons, "International Law and State Behavior: Commitment and Compliance in International Monetary Affairs," *American Political Science Review*, vol. 94, no. 4, December 2000, pp. 819–835; and Beth A. Simmons, "The Legalization of International Monetary Affairs," *International Organization*, vol. 54, no. 3, Summer 2000, pp. 573–602.

37. On the high degree of temporal and geographic clustering and the patterns of economic policy diffusion explained by international economic competition, informational networks or socio-cultural emulation, see Beth Simmons, "Competition, Communication or Culture? Explaining three decades of foreign economic policy diffusion," presented at *Notre Dame University, Kellogg Institute Political Economy Working Group*, October 4, 2001 (unpublished).

38. See Nancy Brune and Geoffrey Garrett, "The Diffusion of Privatisation in the Developing World," *Yale University Working Paper*, August 2000, prepared for presentation at the *Annual Meetings of the American Political Science Association*, Washington, D.C., August 30–September 3, 2000 (unpublished). One of the non-solved questions remain however: why, within a same peer group as Latin America, there are countries that don't participate in the race, some for internal political considerations others because they present low attractiveness. In Latin America, the

cases of Costa Rica and Uruguay are quite interesting from this perspective as both have high international credentials and "offered" very few assets to the private sector during the past decade.

39. However the correlation between pension reforms and savings rates are controversial. Andrew Samwick, e.g., studies seven pension reforms in Latin America, seven in Africa, two in Asia and four in Europe and he finds no evidence that countries that reformed their pension systems and introduced private social security systems increased their savings rates, with the exception of Chile. See Andrew Samwick, "Is Pension Reform Conductive to Higher Saving?", *The Review of Economics and Statistics*, vol. 82, no. 2, 2000, pp. 264–272. In another study, two Princeton economists show that in fact Chilean investment and growth boom during the 1980s is mainly explained by the reduction in the tax rate on corporate retained profits instead of the pension reform per se. See Chang-Tai Hsieh and Jonathan Baker, "Taxes and Growth in a Financially Underdeveloped Country: Explaining the Chilean Investment Boom," *Princeton Working Paper*, presented at the Analytical Country Studies on growth, Centre for International Development, Kennedy School of Government, Harvard University, April 20–21, 2001.

40. See Sarah Brooks, "Who Privatize, When and Why? Pension Privatization Across Space and Time," paper prepared for *The University of Chicago Comparative Politics Workshop*, May 2, 2001 (unpublished); and Evelyne Huber and John D. Stephens, "The Political Economy of Pension Reform: Latin America in Comparative Perspective," paper presented for delivery at the *2000 Meeting of the Latin American Studies Association*, Miami, March 16–18, 2000 (unpublished). On the economics of pension reforms see Salvador Valdés Prieto, ed., *The Economics of Pensions. Principles, Policies and International Experience*, Cambridge, Mass., Cambridge University Press, 1997; Martin Feldstein, ed., *Privatizing Social Security*, Chicago, Chicago University Press, 1998 (see in particular the contribution of Sebastian Edwards on Chile); and more specifically on Latin America, Monika Queisser, *The Second Generation Pension Reforms in Latin America*, Paris, OECD, 1998.

41. For a detailed analysis of Nafta negotiations, see Maxwell Cameron and Brian Tomlin, eds., *The Making of Nafta: How the Deal was Done*, Ithaca, Cornell University Press, 2000; and for an empirical evidence, based on a survey of European corporations (French companies), suggesting that Mercosur has also been perceived as a "signal," a promise of greater economic (and political) stability by foreign investors, see Paolo Giordano and Javier Santiso, "La course aux Amériques: les stratégies des investisseurs européens dans le Mercosur," *Problèmes d'Amérique latine*, no. 39, October–December 2000, pp. 55–87.

42. See Michael Tomz, "Do International Agreements Make Reforms More Credible? The Impact of Nafta on Mexican Stock Prices," Stanford University, prepared for delivery at the *1997 Annual Meeting of the American Political Science Association*, Washington, D.C., August 28–31, 1997; and for a similar analysis of the search of credibility signals through Nafta Aaron Tornell and Gerardo Esquivel, "The Political Economy of Mexico's Entry to Nafta," *NBER Working Paper*, No. 5322, 1995.

43. For analyses testing the "Lipset hypothesis" (prosperity stimulates democracy) and for analyses testing the reverse channel, i.e. the impact of economic development on democratic propensity, see José Tavares and Romain Wacziarg, "How Democracy Affects Growth," *European Economic Review*, vol. 45, no. 8, August 2001, pp. 1341–1378; Dani Rodrik, "Democracies Pay Higher Wages," *The Quarterly Journal of Economics*, vol. CXIV, no. 3, August 1999, pp. 707–738; Robert Barro, "Determinants of Democracy," *Journal of Political Economy*, vol. 107, no. 6, 1999, pp. 158–183; Adam Przeworski and Fernando Limongi, "Political Regimes and Economic Growth," *Journal of Economic Perspectives*, no. 7, Summer 1993, pp. 51–69; and Adam Przeworski and Fernando Limongi, "Modernization: Theories and Facts," *World Politics*, vol. 49, no. 2, January 1997, pp. 156–183. See Adam Przeworski, Michael Alvarez, José Antonio Cheibub and Fernando Limongi, *Democracy and Development: Political Regimes and Economic Well-Being in the World, 1950–1990*, Cambridge, Mass., Cambridge University Press, 2000.

44. Interviews with emerging markets asset managers, Paris, November 9, 2000; London, October 17, 2000; and New York, May 8, 2000.

45. Dani Rodrik, "Participatory Politics, Social Cooperation and Economic Instability," *American Economic Review*, vol. 90, no. 2, May 2000, pp. 140–144.

46. On this "blessings in disguise" of democracy's propensity to moderate social conflicts see the last essays of Albert Hirschman, "Social Conflicts as Pillars of Democratic Market Societies," in Hirschman, *A Propensity to Self-Subversion*, Princeton, Princeton University Press, pp. 231–249; and Albert Hirschman, "Melding the Public and Private Spheres: Taking Commensensality seriously," in Hirschman, *Crossing Boundaries*, New York, Zone Books, 1998, pp. 11–32.

47. For empirical research on political institutions and private investors, see Yi Feng, "Political Freedom, Political Instability and Political Uncertainty: A Study of Political Institutions and Private Investment in Developing Countries," *International Studies Quarterly*, vol. 45, no. 2, June 2001, pp. 271–294.

48. See David L. Richards, Ronald D. Gelleny and David H. Sacko, "Money with a Mean Streak? Foreign Economic Penetration and Government Respect for Human Rights in Developing Countries," *International Studies Quarterly*, vol. 45, no. 2, June 2001, pp. 219–239.

49. As noted by Sylvia Maxfield, international financial asset holders are supposed to be "more willing, *ceteris paribus*, to invest in countries with independent central banks for two reasons. First, investors expect central banks with discretional authority to help keep the national economy on a stable, consistent course. Therefore central bank independence increases the extent to which investors can predict their relative returns." "Central bank independence may also increase the confidence of some international investors in a second way": "international investors may believe that their ability to influence policy is greater the more independent the central bank is from the executive branch." See Sylvia Maxfield, *Gatekeepers of Growth: The International Political Economy of Central Banking in Developing Countries*, Princeton, Princeton University Press, 1997, p. 36; Michael Pastor and Sylvia Maxfield, "Central Bank Independence and Private Investment in the Developing World," *Economics & Politics*, vol. 11, no. 3, November 1999, pp. 299–309. In the same way, central bank independence is linked with more democratic governance and political stability, see Delia M. Boylan, *Defusing Democracy: Central Bank Autonomy and the Transition from Authoritarian Rule*, Ann Arbor, University of Michigan Press, 2001.

50. Citibank Salomon Smith Barney, *Brazil: Independence for the Central Bank?* New York, Citibank Salomon Smith Barney Economic & Market Analysis, January 31, 2001.

51. On the attempt to establish credible rules and institutions, see Charles Calomiris and Andrew Powell, "Can Emerging Market Bank Regulators Establish Credible Discipline? The Case of Argentina, 1992–1999," *NBER Working Paper*, No. 7715, May 2000; and on high inflation destructive process, see Axel Leijonhufvud and Daniel Heymann, *High Inflation: The Arne Ryde Memorial Lecture*, London, Clarendon Press, 1995; and Axel Leijonhufvud, *Macroeconomic Instability and Co-ordination: Selected Essays*, London, Edward Elgar Pub., 2001.

52. Interview of Freddy Thomsen, ING Barings emerging markets economist, *Financial Times*, February 20, 2001, p. 5.

53. For a closer analysis of central banks' skills see the empirical results of a research based on a database of questionnaires received and used from 91 institutions covering 57 countries, Charles Goodhart, Dirk Schoenmaker and Paolo Dasgupta, "The Skill Profile of Central Bankers and Supervisors," Financial Markets Group, London School of Economics, April 2001, paper presented at the *28th Annual Meeting of the European Finance Association*, Universitat Pomepu Fabra, Barcelona, August 22–25, 2001.

54. At the same time, domestic politics included financial regulatory choices and the security of the banking systems. Despite the homogenizing effects of global financial integration, electoral rules and local political dynamics can shape prudential regulation choices. See Frances Rosenbluth and Ross Schaap, "The Domestic Politics of Banking Regulation," *Yale University and UCLA Working Paper*, August 2001 (unpublished).

55. Sources: http://www.banxico.org.mx/; http://www.bcra.gov.ar/; http://www.bcb.gov.br/; and Sylvia Maxfield, *Gatekeepers of Growth*, pp. 101 and 129.

56. See Dani Rodrik, "Governing the Global Economy: Does One Architectural Style Fit All?" Harvard University, John F. Kennedy School of Government, p. 13, paper prepared for the *Brookings Institution Trade Policy Forum* conference on *Governing in a Global Economy*, April 15–16, 1999 (unpublished).

57. See Adam Posen, *Dollarization, Currency Blocs, and US Policy*, Washington, D.C., Institute for International Economics, 2001.

58. Andrew Rose, "One Money, One Market: Estimating the Effect of Common Currency on Trade," *Economic Policy*, April 2000, pp. 7–46.

59. See Bejamin Cohen, "Dollarization: Pros and Cons," *University of California at Santa Barbara*, working paper prepared for workshop on "Dollars, Democracy and Trade: External Influences on Economic Integration in the Americas," Los Angeles, Calif., May 18–19, 2000 (final draft June 2000).

60. See Barry Eichengreen, "What Problems can Dollarization Solve?", *University of California at Berkeley Working Paper*, January 2001 (unpublished).

61. For a discussion see Atish Ghosh, Anne-Marie Gulde and Holger Wolf, "Currency Boards: More Than a Quick Fix?", *Economic Policy*, vol. 15, no. 31, October 2000, pp. 269–335.

62. See Alberto Alesina and Robert Barro, "Dollarization," *American Economic Review*, vol. 91, no. 2, May 2001, pp. 381–385. See also Alberto Alesina and Robert Barro, "Currency unions," *NBER Working Paper*, No. 7927, September 2000.

63. Walter Molano, *Addressing the Symptoms and Ignoring the Causes: A View from Wall Street on Dollarization*, New York, BCP Securities, 2000.

64. See Jeffrey Frieden, "The Political Economy of Dollarization: Domestic and International Factors," *Harvard University*, prepared for a conference in Buenos Aires, May 12–13, 2000 (unpublished).

65. For a view on the economic timing of dollarization see Barry Eichengreen, "When to Dollarize?", *University of California at Berkeley Working Paper*, February 2000, published in the *Journal of Money, Credit, and Banking*, vol. 34, no. 1, February 2002.

66. For an analysis of capital markets' reactions to Argentine policy announcements, see Eduardo Ganapolsky and Sergio Schmukler, "Crisis Management in Capital Markets: The Impact of Argentine Policy During the Tequila Effect," *World Bank Policy Research Working Paper*, No. 1951, 1998 (forthcoming in *Economists' Forum*).

67. Walter Molano, "Adressing the Symptoms and Ignoring the Causes: A View from Wall Street on Dollarization," New York, BCP Securities, 2000. For a closer view on the issues involved in Argentina dollarization game see the article of François Velde and Marcelo Veracierto, "Dollarization in Argentina," *Federal Reserve Bank of Chicago Economic Perspectives*, First Quarter 2000, pp. 24–35.

68. Barep Asset Management, *Emerging Markets Fixed Income Asset Allocation*, Paris, Barep Asset Management, November 2000.

69. From New York to London, the package was seen as a positive (and expected) confidence shock, as stressed, e.g., by Morgan Stanley, *Argentina: Financial Package has Finally Arrived*, New York, Morgan Stanley Equity Research, Latin American Economics, December 19, 2000; BSCH Investment, *Argentina Under the Umbrella of the IMF*, New York, BSCH Santander Central Hispano Investment Latin America daily *Perspectives*, January 9, 2001; or HSBC, *Argentina: Domestic Adjustment, Multilateral Support*, London and New York, HSBC Global Economics and Investment Strategy, November 2000; WestLB, *Global Emerging Markets Monthly Economic Outlook*, London, WestLB Economics Research, January 8, 2001, pp. 70–73. However, the IMF package was also perceived as not solving medium-term and pending issues of Argentina (need for stronger growth), see e.g. CDC Ixis, *Risques émergents*, Paris, CDC Ixis, December 2000, no. 43; ING Barings, *Argentina: One More Chance for Growth*, New York, ING Barings Latin American Economics, December 21, 2000; BBVA, *Latinwatch*, Madrid, BBVA Servicios de Estudios, January 2001.

70. Scotiabank, *Global Views. First Half 2001*, Toronto, Scotiabank Global Economic Research, January 2001, p. 37.

71. Mohamed El-Erian, "IMF Delivers Packages for the Holidays," *PIMCO Emerging Markets Watch*, PIMCO, December 2000.

72. The first weeks of 2001 reflected a complete somersault in investor attitudes. In the fourth quarter of 2000, Latin borrowers hardly raised US$1.7 bn. In January 2001 alone, the figure was US$6.7 bn. Brazil (with a share of 32%) and Mexico (20%) lead Latin sovereign issues during the first three months of 2001. See, "A Reversal of Fortunes," *Latin Finance*, March 2001, pp. 30–34.

73. ING Barings, *Emerging Markets Weekly Report*, London, ING Barings Emerging Markets Research, January 26, 2001.

74. See e.g., the reports of CDC Ixis, "Trade-Driven Spread of a Growth Shock: Simulations on Bilateral Elasticities," *Emerging Regions Report*, no. 9, Paris, CDC Ixis Research, Country Risk and Emerging Markets Unit, Department of Economic and Financial Analysis, December 2000, pp. 17–29; Fortis Investment Management, "Les marchés émergents dans le cas d'un atterrissage brutal aux Etats-Unis," *Tendance des Marchés Emergents*, no. 4, Fourth Quarter 2000, Paris, Fortis Investment Management, 2000; UBS Warburg, "Global Emerging Markets in 2001," London, *UBS Warburg Global Equity Research*, December 19, 2000, pp. 7–11; BBVA Securities, "The US Slowdown, the Fed and Latin America," London, *BBVA Securities Latin American Economic and Equity Research*, January 8, 2001; Standard Chartered, "Economic Update: The US and Its Impact on Latin America," Miami, *Standard Chartered*, January 12, 2001.

75. Goldman Sachs, "The US Downturn: Risks and Effects on Latin America," New York, *Goldman Sachs Latin America Economic Analyst*, New York, Goldman Sachs, January 19, 2001; and HSBC, "How the World will Deal with a US Recession," London, *HSBC Global Economics & Investment Strategy*, First Quarter 2001

76. Morgan Chase, "Mexican Corporates and the US Downturn," New York, *JP Morgan Chase Emerging Markets Research*, March 14, 2001.

77. For a political analysis of the Argentinian crisis, during the de la Rúa (and previously Menem) presidency, see Javier Corrales, "The Political Causes of Argentina's Recession," *Woodrow Wilson International Center for Scholars*, June 2001 (unpublished).

78. Goldman Sachs, "Argentina: It's Déjà vu all Over Again!", New York, *Goldman Sachs Global Economic Weekly*, March 28, 2001; Deutsche Bank, "Argentina Risk Monitor," New York, *Deutsche Bank Emerging Markets, Global Markets Research*, March 30, 2001; JP Morgan Chase, "Argentina at a Critical Juncture," in *Emerging Markets Today*, New York, JP Morgan Chase Emerging Markets Research, March 26, 2001; or Crédit Agricole Indosuez, "Argentina: The Political Gamble," Paris, *Crédit Agricole Indosuez Global Economic Markets Strategy*, March 29, 2001.

79. Morgan Stanley Dean Witter, "Argentina: The White Knight Rides Again," New York, *Morgan Stanley Dean Witter Latin American Economics, Equity Research Latin America*, March 26, 2001.

80. Walter Molano, "High Stakes Poker," New York, *BCP Securities Latin American Advisor*, March 28, 2001.

81. Latin America totaled 66% of all emerging market debt issuance in 2000. See Ingrid Iversen, "Emerging Market Debt: Fundamental and Flows," London, *Rothschild Asset Management*, March 2001 (presented at the European Pensions Symposium in Barcelona). However emerging sovereign bond market represent only 5% of all government bond market in 2000 according to Merrill Lynch, see Merrill Lynch, "Size and Structure of the World Bond Market: 2000," London and New York, *Merrill Lynch Fixed Income Strategy*, April 2000.

82. This was mainly the case of emerging capital market economists who started to point out the positive impacts of the Cavallo. See e.g. Barclays Capital, "Emerging Markets—Latin America," New York, *Barclays Capital*, March 29, 2001. For debt market analysts the worries were also the possible financial contagion to other Latin American markets, analysts trying to convince themselves—and their clients—that they were insulated. See e.g. ING Barings,

"Brazil: Fundamentally Insulated from Argentina, but Still Vulnerable," New York and London, *ING Barings Emerging Markets Weekly Report*, March 23, 2001.

83. ABN Amro, "Daily Strategy," New York, *ABN Amro Emerging Markets*, April 5, 2001.

84. As noted by BBVA's head of Latam Strategies, "the gambling man" Domingo Cavallo has not got much time. "The markets are impatient, Argentines are desperate and the October Congressional are elections looming." "We need to see a quick stabilization of reserves and bank deposits, followed by concrete evidence of an improvement in sentiment and the first signs turnaround in activity. If all this does not occur within the next 90 days or so, a more dramatic outcome could occur." See BBVA Securities, "Argentina: Cavallo Bets all on Growth," London, *BBVA Securities Latin American Fixed Income Economics*, April 6, 2001. Previously these views were expressed also in several other reports by a major security house operating in Latin American emerging markets and one of the most respected Latin American economist of the city according to the interviews realized in London with fund managers and strategists in London and Edinburgh in April, June and October 2000. See also BBVA Securities, "Q2 Outlook: Keep Clipping the Coupons," London, *BBVA Securities Fixed Income & Foreign Exchange*, March 15, 2001.

85. See Dresdner Bank Lateinamerika, "Two Weeks and Five Presidents Later," London and Frankfurt, *Dresdner Latin American Daily Spotlight*, January 2, 2001.

86. See Mark P. Jones, Sebastian Saiegh, Pablo Spiller and Mariano Tommasi, "Políticos profesionales—legisladores 'amateurs': el congreso argentino en el siglo XX," *CEDI Working Paper*, No. 45, Buenos Aires, *Fundación Gobierno y Sociedad*, November 2000 (unpublished). Argentina is one of the major developing countries that has been well documented by institutionalists; therefore there is considerable background research that will be very helpful, see e.g., Pablo T. Spiller and Mariano Tommasi, "The Institutional Foundations of Public Policy: A Transactions Approach with Application to Argentina," *CEDI, Fundación Gobierno y Sociedad, Working Paper*, 2001 (unpublished).

87. See also Mark P. Jones, Sebastian Saeigh, Pablo T. Spiller and Mariano Tommasi, "Keeping a Seat in Congress: Provincial Party Bosses and the Survival of Argentine Legislators," prepared for delivery at the *2001 Annual Meeting of American Political Science Association*, San Francisco, September 2, 2001.

88. See Pablo Spiller and Mariano Tommasi, "Los determinantes institucionales del desarrollo argentino: una aproximación desde la nueva economía institucional," *CEDI Working Paper*, No. 33, Buenos Aires, *Fundación Gobierno y Sociedad*, May 2000; published in *Desarrollo Económico*, vol. 40, no. 159, October–December 2000, pp. 425–464; and Matias Iaryczower, Pablo Spiller and Mariano Tommasi, "Judicial Decision Making in Unstable Environments, Argentina, 1935–1998," *Universidad San Andrés, University of Califorina at Berkeley and Harvard University, Working Paper*, 2000 (unpublished).

89. Jon Elster, *Ulysses Unbound: Studies in Rationality, Precommitment and Constraints*, Cambridge, Cambridge University Press, 2000 (reprinted). This idea (probably without reference to Elster works) was strangely also made by a respected Brazilian economist who wrote about Argentina monetary and exchange rate policies, "the country chose to give up two of its economic policy instruments, for it believed that most likely they would not be used widely, as the country's history eloquently illustrates. This was indeed a measure to tie Odysseus to the mast, and prevent him from being dragged by the siren's song." See Alexandre Schwartsman, "Argentina's last hand," *Indosuez W.I. Carr Securities Research Nullum Gratuitum Prandium*, Sao Paulo, Indosuez W. I. Carr Securities, March 19, 2001.

90. See James Vreeland, "The IMF: Lender of Last Resort or Scapegoat?", *Yale University Leitner Working Paper*, No. 3, 1999 (unpublished); James Vreeland, "Why do Governments and the IMF Enter into Agreements? Statistically Selected Cases," *Yale University Leitner Working Paper*, No. 4, 2000 (unpublished); Adam Przeworski and James Vreeland, "The Effect of IMF Programs on Economic Growth," *Journal of Development Economics*, vol. 62, no. 2, 2000, pp. 385–421;

James Vreeland, "Why Governments Enter into IMF Programs? The Effects of Presidentialism," *Universidad Torcuato di Tella Working Paper*, June 2002.

91. See James Raymond Vreeland, "Why do Governments and the IMF Enter into Agreements? Statistically Selected Cases," prepared for the *2000 Annual Meeting of the Midwest Political Science Association*, April 27–30, 2000. See also James Raymond Vreeland, *IMF and Economic Development*, Cambridge, Mass., Cambridge University Press, 2002.

92. For an empirical test of this argument using data from 179 countries from 1975 to 1996, see James Raymond Vreeland, "Institutional Determinants of IMF Agreements," *Yale University, Department of Political Science*, September 28, 2001 (unpublished).

93. See e.g. the critique of Leslie Elliott Armijo, ed., *Financial Globalization and Democracy in Emerging Markets*, London, MacMillan, 1999.

94. See Chase Fleming Asset Management, *Emerging Equity Markets. Quarterly Review*, London, Chase Fleming Asset Management, November 2000, p. 5.

95. See Sylvia Maxfield, "Globalization, Economic Policymaking and Democratization," speech prepared for the *UNRSID Conference on Technocratic Policymaking and Democratization*, Geneva, April 27–28, 2000 (unpublished); and Sylvia Maxfield, "Understanding the Political Implications of Financial Internationalization in Emerging Markets Countries," *World Development*, vol. 26, 1998, pp. 1201–1219.

96. See, e.g., explicit references to growth dynamics by Michael Cembalest and Paul Dickson, JP Morgan emerging markets debt managers, in their *JP Morgan Markets Debt Fund Quarterly Report*, September 2000 (http://jpmorgan.com/mutualfunds) or Mohamed El-Erian, PIMCO emerging markets debt manager, in his *PIMCO Emerging Markets Watch*, October 2000 (http://www.pimco.com). Julius Baer emerging markets debt team was even more direct concerning Argentina: "Argentina is the simplest to analyse. A rash of debt dynamics studies, qualifications, re-analysis and data-mining has not altered one fact (which the market fully recognize)—a return to growth of say 4% a year will boost tax revenues, restore confidence and prevent a debt spiral while further stagnation will lead to a crisis and possibility a default." Julius Bär, *Fixed Income Essentials. 4th Quarter 2000*, London, Julius Baer Investment Management, 2000, p. 5 (http://www.juliusbaer.com).

97. The long-term horizon of direct investors, among other implications, reduces their sensitivity to financial or monetary crises. Unlike portfolio investors or banking lenders, they are less likely to withdraw capital during financial crises episodes as stressed by several comparative studies, see e.g. Robert Lipsey, "Foreign Direct Investors in Three Financial Crises," *National Bureau of Economic Research Working Paper*, No. 8084, January 2001 (unpublished). On the temporal horizons of foreign direct investors, see the survey results published in Javier Santiso and Paolo Giordano, "La course aux Amériques: les stratégies des investisseurs européens dans le Mercosur," *Problèmes d'Amérique latine*, no. 39, October–December 2000, pp. 55–87; and Javier Santiso, *En busca de El Dorado de las Américas: la internacionalización de las multinacionales y de las pymes francesas hacia América latina*, Paris, CERI (Sciences Po) Working Paper, prepared for the IADB (Inter-American Development Bank) 2001.

98. See interviews with emerging markets fund managers in Paris, April 28, 2000, London, May 2, 2000 and Boston, November 20, 2000. The distribution of emerging market debt fund industry can give an idea of the share of long-term fund strategies. "Dedicated" investors with constant strategic allocation, typically looking to outperform an emerging market index, represent only 25% of all emerging debt market fund holders in 2000 against 40% for "cross-over" investors with tactical short-term allocation policies. The remaining share is distributed among local investors, 20%, and retail and original bank holders, 15%, that can have either short- or long-term strategies. See Ingrid Iversen, *Emerging Market Debt: Fundamental and Flows*, London, Rothschild Asset Management, March 2001 (presented at the European Pensions Symposium in Barcelona).

99. Templeton Asset Management, *Manager's Perspective, Emerging Markets Series*, Templeton Asset Management, September 30, 2000 (http://www.fttrust.com/library/library.htm).

100. Interviews, New York, May 1 and 10, 2000, with emerging bonds markets fund manager and emerging markets fixed income team; interview in London, April 13, 2000, with an emerging bond markets fund manager; and interview in Paris, November 17, 2000, with an emerging bond market fund manager.

101. Interview, London, April 12, 2000, with a mutual fund asset manager in global emerging markets; and interview in Paris, June 9, 2000, with another mutual fund asset manager in global emerging markets.

102. As showed by Frieden, Ghezzi and Stein, who analyzed the behavior of nominal and real exchanges rates within a 19-month window centered on more than 240 election episodes in Latin America, the probability of large real depreciations is typically affected (over 25%) by the electoral cycle. See Jeffry Frieden, Piero Ghezzi and Ernesto Stein, "Politics and Exchange Rates: A Cross-Country Approach to Latin America," in Jeffry Frieden and Ersneto Stein, eds., *The Currency Game: Exchange Rate Politics in Latin America*, Baltimore, The Johns Hopkins University Press, 2001. See currency games and the political economy of exchange rates regimes in Latin America, Carol Wise and Riordan Roett, eds., *Exchange Rate Politics in Latin America*, Washington, D.C., Brookings Institution, 2000.

103. For an analysis centered on the political economy of the crisis, see Jeffry Frieden, "The Politics of Exchange Rates," in Sebastian Edwards and Moisés Naim, eds., *Mexico 1994: Anatomy of an Emerging Markets Crash*, Washington, D.C., Carnegie Endowment for International Peace, 1997, pp. 81–94.

104. See Joseph Stiglitz, "The Insider: What I learned at the World Economic Crisis," *The New Republic*, April 17, 2000. See also http://www.brookings.edu/views/articles/Stiglitz/20000417. htm; and the essay (presented at an IMF meeting) of Moisés Naim, "Washington Consensus or Washington Confusion?" *Foreign Policy*, Spring 2000, pp. 87–103.

Chapter Three   Capital Flows to Emerging Markets: Goodbye the Golden 1990s?

1. This chapter is based on previous studies conducted in 2000 with the support of the SG, see Javier Santiso, "Capital Flows to Emerging Markets: Welcome to Latin America," Paris, *SG Emerging Markets Quarterly*, April 2000; Javier Santiso, "Capital Flows and Perceived Risks: A Latin American and Global Emerging Markets Survey," Paris, *SG Emerging Markets Quarterly*, July 2000; Javier Santiso, "Capital Flows in Emerging Countries: Back to the Future?" Paris, *SG Emerging Markets Quarterly*, October 2000.

2. The peak of capital inflows during the 1990s was reached in 1992, total capital flows representing 2.16% of Latin American GDP. Note however that this peak was lower than the record capital flows reached just before the debt crisis. In 1981, capital flows received by Latin American countries amounted to 3.32% of Latin America GDP. See for a very interesting analysis Guillermo Calvo, Eduardo Fernández-Arias, Carmen Reihnart and Ernesto Talvi, "Growth and External Financing in Latin America," *Inter-American Development Bank Working Paper*, No. 457, prepared for the seminar "What is Holding Back Growth in Latin America and the Caribbean? What Should Governments do?", *IADB Annual Meetings of the Board of Governors*, Santiago de Chile, March 18, 2001.

3. JP Morgan, "Emerging Markets Debt: Outlook for 2002," New York, *JP Morgan Emerging Markets Research*, December 17, 2001, pp. 4 and 6.

4. See Sebastian Edwards, ed., *Capital Flows and the Emerging Economies*, Chicago, Ill., The University of Chicago Press, 2000.

5. See Peter Blair Henry, "Do Stock Market Liberalizations Cause Investment Booms?", *Journal of Financial Economics*, vol. 58, no. 1, October 2000, pp. 301–334; and also for a similar analysis Geert Bekaert and Campbell Harvey, "Foreign Speculators and Emerging Equity Markets," *The Journal of Finance*, vol. 55, no. 2, April 2000, pp. 565–613.

6. See Anusha Chari and Peter Blair Henry, "Capital Account Liberalization: Allocative Efficiency or Animal Spirits," *University of Michigan Business School and Stanford University Graduate School of Business*, September 2001 (unpublished).

7. Geert Bekaert, Campbell Harvey and Christian Lundblad, "Does Financial Liberalization Spur Growth?" *NBER Working Paper*, No. 8245, 2001, a new paper version presented also at the *28th Annual Meeting of the European Finance Association*, Universitat Pompeu Fabra, Barcelone, August 22–25, 2001.

8. See among the last empirical research papers, Carlos Arteta, Barry Eichengreen and Charles Wyplosz, "On the Growth Effects of Capital Account Liberalization," *University of California at Berkeley, Working Paper*, 2001 (unpublished); Sebastian Edwards, "Capital Mobility and Economic Performance: Are Emerging Economies Different?", *NBER Working Paper*, No. 8076, 2001.

9. For a closer analysis of twentieth-century finance (including emerging markets) see Raghuram G. Rajan and Luigi Zingales, "The Great Reversals: The Politics of Financial Development in the 20th Century," *University of Chicago, Working Paper*, June 2001 (unpublished); Maurice Obstfeld and Alan M. Taylor, "Globalization and Capital Markets," in Michael Bordo, Alan M. Taylor and Jeffrey Williamson, eds., *Globalization in Historical Perspective*, Chicago, Ill., NBER and The University of Chicago Press, 2002; Michael Bordo, Barry Eichengreen and Douglas A. Irwin, "Is Globalization Today Really Different than Globalization a Hundred Years Ago?" in Susan M. Collins and Robert Z. Lawrence, eds., *Brookings Trade Forum*, Washington D.C., Brookings Institution, 1999, pp. 1–50.

10. See Michael Bordo, "The Globalization of International Financial Markets: What Can History Teach Us?", *Rutgers University and National Bureau of Economic Research*, March 2000 (unpublished). For more a stimulating historical perspective on globalization see Michael Bordo, Alan M. Taylor and Jeffrey Williamson, eds., *Globalization in Historical Perspective*, Chicago, Ill., NBER and The University of Chicago Press, 2002.

11. See Ashoka Mody and Antu Panini Murschid, "Growing Up with Capital Inflows," IMF, 2001 (unpublished). See also on the policy implications of capital flows volatility Guillermo Calvo and Carmen Reinhart, "When Capital Flows Come to a Sudden Stop: Consequences and Policy Options," in Peter Kenen and Alexander Swoboda, eds., *Reforming the International Monetary and Financial Systems*, Washington, D.C., IMF, 2000, pp. 175–201; Guillermo Calvo and Carmen Reinhart, "Fear of Floating," *Quarterly Journal of Economics*, vol. 117, no. 2, May 2002, pp. 379–408.

12. See Michael Bordo, Barry Eichengreen, Daniela Klingebiel and Maria Soledad Martinez-Peria, "Is the Crisis Problem Growing More Severe?", *Economic Policy*, vol. 16, no. 32, April 2001, pp. 51–82.

13. Barry Echeigreen and Michael Bordo, "Crises Now and Then: What Lessons from the Last Era of Financial Globalization?" prepared for the conference in honor of Charles Goodhart, London, *Bank of England*, November 15–16, 2001.

14. See Sebastian Edwards and Raul Susmel, "Volatility Dependence and Contagion in Emerging Equity Markets," *NBER Working Paper*, No. 8506, October 2001.

15. Charles Kindleberger, *Manias, Panics and Crashes. A History of Financial Crises*, New York, John Wiley & Sons, 1996 and 2001.

16. For a comparative perspective on the "great transformation" of capital markets during the period 1870–1929 and the globalization trends by the end of the twentieth century, see Marc Flandreau, "Le début de l'histoire: globalisation financière et relations internationales," *Politique Etrangère*, 3–4, 2000, pp. 673–686; Marc Flandreau and Chantale Rivière, "La Grande transformation? Contrôles de capitaux et intégration financière internationale, 1880–1996," *Economie Internationale*, no. 78, Second Quarter 1999, pp. 11–58; Daniel Verdier, "Capital Market Internationalization, 1870–1914," *International Organization*, vol. 52, no. 1, 1998, pp. 1–34.

17. Later U.S. bankers followed the British, investing their portfolios in particular in Latin America, see Barbara Stallings, *Banker to the Third World: US Portfolio Investment in Latin America, 1900–1986*, Berkeley, University of California Press, 1987.

18. See the two economist's essay Kevin O'Rourke and Jeffrey Williamson, *Globalisation and History: The Evolution of the Nineteenth-Century Atlantic Economy*, Cambridge, Mass., MIT Press, 2000.

19. See John Coastworth and Alan Taylor, *Latin America and the World Economy Since 1800*, Cambridge, Mass., Harvard University Press, 1998.

20. See Michael A. Clemens and Jeffrey Williamson, "Wealth Bias in the First Global Capital Market Boom, 1870–1913," *Harvard University, Working Paper*, July 2001 (unpublished).

21. For a closer and more detailed analysis, see Piti Disyatat and Gaston Gelos, "The Asset Allocation of Emerging Market Mutual Funds," *IMF Working Paper*, WP/01/111, August 2001.

22. See for a detailed study Juan Yermo, "Institutional Investors in Latin America: Recent Trends and Regulatory Challenges," in *Institutional Investors in Latin American Paris*, OECD, 2000, pp. 21–119; and for pension funds data José Garcia-Cantera and Ramon Portillo, "Latin America Private Pension Funds," New York, *Salomon Smith Barney Latin America Equity Research*, April 18, 2001; and JP Morgan, "Pension Reforms Altering Market Dynamics for Emerging Debt Market," New York, *JP Morgan Securities Emerging Markets Research*, December 21, 2001.

23. For measure of private capital flows for a sample of 67 developing and industrial countries see Philip Lane and Gian Maria Milesi-Ferretti, "The External Wealth of Nations: Measures of Foreign Assets and Liabilities for Industrial and Developing Countries," *Journal of International Economics*, vol. 55, no. 2, December 2001, pp. 263–294.

24. Institute of International Finance, *Capital Flows to Emerging Market Economies*, Washington, D.C., IIF, September 20, 2001. In 2001, net capital flows to emerging countries, due to increasing risk aversion following terrorist attacks in the United States on September 11 and the U.S. slowdown, were expected to fall sharply to less than US$ 110 bn. Net official flows, due in part to Argentina and Turkey rescue packages, were expected to jump to US$30 bn. See also for more data International Monetary Fund, *World Economic Outlook. October 2001. The Information Technology Revolution*, Washington, D.C., IMF, 2001.

25. See UNCTAD, *World Investment Report 2001. Promoting Linkages*, Geneva, UNCTAD, 2001, p. 52.

26. See for more examples Stephen Thomsen, "Investment Patterns in a Longer-Term Perspective," *OECD Working Papers on International Investment*, No. 2, November 2000.

27. On this topic, see Brieuc Monfort and Christian Mulder, "Using Credit Ratings for Capital Requirements on Lending to Emerging Market Economies—Possible Impact of a New Basel Accord," *IMF Working Paper*, No. 69, March 2000. Another study underlines that these patterns are less present in Latin America, with foreign banks in Mexico and Argentina showing sizeable credit growth during crisis periods and, even more, lower lending volatility than domestic banks. This study confirms that foreign banks contribute more than local banks to lower overall credit volatility in emerging markets. Linda Goldberg, Gerard Dages and Daniel Kinney, "Foreign and Domestic Bank Participation in Emerging Markets: Lessons from Mexico and Argentina," *NBER Working Paper*, No. 7714, May 2000.

28. On the specific effects of U.S. bank lending (that typically lend to Latin America when U.S. economy is expanding and reduce flows when the U.S. economy goes into recession), see Linda Goldberg, "When is US Bank Lending to Emerging Markets Volatile?", *Federal Reserve Bank of New York and NBER*, New York, March 2001.

29. See Helmut Reisen and Julia von Maltzan, "Boom and Bust and Sovereign Ratings," *International Finance*, vol. 2, no. 2, July 1999, pp. 273–293; Helmut Resein, "Revisions to the Basel Accord and Sovereign Ratings," in Ricardo Hausmann and Ulrich Hiemenz, eds., *Global Finance from a Latin American Viewpoint*, Paris, OECD, 2000, pp. 71–80.

30. See Avinash Persaud, "Sending the Herd Off the Cliff Edge: The Disturbing Interaction Between Herding and Market Sensitive Risk Management Practices," *Jacques de Larosière Essay on Global Finance*, Washington DC, Institute of International Finance, September 2000.

31. See for more details Graciela Kaminsky and Carmen Reinhart, "Bank Lending and Contagion: Evidence from Asian crisis," *NBER's 10th Annual East Asia Seminar on Economics*, 1999, published in T. Ito and Anne Krueger, eds., *Regional and Global Capital Flows: Macroeconomic Causes and*

Consequences, Chicago, Chicago University Press for the NBER, 2001; Graciela Kaminsky and Carmen Reinhart, "On Crises, Contagion and Confusion," *Journal of International Economics*, vol. 51, no. 1, June 2000, pp. 145–168; Beatrice Weder and Caroline van Rijckeghem, "Sources of Contagion: Is It Finance or Trade?", *Journal of International Economics*, vol. 54, no. 2, August 2001, pp. 293–308; Caroline van Rijckeghem and Beatrice Weder, "Spillovers Through the Banking Centre. A Panel Data Analysis," *IMF Working Paper*, No. 88, May 2000; Jacques Cailloux and Stephany Griffith-Jones, "International Bank Lending and the East Asian Crisis," *Institute of Development Studies Working Paper*, University of Sussex, March 2000 (unpublished).

32. The EMAI is based on an annual survey of 111 international experts in government agencies and private sector organizations in the United States and Canada. The country score is based on 16 measures of market openness that include among others average intellectual property rights protection, tariff levels, import quotas, certification barriers, standard barriers and investment barriers.

33. See JP Morgan Chase, "Latin America Focus: Capital Flows," in JP Morgan Chase, Global Data Watch, New York, *JP Morgan Chase, Economic & Policy Research*, February 15, 2002.

34. See CEPAL, *La inversión extranjera en América Latina y el Caribe*, Santiago de Chile, CEPAL, 2002.

35. See Javier Santiso, "Business as Unusual: The Politicial Economy of Mexican and European Relations," prepared for the forthcoming book edited by Riordan Roett, *Mexico: New Scenarios for the Future*, 2003, and presented at SAIS Johns Hopkins University, Bologna and Washington, D.C., April and June 2001. The Mercosur tropism of European investors is clearly examplified not only by Spanish corporations but also by other major European firms such as French multinationals, see Javier Santiso and Paolo Giordano, "La course aux Amériques: les stratégies des investisseurs européens dans le Mercosur," *Problèmes d'Amérique latine*, No. 39, October–December 2000, pp. 55–87; and Javier Santiso, "France," in Ziga Vodusek, ed., *Foreign Direct Investment in Latin America. The Role of European Investors*, Washington, Inter-American Development Bank, 2002, pp. 143–175.

36. However, the pattern can differ from one country to another; on the impact of U.S. interest rates on domestic interest rates and exchange rates across emerging markets, see Eduardo Borensztein, Jeromin Zettelmeyer and Thomas Philippon, "Monetary Independence in Emerging Markets: Does the Exchange Rate Regime Make a Difference?", *IMF Working Paper*, WP/01/1, January 2001; and for different tests and scenarios of the combined impact of interest rates and exchange rates in the United States on emerging markets, see the study by Carmen Reinhart and Vincent Raymond Reinhart, "What hurts most? G3 Exchange Rate or Interest Rate Volatility?", *University of Maryland and Board of Governors of the Federal Reserve System*, March 2001.

37. See Rui Albuquerque, "The Composition of International Capital Flows: Risk Sharing Through Foreign Direct Investment," *Simon School of Business, Rochester University*, June 2001.

38. See Robert Lipsey, "Foreign Direct Investment in Three Financial Crises," *NBER Working Paper*, No. 8084, January 2001.

39. See Laura Alfaro and Areedam Chanda, "FDI and Economic Growth: The Role of Local Financial Markets," *Harvard Business School and University of Houston*, February 2001 (unpublished).

40. A long-term analysis suggests also that: (1) this kind of trend can be reversed (even if it's difficult; (2) that in the case of Argentina, the number of listed companies per million people did not stop the decrease during the twentieth century falling from 15.29 listed companies per million people in 1913 to 3.63 in 1999 (while the ratio of stock market capitalization over GDP remains stable), according to Raghuram Rajan and Luigi Zingales, "The Great Reversals: The Politics of Financial Development in the 20th Century," *OECD Economics Department*, Working Paper 38, 2000.

41. Lucio Sarno and Mark Taylor, "Hot Money, Accounting Labels and the Permanence of Capital Flows to Developing Countries: An Empirical Investigation," *Journal of Development Economics*, 1999, vol. 59, no. 2, pp. 337–364.

42. Eduardo Fernandez-Arias and Ricardo Hausmann, "Is Foreign Direct Investment a Safer Form of Financing?", *Emerging Markets Review*, vol. 2, no. 1, March 2001, pp. 34–49. However, as stressed by these two economists in another paper, the rise of FDI and in particular the share of FDI in total inflows, is not an indication of good economic health. It can be explained by the simple fact that, after the Tequila crisis in the mid-1990s, international companies tended to prefer more equity and less debt in the composition of their capital in order to avoid financial turbulence. The rise of FDI (which represent nearly 97% of net private capital inflows in 1999 for Latin American countries) was an adaptative response by international firms to a deteriorating environment. See Ricardo Hausmann and Eduardo Fernandez-Arias, "Foreign Direct Investment: Good Cholesterol?" paper prepared for the *Annual Meeting of the Board of Governors of the Inter-American Development Bank*, New Orleans, March 26, 2000.

43. See Marcelo Soto, "Capital Flows and Growth in Developing Countries: Recent Empirical Evidence," *OECD Development Centre*, February 2000 (unpublished); Helmut Reisen and Marcelo Soto, "Which Types of Capital Flows Foster Developing-Country Growth?", *International Finance*, vol. 4, no. 1, Spring 2001, pp. 1–14.

44. See Bear Stearns, "Latin America. Impact of Argentina: Opening Pandora's Box," Bear Stearns, Latin America Watch, New York, *Bear Stearns Emerging Markets Equity Research*, January 10, 2002.

45. See Institute of International Finance, *Capital Flows to Emerging Market Economies*, Washington, DC, IIF, January 30, 2002.

46. See e.g. Trevor Greetham and Owain Evans, *Fund Manager Survey: May 2000*, New York, Merrill Lynch Global Securities and Research Group, May 17, 2000; Douglas Beck and Joshua Mendes, *Country Funds: Emerging Markets Update. Temporarily Defensive, yet Valuations Remain Compelling*, New York, Merrill Lynch Global Funds Research Department, June 1, 2000.

47. See e.g. Crédit Lyonnais Securities Americas, "Emerging Markets Fund Flows," New York, *CLSA Global Emerging Markets Research*, 2000 (one issue per month); Ajay Kapur, Elaine Chu and Narenda Singh, "GEMS Analytics: US Mutual Fund Flows and Investor Risk-Love Charts," New York, *Morgan Stanley Dean Witter Global Equity Research*, May 29, 2000; William Dinning, "US Listed Country Funds," London, *UBS Warburg Global Equity Research*, June 6, 2000. For *AMG Data Services* see www.amgdata.com.

48. See Sergio Schmukler, Richard Lyons and Graciela Kaminsky, "Managers, Investors and Crises: Mutual Fund Strategies in Emerging Markets," *World Bank Working Paper*, 2399 and *NBER Working Paper*, 7855, 2000.

49. Kenneth Froot, Paul O'Connell and Mark Seasholes, "The Portfolio Flows of International Investors," *Journal of Financial Economics*, vol. 59, no. 2, February 2001, pp. 151–193; and Woochan Kim, "Foreign Portfolio Investors Before and During a Crisis," *Journal of International Economics*, 56(1), 2002, pp. 77–96.

50. See Graciela Kaminsky and Carmen Reihnart, "The Centre and the Periphery: Tales of Financial Turmoil," paper presented for the joint Asian Development Bank, International Monetary Fund and World Bank Conference on *Financial Contagion: How it Spreads and How it Can be Stopped?* February 3–4, 2000, Washington, D.C. (unpublished).

51. Robert Shiller, *Irrational Exuberance*, Princeton, Princeton University Press, 2000.

52. Graciela Kaminsky, Richard Lyons and Sergio Schmukler, "Managers, Investors and Crises: Mutual Fund Strategies in Emerging Markets," *World Bank Working Paper*, 2399 and *NBER Working Paper*, 7855, 2000.

53. Kenneth Froot, Paul O'Connell and Mark Seasholes, "The Portfolio Flows of International Investors," *Journal of Financial Economics*, vol. 59, no. 2, February 2001, pp. 151–193. On herding behavior and mutual funds momentum strategies, see Sushil Bikhchandani and Sunil Sharma,

"Herd Behavior in Financial Markets: A Review," *IMF Working Paper*, No. 48, March 2000.

54. For further analysis, see Stephany Griffith-Jones, "The Role of Mutual Funds and Other International Investors in Currency Crises," *Institute of Development Studies Working Paper*, University of Sussex, February 2000 (unpublished); Stephany Griffith-Jones, Manuel Montes and Anwar Masution, eds., *Short-Term Capital Flows and Economic Crises*, Oxford, Oxford University Press, 2001. See also the respective role of U.S. market shifting sentiments and domestic Asian markets during the Asian crisis, Benjamin Cohen and Eli Remolona, "Information Flows During the Asian Crisis: Evidence from Closed-End Funds," *BIS Working Papers*, No. 97, December 2000.

55. See Jorge Mariscal and Kent Hargis, "Money is not Everything. Fundamentals, not Benchmark Indices, will Drive Fund Flows to Emerging Markets," New York, *Goldman Sachs Global Emerging Markets*, November 22, 1999; Kent Hargis and Jorge Mariscal, "Emerging Markets Flow of Funds Monitor. Where is the Money Coming From?", New York, *Goldman Sachs Global Emerging Markets*, November 26, 1999.

56. See Barry Eichengreen, Andrew Rose and Charles Wyplosz, "Contagious Currency Crises: First Tests," *Scandinavian Journal of Economics*, vol. 98, no. 4, 1996, pp. 463–484.

57. See Manmohan Kumar and Avinash Persaud, "Pure Contagion and Investors' Shifting Risk Appetite: Analytical Issues and Empirical Evidence," *IMF Working Paper*, No. 134, September 2001.

58. See Guillermo Calvo and Enrique Mendoza, "Rational Contagion and the Globalization of Securities Markets," *Journal of International Economics*, vol. 51, no. 1, June 2000, pp. 79–113; and for a discussion Gary Schinasi and Todd Smith, "Portfolio Diversification, Leverage, and Financial Contagion," *IMF Staff Papers*, vol. 47, no. 2, 2001, pp. 159–176.

59. See Piti Disyatat and Gaston Gelos, "The Asset Allocation of Emerging Market Mutual Funds," *IMF Working Paper*, WP/01/111, August 2001.

60. Interviews with several fund managers in Madrid, April 7 and 8, 2001; Paris, May 14, June 7 and 14, 2001, July 27, 2001; Washington, March 21, 2001; Edinburgh, November 17, 20 and 21, 2000; New York, January 15, 17 and 19, 2001; London, October 4, 6 and 17, 2000.

61. Interview with a fund manager, London, June 1, 2000.

62. Interview with an emerging markets fund manager, New York, May 12, 2000.

63. Interview with an emerging markets fund manager, London, June 2, 2000.

64. Interview with an emerging market strategist, Paris, July 5, 2001.

65. For a comparative analysis of Latin American sovereign bonds see Martin Grandes, "Country Risk, Intertemporal Solvency and Debt Dynamics: Exploring the Latin American Cases," *OECD, Draft Paper*, August 2001 (unpublished).

66. Later other countries will follow Venezuela in 1990 (30% of debt forgiveness), Argentina in 1993 (35%), Brazil and the Dominican Republic in 1994 (35%), Ecuador, Panama and Peru in 1996 (45%). The cycle of debt buy-backs and swaps started with Mexico in 1996. In 2000, Latin America was still dominating the Brady market with only four countries (Argentina, Brazil and Mexico) accountig for 70% of the outstandings. See for a detailed analysis Inés Bustillo and Helvia Velloso, "Bond Markets for Latin American Debt in the 1990s," *ECLAC Serie Temas de Coyuntura*, No. 12, Santiago de Chile, ECLAC, November 2000.

67. Rodrigo da Fonseca, "Argentina in Numbers," Buenos Aires, *Banco de Galicia Research Department*, October 2001.

68. For a closer analysis of this "euro-ization," see Luis Miotti, Dominique Plihon and Carlos Quenan, "The Euro and Financial Relations Between Latin America and Europe: Medium- and Long-Term Implications," prepared for ECLAC and presented at CDC Ixis, seminar on *L'euro et son impact en Amérique Latine*, Paris, CDC Ixis, September 25, 2001.

69. Technically speaking, this means also that "under this strict definition of 'emerging markets,' there were no emerging markets between the first world war and the 1990s," see Paulo Mauro,

Nathan Sussman, and Yihay Yafeh, "Emerging Market Spreads: Then Versus Now," *Quarterly Journal of Economics*, vol. 117, no. 2, May 2002, pp. 695–733. In 1870–1913 the amounts of emerging market bonds were already impressive representing 45% of Britain's GDP in 1875 and 55% in 1905. By this time, the market value of Russian bonds represented nearly 12% of all government bonds traded in London while Argentina totaled 2% of total bonds traded in London (the same volumes as Brazil bonds). Regarding the development of bond markets and for a historical perspective see in particular the works of Niall Ferguson, "Wars, Revolutions and the International Bond Market From the Napoleonic wars to the First World War," Jesus College, Oxford, prepared to be presented at the *Yale International Centre for Finance*, October 15, 1999. This research project was based on a broader research program on the history of the Rothschild Bank, see Niall Ferguson, *The House of Rothschild: Money's Prophets, 1798–1848*, London, Viking Press, 1998; and Niall Ferguson, *The Cash Nexus: Money and Power in the Modern World, 1700–2000*, London, Basic Books, 2001.

70. By 1870–1913, as shown by Marc Flandreau, investors devoted substantial amounts of highly qualified human resources to monitor emerging economies and analyze economic and financial data, leading analysts to discriminate among countries in important ways. See the fascinating analysis based on archives and data from one of the leading financial operators in emerging countries by the time, Crédit Lyonnais, by Marc Flandreau, "Caveat Emptor: Coping with Sovereign Risk Without the Multilaterals," *CEPR Discussion Paper*, No. 2004, 1998.

71. See Albert Fishlow, "Lessons from the Past: Capital Markets During the 19th Century and the Interwar period," *International Organization*, vol. 39, no. 3, 1985, pp. 383–439; and, for an analysis on the rescue packages by the time, involving a reduced number of private actors, see Albert Fishlow, "Conditionality and Willingness to Pay: Some Parallels from the 1890s," in Barry Eichengreen and Peter H. Lindert, eds., *The International Debt Crisis in Historical Perspective*, Cambridge, Mass., MIT Press, 1989, pp. 86–105.

72. See Hong Min, "Determinants of Emerging Market Bond Spread: Do Economic Fundamentals Matter?" Washington, D.C., *World Bank Working Paper*, No. 1899, 1998; Alberto Ades, Federico Kaume, Paulo Leme, Rumi Masih and Daniel Tenengauzer, "Introducing GS-ESS: A New Framework for Assessing Fair Value in Emerging Markets Hard-Currency Debt," New York, *Goldman Sachs, Global Economics Paper*, No. 45, 2000.

73. See Barry Eichengreen and Ashoka Mody, "What Explains Changing Spreads on Emerging Market Debt: Fundamentals or Market Sentiment?", *World Bank RMC Discussion Paper Series*, No. 123, 1998.

Chapter Four   The Usual Suspects: Timescales, Strategies and Constraints of Emerging Market Asset Managers

1. See Woochan Kim and Shang-Jin Wei, "Offshore Investment Funds: Monsters in Emerging Markets?" Harvard University Center for International Development, *CID Working Paper*, No. 69, June 2001 (unpublished).

2. See Woochan Kim, "Foreign Portfolio Investors Before and During a Crisis," *Journal of International Economics*, 56(1), 2002, pp. 77–96.

3. See Jeffrey Frankel and Sergio Schmukler, "Country Funds and Asymmetric Information," *The World Bank Policy Research Paper*, No. 1886, 1998, published by the *International Journal of Finance and Economics*, no. 5, July 2000, pp. 177–195; and Jeffrey Frankel and Sergio Schmukler, "Country Funds Discounts, Asymmetric Information and the Mexican Financial Crisis of 1994: Did Local Residents Turn Pessimistic Before International Investors?", *NBER Working Paper*, No. 5714, 1996 (unpublished).

4. See, for analysis based on the trading behavior of the mutual funds investing in Latin America, Graciela Kaminsky, Richard Lyons and Sergio Schmukler, "Managers, Investors and Crises: Mutual Fund Strategies in Emerging Markets," *NBER Working Paper*, No. 7855, 2000 and *The World Bank Working Paper*, No. 2399.

5. Avinash Persaud, "Of Virtues and Villains—Reordering the Hierarchy of Capital Flows to Emerging Countries," *State Street Global Markets*, October 16, 2001, Avinash Persaud, "Liquidity Black Holes and Why Modern Financial Regulation in Developed Countries is Making Short-Term Capital Flows to Developing Countries even more Volatile," *United Nations University, World Institute for Development Research*, March 2002.

6. On companies' strategy operations and currency depreciations, see Graciela Moguillansky, "Non-Financial Corporate Risk Management and Exchange Rate Volatility in Latin America," *WIDER United Nations University, Discussion Paper*, No. 2002/30, March 2002, and Kristin Forbes, "How do Large Depreciations Affect Firm Performance?", *MIT-Sloan School of Management and NBER*, July 2002. On bank lending to emerging markets, see David Lubin, "Bank Lending to Emerging Markets," *WIDER United Nations University, Discussion Paper*, No. 2002/61, June 2002.

7. See Sergio Schmukler, Richard Lyons and Graciela Kaminsky, "Managers, Investors and Crises: Mutual Fund Strategies in Emerging Markets," *World Bank Working Paper*, December 1999 (unpublished).

8. Kenneth Froot, Paul O'Connell and Mark Seasholes, "The Portfolio Flows of International Investors," *Harvard University Working Paper*, August 1999 (unpublished). See on the role of mutual funds in emerging markets Stephany Griffith-Jones, "The Role of Mutual Funds and other International Investors in Currency Crises," *Institute of Development Studies, University of Sussex and Commonwealth Secretariat*, February 2000 (unpublished).

9. See Graciela Kaminsky and Carmen Reihnart, "The Centre and the Periphery: Tales of Financial Turmoil," paper presented for the joint Asian Development Bank, International Monetary Fund and World Bank Conference on *Financial Contagion: How It Spreads and How It can be Stopped?* February 3–4, 2000, Washington D.C. (unpublished).

10. See Manmohan S. Kumar and Avinash Persaud, "Pure Contagion and Investor's Shifting Risk Appetite: Analytical Issues and Empirical Evidence," *IMF Working Paper*, No. 134, September 2001.

11. Robert Shiller, "Stock Prices and Social Dynamics," *Brookings Papers on Economic Activity Review*, 2, 1984, pp. 457–498; Robert Shiller, "Speculative Prices and Popular Models," *Journal of Economic Perspectives*, 4, 1990, pp. 55–65; Robert Shiller, "Conversation, Information and Herd Behavior," *American Economic Review*, 85, 2000, pp. 181–185.

12. David Hirshleifer and Tyler Shumway, "Good Day Sunshine: Stock Returns and the Weather," *University of Michigan Business School*, March 2001 (unpublished).

13. See "Loyalty to Emerging Markets Pays Off," *Financial Times Fund Management*, July 29, 2002, p. 5.

14. Mohamed El-Erian, interview published in PIMCO website, April 2002.

15. See Paula Tkac, "The Performance of Open-End International Mutual Funds," *Federal Reserve Bank of Atlanta Economic Review*, Third Quarter 2001, pp. 1–17; based on data provided by the Center for Research in Securities Prices of the University of Chicago, see http://gsbwww.uchicago.edu/research/crsp/.

16. Mohamed El-Erian interview in PIMCO website, April 2002.

17. See interviews with fund managers in London, April 13–15, June 1, 2 and 20–24, 2000; Paris, May 18, June 8 and 17, 2000, June 14 and 15, 2001; Edinburgh, November 17, 2000; Boston, November 19, 21 and 22, 2000; and New York, May 8–12, November 6 and 7, 2000.

18. See Fortis Investment Management, "Indices Emergents!" *Tendances des Marchés Emergents*, Paris, Fortis Investment Management, no. 6, Second Quarter 2001. There has been in fact an explosion in the number of indexes used by fund managers. Barclays Global Investors, a fund manager, uses e.g. more than 200 indexes for its funds, see the Index Atlas with comparative data

on equity indexes produced by Barclays Global Investors, *Index Atlas—Equities*, London, BGI, 2000.

19. See Guillermo Calvo and Enrique Mendoza, "Rational Contagion and the Globalization of Securities Markets," *Journal of International Economics*, vol. 51, no. 1, 1999, pp. 79–113.
20. Interviews in Paris, May 18 and 19, 2000; London, June 22, 2000; New York, January 15, 17 and 19, 2001; and Madrid, May 9, 2001.
21. See Piti Disyatat and Gaston Gelos, "The Asset Allocation of Emerging Market Mutual Funds," *IMF Working Paper*, No. 111, August 2001.
22. Mohamed A. El-Erian, "The Long and Winding Road," *PIMCO Emerging Markets* Watch, October 2000.
23. See BBVA Securities, "EMBI+ Index Changes Bode Well for Brazil," Madrid, *BBVA Securities Fixed Income and Foreign Exchange Strategies*, November 13, 2001.
24. The most underrepresented continent is Africa with only three countries (South Africa, Egypt and Morocco) included in the MSCI ACWI Index in 2001.
25. Santander Central Hispano Investment, "Latin America: Daily Perspectives," New York and Latin American local branches, *BSCH Investment*, October 10, 2001; BBVA Securities, "Andean Update," London, *BBVA Securities Latin America Equities Strategy*, October 30, 2001.
26. This point was underlined by several asset managers that questioned the "Chinese wall" related issue and possible conflict of interests. See interviews in London, June 21 and 22, 2000; Paris, June 8, 2000 and June 15, 2001; Edinburgh, November 17, 2000; and New York, November 7, 2000.
27. See Capital Group Companies website: http://www.capgroup.com/; and for MSAM: http://www.morganstanley.com/im/index.html.
28. See interviews in Edinburgh November 19, 2000; New York, November 5, 2000; Paris, April 27 and 28, 2000; and London, April 10 and 11, 2000.
29. While active managers may have a 2% tracking error, that is a deviation from a chosen benchmark index, index trackers will be closer to 0.5%. They are then less risky funds but also—a major driver of their success—less costly as they charge lower fees and have lower cost expenditures, the research units and active managers being reduced to the strict minimum. On average an active manager might cost a pension fund around 30 basis points of performance in the United Kingdom e.g. while indexing costs are likely to be at maximum ten basis points for their most complex mandates.
30. See "Index-based investing," *Financial Times Survey*, Wednesday, July 18, 2001. In 1990, only 16% of the top pension fund assets were estimated (by Greenwich Associates) to be indexed. In 1999, this figure jumped to more than 28%. Among the biggest tracker managers are companies such as Barclays Global Investors (who manages US$800 bn.) and State Street Global (US$700 bn.). See interview with fund managers, London, April 12, 2000.
31. In 2000 according to William Mercer consultants' *European Pension Fund Managers Guide* there were 172 firms operating in 30 European countries and managing US$ 1,800 bn. Over a quarter of the managers were involved in mergers. The top five manager's worldwide assets totaled US$4,000 bn., that is more than the GDP of Germany and the United Kingdom put together, see "Pension Fund Investment," *Financial Times Survey*, May 21, 2000. In his report on institutional investment in the United Kingdom, Paul Myners, chairman of Gartmore, argues that the consolidation trend must however be relativized at least for the United Kingdom. He revealed that the Herfindahl–Hirschman index, which provides a measure of market concentration, gives a figure of 650 for the U.K. management industry, which is much higher than the figure for global fund management—just 100—but well below the level that cause anti-competition authorities to intervene—1000 or above. See *Investment in the UK: A Review*, London, HM Treasury, 2001. The Myners report is downloadable from: http://www. hm-treasury.gov.uk/pdf/2001/myners_report.pdf.
32. See interviews in New York, November 7, 2000; Paris, June 14, 2001; and Boston, November 21 and 22, 2000 (with the help of Daniel Charron).

33. See interviews in New York, November 6, 2000; Edinburgh, November 19–21, 2000 (with the help of Stewart Amer); and London, April 13 and 14, 2001.

34. Interviews in London, June 22, 2000; and Paris, June 8, 2000, with emerging market fund managers.

35. Interview in London, June 21, 2000 with a (active) fund manager.

36. According to Goldman Sachs, "Catching up with the Times," New York, *Goldman Sachs Emerging Market Strategist*, June 6, 2001. See also on the free float debate and the rebalancing index games of the year 2001, Goldman Sachs, "MSCI Free Float Short-Term Impact Should be Muted," New York, *Goldman Sachs Global Emerging Markets Portfolio Strategy*, May 24, 2001; USB Warburg, "MSCI Methodology Changes and Global Emerging Markets," London, *UBS Warburg Global Equity Research*, December 14, 2000; HSBC, "Free Floats in Developed and Emerging Markets," London, *HSBC Economics & Investment Strategy*, December 18, 2000; and Morgan Stanley Dean Witter, "Sink or Swim? The MSCI Free Float Debate," New York, *Morgan Stanley Dean Witter Global Equity Research Strategy*, January 31, 2001.

37. See for an empirical analysis Giancarlo Corsetti, Paolo Pesenti and Nouriel Roubini, "The Role of Large Players in Currency Crises," *University of Rome & Yale University, Federal Reserve Bank of New York and New York University*, April 2001 (unpublished); Giancarlo Corsetti, Amil Dasgupta, Stephen Morris, and Hyun Song Shin, "Does one Soros make a Difference? The Role of a Large Trader in Currency Crises," *Yale University Cowles Foundation Discussion Paper*, No. 1273, 2000; and Barry Eichengreen and Donald Mathieson, "Hedge Funds: What do we Really Know?" *IMF Economic Issues*, no. 19, September 1999.

38. See "Pension Fund Investment Survey," *Financial Times*, Thursday, Arpil 17, 2001.

39. Paul Myners, *Institutional Investment in the United Kingdom: A Review*, London, UK HM Treasury, 2001.

40. See Morgan Stanley Dean Witter, "LatStrat Monday Comment: MSCI—Changing Its Spots?" New York, *Morgan Stanley Dean Witter*, July 31, 2001.

41. Calculated from Goldman Sachs, *Global Emerging Market Strategist*, New York, Goldman Sachs, June 6, 2001.

42. Overall Latin America represents a small fraction of the world institutional market (1% of those held in OECD countries). One country alone, Brazil, accounts for around 60% of all assets held by Latin American institutional investors. See Juan Yermo, "Institutional Investors in Latin America: Recent Trends and Regulatory Challenges," in OECD, *Institutional Investors in Latin America*, Paris, OECD, 2000, pp. 23–117.

43. Goldman Sachs, "Pension and Mutual Funds and Their Impact on Stock Markets," New York, *Goldman Sachs, Latin America Portfolio Strategy*, August 31, 2001.

44. See William Mercer, *European Pension Fund Managers Guide 2001/2002—Latest Developments in Institutional Fund Management*, London, William Mercer, 2001.

45. See Pierre Laurent, Nicolas Meunier, Luis Miotti, Carlos Quenan and Véronique Seltz, "Le choix de la devise d'endettement pour un pays émergent," in CDC Ixis, *Zones émergentes*, nos. 11 and 12, Paris, CDC Ixis, December 2001 and June 2002, pp. 7–16 and pp. 14–17; and Pierre Laurent, "Risque de marché, risque de crédit et défaut: la problématique particulière de la dette souveraine émergente," *CDC Ixis Etude Marchés Emergents*, no. 2, September 2001. The exact amount invested in emerging bond markets is difficult to evaluate. The market capitalization of the different JP Morgan indexes covering emerging bond markets e.g. ranged in 1999 from US$72 bn. (JP Morgan EMBI) to 170 (JP Morgan EMBI Global). As underlined in a Bank of England report, "by focusing on restructured debts (principally Bradys), the EMBI captures only a subset of emerging economy debt. For example, at the end 1998, the total stock of Bradys had a face value of USD 121 bn, compared to USD 854 bn loans to emerging economies from BIS banks and total gross external debts of USD 2,3 trillion at end-1997." See Alastair Cunningham, "Emerging Economy Spread Indices and Financial Stability," in Bank of England, *Financial Stability Review*, London, Bank of England, November 1999, pp. 115–183.

46. The Hirschman–Herfindahl Index (H) measures the total sum of the squares of the (%) market share of all the firms in an industry: $H = S\ si2$ where s-i measures the market share of firm i.

47. The concentration of assets under management in emerging markets is only another example of the concentration trend in the entire financial industry. It is even more impressive in other markets such as derivates where a single company, JP Morgan Chase (Chase Manhattan Bank and Morgan Guaranty together), represents 60% of the total derivates market controlled by U.S. commercial banks and trusts in 2001. See Adam Hamilton, "JPM Derivatives Monster Grows," January 4, 2002 and "The JPM Derivatives Monster," September 7, 2001, both available through the website: http://www.zealllc.com/.

48. See interviews with fund managers in London, November 3–5, 2000; and Edinburgh, November 17 and 21, 2000.

49. See interviews in New York, May 8, 9 and 11, 2000. See also Paul Myners, *Institutional Investment in the United Kingdom: A Review*, London, UK HM Treasury, 2001, pp. 88–89.

50. Interviews with fund managers in New York, January 15, 17 and 19, 2001.

51. See e.g. for a survey based on top 20 investors, Eric Fine, "Fundamentals Challenging Technicals," New York, *Morgan Stanley Dean Witter Fixed Income Global Research*, March 9, 2001; See also, focusing on firms, Goldman Sachs quarterly surveys of Latin American CFOs, Goldman Sachs, "Resilient Performance Despite Economic Downturn," New York, *Goldman Sachs Quarterly Survey of Brazilian CFOs*, October 2001; and Goldman Sachs, "Adjusting for a Delayed Recovery," New York, *Goldman Sachs Quarterly Survey of Mexican CFOs*, October 16, 2001. In the industry there is several polls, realized in collaboration with firms such as Gallup, on "index investors optimism," see e.g. the UBS Index Investor Optimism http://www.ubs.com/e/index/about/ research/indexofinvestoroptimism.html; and the Merrill Lynch Gallup Fund Manager Survey: http://www.research.ml.com/marketing/content/gallup.pdf.

52. See Torsten Arnswald, "Investment Behaviour of German Equity Fund Managers. An Exploratory Analysis of Survey Data," *Deutsche Bundesbank Economic Research Centre Discussion Paper*, No. 08/01, March 2001. In this survey, 540 questionnaires were sent to executive directors of 62 German mutual companies. A total of 278 questionnaires were completed from 60 different companies or 52% of all questionnaires sent out.

53. See Marianne Demarchi and Solenn Thomas, "Processus de gestion, techniques de transaction et attentes des investisseurs institutionnels français," *SBF Bourse de Paris*, December 1996 (unpublished).

54. Interviews with fund managers in Paris, May 18 and 19, 2000; London, June 22, 2000; and Madrid, May 9, 2001.

55. Interviews with fund managers in London, June 1 and 2, 2000; and Paris, February 21, 2001.

56. Interviews with fund managers in Paris, May 3, 2001, June 7, 2001; Madrid, May 8, 2001.

57. See Fan Hu, Alastair Hall and Campbell Harvey, "Promotion or Demotion? An Empirical Investigation of the Determinants of Top Mutual Fund Manager Change," *Duke University Fuqua School of Business Working Paper*, September 2000 (unpublished).

58. Investment Company Institute, "The Potential Effects of more Frequent Portfolio Disclosure on Mutual Fund Performance," *Investment Company Institute Perspective*, vol. 7, no. 3, June 2001.

59. Sylvia Maxfield, "Effects of International Portfolio Flows on Government Policy Choice," in Miles Kahler, ed., *Capital Flows and Financial Crisis*, Manchester, Manchester University Press, 1998, pp. 69–92.

60. On this impact, see Layna Mosley, "Global Capital and National Economic Policies: The Varying Impacts of Foreign Direct and Portfolio Investment," University of Notre Dame, Department of Government, paper prepared for the presentation at the *2001 Annual Meeting of the American Political Science Association*, San Francisco, August 30–September 2, 2001.

61. On the temporal horizons of foreign direct investors in Latin American emerging countries, see the survey conducted by Paolo Giordano and Javier Santiso, "La course aux Amériques: les

stratégies des investisseurs européens dans le Mercosur," *Problèmes d'Amérique latine*, no. 39, October–December 2000, pp. 55–87.

62. Interview in London, June 22, 2000.

63. Investment Company Institute, "Redemption Activity of Mutual Fund Owners," *Fundamentals Investment Company Institute Research in Brief*, vol. 10, no. 1, March 2001, see also http://www.ici.org/.

64. Brad Barber, Terrance Odean and Lu Zheng, "The Behavior of Mutual Fund Investors," September 2000 (unpublished working paper).

65. See Monks Partnership, *City Paid Guide. Financial Sector*, London, Monks Partnership, November 2000; Monks Partneship, *International Banks and Investment Houses. Remuneration Guide*, London, Monks Partnership, August 1999. See also: http://www.monkspartnership.com/. For an international comparison of CEO's salaries and benefits, see also *The Towers Perrin 2001–2002 Worldwide Total Remuneration*, http://www.towers.com/towers/. The highest paid chief executives, out of a total of 26 countries surveyed, are in the United States (US$2 mn. a year on average). The second highest paid are those in Argentina (US$880,000) with those in Mexico (US$867,000) in third place, far above executives from the United Kingdom (US$670,000), France (US$520,000) or Spain and Sweden (around US$400,000).

66. See AIMR & Russell Reynolds Associates, *1999–2000 Investment Management Compensation Survey*, New York, AIMR, 2000. See their respective websites: http://www.aimr.org/; http://www.russreyn.com/; http://www.roberthalf.com/. For executive compensations around the world, see also the data provided by Towers Perrin: http://www.towers.com/towers/services_products/default.htm. We use also other sources of information to control the importance of bonuses in the industry using also reports of TMP Worldwide, *Financial Services Compensation 2000. A Special Report from TMP Worldwide Executive Search*, TMP Worldwide, November 2000.

67. Interviews in Paris with emerging market economist and fund manager, June 27 and 29, 2001.

68. Interviews in Paris with fund managers, November 18, 19 and 25, 2000.

69. Interviews in London with fund managers, November 3, 4, 6 and 17, 2000, June 22, 2001; and interviews with several asset managers in Boston, November 19, 21 and 22, 2000; and New York, November 6 and 7, 2000.

70. Interview in New York with a fund manager, New York, May 11, 2000.

71. Interview in New York with a fund manager, May 12, 2000.

72. See Randolph B. Cohen, Brian J. Hall and Luis Viceira, "Do Executive Stock Options Encourage Risk-Takings?", *Harvard University Graduate School of Business Administration*, March 2000 (unpublished). See Brian Hall and Jeffrey Leibman, "Are CEOs Really Paid Like Bureaucrats?" *Quarterly Journal of Economics*, 1998, 113(3), pp. 653–691; Joseph Haubrich, "Risk-Aversion, Performance Pay and the Principal Agent Problem," *Journal of Political Economy*, 102(2), 1994, pp. 258–276.

73. See Edwin J. Elton, Martin J. Gruber and Christophe R. Blake, "Incentive Fees and Mutual Funds," *New York University Working Paper*, June 2001 (unpublished).

74. Jennifer Carpenter, "Does Option Compensation Increase Managerial Risk Appetite?" *Journal of Finance*, 55, 2000, pp. 2311–2331; Jennifer Chevalier and Glenn Ellison, "Risk Taking by Mutual Funds as a Response to Incentives," *Journal of Political Economy*, 105, 1997, pp. 1167–1200.

75. Interviews in Edinburgh, November 19 and 21, 2000; New York, November 5–7, 2000; and Boston, November 19, 21 and 22, 2000; and London, April 10, 13 and 14, 2000.

76. Interviews in Edinburgh, November 20, 2000; New York, November 5, 2000; Boston, November 21, 2000; London, June 22, 2000; and Paris, June 8, 2000.

77. Interviews in Edinburgh, November 19, 2000; New York, November 5 and 7, 2000; Boston, November 21 and 22, 2000; and London, April 13 and 14, 2001.

78. Interviews in New York, November 5–7, 2000; Boston, November 19, 21 and 22, 2000; London, April 10, 13 and 14, 2000; and Paris, June 11 and 14, 2001.

Chapter Five   A Small Embedded World: Technopols, Arenas and Trespassers

1. On the diffusion of monetarism in Latin America and the key role of Chilean Chicago Boys, see Juan Gabriel Valdés, *Pinochet's Economist: The Chicago School in Chile*, Cambridge, Mass., Cambridge University Press, 1995. For a more socioeconomic analysis of the elite transformations in Latin America, see Yves Dezalay and Bryant Garth, *The Internationalization of Palace Wars: Lawyers, Economists and the Contest to Transform Latin American States*, Chicago, The University of Chicago Press, 2002; and John Campbell and Ove Kaj Pedersen, eds., *The Rise of Neoliberalism and Institutional Analysis*, Princeton, Princeton University Press, 2001.

2. For a study on this "technocratic vanguard" and the rise of U.S.-trained economists within the Mexican government see Roderic A. Camp, *Mexico's Mandarins: Crafting a Power Elite for the Twenty-First Century*, La. University of California Press, 2002; Sarah Babb, *Managing Mexico: Economists from Nationalism to Liberalism*, Princeton, Princeton University Press, 2001; and Miguel Angel Centeno, *Democracy Within Reason: Technocratic Revolution in Mexico*, University Park, Pa., The Pennsylvania State University Press, 1994.

3. See for an analysis of the political dimensions of financial reforms in Mexico, Timothy Kessler, "Political Capital: Mexican Financial Policy Under Salinas," *World Politics*, no. 51, October 1998, pp. 36–66; and Nancy Auerbach, *States, Banks and Markets: Mexico' Path to Financial Liberalization in Comparative Perspective*, New York, Westview Press, 2000. For a more theoretical approach see Jeffry Frieden, "Invested Interests: The Politics of National Economic Policies in a World of Global Finance," *International Organization*, no. 45, Fall 1991, pp. 440–441.

4. Interview with Domingo Cavallo, Buenos Aires, April 30, 1998.

5. See Javier Corrales, "Technocratic Policy-Making and Parliamentary Accountability: The Argentine Case," Amherst College, Department of Political Science, August 2001, presented at the *2001 Latin American Studies Association Congress* (unpublished).

6. See for the notion of idea carrier and the trajectories of these reformers respectively Peter Hall, ed., *The Political Power of Economic Ideas: Keynesianism Across Nations*, Princeton, Princeton University Press, 1989. For a perspective centered on Chile, see Eduardo Silva, *The State and Capital in Chile, Business Elites, Technocrats and Market Economists*, London, Westview Press, 1996. On Cieplan and Chilean opposition during the Pinochet regime, see Jeffrey Puryear, *Thinking Politics: Intellectuals and Democracy in Chile, 1973–1988*, Baltimore, John Hopkins University, 1994.

7. One of the most famous financial marketers that "invented" the emerging markets label is Antoine W. Van Agtmael, founder, president and chief investment officer of Washington, D.C.-based Emerging Markets Management (EMM). The firm's "generic" name is testimony to Mr. van Agtmael's pioneering spirit: he was one of the first investment professionals to draw attention to the opportunities presented by stocks of firms domiciled in developing countries in the early 1980s. Interesting to note also is that the firm, founded in 1987, was created by six former staff members of the World Bank and the International Finance Corporation. Mr. Agtmael e.g. served as division chief in the World Bank's Treasury operations and as deputy director of the Capital Markets Department at the International Finance Corporation. There he created the first emerging markets equity index, later bought by Standard & Poor's to compete with the index leader MSCI. See the website of EMM: http://www.emi-emm.com.

8. The term Washington Consensus was given in 1989, the same year of the fall of the Berlin Wall, to a list of ten policy recommendations gave by the economist John Williamson for developing country reformers. As stressed by Moisés Naím this Washington Consensus was more a Washington Confusion, as the views shared by prominent individuals that share pro-markets beliefs and distrust of government intervention were divergent. See Moisés Naím, "Fads and Fashion in Economic Reforms: Washington Consensus or Washington Confusion?" *Working Draft for the IMF Conference on Second Generation Reforms*, November 8–9, 1999, see http://www.imf.org/external/pubs/ft/seminar/1999/reforms/Naim.HTM.

9. See Michael Walzer, "The divided self," in Walzer, *Thick and Thin. Moral Argument at Home and Abroad*, London and Notre Dame, University of Notre Dame Press, 1994, pp. 85–103.

10. Interviews in New York, May 10, 2000 with a Wall Street global emerging markets strategist; and London, October 7, 2000 with an emerging markets economist.

11. See Graciela Kaminsky, Saul Lizondo and Carmen Reinhart, "Leading Indicators of Currency Crises," *International Monetary Fund Staff Papers*, vol. 45, March 1998, pp. 1–48; Graciela Kaminsky and Carmen Reinhart, "The Twin Crises: The Causes of Banking and Balance of Payments Problems," *American Economic Review*, vol. 89, no. 3, June 1999, pp. 473–500; Morris Goldstein, Graciela Kaminsky and Carmen Reinhart, *Assessing Financial Vulnerability: An Early Warning System for Emerging Markets*, Washington, D.C., Institute for International Economics, 2000.

12. See Barry Eichengreen, Andrew Rose and Charles Wyplosz, "Speculative Attacks on Pegged Exchange Rates: An Empirical Exploration with Special Reference to the European Monetary System," *National Bureau of Economic Research Working Paper*, No. 4898, 1994; Barry Eichengreen, Andrew Rose and Charles Wyplosz, "Contagious Currency Crises," *National Bureau of Economic Research Working Paper*, No. 5681, 1996; Jeffrey Sachs, Aaron Tornell and Andrés Velasco, "Financial Crises in Emerging Markets: The Lessons from 1995," *Brookings Papers on Economic Activities*, 1996, pp. 147–198; Jeffrey Frankel and Andrew Rose, "Currency Crashes in Emerging Markets: An Empirical Treatment," *Journal of International Economics*, November 1996, pp. 351–366.

13. See Andrew Berg and Catherine Patillo, "Predicting Currency Crises: The Indicators Approach and an Alternative," *Journal of International Money and Finance*, vol. 18, no. 4, August 1999, pp. 561–586; Andrew Berg, Eduardo Borensztein, Gian Maria Milesi-Ferretti and Catherine Patillo, "Anticipating Balance of Payments Crises: The Role of Early Warning Systems," *IMF Occasional Paper*, No. 186, 1999.

14. See Olivier Burkart and Virginie Coudert, "Leading Indicators of Currency Crises for Emerging Markets," *Emerging Markets Review*, vol. 3, no. 2, June 2002, pp. 107–133; Matthieu Bussière and Marcel Fratzscher, "Towards a New Early Warning System of Financial Crises," *European Central Bank Working Paper Series*, No. 145, May 2002; Olivier Burkart and Virginie Coudert, "Les crises de change dans les pays émergents," *Bulletin de la Banque de France*, no. 74, February 2000, pp. 49–61; Peter Vlaar, "Early Warning Systems for Currency Crises," *BIS Conference Papers*, vol. 8, March 2000, pp. 253–274; John Hawkins and Marc Klau, "Measuring Potential Vulnerabilities in Emerging Market Economies," *BIS Working Papers*, No. 91, October 2000; and Claire Dissaux who built a "country seismograph" based on "early warning signals" approaches, Crédit Agricole Indosuez, *Country Seismograph Presentation*, Paris, CAI Global Emerging Markets, October 7, 2000.

15. See Hali Edison, "Do Indicators of Financial Crises Work? An Evaluation of Early Warning System," *Board of Governors of the Federal Reserve System International Finance Discussion Papers*, No. 675, July 2000 (unpublished); and later Steven Kamin, John Schindler and Shawna Samuel, "The Contribution of Domestic and External Factors to Emerging Market Devaluation Crises: An Early Warning Systems Approach," *Board of Governors of the Federal Reserve System, Internationational Finance Discussion Papers*, No. 711, September 2001; Citicorp Securities, "Early Warning System—An Anticipating Balance of Payments Crisis in Latin America," New York, *Citicorp Securities Economic Research*, May 6, 1998; Crédit Suisse First Boston, "Emerging Markets Risk Indicator," London, *CSFB Technical Report*, 1999; Avinash Persaud, *Event Risk Indicator Handbook*, London, JP Morgan, January 29, 1998.

16. See Karin Kimbrough and Stephen Li Jen, "An Early Warning System for Currency Crises," London, *Morgan Stanley Dean Witter, Global Equity Research & Economics*, July 2, 2001.

17. See Arturo Porzecanski, "An Assesment of Sovereign Liquidity Risk," in ABN Amro Emerging Markets Fortnightly, New York and London, *ABN Amro Emerging Markets Research*, December 13, 2000.

18. See Alberto Ades, Rumi Masih and Daniel Tenengauzer, "GS-Watch: A New Framework for Predicting Financial Crises in Emerging Markets," *Goldman Sachs Emerging Markets Economic Research*, December 18, 1998.

19. Andrew Berg and Catherine Patillo, "Are Currency Crises Predictable? A Test," *IMF Staff Papers*, vol. 46, no. 2, June 1999, pp. 107–138; and Andrew Berg and Catherine Patillo, "What Caused the Asian Crises: An Early Warning System Approach," *Economic Notes by Banca Monte dei Paschi di Siena*, vol. 28, no. 3, 1999, pp. 285–334.

20. See Hali Edison, "Do Indicators of Financial Crises Work? An Evaluation of an Early Warning System," Board of Governors of the Federal Reserve System, *International Finance Discussion Papers*, No. 675, July 2000; Olivier Burkart and Virginie Coudert, "Leading Indicators of Currency Crises in Emerging Economies," Banque de France, *Notes d'Etudes et de Recherche*, No. 74, May 2000; and for a synthesis and an evaluation see James Bell and Darren Pain, "Leading Indicator Models of Banking Crises: A Critical Review," in Bank of England, *Financial Stability Review*, London, Bank of England, December 2000, pp. 113–129.

21. Andrew Berg, Eduardo Borensztein, Gian Maria Milesi-Ferretti and Catherine Patillo, "Anticipating Balance of Payments Crises: The Role of Early Warning Systems," *IMF Occasional Paper*, No. 186, 1999, p. 2.

22. For an epistemological critic of the pretension embedded in nearly all social sciences to predict the future, see Karl Popper, *Poverty of Historicism*, London, Routledge, 1988. As stressed by many commentators, scholars and financial operators, too frequently the debates are about crisis prediction versus crisis anticipation or crisis prevention embedded in confusion about the terms of the debates themselves. As pointed out by Jorge Braga de Macedo, "the role of news in generating sudden changes in beliefs is such that crises can hardly be forecast: the success rate at predicting them is less than one third (25–30 percent). The reason is that two types of errors must be balanced against each other: not to predict crises that do occur and to predict crises that do not occur. Detecting vulnerability is very different from predicting the timing of the crisis." Jorge Braga de Macedo, "Financial Crises and International Architecture: A Euro-Centric Perspective," paper prepared for a panel on *The future of Mercosur* held at the Central Bank of Argentina, Buenos Aires, August 24, 2000, p. 10 (unpublished).

23. Goldstein, Kalinsky and Reinhart, *Assessing Financial Vulnerability*, p. 105.

24. See Avinash Persaud, "Sending the Herd off the Cliff Edge: The Disturbing Interaction Between Herding and Market-Sensitive Risk Management Practices," *2000 Essay Competition Essay in Honour of Jacques de Larosière of the Institute of International Finance*, 2000, p. 5.

25. Interview with an emerging market fund manager, Edinburgh, November 17, 2000.

26. See http://www.imf.org/external/am/2000/prague.htm.

27. See http://www.puc-rio.br/lacea-rio-2000/; http://www.dallasfed.org/htm/dallas/archives.html.

28. Interviews, New York, 8, 9 and 11, 2000, Edinburgh, November 17 and 20, 2000, several interviews with a head of emerging market fixed income team, a fund manager on emerging market and an emerging market chief economist; interviews in Paris, November 17, 2000, May 28, 2001 and June 7, 2001, with emerging debt fund managers and economists; confirmed also by fund managers and economists in Madrid, April 7, 2001.

29. Mohamed El-Erian, *PIMCO Emerging Markets Watch*, PIMCO, August 2000 (http://www.pimco.com).

30. Interview, New York, May 12, 2000. The proceedings of panel speakers were published by Deutsche Bank, see Deutsche Bank World Bank/IMF Annual Meetings, *Realignments in Industrial Countries: A Challenge Facing Emerging Markets*, London, Deutsche Bank Global Markets Research, November 1999; and Deutsche Bank IADB Annual Meetings, *Financing Latin American Growth: Sources, Politics, and Outlook*, London, Deutsche Bank Global Markets Research, May 2000.

31. Interview, New York, May 12, 2000 with an emerging markets chief economist.

32. These social events were respectively organized during the IADB 2001 investor forums of Crédit Suisse First Boston and Salomon Smith Barney in March 2001.

33. Chase, "IMF/World Bank Meetings. Update from Chase International Fixed Income Research Meetings in Prague," New York, *Chase International Fixed Income Research*, September 26 and 27, 2000.

34. One of the co-written papers presented by the newly appointed IADB chief economist, Guillermo Calvo, one of the most respected economists on Latin American issues (coming from Maryland University), was precisely on the U.S. downturn impact in emerging countries, see Guillermo Calvo, Eduardo Fernández-Arias, Carmen Reinhart and Ernesto Tavi, "The Growth-Interest Rate Cycle in the United States and Its Consequences for Emerging Markets," Washington, Inter-American Development Bank Research Department, Working Paper presented at the *Annual Meetings of the Board of Governors, Inter-American Development Bank*, Santiago de Chile, March 18, 2001.

35. Deutsche Bank, *A Fresh Look at Latin America Ahead. Special Issue Prepared for the IADB Meetings, Santiago, March 17, 2001*, New York; Deutsche Bank Global Emerging Markets Research, March 12, 2001.

36. This "R-word index" has gained the attention e.g. of ABN Amro economic research team, see ABN Amro Bank, "Euroland View: Is Psychlogy Driving the Economy?" in ABN Amro, Euroland economic update, Amsterdam, *ABN Amro Economics Department*, February 8, 2001, pp. 2–5.

37. See Robert Shiller, "Bubbles, Human Judgement, and Expert Opinion," *Yale University Cowles Foundation Discussion Paper*, No. 1303, May 2001 (unpublished).

38. See Jeff Madrick, "The Influence of the Financial Media over International Economic Policy," Center for Economic Policy Analysis, New School for Social Research, *CEPA Working Paper Series III*, No. 16, June 2000 (unpublished).

39. Gordon Clark and Dariusz Wojcik, "The City of London in the Asian Crisis," *Journal of Economic Geography*, vol. 1, no. 1, January 2001, pp. 107–130.

40. See Ricardo Hausmann, "A Way out of Argentina," *Financial Times*, October 29, 2001, p. 17. This article followed some others written by leading economists on Argentinian perspectives but much less "visible" because they were not published in global confidence arenas like the *Financial Times*, see e.g. the excellent synthesis written by Barry Eichengreen, "Argentina after the IMF," *Berkeley University*, August 27, 2001 (unpublished); available at http://elsa.berkeley.edu/users/ eichengr/website.htm.

41. See Michael Mussa, "Fantasy in Argentina," *Financial Times*, November 12, 2001, p. 15; and for a longer version Michael Mussa, "Argentina Needs Effective not Unthinking Support," *FT.com*, November 9, 2001; Michael Mussa, "Argentina and the Fund: From Triumph to Tragedy," *Institute of International Economics, Policy Analysis in International Economics*, 67, July, 2002, available online at http://www.iie.com/publications/publication.cfm?pub_id=343&source=none.

42. Dresdner Bank Lateinamerika, *Latin American Daily Spotlight*, New York, London and Frankfurt, *Dresdner Bank Lateinamerika*, November 12, 2001.

43. See Barclays Capital, "Argentina: Difficult Just Got Worse," New York, *Barclays Capital, Latam Economics & Strategy*, November 9, 2001. Some leading Wall Street firms in an unusual mea culpa, explicitly recognized debt restructuring as increasingly likely, just a few moments before its official annoucement (however there is frequently a time lag between what is said in a face to face exhange and what is written in reports), see Goldman Sachs, "Argentina: Our Views have Changed," in *Global Economics Weekly*, New York, Goldman Sachs, November 7, 2001.

44. Most of Rudiger Dornbusch papers are available online at http://web.mit.edu/rudi/www/papers.html. As stressed by Paul Samuelson during moments of financial euphoria no one wants to listen to warnings. Before the 1929 financial crisis, Paul Warburg, by that time one of the most respected bankers and a founding member of the Federal Reserve System, warned about a forthcoming collapse but "the reaction to his statement was bitter, even vicious" and the same happened to Economist Roger Babson whose forecast of the crash brought a deluge of criticism. See Paul Samuelson, *A Short History of Financial Euphoria*, New York, Penguin Books, 1994, p. 7.

45. Note also that the trespassing can go the other way round: investment bankers (with Ph.D. credentials) can trespass from Wall Street to the academy. A good example is Carmen Reinhart, a leading scholar, based at Maryland University since 1996, who has published prestigious

234 *Notes*

academic reviews and is also involved as consultant for the World Bank and the IMF. She earned
a Ph.D. from Columbia University and spent nearly four years as an economist at Bear Stearns,
a New York-based investment house, before joining the IMF in 1988 where she developed a
career mainly in the Research Department.

46. See www.friedberg.com.
47. Historically one of the most famous "trespassers" is probably John Maynard Keynes, not only
    one of the most creative economists but also a clever financial investor. On Keynes see Robert
    Skidelsky's exhaustive biography, *The Economist as a Saviour: John Maynard Keynes*, London,
    Macmillan, 1994; and Robert Skidelsky, *John Maynard Keynes: Fighting for Britain, 1937–1946*,
    London, Macmillan, 2000.
48. See http://www.dfafunds.com.
49. See http://www.sinopia.fr and http://www.kmv.com.
50. Interviews in New York, with strategists and economists, May 11, 2000. See http://www.ssglobal
    link.com/marketing/index2.htm and http://www.vbp.com/research/index.html., and for the
    Center for Brazilian Studies at Columbia University http://www.sipa.columbia.edu/ brazilc/.
    Interviews, New York, May 12, 2000, with a senior emerging market economist and an emerg-
    ing market chief economist; and for Stiglitz see The Brookdale Group, Ltd asset management
    website http://www.brookdaleglobal.com/, mentioned by Joshua Chaffin, "High-Profile
    Academics are Streaming to Wall Street Eager to Put Their Theories to the Test," *Financial Times*,
    November 3, 2000 on ft.com. See also their last essays, Rudiger Dornbusch, *Keys to Prosperity:
    Free Markets, Sound Money and a Bit of Luck*, Cambridge, Mass., MIT Press, 2000; Albert Fishlow
    and Karen Parker, eds., *Growing Apart: The Causes and Consequences of Global Village Inequality*,
    Washington, D.C., Council on Foreign Relations Press, 2000.
51. After the devaluation, Ricardo Hausmann published other important personal views as
    "Argentina's Route to Salvation," *Financial Times*, January 4, 2002, p. 13.
52. See Walter Molano, "Argentina: The No Brainer Danger of Devaluation," New York, *BCP
    Securities, The Latin American Adviser*, November 27, 2001.
53. The Economist, "A Tale of Two Economists," September 28, 2000. Andrei Shleifer is the author
    of several essays on international finance, see e.g. Andrei Shleifer, *Inefficient Markets: An
    Introduction to Behavioural Finance. Clarendon Lectures in Economics*, Oxford, Oxford University
    Press, 2000.
54. See http://www.lsvasset.com.
55. Several interviews with Latin American strategists and economists from Wall Street investment
    banks, New York, May 9, 10 and 11, 2000; and with emerging market analysts in Paris, May 18
    and 19, 2000; and fund managers in London, October 3, 5 and 17, 2000.
56. Obviously, Deutsche Bank is not the only boutique to hire from the IMF—an institution at the
    very heart of emerging market financial crises and rescue packages, another key player in the
    confidence game. Federico Kaune and Paulo Leme, e.g. both emerging market economists
    at Goldman Sachs, came from the IMF. The first joined Wall Street from Washington in 1993
    (after spending nine years at the IMF and being, among other functions, responsible for the
    Brady debt restructuring at the IMF of Venezuela and Jordan) and the second joining in 1997
    after three years as an economist at the IMF. Both graduated in economics from the University
    of Chicago.
57. Peter Garber is the author of several important essays, among them see Peter Garber, *Famous
    First Bubbles*, Cambridge, Mass., MIT Press, 2000. He published some of them with leading
    figures of the confidence game as Herminio Blanco who, later in the 1990s, became one of the
    most successful ministers under the Zedillo Mexican government (by the time Peter Garber
    had joined Wall Street). See Herminio Blanco and Peter Garber, "Recurrent Devaluation and
    Speculative Attacks on the Mexican Peso," *Journal of Political Economy*, vol. 94, February 1986,
    pp. 148–166.
58. See http://www.darbyoverseas.com/.

59. Interview with a Latin American economist and a fund manager, Washington, D.C., July 20 and 21, 2001.

60. Interview, New York, May 12, 2000, with a former senior economist of a Washington-based international organization who trespassed into a Wall Street boutique.

61. Interview, Paris, May 3, 2000, with former IMF economists that trespassed into international investment banks and fund management companies.

62. Interview, Paris, June 9, 2000, with a former IMF economist who became an asset manager strategist.

63. On JP Morgan, see the biography by Jean Strouse, *Morgan: An American Financier*, New York, Random House, 1999.

64. See Promperu website: http://www.promperu.gob.pe/ and, for one of the last reports, Promperu, *Peru: Analysts' View on the Peruvian Economy*, Lima, Promperu, June 2001. This kind of report gives also an idea of the country coverage by the financial community of a specific country. In the case of Peru, the September 2001 report referenced for example 18 products and views of leading firms such as BBVA, ABN Amro, BCP Securities, Bear Stearns, BNP Paribas, Crédit Suisse First Boston, Dresdner Bank Lateinamerika, Deutsche Bank Securities, Goldman Sachs, ING Barings, JP Morgan, Lehman Brothers, Merrill Lynch, Morgan Stanley Dean Witter, Salomon Smith Barney, BSCH, Scotiabank Group and EIU. See Promperu, *Peru's Analysts' View on the Peruvian Economy. September 2001*, Lima, Promperu, September 2001. In the case of Coinvertir's report on Colombia the coverage more limited (11 reports).

65. See the online reports in Coinvertir website: http://www.coinvertir.org/02-econ/02-ibank.htm. In the case of Colombia it's also interesting to mention the bimonthly reports covering Wall Street analysts' views realized by the central bank, Banco de la República de Colombia, see e.g. Banco de la República de Colombia, *Como nos ven afuera ? Del 16 al 22 de junio de 2001*, Bogotá, Banco de la República de Colombia, June 2001.

66. See Chilean Foreign Investment Committee, *Chile in the Eyes of Wall Street*, Santiago de Chile, FIC, August 2000; PromPerú, *Peru: A Country in the Move. Analysts' Views on the Peruvian Economy*, Lima, Promperú, December 2000 and December 1999; Coinvertir, *Colombia Investment Banks and Credit Rating Agencies' Views on the Economy*, Santa Fé de Bogotá, December 1999. Other countries like Argentina e.g. also created financial hubs where investors can find precious economic and financial data. See http://www.infoarg.org/.

67. See Dani Rodrik, "How Far will International Economic Integration go?" *Journal of Economic Perspectives*, vol. 14, no. 1, Winter 2000, pp. 177–186. One of the principal insights for which Mundell received the Nobel Prize was precisely to underline that a country cannot have at the same time unhampered international capital flows, a fixed exchange rate system and an independent monetary policy. See Robert Mundell, "Capital Mobility and Stabilization Policy Under Fixed and Flexible Exhange Rates," *Canadian Journal of Economics*, vol. 29, 1963, pp. 475–485.

68. See Jeffrey Frankel, "No Single Currency Regime is Right for all Countries or at all the Times," *Princeton University, Essays in International Finance*, No. 125, 2000.

69. Andrés Velasco, "The Impossible Duo? Globalization and Monetary Independence in Emerging Markets," prepared for the *2001 Meeting of the Brookings Trade Forum*, Washington, D.C., May 10–11, 2001.

70. For a closer analysis see Benjamin Ross Schneider, "The Material Basis of Technocracy: Investor Confidence and Neoliberalism in Latin America," in Miguel Centeno and Patricio Silva, eds., *The Politics of Expertise in Latin America*, New York, St. Martin's Press, 1998, pp. 77–95. For a comparative study on Chile, Mexico, France and Great Britain, see Marion Fourcade Gourinchas and Sarah Babb, "Social Learning in the Global Village: Paths to Neoliberalism in Four Countries," Princeton University and University of Massachusetts, paper presented at the *American Sociological Association*, August 11, 2000, Washington, D.C.

71. See Miguel Centeno and Patricio Silva, eds., *The Politics of Expertise in Latin America*, London, St. Martin's Press, 1998; and Jorge Dominguez, ed., *Technopols: Freeing Politics and Markets in Latin America in the 1990s*, University Park, Pa., The Pennsylvania State University Press, 1997.

72. BBVA Securities, *Peru: Economy Ministry Dream Team*, London and New York, Latin America Fixed Income & Foreign Exchange, BBVA Securities, June 28, 2001. The rumors by the time were that Alfredo Thorne, a JP Morgan economist, and Liliana Rojsa-Suarez, a former IADB and Deutsche Bank senior economist, would join the government as vice minister of the economy and superintendent of banks. See also the research analysis of BBVA Banco Continental in Peru: http://www.bbvabancocontinental.com/. A few weeks later however, the ideological inconsistency within Toledo's cabinet was questioned: "while the presence of Finance Minister Pedro Pablo Kuczynski and Central Bank President Richard Webb, two major proponents of economic orthodoxy, is reassuring to the market, the presence of Vice Minister of Finance Kurt Berneo and Central Bank Director Oscar Dancourt, two well-known proponents of economic heterodoxy, is likewise disconcerting." BBVA Securities, *Peru: Limited Room for Maneuver*, New York, BBVA Latin American Equities Strategy, August 27, 2001.

73. See Peter Evans and Martha Finnemore, "Organizational Reform and the Expansion of the South's Voice at the Fund," *Berkeley University and George Washington University Working Paper*, prepared for the G-24 Technical Group Meeting, Washington, D.C., April 17–18, 2001 (unpublished).

74. See Robert Barro and Jong-Wha Lee, "IMF programs: Who is Chosen and What are the Effects?" *NBER Working Paper*, No. 8951, May 2002 (unpublished). See also on the political economy of IMF lending, James Raymond Vreeland, *The IMF and Economic Development*, Cambridge, Mass., Cambridge University Press, 2003.

Chapter Six The Timing Game: Wall Street, Mexico and Argentina. A Temporal Analysis

1. Rudiger Dornbusch, "A Primer on Emerging Market Crises," MIT, *Working Paper*, January 2001, p. 6 (unpublished), see: http://web.mit.edu/rudi/www/papers.html; published also in Sebastian Edwards and Jeffrey Frankel, eds., *Preventing Currency Crises in Emerging Markets*, Chicago, Ill., NBER and The University of Chicago Press, 2001.

2. See Steven Block, "Political Conditions and Currency Crises: Empirical Regularities in Emerging Markets," *Center for International Development at Harvard University*, Working Paper, No. 79, October 2001 (unpublished). See for a former study focusing on political variables in currency crises, Allan Drazen, "Political Contagion in Currency Crises," *NBER Working Paper*, No. 7211, 1999 (unpublished).

3. For a close study of the 2002 election year in Brazil and the interactions with financial markets, see Juan Martínez and Javier Santiso, "Financial Markets and Politics: The Confidence Game in Latin American Emerging Economies," *International Political Science Review*, 2003 Vol. 24, no. 3, pp. 363–395.

4. Jianping Mei, "Political Risk, Financial Crisis, and Market Volatility," New York University, Department of International Business, *Working Paper*, 1999 (unpublished). The history of economics suggest also plenty of examples on the incidence of political events in framing economic uncertainty and in stock market volatility as suggested by a close analysis of Argentina peso exchange rate during the nineteenth century, see Maria Alejandra Irigoin and Eduardo Salazar, "Looking at Political Events and Economic Uncertainty: An Examination of the Volatility in the Buenos Aires Paper Peso Rate of Exchange, 1826–1866," Torcuato di Tella and Universidad Nacional de Mar del Plata, paper presented at *Stanford University LACLIO Conference*, November 17–18, 2000 (unpublished); and Maria Alejandra Irigoin, *Finance, Politics and Economics in Buenos Aires, 1820s–1860s: The Political Economy of Currency Stabilisation*, London, Unpublished Ph.D. Diss., London School of Economics, 2000.

5. See the empirical evidence based on a portfolio choice model that relates capital flight to rate of return differentials, risk aversion, and the three types of risk mentioned for a panel of 47 developing countries over 16 years, Quan Vu Le and Paul J. Zak, "Political Risk and Capital Flight," *Claremont Graduate University, School of Politics and Economics*, May 2001 (unpublished).

6. See Steven Block and Paul M. Vaaler, "The Price of Democracy: Sovereign Risk Taking, Bond Spreads and Political Business Cycles in Developing Countries," Center for International Development at Harvard University, *CID Working Paper*, No. 82, December 2001 (unpublished). See also for similar results, indicating that share prices in a sample of 33 developed and developing countries, react negatively to uncertainty in the outcome of elections, Christos Pantzalis, David Stangeland and Harry Turtl, "Political Elections and the Resolution of Uncertainty: The International Evidence," *Journal of Banking and Finance*, vol. 24, no. 10, 2000, pp. 1575–1604.

7. See Mathieu Bussière and Christian Mulder, "Political Instability and Economic Vulnerability," *IMF Working Paper*, 99/46, 1999.

8. See Philippe Aghion, Alberto Alesina and Francesco Trebbi, "Endogenous Political Institutions," *Harvard University*, November 2001 (unpublished).

9. For a closer analysis of the relationships between democratic institutions and currency markets, see John Freeman, Jude Hays and Helmut Stix, "Democracy and Markets: The Case of Exchange Rates," *American Journal of Political Science*, July 2000; David A. Leblang, "Democratic Processes and Political Risk: Evidence from Foreign Exchange Markets," *American Journal of Political Science*, August 2001; David Leblang and William Bernhard, "The Politics of Speculative Attacks in Industrial Democracies," *International Organization*, vol. 54, 2000, pp. 291–324.

10. There is an extensive literature that draws on several traditions dealing with these issues, both for developed and developing countries interested in public finances, government expenditure and the size of governments. Among the many papers looking to the systematic effects of electoral rules and political regimes on the size and composition of governments spending, see Torsten Persson, "Do Political Institutions Shape Economic Policy?" *Econometrica*, vol. 70, no. 3, May 2002, pp. 883–905; Allan Drazen, *Political Economy in Macroeconomics*, Princeton, Princeton University Press, 2000; Torsten Persson and Guido Tabellini, *Political Economics: Explaining Economic Politicy*, Cambridge, Mass., MIT Press, 2000.

11. See Alberto Alesina, Ricardo Hausmann, Rudi Hommes and Ernesto Stein, "Fiscal Institutions and Budget Deficits in Latin America," *Journal of Development Economics*, 59, 1999, pp. 233–255.

12. See Barry Ames, *Political Survival*, Berkeley, University of California Press, 1987.

13. See Steven A. Block, "Elections, Electoral Competitiveness and Political Budget Cycles in Developing Countries," *Center for International Development at Harvard University*, Working Paper, No. 78, October 2001 (unpublished).

14. See for an empirical test Witold Jerzy Henisz, "Political Institutions and Policy Volatility," *The Wharton School of Management, University of Pennsylvania*, August 2001 (unpublished).

15. See David Leblang, "The Political Economy of Speculative Attacks in the Developing World," *International Studies Quarterly*, vol. 46, no. 1, March 2002, pp. 69–91. This study underlines that markets respond and react to political events. They tend to take into account the timing of elections but also the political orientation of the government. In particular speculative attacks are more likely under Left than under Right governments.

16. See e.g. the analysis based on four Asian democracies by Jude Hays, John Freeman and Hans Nesseth, "Democratization and Globalization in Emerging Market Countries: An Econometric Study," prepared for the *2001 Annual Meeting of the American Political Science Association*, San Francisco, August 30–September 2, 2001 (unpublished); and on Asian emerging countries Andrew MacIntyre, "Institutions and Investors: The Politics of the Economic Crisis in Southeast Asia," *International Organization*, vol. 55, no. 1, 2001, pp. 81–122.

17. See, for Mexico, Lawrence Whitehead, "Political Explanations of Macroeconomic Management," *World Development*, vol. 18, no. 8, 1990; Herminio Blanco and Peter Garber, "Recurrent Devaluations and Speculative Attacks on the Mexican Peso," *Journal of Political Economy*, vol. 94, 1986, pp. 148–166; Pamela Starr, "Flujos de capital, tipos de cambio fijos y supervivencia política: México y Argentina, 1994–1995," *Política y Gobierno*, vol. 6, no. 1,

238   *Notes*

First Semester 1999, pp. 129–171; and for a more systematic analysis Liliana Rojas-Suarez, Gustavo Cañonero and Ernesto Talvi, *Economics and Politics in Latin America: Will Up-coming Elections Compromise Stability and Reform?*, New York, Deutsche Bank Securities, Global Emerging Markets Research, August 1998.

18. See María de los Angeles González, "On Elections, Democracy and Macroeconomic Policy Cycles: Evidence from Mexico," Princeton University, 2000, paper presented at *Stanford University Conference of the Social Science History Institute on Political Institutions and Economic Growth*, Stanford, April 14–15, 2000 (unpublished).

19. See María de los Angeles González, "On Elections, Democracy and Macroeconomic Policy Cycles," Princeton University, 1999 (unpublished).

20. See e.g. the demonstration based on the analysis of market expectations and stock market returns prior to the March 2000 presidential election in Taiwan by Tse-Min Lin and Brian Roberts, "Parliamentary Politics and Exchange Markets," paper delivered at the *Annual Meeting of the Midwest Political Science Association*, Chicago, 2001 (unpublished).

21. See Christos Pantzalis, David Strangeland and Harry Tuttle, "Political Elections and the Resolution of Uncertainty: The International Evidence," *Journal of Banking and Finance*, vol. 24, 2000, pp. 1575–1604.

22. In October 2001, Lehman Brothers fixed income research and Eurasia Group's political science expertise launched a joint venture in order to cover political risks in emerging markets and analytical tools such as the Lehman Eurasia Group Stability Index (LEGSI), which incorporates political factors (65% of a country's weight) and economic factors (35%). See http://www.lehmaneurasiagroup.com/.

23. Interview, Paris, June 21, 2001.

24. See, e.g. the reports produced by JP Morgan, "Argentina: The 'Model'—Not Just the Peg—Suffers," New York, *JP Morgan Economic Research*, December 27 and 31, 2001.

25. See for a general assessment, Stephan Haggard, *The Political Economy of the Asian Financial Crisis*, Washington, D.C., Institute of International Economics, 2000; and Allan Drazen, *Political Economy in Macroeconomics*, Princeton, Princeton University Press, 2000.

26. See Sebastián Saiegh, "Is There a Democratic Advantage? Assessing the Role of Political Institutions in Sovereign Borrowing," prepared for the *Annual Meeting of the American Political Science Association*, August 30–September 2, 2001 (unpublished). From the point of view of foreign direct investors, some democratic advantage seems to exist. Democratic political systems tend to attract higher levels of FDI both across countries and within countries over time (70% more FDI goes into democratic countries than their authoritarian counterparts). The major reasons for this democratic FDI propensity are better transparency and commitments to external actors; the possibility for foreign investors to lobby government officials seeking electoral outcomes; and the credibility factor, democratic governments being perceived as more credible regarding their agreements in the international area. See Nathan Jensen, "Global Corporations and Domestic Governance: The Political Economy of Foreign Direct Investment," Yale University, Department of Political Science, *Working Paper*, 2001 (unpublished).

27. See for a temporal analysis of the Mexican financial crisis Javier Santiso, "Wall Street and the Mexican Financial Crisis: A Temporal Analysis of Emerging Markets," *International Political Science Review*, vol. 20, no. 1, 1999, pp. 49–71; Jonathan Heath and Sidney Weintraub, eds., *Mexico and the Sexenio Curse: Presidential Successions and Economic Crises in Modern Mexico*, Washington, D.C., Center for Strategic & International Studies, 1999; Sebastian Edwards, ed., *Mexico 1994: Anatomy of an Emergency-Market Crash*, Washington D.C., Carnegie Endowment for International Peace, 2000.

28. Rudi Dornbusch, "Fewer Monies, Better Monies: Exchange Rates and the Choice of Monetary-Policy Regimes," *American Economic Review*, vol. 91, no. 2, May 2001, pp. 238–242.

29. See Beatriz Magaloni, "Institutions, Political Opportunism and Macroeconomic Cycles: Mexico 1970–1998," Stanford University, paper presented at *Stanford University Conference of the Social Science History Institute on Political Institutions and Economic Growth*, Stanford, April 14–15,

2000. As underlined there is a "Mexican paradox" in the fact that in spite of sound economic performances the PRI regime (and system) took several decades to survive. For an explanation based on central government's fiscal resources distribution among the federation and the incentives to "voice" or "exit" among voters, Alberto Díaz Cayeros, Beatriz Magaloni and Barry Weingast, "Democratization and the Economy in Mexico: Equilibrium (PRI) Hegemony and Its Demise," *Stanford University, Department of Political Science,* June 2000.

30. Interview, New York, February 15, 1997.

31. On the financial crisis of 1994, see Maxwell Cameron and Vinod Aggarwal, "Mexican Meltdown: States, Markets and Post-NAFTA Financial Turmoil," *Third World Quarterly,* vol. 17, December 1996, pp. 975–987; and Riordan Roett, ed., *The Mexican Peso Crisis. International Perspectives,* Boulder, Lynne Rienner Publishers, 1996.

32. On the socioeconomic transformation of Mexican elite and the rise of economists over the last decades, see Sarah Babb, *Managing Mexico: Economists from Nationalism to Neoliberalism,* Princeton, Princeton University Press, 2001.

33. See on Nafta negotiations and related issues Maxwell Cameron and Brian Tomlin, *The Making of Nafta: How the Deal was Done,* Ithaca, Cornell University Press, 2000; and for business perceptions within Mexico and outside Strom Cronan Thacker, *Big Business, the State and Free Trade: Constructing Coalitions in Mexico,* Cambridge, Mass., Cambridge University Press, 2000.

34. See William Goetzmann and Philippe Jorion, "Re-Emerging Markets," *NBER Working Paper,* No. 5906, January 1997; published in *Journal of Financial and Quantitative Analysis,* vol. 34, no. 1, March 1999. For a specific study of the integration of emerging markets into the world capital markets, see Geert Bekaert, Campbell Harvey and Robin Lumsdaine, "Dating the Integration of World Equity Markets," Columbia University, Duke University, Brown University and NBER, paper presented at the *28th Annual Meeting of the European Finance Association,* Universitat Pompeu Fabra, Barcelona, August 22–25, 2001.

35. Between 1990 and 1994 Mexico alone received some US$ 102 bn., which accounted for almost 20 percent of total world capital flows over the same period. For comparative purposes, the Asian emerging economies taken together received US$ 261 bn. over the same period.

36. Barry Eichengreen, "The Baring Crisis in a Mexican Mirror," *International Political Science Review,* vol. 20, July 3, 1999, reprinted in Barry Eichengreen, Capital flows and crises, Cambridge, Mass., MIT Press, 2003.

37. See for a comparison between Mexican and Chilean financial crises Sebastian Edwards, "A Tale of Two Crises: Chile and Mexico," *NBER Working Paper,* 5794, October 1996; reprinted "Two Crises: Inflationary Inertia and Credibility," *The Economic Journal,* vol. 108, no. 448, May 1998, pp. 680–702.

38. See, on the politics of Mexican finance during the 1990s, Timothy Kessler, "Political Capital: Mexican Financial Policy Under Salinas," *World Politics,* vol. 51, October 1998, pp. 36–66.

39. During the 1960s and 1970s, the American universities were the compulsory education and socialization centers for the Latin American elites. Aspe completed his doctoral thesis at MIT in 1978, one year after Domingo Cavallo, the future architect of Argentina's move toward liberalism, had finished his dissertation at Harvard. Indeed it was in Cambridge, Massachusetts that the two young economists met one of the major Latin American reformers of the 1990s, the Chilean Alejandro Foxley, who at that time was a visiting scholar at MIT. For more information on the lives of this Latin American generation, see Jorge Domínguez, ed., *Technopols. Freeing Politics and Markets in Latin America in the 1990s,* University Park, The Pennsylvania State University Press, 1999.

40. Interviews, New York, February 14 and 15, 1997.

41. Tesobonos are short-term Mexican Treasury bills payable in pesos but indexed on the dollar. Cetes are short-term (28 days) peso-denominated treasury bills.

42. See Guillermo Calvo, Leonardo Leiderman and Carmen Reinhart, "Inflows of Capital to Developing Countries in the 1990s," *Journal of Economic Perspectives,* vol. 10, no. 2, Spring 1996, pp. 123–139; Ricardo french-Davis and Stephany Griffith-Jones, eds., *Coping with Capital*

Surges. The Return of Finance to Latin America, Boulder, Lynne Rienner, 1995; and for later dynamics Felipe Larraín, ed., *Capital Flows, Capital Controls and Currency Crises: Latin America in the 1990s*, Ann Arbor, University of Michigan Press, 2001; Stephany Griffith-Jones and Manuel Montes, eds., *Short-Term Capital Flows and Economic Crises*, Oxford, Oxford University Press, 2001.

43. The timing of the capital flows confirms the predominance of exogenous factors. Capital flows are not linked to the implementation of economic reforms or to the performance registered by the recipient country. Certain countries received financing although they had not embraced any reforms while others began to receive foreign investment only after having finalized reforms.

44. Interview, New York, February 11, 1997.

45. See Guillermo Calvo and Enrique Mendoza, "Mexico's Balance of Payments Crisis: A Chronicle of a Death Foretold," *Journal of International Economics*, vol. 41, no. 3–4, November 1996, pp. 235–264; Jeffrey Sachs, Aaron Tornell and Andrés Velasco, "The Mexican Peso Crisis: Sudden Stop Death or Death Foretold," *Journal of International Economics*, vol. 41, no. 3–4, November 1996, pp. 265–283.

46. Since 1991 Rudiger Dornbusch, an economist at MIT and the former mentor of Pedro Aspe, had continually argued in favor of a devaluation, especially in the columns of *La Epoca*. In June 1992 he repeated his recommendations to no avail to Carlos Salinas de Gortari and again to Pedro Aspe during the latter's visit to MIT the following winter. His campaign in favor of devaluation culminated with a speech delivered at the Brookings Institution in Washington in April 1994, when he strongly recommended a 20 percent devaluation so as to boost Mexican exports. See "Picking up Pieces. Mexico's Near Default can be Traced Back to Lost Opportunity," *The Wall Street Journal*, July 6, 1995. See also the paper published prior to the crisis and ex-post, Rudiger Dornbusch and Alejandro Werner, "Mexico: Stabilization, Reform and No Growth," *Brookings Papers on Economic Activity*, no. 1, 1994, pp. 243–315; and Rudiger Dornbusch, Ilán Goldfajn and Rodrigo Valdés, "Currency Crises and Collapse," *Brookings Papers on Economic Activity*, no. 2, 1995, pp. 735–754.

47. New York investment bank analysts were well aware of this and most paid close attention to Mexican political developments in 1994. See, e.g. the analysis of Arturo Porzecanski, *Quo Vadis Mexico*, New York, ING Securities, New York, June 17, 1994.

48. See the introduction of Charles Kindleberger, *Manias, Panics, and Crashes: A History of Financial Crises*, New York, John Wiley & Sons, 4th edition, 2001.

49. See Arturo Porzecanski, *Emerging Markets Weekly Report*, New York, ING Securities, December 2, 1994.

50. Interview, New York, February 12, 1997.

51. Quoted by Sebastian Edwards, "The Mexican Peso Crisis: How Much Did we Know? When Did we Know It?" *NBER Working Paper*, No. 6334, December 1997, p. 8.

52. David Malpass and David Chon, *Mexican Pesos and Cetes are Attractive*, New York, Bear Stearns, November 7, 1994; JP Morgan, *Emerging Markets Outlook*, New York, Several Issues, 1994.

53. Interviews, New York, February 11, 12 and 14, 1997; telephone interview, New York, February 5, 1997.

54. See Andrés Oppenheimer, *Bordering on Chaos. Guerrillas, Stockbrokers, Politicians and Mexico's Road to Prosperity*, New York, Little, Brown & Co, 1996.

55. A number of these arguments, in particular those citing the lack of reliable information, reappeared a few years later during the crisis in Thailand and other countries of Southeast Asia. However, as we have been reminded by many economists, including Morris Goldstein of the Institute for International Economics, the financial markets and the international institutions had the necessary information for both Mexico and Thailand. He even demonstrates that there were warning signs that should have enabled the financial markets to forecast each of the 31 banking and monetary crises he analyzed.

56. Interview, Paris, March 6, 1997.

57. The overreaction can thus be explained as a downward spiral where information asymmetries led to moral hazard and adverse selection.

58. Interview in Paris on March 17, 1997. In this regard the analysis of the Mexican crisis leads one to look deeper into the conflicts that destabilized the increasingly fractured pyramid of the Mexican government. See Jong Gook Back, "The Mexican Crisis and the Internationalization of Finance," prepared for the XVIIth World Congress, *International Political Sciences Association,* Seoul, August 17–21, 1997 (unpublished).

59. See, on the distribution of congressional positions regarding the executive's pro-bailout agenda, Lawrence Broz, "The Political Economy of International Bailouts: Congressional Voting on Bailout Legislation in the 1990s," New York University, Department of Political Science, prepared for the *2001 Annual Meeting of the American Political Science Association,* San Francisco, August 30–September 2, 2001. U.S. Congress member position increases as the proportion of low-educated and low-skilled workers increases in their districts. At the same time, the most supportive members were those coming from states where the proportion of individuals employed in export competing sectors increases.

60. On the Clinton administration efforts to grapple with the Mexican crisis and more generally with monetary crisis in emerging markets during the 1990s see Riordan Roett, "The Mexican Devaluation and the U.S. Response: Potomac Politics, 1995-Style," in Riordan Roett, ed., *The Mexican Peso Crisis: International Perspectives,* Boulder, Col., Lynne Rienner, 1996, pp. 33–48; J. Bradford DeLong and Barry Eichengreen, "Between Meltdown and Moral Hazard: the International Monetary and Financial Policies of the Clinton Administration," University of California at Berkeley, prepared for the *Conference on the Economic Policies of the Clinton Administration,* Kennedy School of Government, June 26–29, 2001 (unpublished).

61. On the role of the IMF and more generally of industrial countries in emerging market crises see Jeffrey Frankel and Nouriel Roubini, "The Role of Industrial Country Policies in Emerging Market Crises," in Martin Feldstein, ed., *Economic and Financial Crises in Emerging Market Economies,* Chicago, Ill., University of Chicago Press, 2001. For a historical perspective on the IMF Michael Bordo and Anna Schwartz, "From the Exchange Stabilization Fund to the International Monetary Fund," *NBER Working Paper,* No. 8100, January 2001.

62. Telephone interview, Washington, October 7, 1997.

63. For a comparison of IMF bailouts, see Michael Bordo and Anna Schwartz, "Measuring Real Economic Effects of Bailouts. Historical Perspectives on How Countries in Financial Distress have Fared with and without Bailouts," *NBER Working Paper,* No. 7701, May 2000; and Michael Bordo and Anna Schwartz, "Under What Circumstances, Past and Present, Have International Rescues of Countries in Financial Distress been Successful?" *NBER Working Paper,* No. 6824, December 1998.

64. See the IMF's 1996 Annual Report, Washington, p. 137. See also for an analysis of the Mexican crisis issues by the IMF David Folkerts-Landau and Takatoshi Ito, eds., *International Capital Markets: Developments, Prospects and Policy Issues,* Washington, D.C., IMF, 1995.

65. In a study of some 100 developing countries over the period 1971–1992, Frankel and Rose concluded that a fairly weak FDI/debt ratio is associated with a monetary crisis. See Jeffrey Frankel and Andrew Rose, "Currency Crashes in Emerging Markets: Empirical Indicators," *NBER Working Paper,* No. 5437, January 1996, published in *The Journal of International Economics,* vol. 41, no. 3–4, November 1996, pp. 351–367.

66. See Jeffrey Frankel and Sergio Schmukler, "Country Fund Discounts and the Mexican Crisis of December 1994," *Open Economies Review,* vol. 7, no. 1, 996, pp. 511–534; Jeffrey Frankel and Sergio Schmukler, "Country Funds and Asymmetric Information," *International Journal of Finance and Economics,* vol. 5, July 2000, pp. 177–195. The U.S. Federal Reserve (FED) bulletins for the first half of 1996 also confirm the loss of confidence among Mexicans themselves in their own currency. While the government was negotiating financial support from the

international community to reimburse its short-term debt, contracted partly in the aftermath of the peso's devaluation, holders of Mexican capital continued their massive transfers to the United States. In its June 1996 report the FED disclosed that the funds of Mexican origin deposited in the United States totalled some US$ 25 bn. on December 31, 1995, twice as much as a year earlier. Mexicans alone hold 27.5% of all Latin American deposits in U.S. financial institutions, far ahead of Brazil, Argentina, Venezuela and Colombia, whereas in 1994 Mexico was in third place after Argentina and Venezuela. In 1995, apart from the Mexicans, only the Brazilians had considerably increased their deposits abroad.

67. On financial crisis contagion see the essays reproduced in Stijn Claessens and Kristin Forbes, eds., *International Financial Contagion*, New York, Kluwer Academic publishers, 2001; Michael Pettis, *The Volatility Machine: Emerging Economies and the Threat of Their Financial Collapse*, Oxford, Oxford University Press, 2001; Graciela Kaminsky and Carmen Reihnart, "On Crises, Contagion and Confusion," *Journal of International Economics*, vol. 51, no. 1, June 2000, pp. 145–168.

68. Empirical tests carried out by Barry Eichengreen, Andrew Rose and Charles Wyplosz on some twenty industrialized countries between 1959 and 1993 tend to give less weight to transmission via comparison of the fundamentals. They show in their survey that, in contrast to the tequila effect episode, the predominant transmission channel is still that of trade relations. See Barry Eichengreen, Andrew Rose and Charles Wyplosz, "Contagious Currency Crises," *NBER Working Paper*, 5681, July 1996.

69. See André Orléan, *Le pouvoir de la finance*, Paris, Editions Odile Jacob, 1999; André Orléan, "Contagion spéculative et globalisation financière: quelques enseignements tirés de la crise mexicaine," in André Cartapanis, ed., *Turbulences et spéculations dans l'économie mondiale*, Paris, Economica, 1996, pp. 27–45; André Orléan, "Le rôle des influences interpersonnelles dans le détermination des cours boursiers," *Revue Economique*, 5, September 1990, pp. 839–868.

70. Interview, New York, February 11, 1997.

71. Henry Kaufman, "Opening remarks," in *Mexico: Why didn't Wall Street Sound the Alarm?* New York, Group of Thirty, 1995 (not published).

72. Interview, New York, February 14, 1997. From this viewpoint Mexico, following in Thailand's footsteps, also illustrates the thesis developed by Robert Shiller, Yale University economist, who conducted a poll to investigate investor behavior in the face of a financial shock. After the crash of October 19, 1987, he questioned a panel of 1,000 investors, the result being that, at that time, operators' reaction was not triggered by new information or data that would have polarized their attention (and explained the overreaction), but rather to the actual news of the crash, which then led to a mimetic self-nurtured collapse. See Robert Shiller, *Market Volatility*, Cambridge, Mass., The MIT Press, 1989.

73. Paul Krugman, "Dutch Tulips and Emerging Markets," *Foreign Affairs*, vol. 74, 1995, p. 33. See also Paul Krugman, *Currency Crises*, Chicago, Ill., University of Chicago Press, 2000.

74. See for a coverage by *The Economist* of the events "Viva Amexica. A Survey of Mexico," *The Economist*, October 28, 1995; "Financial Markets. Who's in the Driving Seat? A Survey of the World Economy," *The Economist*, October 7, 1995; "Still Volatile. A Survey of Latin American Finance," *The Economist*, December 9, 1995.

75. See Robert Gilpin, *The Challenge of Global Capitalism*, Princeton, Princeton University Press, 2000; Guillermo Calvo, "Capital-Markets Crises and Economic Collapse in Emerging Markets: An Informational-Frictions Approach," *American Economic Review*, vol. 90, no. 2, May 2000, pp. 59–64.

76. See Layna Mosley, "Are Global Standards the Answer? National Governments, International Finance, and the IMF's Data Regime," *Notre Dame University, Department of Government*, 2001 (unpublished). Another survey conducted by the author in 2001 confirmed that the awareness of the SDDS among financial analysts is not much higher (the awareness score for analysts was marginally higher than of fund managers with an average score of 3, 1 being the

greatest awareness and 4 the least—the number of respondents were 22). Only for rating agencies analyst (*n* = 10) the average awareness is very significative (1.6), substantially higher than fund managers and financial analysts. See also Layna Mosley, *Room to Move? Capital Markets and Government Policymaking in the Contemporary Era*, Cambridge, Mass., Cambridge University Press, 2002.

77. Obviously the social recovery of the 1994 crisis have been much more longer and the related issues remained without being solved. See on the post-crisis economics Nora Lustig, "Life is Not Easy: Mexico's Quest for Stability and Growth," *Journal of Economic Perspectives*, vol. 15, no. 1, Winter 2001, pp. 85–106; Nora Lustig, *Mexico: The Remaking of an Economy*, Washington, D.C., Brookings Institution Press, 1998; Richard Snyder, *Politics after Neoliberalism: Reregulation in Mexico*, Cambridge, Mass., Cambridge University Press, 2001; and for an analysis of the Mexican great transformation and the Mexican economic trajectory after the crisis Javier Santiso and Christophe Cordonnier, "Mexique: Croissance ou développement?", *Problèmes d'Amérique latine*, no. 40, January–March 2001, pp. 31–53.

78. See AT Kearney, *FDI Confidence Index*, Alexandria, Virginia, AT Kearney Global Business Policy Council, vol. 4, no. 1, February 2001 and AT Kearney, *FDI Confidence Index*, Alexandria, Virginia, AT Kearney Global Business Policy Council, vol. 3, no. 1, January 2000.

79. See Jorge Mariscal, *Latin American Stocks in 1996: A Bravo New World*, New York, Latin American Research Equity Markets Strategy, Goldman Sachs, January 1996.

80. Interviews, New York, February 12, 13 and 16, 1997.

81. See Deutsche Bank, *Mexico's Economic Outlook for 1997: Ready to Take Off?* New York, Deutsche Bank Emerging Markets Latin America, Deutsche Morgan Grenfell, January 1997; Salomon Brothers, *Latin America—Economic and Financial Projections*, Latin America Economic & Market Analysis, New York, Salomon Brothers, January 30, 1997; Credit Suisse First Boston, *Mexican Banking System: Beyond the Crisis*, New York, CS First Boston, Economic Research Americas, November 14, 1996; Standard & Poor's, *Sovereign Reports: United Mexican States*, New York, Standard & Poor's, April 1996.

82. See Fitch Ratings, "Mexico: Investment Grade," New York, *Fitch Ratings Sovereign Comment*, January 22, 2002; and Standard & Poor's, "United Mexican States. Upgraded to investment grade; Outlook Stable," New York, *Standard & Poor's*, February 7, 2002.

83. The "breaking" of the sexenio cycle, the political and economic linked cycles, was seen by Wall Street as a major issue in 2000 for Mexico, see e.g. Liliana Rojas Suárez and Gustavo Cañonero, "Mexico: Breaking the Sexenio Pulse," New York, *Deutsche Bank Global Emerging Markets Research*, March 22, 2000; Alexandre Schwartsman and Alexandre Bassoli, "Why Mexico will Finally Beat 25-year Election Curse," Sao Paulo, *Indosuez W.I. Carr Securities, Latin America Economics Research*, June 2, 2000. For a post-election analysis, see "Mexico: Un Tequilazo invertido," Madrid, *BBVA Latinwatch*, September 2000.

84. See for a detailed analysis of Wall Street's views on the U.S. tropism of Mexican economy (and lack of European diversification), Javier Santiso, "Business as Unusual: The Political Economy of Mexican and European Relations," Paris, *CERI (Sciences Po) Working Paper*, presented at SAIS Johns Hopkins University, Bologna and Washington, April and June 2001. See also JP Morgan, "Emerging Markets and a US Slowdown Hard Landing: To Worry or Not to Worry?" New York and London, *JP Morgan Securities Emerging Markets Research*, November 6, 2000; Salomon Smith Barney, "Mexico: The Undiscovered Country. Policy Challenges in 2001 and Beyond," New York, *Salomon Smith Barney Economic & Market Analysis*, December 12, 2000; Deutsche Bank, "The Impact of a Hard Landing on Latin America," New York, *Deutsche Bank Global Markets Research*, December 22, 2000; UBS Warburg, "Global Economic Perspectives," London and New York, *UBS Warburg Global Economic & Strategy Research*, January 11, 2001; Goldman Sachs, "The US Downturn: Risks and Effects on Latin America," *Goldman Sachs Latin America Economic Analyst*, January 19, 2001; BBVA Securities, "Mexico: No Honeymoon for Fox, but Better Prospects in Second Half," London, *BBVA Securities Latin America Equities*, February 1,

2001; and, for a detailed analysis by the IADB economists, see Guillermo Calvo, Eduardo Fernández-Arias, Carmen Reinhart and Ernesto Talvi, "The Growth-Interest-Rate Cycle in the United States and its Consequences for Emerging Markets," *Inter-American Development Bank Research Department, Working Paper*, No. 458, August 2001.

85. See for a detailed analysis Roberto Rigobon, "The Curse of Non-Investment Grade Countries: Excess Vulnerability," *Journal of Development Economics*, vol. 69, no. 2, December 2002, pp. 423–449.

86. For more analysis on the meaning of the crisis for the United States, see Jorge Castañeda, *The Mexican Shock: Its Meaning for the US*, New York, The New Press, 1995.

87. See the interesting analysis, comparing the Mexico solution after 1995 and the English Crown solution in the seventeenth century analyzed by Douglass North and Barry Weingast, Aldo Flores-Quiroga, "Economic Crisis and the Mexican State: Toward a New Institutional Interpretation," *Claremont Graduate University, School of Politics and Economics*, 2000 (unpublished); Douglass North and Barry Weingast, "Constitutions and Commitment: The Evolution of Institutions Governing Public Choice in 17th Century England," *Journal of Economic History*, vol. 39, 1989, pp. 803–832.

88. See Raquel Fernández and Dani Rodrik, "Resistance to Reform: Status Quo Bias in the Presence of Individual-Specific Uncertainty," in Federico Sturzenegger and Mariano Tommasi, eds., *The Political Economy of Reform*, Cambridge, Mass., MIT Press, 1998, pp. 61–75. See also in this same book the articles of Alberto Alesina and Allan Drazen, "Why are Stabilizations Delayed?" op. cit., pp. 77–105; and Allan Drazen, "The Political Economy of Delayed Reforms," op. cit., pp. 39–60.

89. See on balance of payments crises and the role of short-term debt in the Mexican experience of 1994 (and also Indonesia in 1997 and Brazil in 1998), Michael Kumhof, "A Quantitative Exploration of the Role of Short-Term Domestic Debt in Balance of Payments Crises," *Journal of International Economics*, vol. 51, no. 1, June 200, pp. 195–215.

90. Nearly one year before the Brazilian presidential election, financial analysts and economists in Wall Street started, to foresee and forecast the possible impacts and issues involved as suggested by reports like Goldman Sachs, "Focus Brazil: A Roadmap to the 2002 Presidential Elections," New York, *Goldman Sachs Latin America Economic Analyst*, September 27, 2001.

91. On this issue see Felipe Larraín and Andrés Velasco, "Exchange-Rate Policy in Emerging-Market Economies: The Case for Floating," *Princeton University Essays in International Economics*, no. 224, October 2001; and for analysis of regime exchange exit options and their trade impact in the case of Argentina, see Sophie Chauvin, "Exit Options for Argentina with Special Focus on their Trade Impact on External Trade," *CEPII Working Paper*, No. 07, October 2001 (unpublished).

92. See Mohamed A. El-Erian, "The Ant Trail," *Pimco Emerging Markets Watch*, Newport Beach, Calif., August 2001.

93. For a closer analysis of the developments of emerging bond markets, see Pierre Laurent, Nicolas Meunier, Luis Miotti and Véronique Seltz, "Le choix de la devise d'endettement pour un pays émergent," in CDC Ixis, *Zones émergentes*, no. 11, Paris, CDC Ixis, December 2001, pp. 7–16; and Pierre Laurent, "Risque de marché, risque de crédit et défaut: la problématique particulière de la dette souveraine émergente," *CDC Ixis Etude Marchés Emergents*, no. 2, September 2001. As underlined by these researches, one of the surprising facts during the end of the 1990s has been the development of bonds in Euros for Latin American sovereigns. Argentina alone issued the equivalent of more than US$ 5.5 bn. of bonds denominated in Euros since the creation of the Euro (against US$ 3.9 bn.). For an analysis of the development of the Eurobond markets see Luis Miotti, Dominique Plihon and Carlos Quenan, "The Euro and Financial Relations Between Latin America and Europe: Medium and Long-Term Implications," *Caisse des Dépôts et Consignations, Série Economie Internationale*, 52, February 2002.

94. For a discussion by a fund manager of such index game weightings issue see, Fortis Investment Management, "Indices émergents!," Paris, *Fortis Investment Management Tendances des Marchés Emergents*, no. 6, Second Quarter 2001.

95. Walter Molano, "Overview: Why I Cry for Argentina," New York, *BCP Securities, The Latin American Adviser*, January 8, 2002.

96. Currency boards in Argentina were not new, these monetary arrangements being part of the (partly failed) search for macroeconomic stability in Argentina, see for a historical perspective Gerardo della Paolera and Alan M. Taylor, *Straining the Anchor: The Argentine Currency Board and the Search for Macro-Economic Stability 1880–1935*, Chicago, Ill., NBER and The University of Chicago Press, 2001. For an economic perspective on Argentina, see also Gerardo della Paolera, *A New Economic History of Argentina*, Cambridge, Mass., Cambridge University Press, 2003.

97. Each additional IMF disbursement has been perceived by market analysis as giving more time for Argentina in order to pursue the game but all stressed that the road ahead remained difficult. See e.g. after the second package in September 2001, Goldman Sachs, "Argentina: Another Breath of Life from the IMF," New York, *Goldman Sachs Global Economics Weekly*, September 5, 2001, p. 14; or Neil Dougall, "Argentina and the IMF: More Oxygen. But will it Revive the Patient?" London, *Dresdner Kleinwort Wasserstein Latin American Economics*, September 3, 2001; Arnab Das, "Launching: Argentina Financial Markets Focus," London, *Dresdner Kleinwort Wasserstein Latin America Emerging Markets Research*, September 3, 2001.

98. For financial operators, see e.g. ING Barings, "Argentina: Frozen Until the October Elections," New York and Buenos Aires, *ING Baring Latin American Economics Team*, October 1, 2001.

99. Obviously with the election day approaching the reports multiplied, see e.g. Crédit Agricole Indosuez, "Argentina Elections: Political Governance . . . wanted!" Paris, *Crédit Agricole Indosuez Economic & Markets Strategy Analaysis*, Special Focus, October 11, 2001; Goldman Sachs, "Focus: Argentina. What Should we Expect after the Elections?" in Goldman Sachs, *Latin America Economist*, New York, Goldman Sachs, October 11, 2001; JP Morgan Chase, "Argentina's Peculiar and Pivotal Mid-Term Elections," in JP Morgan Chase, *Global Data Watch*, New York, JP Morgan Chase Economic and Policy Research, October 5, 2001.

100. See the risk warnings issued by leading Wall Street firms JP Morgan, "Argentine Corporates & Banks: Testing the Strength in Highly Negative Scenarios," New York, *JP Morgan Emerging Markets Research*, July 26, 2001; Bear Stearns, "Argentine: Update on Our Views," New York, *Bear Stearns Global Sovereign Debt Research*, July 12, 2001; Bear Stearns, "Pandora's Box in Argentina," New York, *Bear Stearns Equity Research*, July 25, 2001; Bear Stearns, "Argentina: Talk of a Bailout," New York, *Bear Stearns Equity Research*, July 30, 2001; Crédit Agricole Indosuez, "Argentina: Last Tango in Buenos Aires," Paris, *Crédit Agricole Indosuez, Economic & Markets Strategy & Analysis*, Special Focus, July 27, 2001.

101. See Dresdner Bank Lateinamerika, "Latin American Spotlight. Update October 2001," Hamburg, *Dresdner Bank Lateinamerika Economics*, October 2001; JP Morgan, "Sizing up Argentina's Resistance to Financial Stress" and "Latin America Facing a New Balance of Payments Shock," in JP Morgan, "Global Data Watch," New York, *JP Morgan Chase Economic Research*, September 28, 2001; Goldman Sachs, "Latin America: A Weaker Outlook for Latin America," New York, *Goldman Sachs Latin America Economic Analyst*, September 18, 2001; JP Morgan, "Focus: Latin America. The Peace Dividend Gives Way to the War Levy," New York, *JP Morgan Chase Global Emerging Markets Equity Strategy*, September 19, 2001; and on the global impact analysis by one of the leading Wall Street economists Stephen Roach of Morgan Stanley, "Special Edition Aftershocks of the Terrorists Attacks. Tragedy and Macro-shock," New York, *Morgan Stanley Dean Witter Global Economics Group*, Weekly International Briefing, September 17, 2001.

102. See Goldman Sachs, "Argentina vs the Rest of the World: Debt Dynamics after the Local Exchange," New York, *Goldman Sachs, Emerging Markets Strategy*, November 15, 2001; BBVA

Securities, "Recent Crises in Emerging Markets and a Closer Look at Argentina," London and New York, *BBVA Securities, Latin America Equities*, November 7, 2001; BBA Creditanstalt, "No Free Lunch: The Debt Restructuring or Hunting with Jimbo and Ned," Sao Paulo, *BBA Economic Research on Brazil*, November 5, 2001; ING Barings, "Argentina Debt Re-Profiling Options," New York and London, *ING Barings, Emerging Markets Weekly Report*, November 2, 2001.

103. See Ricardo Hausmann, "After 10 Years of Convertibility: Should Argentina Move to Greener Pastures?," Kennedy School of Government, Harvard University, paper prepared for the *Conference on the 10th Anniversary of the Convertibility Law, organized by the Banco de la República Argentina*, Buenos Aires, April 5–6, 2001 (unpublished); or the one, written after a round trip to Buenos Aires, of Barry Eichengreen, "Argentina after the IMF," *Berkeley University*, August 27, 2001 (unpublished).

104. See JP Morgan, *Emerging Markets Outlook*, New York, *JP Morgan Emerging Markets Research*, December 6, 2001, p. 7.

105. Goldman Sachs, "The Argentina 'Tango' Effect on Latin America," New York, *Goldman Sachs Latin America Economics and Equity Research*, November 15, 2001.

106. See Fitch Ibca, "Argentina Debt Restructuring Scenario," London and New York, *Fitch Ibca Sovereign Research*, October 17, 2001; Richard Fox, "Argentina: Calm Before the Presentation?" London, *Fitch Ibca* presentation in Milan, September 14, 2001; Fitch Ibca, "Argentina: Imminent Default or Merging of Manoeuvre?" London and New York, *Fitch Ibca Sovereign Research*, August 2001; and for Wall Street research Goldman Sachs, "Argentina's Choices: Default, Dollarization, Devaluation or All?" New York, *Goldman Sachs Emerging Markets Bond Views*, December 6, 2001; Morgan Stanley, "Argentina: Tipping has Begun," New York, *Morgan Stanley Latin America Economics*, December 2, 2001; and Dresdner Kleinwort Wasserstein, "Argentina Financial Markets Focus: Close to Breaking Point," London, *Dresdner Kleinwort Wasserstein Emerging Markets Research*, December 7, 2001.

107. On the resignation of Cavallo, see Credit Suisse First Boston, "Argentina Update: Congress to Discuss Succession in the Coming Days; Monetary Clarification Unlikely," New York, *Credit Suisse First Boston Emerging Markets Economic Research*, December 20, 2001.

108. See comments on Wall Street e.g. Dresdner Bank Lateinamerika, "Argentina: Peso Devalued but Two-Tier Regime Adopted as Temporary Measure," New York, London and Hamburg, *Dresdner Bank Lateibamerika Latin American Daily Spotlight*, January 7, 2002; Morgan Stanley, "Argentina: Exiting Convertibility," New York, *Morgan Stanley Latin America Equity Research, Economics*, January 7, 2002; UBS Warburg, "Argentina 2002: Argentino DOA; But What Next?" Stamford, *UBS Warburg*, January 3, 2002; and BBVA Securities, "Argentina Strategy: Saying Goodbye to Convertibility," London and New York, *BBVA Securities Latin American Equities*, January 10, 2002.

109. See Dresdner Bank Lateinamerika, *Latin American Daily Spotlight*, Dresdner Bank Lateinamerika, January 30, 2002.

110. See Alex Schwartsman, "No Free Lunch: The Library of Babel," Sao Paulo, *BBA Economic Research on Brazil*, January 7, 2002; and previously an extended and accurate analysis of Argentinian developments (labelled as a chronicle of a foretold death) Alex Schwartsman, "No Free Lunch: Crossroads," Sao Paulo, *BBA Economic Research on Brazil*, January 2, 2002.

111. See JP Morgan, *Emerging Markets Outlook*, New York, *JP Morgan Emerging Markets Research*, December 6, 2001, p. 12.

112. JP Morgan, "Emerging Markets Client Survey: Results for 20th December 2001," New York, *JP Morgan Emerging Markets Strategy*, December 20, 2001.

113. See e.g. Dresdner Kleinwort Wasserstein, "Quarantining Argentina. New Executive Lets Cat out of the Bag: Devaluation; Default. But What About a New Economic Model?" London, *Dresdner Kleinwort Wasserstein Latin America Emerging Markets Research*, December 28, 2001.

114. For a detailed study of the economic policy of currency regimes in Latin America, please refer to the study by Jeffrey Frieden, Piero Ghezzi and Ernesto Stein, economists at Harvard,

Deutsche Bank and the Research Department of the Inter-American Development Bank respectively: Jeffrey Frieden, Piero Ghezzi and Ernesto Stein, "Politics and Exchange Rates: A Cross Country Approach," in Jeffrey Frieden and Ernesto Stein, eds., *The Currency Game: Exchange-Rate Politics in Latin America*, Washington D.C., John Hopkins University and Inter-American Development Bank, 2001, pp. 20–63.

115. See the study by Héctor Schamis and Christopher Way, "The Politics of Exchange Rate-Based Stabilisation," *Cornell University Working Paper*, 2001 (unpublished).

116. See the study by David Leblang, "To Devalue or Not to Devalue? The Political Economy of Exchange Rate Policy," *University of Colorado Working Paper*, 2001 (unpublished). A close study of Latin American exchange rate regimes from 1960 to 1994 underlines also that the probability of the maintenance of a fixed exchange rate regime increases by about 8% as an election approaches, while the aftershock of an election conversely increases the probability of getting out of the peg by 4%. Economic factors such as the size of the tradable sectors exposed to international competition help also to explain the propensity to maintain or not a fixed exchange rate regime. See Brock Blomberg, Jeffry Frieden and Ernesto Stein, "Sustaining Fixed Rates: The Political Economy of Currency Pegs in Latin America," *Wellesley College, Harvard University and Inter-American Development Bank, Working Paper*, July 2001.

Chapter Seven   Conclusion: Financial Markets and the Memory of the Future

1. Richard Sylla, "Emerging markets in History: the United States, Japan and Argentina," in R. Sato et al., eds., *Global Competition and Integration*, Boston, Kluwer Academic Publishing, 1999.

2. For an analysis of the "credibility policy" signaling through the 1990s decade see also Ilene Grabel, "The Political Economy of Policy Credibility: The New-Classical Macro-Economics and the Remaking of Emerging Economies," *Cambridge Journal of Economics*, vol. 24, no. 1, 2000, pp. 1–19.

3. Barry Eichengreen and Albert Fishlow, "Contending with Capital Flows: What is Different About the 1990s?" in Miles Kahler, ed., *Capital Flows and Financial Crises*, Ithaca, Cornell University Press, 1998, pp. 23–68.

4. See Philippe Martin and Hélène Rey, "Financial Globalization and Emerging Markets: With or Without Crash?" *Federal Reserve Bank of New York and Princeton University*, May 2002.

5. The terrorist attack of September 11, 2001 has been commented on by Wall Street in depth. See, e.g. on the impact on Latin America, oil sectors or Europe, Walter Molano, "Latin America: The Outlook after the World Trade Center," New York, *BCP Securities*, November 7, 2001; Bank of America Securities, "Energy Sector Update: Terrorist Attacks' Impact on Oil and Gas Sector," New York, *Bank of America Securities High Yield Research*, September 21, 2001; Morgan Stanley, "Macroscope: US Recovery in Question: Global Market Implications," New York, *Morgan Stanley*, September/October 2001; and Barclays Capital, "Euro-zone: What Scenario after the Terroist Attacks?" London, *Barclays Capital European Economics*, October 5, 2001. For a broader analysis, see Miles Kahler, "Networks and Failed States: September 11 and the Long Twentieth Century," University of California at San Diego, paper prepared for the *Annual Meeting of the American Political Science Association*, August 29–September 1, 2002, Boston, Mass.

6. Andrés Velasco, "The Grand Illusions," *Harvard University*, unpublished paper 2002. See also the website: http://www.cid.harvard.edu/cidspecialreports/papers/grandillusions.html.

7. See David Hale, "The Fall of a Star Pupil," *Financial Times*, January 7, 2002, p. 15.

8. See for an econometric test, Philip Keefer, "When do Special Interests run Rampant? Disentangling the Role of Elections, Incomplete Information and Checks and Balances in Banking Crises," *The World Bank Development Research Group*, August 2000 (unpublished).

9. See the analysis of Luc Laeven and Enrico Perotti, "Confidence Building in Emerging Stock Markets," *CEPR Discussion Paper*, No. 3055, November 2001.

10. See Dani Rodrik, "Reform in Argentina, Take Two." *Trade Out," The New Republic Online*, January 14, 2002. See http://www.thenewrepublic.com/011402/rodrik011402.html. The metaphor of Ulysses and the sirens has been used also by some leading scholars to underline the bounded rationality of human decision-making, see in particular the essay of Jon Elster, "Ulysses and the Sirens: A Theory of Imperfect Rationality," *Social Science Information*, 16(5), 1977, pp. 469–526; Jon Elster, *Ulysses and the Sirens: Studies in Rationality and Irrationality*, New York, Cambridge University Press, 1979; and Jon Elster, *Ulysses Unbounded. Studies in Rationality, Precommitment and Constraints*, New York, Cambridge University Press, 2000.

11. On the (unfinished) transformation of the style of political economy in Latin America and the emergence of possibilism, see Javier Santiso, "La mirada de Hirschman sobre el desarrollo o el arte de los traspasos y las autosubversiones," *Revista de la CEPAL*, no. 70, avril 2000, pp. 91–107; and Javier Santiso, "Du Bon Révolutionnaire au Bon Libéral? A propos d'un étrange caméléon latino-américain" in Javier Santiso, ed., *A la recherche de la démocratie. Mélanges offert en l'honneur de Guy Hermet*, Paris, Karthala, 2002, pp. 227–257 (also in *Problèmes d'Amérique latine*, no. 44, Spring 2002, pp. 103–130; and Javier Santiso, "¿Del Buen Revolucionario al Buen Liberal? A propósito de un extraño camaleón latinoamericano," in Guy Hermet, Soledad Loaeza and Jean-Francois Prud'homme, eds., *Del populismo de los antiguos al populismo de los modernos*, México, El Colegio de México, 2001, pp. 215–250.

12. There is an extensive and growing literature on this issue, see for a synthesis, Peter Kenen, "The Intentional Financial Architecture: Old Issues and New Initiatives," *International Finance*, vol. 5, no. 1, Spring 2002, pp. 23–45; Barry Eichengreen, *Capital Flows and Crises*, Oxford, Oxford University Press, 2003; Sebastián Edwards and Jeffrey Frankel, eds., *Preventing Currency Crises in Emerging Markets*, Chicago, Ill., University of Chicago Press, 2002; Martin Feldstein, ed., *Economic and Financial Crises in Emerging Markets*, Chicago, Ill., University of Chicago Press, 2002; Michael Dooley and Jeffrey Frankel, eds., *Managing Currency Crises in Emerging Markets*, Chicago, Ill., University of Chicago Press, 2002; and Jérôme Sgard, *L'économie de la panique. Faire face aux crises financières*, Paris, La Découverte, 2002.

13. A problem addressed by the IMF with Anne Krueger IMF first deputy managing director proposal, see Anne Krueger, "International Financial Architecture for 2002: A New Approach to Sovereign Debt Restructuring," address given at the *National Economists' Club Annual Members' Dinner, American Enterprise Institute*, Washington D.C., November 26, 2001; and for the following amendments made to the first proposal, see IMF, *Sovereign Debt Restructuring Mechanism— Further Reflections and Future Work*, Washington, IMF, 2002. For an overview of the issues see Nouriel Roubini, "Private Sector Involment in Crisis Resolution and Mechanisms with Sovereign Debt Problems," *Stern School of Business, New York University*, July 2002; and Richard Cooper, "Chapter 11 for countries?" *Foreign Affairs*, vol. 82, no. 4, July–August 2002, pp. 90–103.

14. See Graciela Kaminsky, Richard Lyons and Sergio Schmukler, "Mutual Fund Investment in Emerging Markets: An Overview," *George Washington University, UC Berkeley and The World Bank*, September 2000 (unpublished). See also for an overview Luisa Palacios, "Sovereign Bond Defaults and Restructurings in Emerging Markets: A Preliminary Review," *JBIC*, Working Paper, June 2002. For a detailed analysis of the dispersion of Argentina bondholders see BBVA, *Informe Económico 2001*, Madrid, BBVA, 2002, pp. 110–113.

15. We made the calculation using data released by one of the most detailed and complete data report on assets managed by Latin American companies, Goldman Sachs, "Latin America: Pension and Mutual Funds and Their Impact on Stocks," New York, Goldman Sachs Global Equity Research, August 31, 2001. The players were subsidiaries of the following firms: Santander Central Hispano, BBVA, HSBC, Citigroup, ABN Amro, Lloyds, BNL, all foreign operators and several fully Argentina ones among the most important, Banco de Galicia and Banco de la Nación.

16. See Woochan Kim and Shang-Jin Wei, "Foreign Portfolio Investors Before and During a Crisis," *Journal of International Economics*, 56, 2002, pp. 77–96; Huyk Choe, Bong-Chan Kho and René Stulz, "Do Domestic Investors have more Information About Individual Stocks than Foreign Investors," *NBER Working Paper*, No. 8073, 2001; and for a recent study that provides opposite evidence in emerging markets, see Mark Seasholes, "Smart Foreign Traders in Emerging Markets," *Harvard Business School Working Paper*, 2000 (unpublished).

    This problem of assymetric information is more pregnant in emerging countries. Developed markets appear in fact to have greater liquidity and greater informational efficiency than emerging markets, see on this aspect the findings, based on an empirical investigation using data from State Street Bank, which encompass over 3 mn. trades by client institutions, of Kenneth Froot, Paul O'Connell and Mark Seasholes, "The Portfolio Flows of International Investors," *NBER Working Paper*, No: 6687, August 1998, published and revised in the *Journal of Financial Economics*, vol. 59, no. 2, 2001, pp. 151–193; and for a discussion Kenneth Foort and Tarun Ramadorai, "The Information Content of International Portfolio Flows," *NBER Working Paper*, No. 72, September 2001.

17. Pamela Druckerman, "Argentina's Bankers have New Role. Now They are Helping Restructure the Debt They Once Sold," *The Wall Street Journal Europe*, Friday–Saturday, November 30–December 1, 2001, p. 8.

18. In the first debt swap of June 2001 the syndicate of bankers who managed the operation collected around US\$130 mn. for the deal. According to Dealogic, the leading underwriters of Argentina's bond issues during the 1990s ranked by percentage share were: JP Morgan (22%), Deutsche Bank (14%), Credit Suisse First Boston (12%), Morgan Stanley Dean Witter (10%), Salomon Smith Barney, Goldman Sachs, UBS Warburg, Nikko Securities, Merrill Lynch and BNP Paribas with around 3–5 percent each.

19. On the imperative of speed and the crushing temporalities, see also Javier Santiso, "Political Sluggishness and Economic Speed: A Latin American Perspective," *Social Science Information*, 39(2), 2000, pp. 233–253. One of the most stimulating analyses on the issue of the compression of the temporal and of geographic constraints brought about by the financial markets is that of Richard O'Brien, *The End of Geography. Global Financial Integration*, London, Pinter, 1992; Nigel Thrift, "A Phantom State? The De-traditionalization of Money, the International Financial System and International Financial Systems," *Political Geography*, vol. 13, no. 4, July 1994, pp. 299–327; and Benjamin Cohen, *The Geography of Money*, Ithaca, Cornell University Press, 1998.

20. Figures collected by Philippe Delmas, *Le maître de horloges. Modernité de l'action publique,* Paris, Odile Jacob, 1991, p. 97.

21. See Susan Strange, *Casino Capitalism*, Oxford and New York, Basil Blackwell, 1986; and Susan Strange, *States and Markets*, London, 1988 and 1994; as well as her latest work, Susan Strange, *Mad Money. When Markets Outgrow Governments,* Ann Arbor, The University of Michigan Press, 1998. On the interactions between governments and the financial markets, one may also consult the work of Jeffrey Frieden, "Invested Interests: The Politics of National Economic Policies in a World of Global Finance," *International Organization*, vol. 45, no. 4, 1991, pp. 425–451. The interactions between governments and markets are in reality much more complex than those of a zero-sum game; they allow a number of other balancing acts. See in particular Alberto Alesina and Geoffrey Carliner, eds., *Politics and Economics in the Eighties*, Chicago and London, The University of Chicago Press, 1991.

22. For a history of instruments measuring time, one can refer to the work of Arno Borst, *The Ordering of Time. From Ancient Computus to the Modern Computer*, Chicago, Chicago University Press, 1993.

23. Paul Valery, *Regards sur le monde actuel et autres essais*, Paris, Gallimard, 1945.

24. Stephen Hawking, *Brief History of Time. From the Big Bang to Black Holes*, London, GK Hakk & Co., 1989.

25. Translated from the French "L'éternel retour des crises financières semble suggérer qu'au mieux nous n'apprenons rien du passé, qu'au pire nous finissons par tout oublier." Eric Barthalon, "Nouvelle économie et capacité d'oubli. Pas de bulle sans nouvelle économie," in Jacques Gravereau and Jacques Trauman, eds., *Crises financières*, Paris, Economica, 2001, p. 415.
26. On these temporalities see also Jean-Pierre Dupuy, "Convention et common knowledge," *Revue Economique*, vol. 40, no. 2, 1989, pp. 361–400.
27. See Frédéric Lordon, *Les quadratures de la politique économique*, Paris, Albin Michel, 1997.
28. See Interview, Emerging Markets Chief Economist, Paris, February 5, 1997.
29. Interview, Emerging Markets Chief Economist, Paris, February 5, 1997.
30. Eric Barthalon, *From Here to Eternity*, Paris, Paribas Economic Research Conjoncture, October 1998, pp. 10 and 12. Translated from Eric Barthalon, *Tant qu'il y aura des hommes: libres réflexions sur les crises financières*, Paris, Paribas Economic Research Conjoncture, October 1998 (the paper is forthcoming in the *International Political Science Review*, in a Special Issue on "The Political Economy of International Finance," in 2003).
31. See Fernand Braudel, *Ecrits sur l'histoire*, Paris, Flammarion, 1969, p. 22.
32. Haldane et al. report that the two leading rating agencies, Moody's and Standard and Poor's, downgrade sovereign ratings prior to a crisis in only 25 percent of cases. See A. Haldane, G. Hoggarth and V. Saporta, "Assessing Financial System Stability, Efficiency and Structure at the Bank of England," *BIS Papers*, No. 1, Basel, March 2001.
33. See Ariel Colonomos and Javier Santiso, "Vive la France! French Multinationals and the Global Genealogy of Corporate Responsibility," Paris, *CERI-Sciences Po Working Paper*, February 2002 (unpublished), presented at the *International Conference on World Civility? Ethical Norms and Transnational Diffusion*, Paris, CERI-Sciences Po, October 3–4, 2002; presented also at the ABCDE World Bank Conference, Paris, May 16th 2003.
34. See Robert Barro and Jong-Wha Lee, "IMF Programs: Who is Chosen and What are the Effects?" *Harvard University and Korea University*, November 2001; published also as a *NBER Working Paper*, No. 8951, May 2002.

INDEX